The
Beacon
On
Kill Devil
Hill

A HISTORICAL NOVEL

By

Thomas J. Morrow

&

James H. Martin

The Beacon on Kill Devil Hill

ISBN: 978-0-9779119-5-0

Printed in the United States of America

By

Lightning Source
1246 Heil Quaker Blvd.
La Vergne, TN 37086

On the web: www.oldwarriorbooks.com

E-mail contacts: *quotetaker@msn.com*

jim_martin51@embarqmail.com

About the authors

Tom Morrow graduated from Arizona State University with a degree in journalism, and for the past 41 years has worked at a number of daily and weekly newspapers throughout the West, including 10 years experience in public relations along the way. He was vice president for communications at the historic Hotel del Coronado during the 1980s and owned a small advertising and PR agency in San Diego until 1988 when he returned to newspapers. Since 1991, he has been with the Blade-Citizen, now known as the North County Times in Oceanside, California.

A native of Charlotte, North Carolina, Jim Martin attended Hargrave Military Academy and Brevard Junior College. After college and chasing a childhood dream, he went to work for his father in the textile industry for 26 years eventually taking over the firm and managing it for the last 13 years. With the advent of worldwide outsourcing of textile products, the firm was forced to close in early 2001. Jim then moved to Rocky Mount where he began pursuing another dream of writing. Jim's first book was a biography of his father's war experiences in Europe during World War II. This is his first challenge in fiction.

Jim's writing abilities have come to life in the crafting of "The Beacon on Kill Devil Hill," a story that takes place right in his backyard – the Outer Banks of North Carolina, where German U-boats sank or damaged 285 Allied merchant cargo ships and tankers in the first seven months of 1942.

The writing team of **Morrow and Martin** is just getting started. Go to our web site for all three books in the Old Warrior Publishing Company's library of novels ii

Note to Readers

The German U-491 submarine used in this story was in fact a real boat with its keel laid down on 31 July 1943 at the Deutsch Werke Shipyard in Kiel, Germany. Save for the approximately 1,288 submarines manufactured throughout Germany during World War II, 135 U-boats were never finished. The U-491 was one of those boats. On 23 September 1944, with seventy-five percent of the U-491 completed, work was cancelled and the boat was broken up into salvage. The authors chose this boat because they liked the number.

The fictional mission surrounding this submarine and its crew is purely the creative imagination of the authors. The military freighters and tankers torpedoed by the U-491 were imaginary ships, but the attacks themselves are loosely based on real events.

The actual procedures depicted in this story for operating the U-491 such as submerging, surfacing, releasing a torpedo, and other functions as well as its replenishment of fuel, supplies, and torpedoes are based on factual information researched by the authors and should be considered accurate. The repair of the head (toilet) in the water closet on the U-491 by civilian Mr. Webber is purely fictitious. However, it is true that some Allied individuals, retrieved from the sea, were at times taken aboard German submarines, interrogated, and later released with alcohol and cigarettes and safely returned to their lifeboats.

The mention of all other U-boats, U.S. warships, and merchant ships, and the officers and sailors, who were aboard them, are true-to-life characters as are their stories. Historical characters mentioned in the upper echelon of the United States Navy, the Coast Guard and the *Kriegsmarine,* (the German Navy), are real and well-known figures. All other characters in the story are fictitious and any similarities between actual persons living or dead are purely coincidental.

Acknowledgment

The Wright Brothers Monument in Kill Devil Hills, North Carolina plays an integral part of our story, and the authors would like to thank **Darrell M. Collins**, the Head Historian of the Monument, for his help in supplying various copies of detailed documents regarding its structure, as well as pointing out the location of the former caretaker's cottage located some four hundred yards behind the monument that is used many times throughout our story.

Author Jim Martin would like to give a special thanks to Darrell for his undivided personal attention and also, for giving him a private tour of its recently restored interior, which currently is not open to the public. It was this tour that provided us with the exquisite details we could use for telling the various story events that unraveled on the inside of this structure. However, because of the actual position of the rotating beacon light inside the dome, the author took artistic license by slightly re-adjusting its position, making it feasible for this story to take place.

Jim Martin & Tom Morrow

FOREWORD

My name is Joshua Scoggins. Growing up in rural North Carolina was idyllic, at best, even though my formative years witnessed a world at war. Living on the Outer Banks was about as close to nowhere as one could get; yet, it was my only world.

Of course, we had our notoriety where Orville and Wilbur Wright learned how to fly. And there was the outdoor drama called the "Lost Colony" that became a popular summertime tourist attraction. But probably the most infamous of all was the more than 500 worldly ships that foundered on the shallow shoals of the Outer Banks. From the north of Nags Head to the south of the Core Banks and intertwining with a forsaken patch of land aptly named Cape Lookout, many a ship died an unmerciful death. But the real Graveyard of the Atlantic was the dreaded Diamond Shoals jutting from the Cape Hatteras cusp and its largely famous lighthouse. It was this body of water that ruthlessly shredded ship after ship when their captains dared its coast in a press for time. It was always a bad decision.

My dad, R.W. Scoggins, was the Deputy Sheriff of Dare County and, along with his friend and fellow deputy, George Washington Dawkins, was the only sense of law and order on the skinny set of drawn-out barrier islands curiously known as Bodie, Pea, Hatteras, and Ocracoke. Access to the lower Banks was largely by ferry, and the only coastal road was soft sand that could sink a car to its axels. Behind the upper Banks, and located between the lower Albemarle Sound and the enormous upper Pamlico Sound, was the historically rich and famous Roanoke Island. To the north end of the island was the small cultural village of Manteo and to the south was the diversified Wanchese fishing village. It was Manteo in 1585 where

America's first immigrants cautiously settled on the tree lined shores of the Roanoke Sound—then strangely disappeared.

Manteo was also the county seat and the home to Dad's office. Thanks to Wash Baum in 1928, you could get there by car from Bodie Island over a rock and sand causeway, a short bridge named after Melvin Daniels, and then the one and a half mile wooden bridge appositely named for Baum. Near the middle of the bridge was a draw allowing small fishing vessels to pass.

In 1930 automobile access from the mainland to the upper Banks, below the community of Duck, became a welcomed relief when an influential group of businessmen from Elizabeth City engineered the construction of the Wright Memorial Bridge—an eighteen-foot wide three-mile wooden structure over the Currituck Sound from Point Harbor to Martins Point—a short jaunt north from Kitty Hawk. It was this bridge that allowed us easy access to the mainland and Elizabeth City. We could also get to the Hampton Roads area of Southeastern Virginia and the mouth of the Chesapeake Bay; but that was a long haul over marshland roads, and we didn't go there very often.

Commercial fishing had always been the mainstay on the Outer Banks for many decades. Because the skinny barrier islands fronted the Atlantic Ocean and backed up to the large salt and fresh water sounds and the upper mainland rivers, avid anglers from all around descended to the islands to catch the variety of fish that schooled in abundance. And after the construction of the Wright Memorial Bridge, tourism began to flourish and many medium-sized hotels and cottages began to fill the twenty-miles of sand dunes from Nags Head north to Duck.

One of the more popular tourist attractions was the tall sixty-one foot wing-like granite monument dedicated to the Wright Brother's flying achievement. It sat atop a ninety-foot bush and grass covered sand dune called Kill Devil Hill and was the highest point for miles and miles around. It was from this sand dune that the brothers launched their gliders, learning how to fly.

For years folks got Kill Devil Hill confused with Kitty Hawk because back around the turn of the 20th century, the entire area was known as "Kitty Hawk, a small-unincorporated town two miles to the north. Nevertheless, it was always a treat to visit the sacred grounds where, in 1903, the world's first self-powered plane actually took off.

Perhaps the most treasured establishment on the Outer Banks was the effervescent two-story Nags Head Casino that was built in the early thirties to provide the social entertainment to the area's young adults. The bottom floor had several duckpin bowling alleys, numerous eight-foot pool tables, and an entire section of buffalo-nickel pinball machines. At the end by the entrance was a well-stocked snack bar. On the upper floor, there was a huge and highly polished wooden dance floor that was sleek, smooth, and slippery. On the one end was a stage for the popular Big Bands of that era; on the other end was a lengthy mahogany bar serving the islands favorite Pabst Blue Ribbon Beer.

As far away as it may have seemed, the Nags Head Casino was the foremost energetic social center for counties all around, attracting hoards of youth to the beat of the swing bands. Dancing in stocking feet was the rule of the day and the slick wooden floor did produce a bump or two. And during the war, the coastal servicemen stationed at the Naval Air Station in Elizabeth City and at the nearby Navy's Lighter Than Air Station in Weeksville, knew the Casino all too well as the sailors' favorite watering hole. On Saturday nights, they loaded up their cars and headed to "The Banks." It was certainly a relief from the stress of duty.

Rags Truscott was the owner, and he was a man of means with a heart of gold. He hired many of the local youth to manage the snack bar or set-up the duckpins; and of course there were many jobs in-between. For many of the youngsters, he was their second father as most of the real fathers were off to war. And to many of his kids, Rags had a soft shoulder to lean with a kindly, encouraging word. He never let his little buddies down.

Through the years, Dad and Rags became good friends and developed a mutual understanding concerning the orderliness of the watering hole's business. With the Casino's popularity, skirmishes were evident when alcohol mixed with anger. But in the rule of order and in lieu of the police, Rags meted out his own judicial justice. If the fight spilled out and beyond the bounds of his property, then Dad would brandish his cuffs. As I recall, that only happened once. Word spread quickly and fights never got beyond the front door.

With a countywide population of six thousand and forty-one, Pop was eminently known far and wide as a good and descent lawman who fairly dispensed his justice with nary a thought of discriminating. It just wasn't in his nature.

During the early 1940s, a colored person endured a challenging life. In the many rural counties of Eastern North Carolina, lawmen were feared protectors, looking for any mundane excuse to fling a colored man in jail; but not my pops. He was a friend to everyone and, in return, was duly treated with the utmost of respect.

And, about those 500 shipwrecks? Well sir, they started back in the sixteenth century and they've been piling up ever sense. Even Edward Teach, better known as Blackbeard the Pirate, scuttled his ship the *Queen Anne's Revenge* in 1718, in the Beaufort Inlet. She buried in time, somewhere just below the Shackleford Banks west of the Cape Lookout cusp. But the ones that began piling up in January 1942 had a little help—and it wasn't coming from foul weather, bad karma, or poor seamanship. It was from German U-boats (*Deutsch Unterseebootes*) and it didn't take long before the coastal community realized we all were under attack.

On Dec. 11, 1941, just after Germany declared war on the United States, German Admiral Karl Dönitz, the commodore and commander of the Submarines, began implementation of Operation Drumbeat (*Unternehmen Paukenschlag*): the destruction of American shipping along the East Coast of the United States.

Around Christmas time December 1941, Dönitz secretly sent a small group of five U-boats across the Atlantic, arriving in mid-

January 1942, to the sleepy American coast and placed them into prearranged quadrants. His mandate was simple: "Sink anything and everything that moves." But just after arriving, the boats' commanders realized the best killing fields were plentiful off the North Carolina Coast. Infamously known as "Quadrant CA, Section 87," the coastal area from Cape Lookout to the mouth of the Chesapeake Bay, it was to be forever etched in my mind as "Torpedo Alley."

But while these boats were destined to indiscriminately sink anything that moved, there was one specially-equipped submarine the German Admiral sent that arrived in mid-February with an entirely different agenda: to specifically sink targeted military cargo leaving the Chesapeake Bay headed to England. It was this boat that was tied to a well-placed German infiltrator within Hampton Roads, who had recruited a handful of American collaborators to join him in this plot. What we didn't know at the time was some of these conspirators where living amongst us, right here on the islands.

The Norfolk Naval Shipyard, the largest on the American East Coast, is actually located in the city of Portsmouth, which is situated at the mouth of the Chesapeake Bay in a large tidal basin known as Hampton Roads. During the colonial days, it was named in honor of Henry Wriothesley, the Third Earl of Southampton, who was a great supporter of colonization in Virginia. The term "roadstead" was an old nautical term meaning a place less-sheltered than a harbor where ships could ride at anchor. Thus, the entire area was recognized as Hampton Roads because of the numerous rivers and creeks flowing into it. Other cities with harbors in this immediate area were Chesapeake, Hampton, Norfolk, Suffolk, Newport News, and Virginia Beach which was at the very top of the Outer Banks just south of the Cape Henry lighthouse.

Hampton Roads was formed by the confluence of the James, Elizabeth, and Nansemond Rivers; with their hundreds of miles of tributaries, the fastest way inland was by navigating these waterways symbolizing a "network of roads." Before and during World War II, various other naval ports were established within this basin where more than 42,000 civilian workers built over one hundred troop carriers, cargo, tankers, and warships.

After the American Revolution and between 1794 and 1799, two of the Navy's first ships, the *USS Chesapeake* and the *USS Constitution*, were built at the Norfolk shipyard. In 1833, the western hemisphere's first dry-dock opened there when the *USS Delaware* needed refitting.

During the Civil War, the Confederate Navy converted the captured ironclad *USS Merrimack* into the *CSS Virginia*. In March 1862, she then engaged the wooden Union ships *USS Cumberland* and the *USS Congress* along with the U.S. Navy's ironclad *USS Monitor* off Sewells Point in Hampton Roads. It was the world's first ironclad confrontation that changed naval warfare forever.

In the years to come, America's first true battleship, the *USS Texas*—the first of three ships named Texas—was built at the Norfolk Naval Shipyards along with the nation's first modern cruiser, the *USS Raleigh*. Both were launched in 1892. And in 1922, the Navy converted the *USS Jupiter* to America's first aircraft carrier, the *USS Langley*. Because Hampton Roads was such a naturally huge deep-water harbor, the importance of this facility became paramount to the defense of the United States. It also became an important spot for German infiltrators to see what was being loaded onto ships going to England.

When Pearl Harbor was bombed on 7 December 1941, the sea and air defenses along the Atlantic Seaboard were sparse at best. Admiral Ernest J. King, the Commander in Chief of the Atlantic Fleet, berthed his flotilla in Hampton Roads for protection, only sparingly using some vessels to support the Coast Guard in their East Coast defense. The Naval Air Station (NAS) at Norfolk, which had both land and seaplanes, did begin flying anti-submarine patrols off the Outer Banks and the Chesapeake Bay areas. Though, at first, these patrols were meager at best.

By mid 1942, NAS Norfolk soon became home to twenty-four fleet squadrons. The amphibious aircraft stationed there were twelve

Kingfisher seaplanes and a small number of the huge PBY Catalina flying boats. The training facilities became so important that a large number of U.S. Navy patrol squadrons, as well counterparts from the British Royal Air Force, the French, and the Soviet Union, were also trained at those bases.

Using NAS Norfolk as the hub of command, these air operations were deployed to Chincoteague, Whitehurst, Reservoir, Oceana, Pungo, Fentress, Monogram, and Creeds, all in Virginia. In North Carolina, Naval Air Auxiliary fields were built in Elizabeth City, Edenton, Manteo, and Harvey Point. Later, a "Lighter Than Air" blimp base was constructed at Weeksville, just south of Elizabeth City. All of the U.S. Navy's air squadrons during World War II, some 326 in all, were trained at these Naval Air facilities before heading for the fleet.

During the early stages of the war, the Civil Air Patrol, a group of volunteer civilian pilots using their own aircraft, provided a great deal of coastal patrols to supplement the military wings. These CAP units were from Charlotte, Asheville, Elkin, and Winston Salem, North Carolina. Later in 1943, the Navy and Coast Guard relieved the Civil Air Patrol squadrons, taking over all coastal anti-submarine patrols.

Aside from civilians using their planes, there was a faction within the Cruising Club of America to have its civilian members use their sailing and motorboats to patrol the coastline as well. The idea, while seemingly preposterous, was passionately passed to Admiral King, now Chief of Naval Operations 26 March 1942, who approved this creative fleet with verve. Many of the larger craft were fitted with fixed machine gun mounts and a small rack of depth charges. Needless to say, there was a contingent of qualified Navy sailors to handle these weapons. While serving with distinction and a get-up-and-go attitude, the civilian flotilla became known as the Coastal Picket Patrol but more infamously as the "Hooligan Navy."

On a clear day, us kids would climb atop Jockey's Ridge or Kill Devil Hill to see if we could spot a U-boat. I swear I saw at least three during the war, but sometimes just staring at the cold, green waters of the Atlantic can play tricks on your mind.

I didn't know it at the time, but Kill Devil Hill and the Wright Brothers Monument played an important part of the war for the Germans in how they were using their U-boats to sink our crucial military cargo.

This is the story of how two gentle giants unknowingly did their part in fighting the Nazis; although at the time, they had no idea how much they were contributing.

Chapter 1

Kapitänleutnant Hans Vogel brought his submarine to the surface and looked for survivors. It was doubtful he would find any. If there were, there wasn't much he could do. His orders were specific— no survivors allowed to board. All he could do was guide them to their lifeboats. Beyond that, they were left to fate. And tonight there'd be no fate.

What he saw were hapless men gyrating about the oil slick deck as devilish flames engulfed their bodies. What he could hear were voluminous cries for help. And as the funeral pyre grew larger and larger, the wailing for help grew less and less. What few brave souls that scrambled to the bow gambled their fate into a boiling sea of oil. There was no chance for survival.

Vogel moved closer to the scorching hulk. He needed his victim's name. It was required by their commander—Admiral Karl Dönitz. But the radiation was excruciating and the radiance too bright; it was impossible to read the nameplate. He quickly backed off his Type VII-C U-boat.

While pausing to ponder, he softly ordered. "Turn us about and give us some room. She is only wounded and slightly heeled. We will send her to the bottom with another crushing blow."

From 400 meters and firing from the hip, the second torpedo coldly ripped into its red-hot hull. Amidships the tanker exploded spewing gobs of lava-like oil and choking black smoke; its backbone broken, torn asunder, swiftly settling into the depths of the sea; its bow and stern awkwardly leaning engulfed in blistering blazes of burning sea. Within seconds the ship was spent and the sibilant sound of gushing air ceased; nothing was left but rolling seas of flickering flames and badly charred bodies. In the hours to come, the surging waves would squash its glow; the remains would sink. A gravesite—unlike no other—vanished from sight.

"Kapitän! It is imperative that we leave if we are to make our rendezvous point. We must leave now," said the Executive Officer Peter Staats.

"Ja ... Ja. Come about ... plot our course. We shall make it in time. I have no doubt. It is so sad to see such innocent sailors meeting this kind of fate. It is a terrible waste ... so vain and senseless. But such is war and there is no other. It is likely that we too shall one day meet this abysmal fate. But we must stay the course. It is our duty to the Fatherland."

Kapitänleutnant Hans Vogel was the Lieutenant-Commander of the U-491 and was considered one of the finest U-boat leaders in the fleet. Although diminutive in stature, his thick broad shoulders and steely blue eyes cast a lengthy shadow of authority. To all the crew, he was heartily respected as a strong and focused leader in pursuit of his mission—a secret mission like no other. He was the epitome of a true Aryan.

This was Hans Vogel's first mission to the American coast. He left La Pallice, France on 25 January 1942 and made his way to the New Jersey coast, fighting rough seas most of the way. To conserve his batteries, Vogel was forced to run on top; to his crew, it was running the gauntlet. It wasn't until he reached the brightly-lit Maryland coast that the seas finally calmed. He was astonished to see such incredibly bright lights illuminating the shore. He could use this to his advantage.

The U-491 was a Type VII-C submarine and considered the workhorse of the fleet. It had a range of 8,500 miles and, on the surface, could cruise at seventeen knots. Under the surface it was considerably slower and only a skilled and a cunning leader could keep the enemy's depth charges from blowing her apart. If he was caught near the surface, he could escape to a 240-meter depth to avoid the blast; but in the coastal waters off North Carolina, those areas were few and far between. It was far better to stay out of harms way.

Once Vogel left the U-491's first tanker kill, passing twenty miles due east off the dreaded Diamond Shoals, the boat commander took a compass heading of 340 degrees until he reached latitude 36° 01' north, which was approximately fifteen miles from the shoreline. This was the line of sight to the west needed to receive the specially designed coded beacon signal. He had to be in position by exactly 0215 hours. He knew he was cutting it close but was confident he'd be there in time.

When he arrived, Vogel was to wait no longer than five minutes. If there was no signal, he would move forward and return the following night. After all, his orders were to sink any vessel that moved. But he had to be careful with his prey. His torpedoes were meant for special military cargo. He already had expended two torpedoes, leaving him with twelve. To preserve those weapons, he

2

could use his powerful 88-millimeter cannon mounted on the deck just below the conning tower, but conditions had to be ideal for that to happen.

After spending two hours in his less-than-spacious stateroom while the boat headed to its rendezvous point, Kapitänleutnant Vogel joined Executive Officer Staats, the Senior Lieutenant (*Oberleutnant*) and First Watch Officer, on the bridge of the conning tower.

As they crawled through the conning tower hatch, Vogel motioned to a Petty Officer (*Unteroffiziere*) and an Able Seaman (*Matrose*), who were on watch, that he and Staats would temporally observe for awhile. The enlisted sailors returned to the confines of the boat. Each officer then grabbed binoculars from around their neck and began scanning the dark horizon—and it was dark.

Today was 15 February 1942, the beginning of the new moon. With a clear brisk sky, every star in the universe was seemingly visable. What else they could see were few and far between lights on the nearby shore. The two men knew they were opposite the infamous Outer Banks of North Carolina. For the past five hundred years, it's been a desolate, dangerous place for seaman.

Kapitänleutnant Vogel had two previous duties with the U-boat fleet: in the North Atlantic fighting British convoys, and patrolling the waters of the Skagerrak and the Kattegat off Norway, Sweden, and Denmark, where British mine layers planted their deadly bombs. Because of his crafty skill and clever tactics fighting the homebound convoys, Vogel had been handpicked by Admiral Dönitz for this special mission. In return, he was allowed to handpick the crew of the U-491.

"Do you think we will receive a worthy target from our operative tonight, Herr Kaleun?" (Kaleun was a warm and affectionate term for Kapitänleutnant and often was used by both officers and crew to address their captain.)

"I really can't say, Peter. This whole operation is so new right now. Getting everything in place, picking the right people, coordinating the details. It all has taken so much time ... especially the new codes and the training of Victor Krech to decipher them. That of course is critical to the operation as well as our operative stationed on the coast. So long as those two factors work in our favor, then our job is really quite simple. But, to answer your question ... tonight is the first night of the operation. Our operative on shore, by now, should have had time to exploit the Americans ... to filter in and build their confidence. I feel a good target tonight."

"Ja, Kaleun ... perhaps you are right. Fortunately you have chosen a good Navigator and Helmsman for our mission. Obersteuermann Kurt Heinz, our Third Watch Officer, will be a very capable guide and he seems to have exceptional senses of these curiously shallow waters.

I feel comfortable that you have picked the right man. Do you know who our operative on the coast is?"

"Nein. That person was planted many months ago. I understand the *Sicherheitsdienst* put him on the coast just before the war started with Poland. But when war broke out with Britain, he devised the plan to stop the special military cargo on this coast before it reached England. Apparently he has key knowledge of which ships to target. He then passes that information to us and, hopefully, we can sink it before it leaves the coast."

Just as Kapitänleutnant Vogel finished his cigarette, the conning tower hatch opened. It was the Obersteuermann Heinz alerting the commander they were within ten minutes of their rendezvous point. Vogel asked Staats to send up Victor Krech with his gear. He wanted him to get acclimated to the cold weather, the darkness, and be ready to receive the message. He wanted no one else on the bridge.

A few minutes later Krech joined Vogel in the conning tower. It was now just the two of them. "Are you ready son," Vogel said in a calming tone.

"Aye sir ... I am ready. I see that it is very dark. This will make for good observation. I should have no problem."

"Good then. We are approaching our latitude. The west is in that direction."

Victor Krech had no rank on the boat. He was given a uniform and was classified as a radioman (*Funkmaat*) and put in charge of special communications. Even though his status carried no weight in the actual operating of the boat, his job was vital for the success of the mission. Without his trained skills, the operation could not function.

Victor Krech was not handpicked by Kapitän Vogel. He was specifically assigned to him from the State Security Service known as the SD (*Sicherheitsdienst*). This function was considered a sister organization to the dreaded Secret State Police (*Gestapo*). Through the SD, Krech was trained to decipher the coded signal.

In 1938, Krech was studying math at the Berlin University. His outstanding performance was noticed by certain people. After his sophomore year, he was approached by an eerie Gestapo Agent named Conrad Kruger. Because of his exceptional mathematical abilities, he suggested to Krech to think about working for the Nazis in the field of codes. At first, he refused saying he wanted no part of the Nazi regime. Unfortunately, it was not the answer they wanted to hear. For that reason, the Gestapo put pressure on his parents. Fearing for their safety and well-being, he reconsidered his position and joined the regime.

While at the university, Victor became fast friends with a fellow student named Johann Krauss, who was studying medicine to become a doctor. He also was contacted by Agent Kruger about working for

4

the Nazis in the field of linguistics. American-born, Johann had excellent knowledge of the English language and could speak it fluently—but there was a reason. He was an American citizen.

He explained to Agent Kruger that he was born in America to German parents who were currently still living there. He therefore had no reason to work for the Nazis. But to Agent Kruger, it made no difference. As far as he was concerned, Johann Krauss was a German. Because of his refusal to join the regime, he was removed from school and forcibly conscripted into the German Army. There appeared to be no hope for his escape when war broke out. *

Kapitänleutnant Vogel had some knowledge of Victor Krech's past and felt more sympathy than apathy knowing he was forced into an undesired situation. Nonetheless, Krech was now charged with an important roll and was required to accomplish the mission regardless of the cost.

Only the officers aboard the U-491 were privy to their mission. The crew was not. They were only aware of going to the vast coast of America to sink cargo ships. But what they did know was that Victor Krech had an important part in the mission. What part, they had no idea.

By 0210 hours at latitude 36° 01' north, Kerch began an early scan of the coastline with his M IV/1T Carl Zeiss 7 x 50 binoculars. These glasses were considered far superior than the British Barr and Stroud Pattern 1900A binoculars. The unit weighed one pound less, and its internal glass surfaces were bloomed to reduce reflection losses, thus increasing the light transmission to eighty percent, compared to sixty-six percent for the British glass.

Another advantage to the Zeiss lens was allowing the observer's eye to move across the axis with no ill effect on the quality of definition in the various regions of the field of view. In as much as receiving a faint signal fifteen miles from shore on a bobbing submarine, these binoculars were an excellent choice for the task.

Vogel, using the same type of glasses, also began scanning the horizon. After five minutes, there was nothing but empty space. With his arms getting tired, Kerch lowered his glasses. Vogel continued scanning.

Just as Kerch was about to resume, Vogel spotted a series of flashes low on the horizon and quickly told Kerch to look. Vogel thought the flashes he saw were part of the code. What he saw was a preliminary signal signifying the entire code was about to start.

Ten seconds later, a series of flashes, similar to a Morse code, popped across the horizon. Kerch was glued to the tower rail, deeply

---

* To discover the fate of Johann Krauss, read "Nebraska Doppelganger" by Thomas J. Morrow.

concentrating on the signals. Vogel also remained very still, observing the flashes, oblivious as to what they meant. In reality, so was Kerch. He wouldn't know until he went below to translate its meaning from a specially prepared notebook.

After forty seconds, the flashes stopped. Kerch told the Kapitän he had it sequenced and needed to get below. Vogel opened the hatch and allowed Kerch to enter first. After Vogel went below, he immediately ordered the three seamen and watch officer to retake their positions on the bridge.

Kerch promptly went to work scanning his notebook. Within five minutes, he had the message in hand. Before taking it to Vogel, he double-checked his translation. After verifying the message, he passed them forward to Vogel, who was standing at the small chart table ready to plot his new course. Also standing by was Obersteuermann Heinz.

Vogel read the message. The first sequence in the signal read: Quadrant CA, Section 7665—a point outside the southern entrance to the Chesapeake Bay. The second sequence revealed its target: a very large freighter packed with important military cargo. Heinz immediately plotted his course.

In an effort to thwart Allied military intelligence and to simplify the complicated and laborious task of plotting latitude and longitude, Admiral Dönitz devised an abridged mathematical grid system to track his submarines as well as the ships of his enemy. This matrix was charted throughout the waters of the world even to where many of his boats would never go. Some grids were irregular by virtue of the shape of the earth and some grids overlapped onto land. This made no difference.

This specialized map, known as Chart 1870G, composed of a grid system equally divided into square quadrants of 486 nautical miles starting in the North Atlantic Ocean above the Arctic Circle to the South Atlantic Ocean just above the Antarctic Circle. These large quadrants were designated with two letters of the alphabet.

The first letter of the quadrant designated north to south while the second letter designated west to east. There were some slight deviations in the lettering based on design; but essentially the northwestern top row started with "AA."

The quadrant that covered the eastern coast of the United States from Portsmouth, New Hampshire south to Cape Fear, North Carolina and inland to about the longitude of Northeast New Hampshire was designated "Quadrant CA." Again, the submariners dismissed the sections over land. Moving from west to east across the Atlantic, the eastern most section was "Quadrant CG" where it adjoined the coasts of Spain, Portugal, North Africa, and the Straits of Gibraltar.

To achieve exactness, the quadrant was then divided into nine equal squares, each being 162 nautical miles representing numbers eleven through ninety-nine and excluding numbers with zeros. These were the first two numbers of the sequence after the quadrant letters.

Following this division, each section was further reduced into another nine squares representing fifty-four nautical miles and numbered one through nine. This was the third number of the sequence. For the final reduction, this section was divided into nine squares, also numbered one through nine. This last reduction of squares was only six nautical miles or thirty-six square miles. It represented the fourth and last number in the sequence.

Vogel asked Heinz what time he could expect to reach his destination. "Sir, if we get underway by 0245 hours, we should be at the rendezvous point by 0623 local time."

"Good ... very good! Our target is a very large military cargo ship leaving Norfolk. Based on our information, we should make contact by 0630. From there, the freighter should make a course adjustment to the northwest. It will be in a convoy of three ships with our target ship in the middle. We should recognize it as the biggest of the three. They will not be running with their lights."

"Sir, do we know what type of cargo it is carrying?" asked Staats.

"Military, nothing but high-grade military wares. We are not to bother ourselves with the other two ships. With sunrise approaching during this time, we must immediately return to deeper waters. We will need to find a nice sandy bottom and settle down for the day and rest until dusk. Then we will go back on patrol and check for another signal. I'm sure the American destroyers will begin looking for us ... and I want to be miles away. Staats, get us underway! We must run on the surface and maintain seventeen knots if we are to get there in time. When we get within firing range, we will attack submerged."

"Aye aye sir ... helmsman ... heading 3 – 4 – 0 degrees. Both diesels all ahead full!"

Running at night on the surface was common practice for the German submarines. As predators, they had the advantage of darkness and the ability to vanish at a moment's notice. It was the perfect choice to create chaos on the American coast. But the subs were fallible. While their speeds on the surface were quick and agile, their ability underwater was less than desirable. The U-boats were slow and cumbersome, limited to the power provided by their batteries. If detected by a destroyer, they could be doomed to destruction in short order. Only a cunning skipper could quickly dive them to safety. But there was a curiosity among the U-boat skippers: why weren't the American defenses fighting back?

The Commander-in-Chief of U.S. Naval Operations was Admiral Ernest J. King. He was a crusty ol' salt who was blunt and rude, often basing his decisions on personal whims. In 1941, the United States Coast Guard merged under the auspices of the United States Navy. With the outbreak of war and the East Coast erupting in flames, on 6 February 1942, King put Rear Admiral Adolphus "Dolly" Andrews, commandant of the Coast Guard, in charge of the newly-created Eastern Sea Frontier (ESF). The ESF previously had been known as the old Northern and Southern Atlantic Naval Coastal Frontiers. It was a daunting task Admiral Andrews met with trepidation.

In a report to Admiral King, Andrews lamented his only vessels could be out-distanced by U-boat running on the surface, plus a Coast Guard cutter's meager guns were greatly out-ranged. To protect the vast American coastline, he pleaded for help. With a massive fleet of unlimited firepower bottled up in the Norfolk area harbors, King wanted to save his Atlantic fleet for a potential sea battle with the Germans—or send it to the Pacific to fight the Japanese. In any case, Andrew's request was denied and told to defend the coastal waters with what he had. It was an arbitrary decision that cost many seamen's lives. The U-boats had a free hand to roam without provocation.

Kapitänleutnant Vogel, through the conning tower voice tube, yelled to Chief Stresemann down in the control room (*Zentrale*), "I'm going to pull the plug. Let's trim the boat. Clear the bridge for dive!"

Immediately, and with the utmost of speed, the five-man bridge party shimmied down the aluminum ladder into the conning tower (*Kommandoturm*), and then into the control room.

"Herr Kaleun, tower hatch secured, bridge watch below!" Staats yelled.

"Chief, take us to periscope depth. E motors half-speed. Flood!" said Vogel.

"Yes, Herr Kaleun. Flood negative!" yelled Stresemann. While doing so, he rang the dive bell; its shrillness clanging throughout the boat; red lights flashing in every compartment. Immediately the crew came alive, moving in different directions throughout the boat; their voices reporting to the Chief in sequence, by loudspeaker, the boat's present condition. By intently listening to the crewmembers' reports, he smoothly submerged the boat.

Unteroffiziere Ralf "Viti" Stresemann was Chief of the Boat and the Leading Engineer (*Leitender Ingenieur*). He was directly responsible for the entire operation of the submarine, including the submerging and surfacing of the boat, as well as keeping it trimmed out at all times. Because he was the oldest member of this crew, he was fondly referred to as "Papa."

"Air vents open – one, two, three, five!"

"Flood valves open!"

"Diesel air valve closed!"

"Diesel engines shut down and dis-engaged! Fuel levers set to zero!"

"Ready to dive!"

"Electric motors engaged to shafts! Half speed!"

"Ventilators closed!

Chief Stresemann leaned towards the hydroplane operators. The sounds of activity still resonated throughout the boat: orders, signals, bells.

He ordered: "Forward plane down ten degrees. "Aft plane down five degrees."

As the U-491 slowly slid beneath the surface, the clamor inside the boat came to an immediate halt; it was dead quiet except for gurgling sounds of bubbling air and the faint hum of electrical motors. The chief watched the column of mercury in the periscope elevation indicator that showed the depths the boat was passing. What he saw was not to his liking. The boat was out of balance.

"Herr Kaleun, we are stern heavy. The torpedoes we earlier launched have thrown us out of balance."

"Get us level and balanced out, Chief!"

"Aye sir. Forward plane up five. Aft plane up five. Close flood valves. Close air vents. E motors slow ahead. Rudder amidship. Prepare to trim!

"Pump four hundred kilograms from aft trim to forward trim!" Throughout the boat, water could be heard running through overhead pipes. It wasn't enough to level her out.

"Pump one hundred kilograms from sea to forward trim." The trimming scales showed the boat gradually settling into a static horizontal plane. The trim finally settled on the number he was seeking: zero. The chief was satisfied the boat was trimmed.

"Herr Kapitän, boat is trimmed." Vogel wasn't pleased.

"Chief, look at you mercury! We are rising."

The chief immediately looked at his depth manometer (*Tiefenmesser*). The captain was correct. While the boat was level, it was experiencing more buoyancy than he expected. It was slowly rising. It was a mental error. Aside from properly balancing the boat, he neglected to adjust the weight. He quickly ordered an adjustment.

"Pump two hundred kilograms seawater to regulator cells!" Within minutes, the boat properly settled at the right periscope depth—thirteen and a half meters. Kapitän Vogel was now ready to find and kill his prey. The event had taken longer than expected. But not all was lost; his target was late.

The command was given to prepare bow tubes one, two, three, and four. The target was big and Vogel believed he might need them all.

Now at periscope depth, Vogel entered the small confines of the conning tower just above the control room. He peered into his attack periscope (*Standzielsehrohr*) while sitting on a tiny swivel saddle resembling a bicycle seat. The closer they got to the target, the more tensions built.

"Course, steady at 3 – 4 – 0. Speed, five knots," Staats relayed to Vogel.

When the boat reached its rendezvous point, there were no signs of any big ships lugging about. What Vogel did see were other smaller freighters. If he couldn't find his target, he pondered an alternate ship.

"Kapitän, it is 0645 hours local," Staats relayed.

No sooner had the five come out of his mouth, Vogel excitedly exclaimed, "There she is -- just where she is supposed to be. And she is in the middle of two smaller freighters ... just as predicted!" Vogel ordered a slight change in course to better his firing position.

The periscope slowly sliced through the calm waters twenty miles off the Chesapeake Bay. Its' wake could not be seen at this pre-dawn hour. Unknown to the crew aboard the freighter, their fate had been sealed.

Kapitän Vogel continued peering through his periscope, zeroing in on his target. Quickly spanning the area, he ordered the boat's speed to three knots. He then asked Staats to compute a firing solution from the electromechnical deflection calculator (*Vorhaltrechner*) from the numbers he called out.

"Distance 1,800 meters ... target speed seventeen ... angle on the bow green [Starboard] twenty-eight ... depth three." Staats worked the torpedo calculator finding the correct values to set the gyro-angle on the torpedoes. Vogel ordered tubes flooded and ready for firing.

"Kapitän, solution computed ... torpedo room reports tubes one, two, three, and four made ready in all respects," Staats reported.

"Open tube doors one and two. Prepare to fire," Vogel ordered.

Vogel continued adjusting his course and speed for better position. He gave Staats a new set of numbers for calculation.

"Correct distance 1,700 meters ... angle on the bow green twenty-five ... speed sixteen ... depth three ... ready tubes one and two."

"Sir, new solution computed ... torpedo tubes are ready!"

"On my command...." There was a brief pause. The control room remained quiet.

"Release torpedo one," Vogel ordered, waiting a split second before firing his second fish.

"Release torpedo two!" Vogel said in a matter-of-fact fashion.

With high-pressure water forcibly ejecting the torpedoes from their tubes, the boat slightly trembled with a pneumatic jolt of air echoing throughout the hull. The submarine briefly rose several meters. Quickly, Chief Stresemann adjusted the ballast tanks and the boat slowly settled down. Death had just been delivered.

Given the distance and speed of the torpedoes to their mark, the helmsman reported a time of one minute and twenty-six seconds to target. After one minute, Heinz quietly counted the seconds. "Five ... ten ... fifteen ... twenty ... twenty-five seconds, Herr Kapitän." Vogel and Staats looked at each other. Were their torpedoes duds or did they miscalculate their firing solution?

"Thirty seconds Herr Kapitän!"

At that moment, a heavily muffled explosion vibrated the boat. Within seconds another sharp explosion was detected. The torpedoes hit their mark. The crew clapped with excitement. Vogel quickly quieted them.

The Kapitän raised the scope and lowered his eyes to the lens. What he saw were massive flames violently erupting into the sky, followed by black charcoal-like smoke, aimlessly curling in all directions. Ammo deep within the hull was igniting its shells, sending wayward bullets streaking through the air. Moments later, and with a thunderous roar, the ship exploded, sending helpless sailors tumbling through the air, engulfed in flames. It was unthinkable to believe anybody could have survived this blast. Within minutes, the ship was no more—sinking to the bloody depths of a cold dark sea.

Vogel then allowed Staats a look. Following him was head radioman Junior Lieutenant (*Leutnant*) and Second Watch Officer Josef Brückner.

"Sir, shall we go find her name?" asked Staats.

"Nein ... nein. That will not be necessary. Have Leutnant Brückner tune in on the six-hundred-meter band and monitor the international traffic. They will, in due course, report her name as well as the tanker we sunk. It is best we leave the area. Sunrise is quickly approaching and we should leave. We will soon have another new target to attack. Our first mission to America has been a grand success. *BdU* will be pleased.

"Exec ... take us south to deeper waters and have the Chief settle us on a sandy bottom. There has been enough killing for the day."

Chapter 2

Thirty-five-year-old Dare County Deputy Sheriff R.W. Scoggins was a fine looking, sinewy man, whose six-foot frame and brawny shoulders always garnished a second look from both men and women. With deep-set blue-gray eyes, brownish-blond hair, and a strong angular jaw, R.W. spoke with a hint of Gaelic brogue, mixed with a Carolina drawl so widely spoken throughout the small populace of the Outer Banks.

The Gaelic burr was brought to the barrier islands years before from sections of settlers from Tidewater Virginia and the Eastern Shores of Maryland from families that had previously migrated many years before from the southwest portion England and the Ulster province of Ireland. Mixed with a moiety of southern-speak from the states well below the Mason and Dixon Line, the dialect was rather uncommon but pleasing to hear.

Cruising the roads along the Banks in his sun-faded green 1937 Pontiac Deluxe sedan, Deputy Scoggins was easily recognized by his non-descript khaki colored uniform and neatly rolled sleeves to just above his elbow. His well-worn engineer boots, continually in need of a polish from the constant dulling of finely powdered sand, usually snagged a pant leg in his boot top just below his shin. And with searing hot days under a sizzling Carolina summer sun, he always wore his wide-brown sweat-stained green felt fedora trimly folded down all around.

R.W. was well-known throughout the islands of the Outer Banks and rarely wore his badge. He opted instead to keep it veiled in his rear pocket wallet. And because of his worthy reputation, he didn't need a sidearm; he always had a large, dutiful and loyal companion at his side.

Standing six-foot-six and thicker than a sack of wholegrain oats, George Washington Dawkins was a trueborn American Indian. Coming from the southeast portion of the state in the Roberson County area where his descendant Lumbee Tribe had migrated, George's heritage was directly linked to the original Algonquian Indian band of the Pamlico, Hatteras, and Croatan Tribes.

His roots were genuine to the Outer Banks when the first European colonist arrived. While it's virtually impossible to determine, because of the extreme chaos that existed during the early years of European colonization, it was entirely possible George was a direct descendent of the Croatan Tribe, who adopted the original colonists from Roanoke Island. When that settlement mysteriously disappeared, its legend became infamously known as "The Lost Colony." Though it was by and far a long stretch of the imagination, George always joked to R.W. that his family was the first to cook a turkey dinner on Thanksgiving Day in 1587. And R.W. always joked that his family was the first to invent the wheel. It was this type of jovial camaraderie that kept their friendship close.

R.W. and George met back in the summer of 1930 when both were laboring on the Wright Memorial Bridge being constructed over the Currituck Sound.

R.W. was a native of the Outer Banks by virtue of his father's life-long job as a commercial fisherman from the small fishing village of Wanchese on the south side of Roanoke Island. George, on the other hand, was a native from Lumberton, North Carolina.

In 1922, fifteen-year-old George got wind of an outstanding American Indian athlete by the name of Jim Thorpe. Aside from learning of his great physical abilities in the 1912 Olympics in Antwerp, Belgium, and also of his adeptness at the game of football, George wanted to be an athlete like Thorpe.

Studying hard and staying out of trouble, In 1925, George's prowess got him into the Indian Normal School of Roberson County. They had a football team, and he was determined to hit the field and make his mark. While studying the books was infinitely important, football was his ultimate goal. He heard that Thorpe was coaching an all-American Indian pro football team, called the Oorang Indians, and wanted to play for them. Unfortunately for George, during his second year of school while playing in an off-season football game, he was accidently clipped by an inexperienced player and George's right knee was badly injured. From that moment onward, he was never again able to play the game he loved so much.

In 1929, after rehabilitation and finishing his education, he decided it was time to help his cash-strapped family. George went looking for work. With the beginning of the Great Depression, that was easier said than done. Nevertheless, with his large sturdy frame and exuberant desire to work, he was able to find an array of jobs where muscle was the key. In the following spring, he was alerted to a lengthy bridge construction job over the Currituck Sound in the northeastern part of the state. He headed in that direction.

George and R.W. became fast friends and enjoyed each other's company. When the bridge was completed in the fall, R.W. rejoined his father's fishing boat to support his wife, Emily Mae, and their newborn son, Josh.

George headed north where he found an abundance of work in the bustling business of construction. With his dauntless agility at wuthering heights and his awesomely incredible Samson-like strength, George helped construct a many of the towering structures dotting the skyline of New York City.

By the summer of 1941, George decided to return to the South and, with time on his hands, ventured a trip to the Banks to visit his buddy—if R.W. was still around. To his good fortune, he was. But by now, R.W. had taken station as a deputy sheriff. Several years before, another deputy, who was patrolling the lower Banks, accidentally drowned when he slipped and fell into the treacherous Oregon Inlet at a ferry crossing. Several days later, from the Pamlico Sound, R.W.'s fishing boat retrieved the body. It had been carried inland with the rising tide.

With the loss of his deputy, Dare County Sheriff Roscoe Simmons began looking for a replacement. At the time, R.W.'s dad was contemplating cutting back his business because of an assortment of minor health problems related to his years at sea. Finding it challenging to continue the grind, he offered to his son command of the boat. R.W. seriously scrutinized the offer; but he, himself, was tiring of the toil. Though in a quandary of muddled deliberation, and a dilemma all its own, Sheriff Simmons, in a quirk of fate, cajoled R.W. into joining the small force. After discussing the various points of interest, R.W. made the move. While the salary could have been better, there would be considerably less stress; and there were some office perks—free meals and gasoline for his car.

A man of George's stature was certainly well-noticed. After hitching a ride to Martins Point, where the bridge he helped build eleven years earlier adjoined the sound side of the Banks, George started walking east then south along the sandy coastal road, more commonly known as Highway 12, or as locals called it, "the Virginia Dare Trail." Sam Beatty, one of Sheriff Simmons's deputies, noticed George and picked him up for vagrancy. He hauled the Indian off to the Manteo jail. George didn't seem concerned of the charge; he gladly welcomed the ride. As far as George was concerned, he was being chauffeured into town. It sure as hell beat pounding the pavement for the next nineteen and a half miles in the searing summer heat.

When deputy and prisoner made their way to the Sheriff's office, Roscoe was sitting behind his desk working on an assortment of mundane paperwork. When George walked in, and ducking beneath the top of the doorway jam, Roscoe's mouth flew open. He'd never seen such a colossal person.

"Sheriff ... found this here Indian walk'en down Highway 12 up there by Martins Point ... didn't give me no information as to who he was or what he was doing ... just grunted a bit want'en to know if this was where the 'deer and antelope play.' I think he was just being a smart ass ... we ain't got no deer and antelope out here! So, I hauled his big ass down here. Want'a throw 'em in the cooler for being a smart ass?"

"Now hold on Sam ... let's see if we can find out just who this feller is before we get too drastic." Turning to the Indian, Roscoe calmly spoke.

"Okay son, now ... what's your name?"

"Big Chief Whoompass from hills out west. On trail long time looking for fire-water at end of rainbow," George said in a very serious slow and deep mocking monotone.

"Now see Sam, that was real easy. You just got'a know how to handle these situations. Now we know who he is, where he's from, and what he's doing here. Okay now, let's get serious a bit. What'cha really doing out here, boy?"

Looking the Sheriff squarely in the eye and speaking clearly, George said, "Well Sheriff, I'm looking for an old friend of mine I met out here years ago ... a white guy I worked with on the Wright Memorial Bridge back in 1930. He's from this area. I just wondered if he's still around."

"Now just who in the hell might that be 'Tonto?' 'The Lone Ranger'?" Sam interjected.

George ignored the remark.

"Maybe you know him ... fellow by the name of R.W. Scoggins. The last I heard, he was working on his dad's fishing boat. You know if he's still around?"

"Well I'll be John Brown! You know ol' R.W. does ya?" Roscoe replied.

"Yes, Sheriff, I do. Know where I can find him after I post bail?"

"Ah shit son, we ain't gonna lock ya ass up. Sam! Get on the horn and call over to R.W.'s house. He's take'en the day off. Now get to it now!"

"Yeah ... okay Chief."

While Sam got on the phone, Sheriff Simmons offered George a seat and asked him to try and not shatter the chair. The last fellow they hauled in was drunk and slammed the chair up against the wall. They fixed it, but it was still wobbly.

16

"Now just what in Sam Hill brings you all the way out here? You know ol' R.W. works for me now … been here going on 'bout three years. Good man he is. Has a lot of respect of the folks 'round here … covers the barrier islands by his self. Usually don't have much trouble out there with him on patrol."

"Well Sheriff, I'd been up north in New York building skyscrapers and then one day I just decided to come home."

"Now just where in the hell is home, son … and by the way, what's your name?"

"George Washington Dawkins and I'm from Roberson County. Know where that is?"

"Yeah, I think so. Down there 'round the Lumberton area. You a Lumbee?"

"Yes, I am. But you know, my great, great, great, great, great granddaddy was born right here on this island."

"Naw … you shit'en me ain't 'cha?"

"Now Sheriff, would I do that?"

Sam walked over and told Simmons that R.W. would be over in a jiffy. He said he was curious as to know who was looking for him. He was bringing his son with him.

After a little more chin-wagging, R.W. pulled up to the two-story brick courthouse and parked on the street. He hurriedly walked into the office with Josh tagging along. Standing right before his eyes was big George Washington Dawkins. Scoggins walked over with a gleaming grin and shook George's hand also putting his left hand on George's thick right forearm.

"Well, I see you met my boss here," R.W. said to George,

"Yes, I sure did. Met Sam over there too!"

"Hi there George!" Sam meekly said standing by the window.

"Have any problems, George?"

"No, everything went smooth. Didn't it Sheriff?" George said winking to Simmons.

"Oh yeah … no problem. No problems a'tall. Ain't that right Sam?"

"Yeah … no problem. Good to meet you, George."

With that, the three left the office and got into R.W.'s car and headed back to his house in Wanchese. R.W. was anxious to catch-up on the past years. It had been a long time. Even though the two hadn't seen each other in eleven years, their friendship endured. George was a man to reckon with; but in actuality, he was gentle as a lamb.

R.W. had a small modest wooden frame house he built years ago on a small parcel of land he purchased during his glory days of fishing with his father. Because the land was in a lower section of the island, the house was built three feet off the ground. This was to help keep the water from flooding the interior of the house by the monstrous sea storms that always seemed to come out of nowhere. While it wasn't a part of the standard building code, it was just common sense to do so. Some residents along the shore built their homes even higher to take advantage of the pretty views of the surrounding sounds of the Roanoke, Croatan, or Pamlico.

One of the nicer touches to R.W.'s house was a large screened-in porch just off the living room. He and Josh would spend many a night talking and listening to the tree frogs croak the night away. It was a soothing place to be after spending many long hours in the dreadful sun that continually drenched the Banks.

After about thirty minutes of catching up on the past, R.W. finally got around to asking George what he was doing back on the islands.

"My knee finally gave out on me. I was working on the thirtieth floor of some skyscraper in New York, and I damned near fell to my death. The doctors took one look at it and said my days as a steeple jack in the skies were over. While I thought my knee had healed from the old football injury, it never really did. Oh, it seemed okay, but the real damage had already been done. I saved some money and had it operated on, but they said it'd never fully heal properly ... just told me to keep it wrapped up and don't lift anything real heavy. That's about all I can do for now. Sometimes it acts up ... sometimes it doesn't; though, most of the time it's okay.

"I came this way to see if you could help me find a job on a fishing boat. I thought I'd learn fishing. You know us Indians are supposed to be fishermen! But, to tell you the truth, I never once ever baited a hook ... don't know a damn thing about it. Thought you might be able to 'hook me up'... but it looks like you're already in another profession right now."

"Yeah, that sort of turned out to be a quirky thing. But so far is fishing is concerned, I don't know what I can do for you, George. Dad sold his boat awhile back and has pretty much retired. Most of the other older fishermen have kind'a done the same thing. We got a whole new breed out there now ... can't say that I know too many of 'em right now. Oh ... they for sure know me, but it ain't quite like it used to be."

George understood what R.W. was saying. He knew it was a gamble to ask in the first place. George thought he might get lucky. He seemed a little disheartened. Then R.W. had an idea.

"Hey George, how'd you like to be a deputy?"

"You're kidd'en me aren't you?"

"No really, I've got an idea. When I go in tomorrow, I'll talk it over with Sheriff Simmons. Something just popped into my mind, and I think he'll go for it."

"But how ... Kemo Sabe?" George said in a mocking Indian tone.

18

"You leave that to me. In the meantime, why don't you stay here with me and Josh awhile until I can get things squared away. It'll be okay, George. Wanchese is a diversified area and folks 'round here don't make much a fuss over such matters. Aside from the white fisherman, the other half of the population here in Wanchese is colored folk and everybody gets along just fine. Besides, ain't nobody gonna mess with me anyway. And you George, hell ... you're 'bout as big as that damn Wright Brothers Monument up there on Kill Devil Hill and ain't nobody crazy enough to be messing with your ass!"

"But Kemo Sabe," George said humorously. "I ain't worrying about those other folks. What about Emily Mae, your wife? What she going to say?"

"Ah hell George, I forget to tell you. She left us ... me and Josh. Left right after I took this job with Simmons ... just packed up one day and left. Took Josh over to Dad's house and then disappeared. When I got home from duty one evening, I found a note pinned to my pillow ... said she didn't want to be an island girl anymore ... wanted more in life than peeling raw shrimp and brushing sand off the sheets. I really don't know where she went. I tried finding her, but she hid herself purty good. After awhile I sort of figured she might come home one day. Then again, maybe not. So me and Josh just kept right on living ... going about our business. At first Josh was upset, but he got over it purty quick when he realized she didn't love 'em anymore by taking off the way she did. Ever since, he's been just fine.

"A couple of weeks ago, and out of the damn blue, I got a letter from some fancy Washington, D.C. lawyer serving me divorce papers ... said she just wants out of the marriage ... nothing else. Inside the papers was a handwritten note from her. She said she was sorry for any heartache she caused but couldn't take it anymore ... just wanted a better life for herself and she knew I couldn't provide that. So off she went and found herself a man of means ... wants to marry 'em.

You know George, we were high school sweethearts. We got along fine. But I tell ya, it sure as hell threw me for a loop when she took off. I never once figured she'd ever do that. But hell, that shit happens and sometimes there just ain't nothing you can do about it!

"I never said nothing to anybody 'bout it. Then one day last week I was over at the Midget Market in Whalebone when one of the local seasonal residents, a lawyer named Michael from Raleigh, told me he was sorry to hear about my divorce and, if I needed any legal help, to give him a call ... said he'd heard about it through Jenny Smith, our Postmistress. Damned if she ain't the 'Mouth of the South' 'round these parts! Well, I reckon sooner or later word was gonna leak out, so I let it go. Anyway, I gave this ol' boy a call and he said he'd make sure I didn't get bamboozled by some slick attorney ... said he'd make sure she couldn't ever get her paws on Josh. That's really all that mattered. Well, we shall see!

"Hey, let's stop talk'en 'bout this nonsense. You want a brew?"

"Humph, me Big Chief Whoompass looking for firewater under rainbow!"

"I guess that's a 'big' yes ... huh?"

"Yeah," George said with a laugh.

Chapter 3

The weather on the Outer Banks in late February 1942 was about as typical as it could get—cold and windy with white puffy cumulus clouds rolling in the far Atlantic sky. In the late afternoon, the slowly setting sun usually projected a vast array of soothing reds, yellows, and oranges, inspiring one's mind to far away places. And this afternoon was no exception.

After finishing their daily patrol and cruising south from the upper Banks far above the small township of Duck, R.W. and George decided to call it a day and head towards the office and prepare their daily paperwork. At this time of year, the roads were virtually empty except for the few lonely beach fishermen that were taking their catch-of-the-day home for a freshly cooked meal.

Just before turning onto the Wash Baum Bridge in the little community of Whalebone, then heading back over to Manteo, George noticed four gangly characters being loud and boisterous in the parking lot of Shanklyn's beer joint across from Jennette's Fishing Pier. They were standing next to a white 1940 Ford Tudor Deluxe with Georgia license plates. R.W. noticed them as well, but what caught his eye was the whisky bottle they were passing back and forth.

In this county, a person could only purchase beer and wine, then it had to be consumed inside the premises. Drinking whiskey was one thing, but drinking it out in the open was another. Such things were forbidden and against the law. R.W. turned his Pontiac around and pulled into the parking lot about twenty feet away with the driver's side of his car facing the passenger side of theirs. He casually got out and approached the boys. George stayed inside the car keeping a steady bead in their direction. He knew what to do.

"What's going on there fellas?" R.W. said in a jovial sort of way.

"Who wants to know there ... asshole?" said the smart aleck in the group.

"You fellas look like you're having a little snort there. Mind tell'en me where you got the bottle?"

"Well, it just fell right out'a the sky over thar and hit ol' Curtis upside the head," said the smart one again.

Yep, that's where it come from ... just fell out'a the sky and hit me upside the head," snickered the one called Curtis.

"Now looky here fellas, don't be piss'en down my back and be tell'en me it's rain'en?"

"Look asshole, I don't give a shit if'n it's rain'en or not. Now why don't you just get back in that piece-o'-shit you just pulled up in and get the hell out'a here before Bubba here plants five knuckles upside yo' head!"

"Now fellas, I don't know how you folks do things down there in Georgia, but up here, drink'en whisky in this county on a public street ain't exactly what we folks call legal. Now if you just hand me the bottle, get in your car, and head back from whinst ya came from ... we'll just call it a day and nobody'll get hurt."

"And just who the hell are you ... the *goddamned* Lone Ranger?"

"Well, in a manner of speaking...."

Just moments before, George saw the commotion building, so he unnoticeably slid from the passenger door and walked to the back of the Georgia boys' car, carrying a Remington Model 31 twelve-gauge shotgun. He pumped its chamber making that unmistakable "slick-slick" sound that echoed off the front of the building. He lowered the weapon waist high and pointed it directly at the belligerent youths – in particular the one doing most of the loud-mouth talk en.'

"What's that *goddamn* big Indian do'en with that shotgun!" Curtis said wide-eyed with an unusually high-pitched voice.

"I'm Deputy Sheriff Scoggins, and oh, and by the way fellas ... that's Tonto!

R.W. squared himself toward the group as if to draw a sidearm, even though he had none. He slowly crossed his arms.

"Tonto here has taken the notion you fellas have pissed me off. Fortunately *he's* in a good mood right now, but if you start piss'en down *his* back, he's liable to loosen your load and stiffen you up, and that's gonna cause me a whole lot of extra paperwork ... and I really hate paperwork. So, why don't you be good little puppies and just hand me over that bottle and whatever else ya got there so's that we can all go home real peaceful like."

"O' yes sir, yes sir ... no problem. Bubba, quick ... open the trunk and give this nice officer the rest of what we got. We sho' as hell don't mean no harm ... *no sir*, we didn't mean that a'tall!"

Curtis put the lid on the bottle they were drinking from and quickly handed it to R.W., along with six other bottles Bubba had gathered out of the trunk.

"Now, gee fellas, that wasn't too hard now, was it?' R.W. said in a slow, country-like drawl.

"No sir, no sir ... no it weren't!"

R.W. then got a stern look on his face. The country bumpkin tone in his voice was gone.

"Ya'll just mosey on out'a here, nice and easy like, and be careful. I don't ever want'a see your nasty asses 'round here again ... you got that?"

"But sheriff, we're supposed to be go'en out deep sea fishing tomorrow!"

"I don't believe that's gonna happen here, Curtis ... as matter of fact, if I ever do see your ugly faces anywhere on The Banks, I'm just gonna have Tonto here throw your asses under the jail ... you know what I mean there, Bubba!"

"O' yes sir ... yes sir we do. We're out'a here!"

And with that the boys jammed into their little Ford and took off nice and easy, heading north up Highway 12 to the Currituck Bridge – going well under the speed limit. Just as they were out of sight, R.W. and George looked at each other and broke out laughing.

"Think those Georgia crackers will ever come back," George laminated.

"Naw, even though they were piss'en vinegar when they left, I don't think we'll see 'em again ... not after see'en your big ass with that young cannon of a shotgun. Come on 'Tonto' ... let's put this whisky in the trunk and head on over to Bessie's Café and grab something to eat. Hell, I'm so hungry right now I could eat the south end out of a northbound polecat. We'll do the paperwork first thing in the morning. I do believe I'm not too much in the mood to be push'en a pencil right now."

Located on a thickly-crushed seashell-bed, some three-foot off the ground in the widely diversified Wanchese fishing community, stood Bessie's Café. It was a landmark to folks on The Banks, and a short stones throw away from the largest marina on the wharf where all the fisherman docked their boats. It was the only restaurant in Dare County where both the whites and coloreds could gather and avoid the racism so ripe for the times throughout the rest of the South.

The South was segregated and it was taboo for a colored person to come into a white restaurant and expect to be served. As a matter fact, it just never happened. It was always understood that it wasn't the proper thing to do. But on the other hand, it was okay for a colored to enter a white restaurant through the kitchen, which was usually located in the rear, order a meal, and eat it on the picnic tables that some owners had put behind their store just for that purpose.

Many restaurant owners were sympathetic to the colored folk. It was an unwritten law of the South that prevailed for decades.

But, it was acceptable for a white person to patronize a colored restaurant if he so desired, but in most parts of the South, that didn't happen. Such occasions were either because the white folks were Yankees and didn't know any better, or they were locals accustomed to the culinary delights of colored cooks. What it really boiled down to was colored folk preferred to eat with colored folk and white folk preferred to eat with white folk. But here it was different. At Bessie's, all the social graces were hurled to the wind blow en' off the Atlantic. It was considered by and far the most popular restaurant on the island and an enjoyable place to eat. Bessie cooked the best home-cooked meals in the whole of the county. Even area white café owners could be seen sneaking in for a bite of her ham biscuits – always trying to figure out her recipe by taste alone.

Being a fourth generation islander, Bessie Potts was a gregarious, albeit portly lady who knew her patrons well. With her round, brown face and jovial sense of humor, she welcomed her customers to their delight. Here, segregation held no quarter. Even the meanest of bigots meekly and quietly sat to enjoy her cuisine. It was a colorless corner along the American coast.

When her father died in a fishing mishap several years before, Bessie took over the restaurant and re-established its look. Although the food remained the same, having been a cook there for many years herself, she decided to bestow a new name. Purely on a whim, and suggested by a wealthy patron, she named it "Bessie's Café."

Aside from her delicious food that was so well-known, the folks all around respected her outwardly and generous deeds. She provided a gracious meal to anyone in need. Her customers supported her occasional acts of charity toward needy folks by slipping a few coins into a big jar Bessie kept by the cash register – which was nothing more than a White Owl cigar box.

Bessie's was always open for the pre-dawn fishing crowd. Aside from her tasty and filling plates, she also served the saltiest country ham biscuits this side of the Dismal Swamp. Practically all the fisherman packed away an extra sack to eat while rolling with the white caps.

For the noon dinner crowd and the evening supper circle, Bessie usually served an array of meats with her legendary pork spare ribs as the every Friday dinner special. It was always a customer favorite. And to complement her meats, there were the always-present red-boiled taters, candied yams, turnip salit, hot cressie greens, vinegary collards, dressed eggs, corndodgers and fried hoecakes, and hot cathead scratch biscuits from an old family recipe always served with a healthy slab of butter. It was a hungry mans delight to chow-down at Bessie's Café.

While George and R.W. where finishing up their wedge of sweet potato pie, George humorously brought to close the day's events.

"You know R.W. ... if I had'a pulled the trigger on those crackers, I doubt seriously there'd been a whole lot of paperwork." he said.

"How's that, George?" R.W. said looking puzzled.

"Well, I forget to tell you. I didn't put any shells in the chamber!"

"No kidd'en! Well, I guess it makes no difference no how. But it sho' as hell made a racket when you pumped that sucker, didn't it?"

"Didn't it though!" George said with a light belly giggle.

"Still, I'm glad you left the shells out. I hate paperwork," R.W. lamented, shaking his head. "Come on ya big lug, finish up that pie and let's go and get Josh and head for the house."

As far as the politics of Dare County was concerned, George Washington Dawkins was not yet officially considered an employee of the county. Because he was an Indian and categorized as colored, it wasn't considered proper for him to be a duty-sworn lawman. But unofficially, George *was* considered part of the County Sheriff's Office and was treated with dignity and respect by his fellow lawman. Thanks to R.W. and Sheriff Simmons, George was enlisted into the ranks when an unusual situation occurred several months before his arrival in the summer of 1941.

One day in the spring, Currituck County Sheriff Jacob Wiggins contacted Sheriff Simmons about working out a deal having one of Sheriff Simmons' deputies patrol a section of the Outer Banks that was under Wiggins's supervision. That particular section of land in Currituck County was just north of Duck, where the county dividing line was located.

Dare County patrolled up to the line and Currituck County was responsible for the land above that and all the way up to the Virginia State line at Virginia Beach. Sheriff Wiggins was only concerned about patrolling only up to Corolla, which was about eleven miles from the county line. The one single road to that area was over the Wright Memorial Bridge and through Dare County to the north end of Duck. It was a very long haul and quite cumbersome to reach. Wiggins lost his deputy who patrolled that area to the Army's draft and Currituck County wasn't going to replace him. Could Sheriff Simmons help?

Simmons was one man short himself, but he thought of an idea that might work. He asked Deputy Scoggins, who was already patrolling from the Oregon Inlet to Duck, if he wouldn't mind covering the extra territory if Sheriff Wiggins reimbursed him for the extra expense of traveling there a few times a week. R.W. had been up that way many times before when he picnicked with Emily Mae. Aside from a large habitat of ducks and geese, the only human habitants he knew of were the Currituck Beach lighthouse keeper and the owner of an opulent hunt club called Corolla Island. It was a quiet area in the sense there was very little human activity.

After settling on a price of $17.50 a week, R.W. started patrolling. A few months later, when George suddenly arrived, looking for a job, R.W. considered forgoing his extra expense money only if Roscoe would hire George. Of course, R.W. and George would patrol the upper Banks together as agreed; but the Currituck County money would, instead, go to George.

At first Simmons was reluctant to the idea. However, believing George could be of value in the Wanchese community when a select few of the local folk regularly got liquored-up, he agreed with stipulations: George was considered only a temporary officer and would patrol with Deputy Scoggins. As time progressed, and he was shown respect from the public, Roscoe would consider bringing him on as a full-time deputy and allow him to patrol on his own. An extra person on the force would be of great help – especially since another county was paying his wages. And Simmons knew with R.W.'s reputation and George always at his side, he believed the townsfolk would readily accept the Indian. He was a likable sort of fellow, who seemed to have a good head on his shoulders. Because of George's demeanor, it didn't take long before Roscoe brought him on full time, finding some extra Dare County money to supplement his income.

Early the following morning, George and R.W. motored to the office to take care of the paperwork needing to be done from the previous evening. Fortunately, none of it was pressing. Sheriff Simmons was already there walking around the office with his usual cup of coffee. He walked over to R.W. and George.

"I hear tell you boys had a little ruckus over at Shanklyn's beer joint late yesterday afternoon. You send them fellers back home to pick peaches?"

"Now Roscoe, just where the hell did you hear that from?" R.W. said looking up from his paperwork.

"Who do you think?" Roscoe said slightly laughing.

"Jenny?" R.W. said, fathoming a guess.

"The ol' 'Mouth of the South' herself! She's just like having a radio in the car."

"No doubt. I didn't see her around, but I guess word travels fast 'round here. Who needs a newspaper?"

Sheriff Simmons had a job for his boys after they finished up their paperwork. In the jail was a thief Roscoe had apprehended the previous afternoon. He had been passing bad checks around town, thinking he could hoodwink a few of the local merchants.

"Look, after you boys finish up your paperwork, I want ya'll to haul this feller up to the Elizabeth City jail. I got with the sheriff up there and he's got room for 'em. Seems this felon is wanted all up and down the Eastern Seaboard ... pretty nasty feller, he is. The Feds are awantin' this guy, so that's why we need to get 'em up there.

"And why ya'll are up there R.W., why don't you take Big George here over to the J.O. Jones Department Store and fix 'em up with some new khakis. With the war just get'en started, I think they'll probably have something that might fit him. It might be a stretch with his size and all, but give it a look-see anyhow."

Roscoe walked over and handed George a thick envelope. He opened it up. There was a wad of one-dollar bills neatly stacked inside. It totaled fifty-eight dollars. George was awestruck.

"Some of the fellers here in the office and the merchants 'round town took up a little collection for ya the other day, George, so you could get a new uniform and blend in with the rest of us. Everyone just wanted to show their kindness and thought you'd look a little more official-like now that you're on the clock full-time. Besides, you've been here pert-near seven months now and it's 'bout time you started look'en a little more like a real deputy."

Big George grinned, showing his appreciation for his new-found friends. He stood up and shook Roscoe's hand, thanking him. He also shook R.W.'s hand, believing the sheriff probably was the one who had something to do with this kindly gesture.

* * * * * * * *

In early March, life on the Outer Banks was slow—very slow. Aside from a little excitement here and there usually revolving around the spirits of alcohol, not much else happened. But with the summer season just around the corner, and soon the rich folks from the Raleigh and Durham areas, as well as other Eastern North Carolina towns, would venture to their cottages. Anglers from everywhere would head to the fishing piers. Many of these sportsmen would go to sea in quest for the larger game fish, unaware as to what was really lurking below the surface or sitting on the sandy Atlantic bottom.

When George and R.W. returned from their appointed trip to Elizabeth City, George was wearing a brand new khaki Army uniform and matching waist jacket. It was quite a chore, but he was able to find a uniform that fit his large frame. The clothes changed George's entire appearance. But, before heading back to the office to hand Roscoe the reciprocal papers regarding his prisoner, R.W. wanted to stop by the post office and pick up his mail.

"You hear about the sinking outside the Chesapeake Bay last night," Jenny, the local Postmistress, said to R.W. as he was thumbing through his mail.

"Yeah, George and me heard about it whilst we were up in Elizabeth City. I understand it was a large military shipment go'en to England. I believe most all the crew was killed ... went up in a huge ball of flames is what I hear."

"Looks like those damn U-boats just about got their way 'round here. From what I hear, the Navy's got their hands tied ... just what I hear, though," Jenny remarked, nodding her head in knowing fashion.

"Well, I wouldn't know too much about that," R.W. said reading the envelopes, not looking up at Jenny as he headed out the door to his car.

To all the folks on the islands, thirty-five year old Jenny Smith, the Postmistress of Dare County, seemed intuitively perceptive on privy issues known only to some. A lot of people thought she was clairvoyant, but others thought she was just down right nosey. But if a person was interested in another person's business, Jenny would be in the know. She was, after all, supervisor of the local postal system. That position, alone, could decipher and determine a person's business by virtue of the type mail they received.

Because of her energetic and fast-paced job, Jenny was blessed with a firm and well-toned body, mostly developed from years on the line moving manly-sized boxes and bulky sacks of mail. For as long as anybody could remember, Jenny always wore her brown hair short, perfectly matching her wide, brown eyes. She was quite attractive and well-preserved for a woman in her mid-thirties. Jenny always presented herself in friendly sorts of ways, but behind closed doors she was an iniquitous, self-seeking scoundrel, whose cussing could redden the most ardent of sailors.

Just as R.W. slid behind the wheel of his Pontiac, Deputy Sam Beatty pulled up beside him.

"Roscoe wants to see ya'll. Some gov'ment men got here a short while ago."

"Now Sam, how do you know they're government men."

"Well, they're wear'en them fancy grey suits and those black trilby-style hats. They look official all right ... driv'en a big ol' black Buick too. Anyway, you two need to get over there mighty quick."

"Come on George, let's go see what all the ruckus is about."

The door was shut to Sheriff Simmons's office when the two deputies walked into the courthouse. It was usually opened, but today something really must be in the wind for Roscoe to have it closed.

"Ya'll can go right on in," the secretary, Rose Ellen Harris told the two men. They walked through the little wooden gate separating the sheriff's area from the county assessor's area. This was in a large room surrounded by various offices. The sheriff and the tax collector were neighbors in this arrangement. The county recorder had the other side of the room because of the amount of walk-in traffic from folks getting license plates, marriage licenses, paying taxes and such.

R.W. knocked on Roscoe's door a couple of times, then opened it a crack.

"Sheriff ... it's me and George. You want'en to see us?"

"Sure, come on in fellers."

Sheriff Simmons was about what you'd expect from a southern small-town lawman. He had a full head of pink skin, usually covered with a straw-colored fedora, slightly cocked to the side. When he wanted to feel extra important, he'd wear his daddy's Colt 45 Peacemaker strapped low to his side. When he chatted with the townsfolk on the street, he'd often lean his hand against pistol's handle, causing the holster to bend around to his side. If the gun was to ever go off, Roscoe would probably blow a hole in his butt. Nevertheless, he always seemed to be careful.

Roscoe was in his early fifties and six-feet tall. He carried his physique well, except for a small potbelly earned from all the meals at Bessie's Café. While R.W. rarely wore his badge, Roscoe always wore his proudly on a clean white shirt, along with everyday freshly-pressed khaki slacks. His boots, like his deputies, were always in need of a shine because of the powdery sand so prominent for the area.

"These fine gentlemen here are from the F-B-I," Roscoe said, smiling. This is Special Agent Jones and this is Special Agent Johnson. They're out'a Norfolk," Roscoe said introducing the men.

R.W. and Roscoe never could figure what was "special" about an FBI agent.

"Special Agent Johnson, would you please be so kind as to explain what you need from us," the sheriff opened, with a slight, but subtle hint of sarcasm.

"Yes Sheriff ... thank you," the agent began. "Whether you know it or not, we're losing cargo ships and tankers all up and down the East Coast. Our Coast Guard, which is now responsible for the protection of our coastline, is having one helluva time trying to catch these German U-boats."

R.W. and George looked at each other, both thinking the same thing – of course the Coast Guard would be charged with protecting the Coast.

"On numerous occasions, Admiral 'Dolly' Andrews, who is the commander of the Eastern Sea Frontier, has requested to his boss, Navy Admiral King, that he needs ships and planes to defend and to hunt down these kraut scoundrels. Unfortunately, King keeps turning him down. We're losing massive amounts of our economy to the depths of the sea, and because of King's arrogance, it's been a tough row to hoe. But Andrew's is making some headway with what he's got ... but it's been real slow."

29

Although the agent was trying hard to sound like common, everyday folk, certain words were slipping through, hinting a tone of arrogance and superiority.

"Well now, all that's well an' good there fellers, but what's that got to do with us?" Sheriff Simmons inquired.

"Quite a bit. Admiral Manley Simons is the commander of our Fifth Naval District, which covers the coastline from Assateague, Virginia down to the New River Inlet at Sneed's Ferry, North Carolina. He believes the Outer Banks is a prime target for German infiltrators, who could come ashore undetected, spread out inland, and start sabotaging key military installations, such as our Navy installations and merchant fleet facilities in the Hampton Roads area.

"Right now, we're concentrating a lot of energy in that area and we think the Germans know what we're doing. That's why we believe they might come in from the south, where the population is thinner and the shores are less-protected. We know the Coast Guardsmen down at the Bodie Island Station are spread way thin themselves, so that's why we're asking the local law enforcement departments throughout the area to help us out. We're approaching all the municipalities and sheriff stations up and down the coast to keep a lookout for anything unusual. Our federal government doesn't have enough manpower and equipment to patrol the islands of the Outer Banks, so we're asking you to lend us a hand. Besides, you folks already know every bead of sand around these parts as it is, and we need you to be our eyes and ears. Anything you see unusual ... give us a call and we'll check it out. Think you can help us out there, fellows?"

"Sure, we'll be of any assistance we can to the government. We'll report anything we get right to your office," Sheriff Simmons told the two agents.

Everybody stood up and shook hands. Special Agent Johnson was quite overwhelmed at the size of the big Indian deputy, who was sitting in on the meeting. He looked up at George and remarked, "Son, I sure am glad you're on our side!"

Simmons walked the two agents out of the office to their car, reassuring them his department would cooperate any way it could. As they pulled out of their parking space and left, Roscoe grunted under his breath.

"In a pig's eye we will!"

Among the two deputies in the department it was no secret that Sheriff Simmons held a certain disdain for anyone from the federal government – especially if they were a Yankee. No one knew why, but any time someone from any federal agency came around, Roscoe gave him his Sunday morning church face; but after they left, he'd flash his Saturday night smile. For the moment, George was oblivious as to what was happening, but soon caught on.

"How do you want us to handle this, Roscoe?" R.W. inquired.

"Ah shit, fellers, we'll just keep on doing what we normally do. We know what's going on 'round here. If we do see something funny, hell ... we'll take of it. But that agent was right. We need to keep this under our hat. Don't even tell Sam. His mouth is 'bout as loose as Jenny's. I'll just feed him some kind of bullshit that'll satisfy him. Meantime, you fellers go on about your patrolling. I'll see ya'll over at Bessie's 'bout suppertime."

Chapter 4

The commander of the Bodie Island Coast Guard station slammed down the phone and sat looking off through his office window out onto the Pamlico Sound. Aside from providing rescue services along the coast, his latest orders were to station night patrols along the beaches from dusk to dawn, making sure the enemy stays at sea.

"Goddamnit ... I can't cover the entire northern Outer Banks with just twenty men per watch," Lieutenant Mark Fleming's voice snapped at no one in particular. "For one thing, I'm deal'en with World War I rifles and pubescent teens. I don't even have enough ammunition to give each man more than two full clips ... just ten rounds!"

Mark Fleming hailed from Tennessee, but, talked like a Yankee when he was mad.

Standing six-foot nothing, and wiry as a whippet, Fleming loathed to say he was less-than satisfied with command decisions that affected his realm of authority. His close-set, blue-grey eyes radiating from a boyish face was anything but youthful when he conveyed his request to headquarters. Given their perverseness in supplying his command's basic needs, Fleming was forced to weave and dodge in roundabout ways to find the wares he needed. It was a time-honored naval tradition.

Before America's entry into war in late 1941, the United States Coast Guard unceremoniously was merged under the auspices of the Department of the Navy. In Fleming's view, merging with the Navy was not a good meld because he flat-out knew the higher-ups in Navy command didn't have a stinking clue of just how few men the Coast Guard really had, nor did they care. But Admiral Adolphus "Dolly" Andrews, Commandant of the Coast Guard, did understand and heartedly fought a battle from within to gain the strength he needed. It was to be long, uphill fight.

After 7 December 1941, Admiral Harold R. Stark appointed Admiral Andrews as commander of the North Atlantic Naval Coastal Frontier, later renamed the "Eastern Sea Frontier." On 3 February 1942, Stark ordered Andrews to protect the entire East Coast. By this time, merchant shipping was sinking faster than a sack full of lead swivel sinkers and Andrews was at odds with his Navy superiors in trying to obtain the proper ships to fulfill the Coast Guard's obligation. But even with the struggles Andrews faced from within, there was some hope in the lower echelons of the Coast Guard that they would, at least, be taken care of in this monumental task. A small bit of hope—but not much.

While Andrews finally was able to finagle a handful of vessels and an assortment of planes to cover America's vast coastal waters, he regrettably found it impossible to allocate enough ammunition to do the job that might need to be done. The supplementary manpower forces need for the defense of the coastal shore, especially the long stretches of dunes along the Outer Banks, were not to be found.

But Lieutenant Fleming did have one bright spot to his little problem—a friend in the Army supply depot in Elizabeth City.

After bartering with a hundred pounds of shrimp and a bushel of oysters, Fleming was able to secure an extra 1,000 rounds of .30-6 caliber ammunition for his outmoded M1917 US Enfield rifles his men were lugging about throughout each long and lonely nights. Fleming didn't dare let the Navy know he had that much ammunition for fear they'd start poking around as to where he got it. Still, Fleming's station was so thinly stretched, each Guardsman had well over two miles of sand to defend each night. And to make matters worse, the few SCR-536 walkie-talkie transceivers they had for communication were about as useless as a screen door hatch on a submarine. With the long distances the Guardsman had to cover, the one and a half mile range limit simply made the transceivers ineffective. If any patrolling Guardsman fell into distress, he'd most likely have to high-tail it to the nearest telephone. In most cases that was next to impossible.

Trying to protect the waters from German U-boats with a less-than-desired fleet of aging ships, and trying to protect the homeland shores with a modicum of men with even older rifles—it didn't get any better when, each night, one of Fleming's two chief petty officers checked on their men. With a line of defense over forty-miles long and located in one the most inhospitable sections of the Barrier Banks, the chief used a prototype 1940 Bantam Jeep to bounce his way around. How this vehicle ever made its way to the Bodie Island Coast Guard Station was nothing short of a mystery; nonetheless, it was transportation and, for the most part, it was the best vehicle suitable to scour the land. But with such an expanse of desolate territory and so few men, a platoon of German sailors could easily sneak through the thin line of defense. If, by happenstance, a Guardsman did find the need to fire his rifle, the best he could do was a meager ten rounds. After that, he'd have to resort to pelting the invaders with a handful of broken seashells.

To say the least, this was the situation in early March 1942, for the beach defenses along the Carolina coast of the Eastern Seaboard. The situation was ludicrous and virtually unknown to most American citizens.

Lieutenant Fleming's executive officer was an ensign fresh out of Officer Candidate School. Ensign Jeremy Hargrove was a good kid, but wasn't any more trained than most of the enlisted young Guardsmen. He was green as all get-out. Fleming thought, *"Hell, I've got more time in the chow line than that kid's got in the Coast Guard."*

The only men Fleming could truly trust were his two chief petty officers: Chief Gunner's Mate Jim Bleu and Chief Boatswain Sam Hatfield. The two senior enlisted men, each, had been in the Guard for more than ten years—three years more than their commanding officer, so it was somewhat comforting to know Fleming could rely on them. The two chiefs took turns on night duty. Each stayed on duty for twelve hours, making sure the troops were okay and staying awake. Most of Fleming's men were under twenty years of age, so staying awake for twelve straight hours was always a problem. Slogging through ultra-soft sand and carrying a seven-pound rifle wasn't an easy task. Still, the security of the nation was at risk. Every time Fleming thought of it, he chuckled. Though, there was one good thing about the approaching summer months: the dawn broke early, and it stayed light much longer; those night watches weren't quite so long and tough.

With little more than forty Guardsmen at what used to be a rescue station, Fleming was fortunate he could keep the beach watch rotating every other day. Rescue boats had to be manned as well as support staff such as cooks, supply, and transportation personnel. Many of the Guardsmen were doing double duty.

* * * * * * * *

Through the salt stained window of his office, Fleming saw a faded green Pontiac drive up. It was Deputy Sheriff R.W. Scoggins and his constant companion, Deputy George Dawkins. In the wintertime, R.W. rarely trekked this far south because nothing was there except the Bodie Island lighthouse and the U.S. Coast Guard Station. Though in the summertime, the circumstances were much different. With sightseers to the lighthouse and vacationers flocking to the shores, the population of The Banks swelled. There were no cottages or motels on this section of island, so visitors had to camp out among the sand dunes. Many stayed through the summer, but most came for just a week or two. It was during this time R.W. ventured down the coast more often.

Getting to the end of the island and safely back usually required precaution. Once a person left Whalebone Junction at the Wash Baum Bridge, heading south along only a bare semblance of a road, the pavement stopped. The remaining six-miles to the Oregon Inlet, where the lighthouse and station were located, were nothing more than very soft sand. To keep from bogging down, the driver had to lessen the tire pressure on each wheel to a meager eighteen pounds. This allowed the tires to flatten and gain a better grip. Failure to do so usually resulted in burying the car to the chassis. To the many locals and the long-time vacationers, this was a well-known routine verity. The newcomer learned his lesson the hard way.

"Lieutenant ... good to see you again. How's your day going?" R.W. asked.

"Well, I could use another fifty or so men," Fleming quipped.

"I know what ya mean. I'm sure you can imagine our dilemma with our lack of resources. George and me have about twenty miles to cover by our lonesome most every day ... so don't feel too out'a kilter."

"Ah hell, I understand that. But we all could have a problem any day now. If those damn Nazis ever decide to come ashore, there ain't a whole lot we can do about it. I've got enough ammo now to give each man thirty shots ... and if we can't nail 'em with what we've got, then we're screwed," Fleming said half-heartedly with a nervous laugh.

"Those FBI Agents come down your way the other day?" R.W. asled.

"Yeah, they came down here giving us the 'rah, rah' speech. They're almost as bad as what the Navy expects us to do. By the way, did you hear about the request for blacking out the shore lights?"

The two deputies looked at each other with a quizzical stare.

"No ... didn't hear 'bout that. But I figured it was com'en sooner than later. I imagine those U-boats are using the silhouette of the ships against the shore lights as they run up and down the coast ... 'bout like shoot'en tin ducks at the carnival.

"The blackout's a good thing. You know, men are dying when those ships go up in flames and we all need to be good stewards. But I don't think the bar owners and hotel folk are gonna like it too much," R.W. said.

"Well they damn well better get used to it! We got a war going on right here in our own backyard and it's amaz'en how so few people know about it! I got my weekly report yesterday, and we've lost about thirty-five merchant ships and tankers to the U-boats just off our own damn coast. God knows how many we've lost all up and down the seaboard.

"And to top it off, just a little while ago, I got this disturbing report that the *USS Jacob Jones,* one of our oldest World War I destroyers was torpedoed in the early pre-dawn hours. Admiral King done released her full time to the Coast Guard. She sank 28 February off the Delaware Capes heading for the Jersey Coast," Fleming said. "The destroyer had only been at sea about a day when she left the Chesapeake," Fleming continued. "The report said one torpedo detonated just below the magazine and the other one blew off the fantail. The whole damn ship just ignited! Out of nearly two hundred sailors, only eleven survived."

Fleming said the death toll could have been more.

"When the ship was sinking, her own depth charges started igniting below the surface, shredding the guts of anybody float'en nearby. God ... it must've been awful!"

"What's the Navy doing about it?" R.W. asked.

"Right now, they're stretched thin as hell," Fleming replied. "King has most of his fleet bottled up in Newport News, wait'en to go to the North Atlantic, or to the Pacific. As many destroyers as possible are already escorting the cargo ships halfways to England. What ships that're left and don't have any orders, which ain't that many, are working our coastal areas with the Coast Guard. I don't know what those 'Big-Wigs' are doing, but I sure as hell hope they'll start sing'en out'a the same song book purty soon. We're get'en our butts wiped off the map."

"Well I knew it was bad, but I didn't realize it was that bad! It's going to be hard enough just mak'en sure the folks keep their lights off or black-out their windows," R.W. said. "That'll be a full-time job in itself."

"Say, R.W., why don't you get your boss to organize a civil defense squad and let them take care of stuff like that?"

"Easier said than done, but if Roscoe hasn't already thought of it, I'll suggest it and tell him it was your idea. That way if he thinks it's a bad one, you can get the blame," R.W. said with a chuckle.

"Thanks a lot. Deal'en with the Navy is hard enough. I don't need you 'silly-villains' on my ass," Fleming replied with a chuckle.

R.W. and George made their farewells and left. Fleming went back to his paperwork, but couldn't get the thought out of his mind that, if there ever was an East Coast invasion, there wouldn't be much to stop it.

Fleming was a Coast Guard Academy graduate. He was taught that a good officer makes do with what he has. In his case, it's very little. Senior Coast Guard officers in command of his sector of the region were in Norfolk, under Navy control. Even though things were supposed to be equal, "Coasties" were always treated like bastard children of the Navy. As one Navy commander told Fleming in joking fashion during a cocktail party, *"You guys aren't real sailors."*

The remark itself was half-hearted, but that pretty much summed up the attitude of most Navy personnel. Recruiting efforts for the Coast Guard were tough enough because most prospects were scooped up by the Navy; hence, the ranks didn't grow too much.

Though, Fleming did have one ace up his sleeve. His baby sister was a Navy lieutenant junior grade at the Bureau of Personnel in Washington. She could get access as to what commands sailors were being dispatched. Those sailors included all Coast Guardsmen.

"Little sister, I need a favor," Fleming said into his telephone.

Chapter 5

When Kapitänleutnant Hans Vogel surfaced his U-491, he was cautious. His "Type VII-C" boat was built in 1939. Underwater it was slow at only seven knots but, on the surface, it could muster seventeen knots and was faster than most of the merchant vessels. On the other hand, roaming destroyers were quite another matter. They were faster and more heavily armed, and it was always best to avoid them by heading for the depths of the sea. It took twenty-eight seconds to completely submerge. A keen eye by the always-present four-man watch group on the conning tower bridge, and a well-executed system of submerging, meant everything to staying alive.

Ironically, when war erupted in September 1939, Germany's War Navy (*Kriegsmarine*) was caught unprepared. Admiral Karl Dönitz had wanted a fleet of 300 U-boats to attack the heavy-laden Allied convoys and escorting warships crossing the North Atlantic. But because of earlier restraints from the World War I Treaty of Versailles and opposition from Adolf Hitler, Dönitz was positioned with only fifty-seven commissioned boats, with which fifty-two were the lighter 250-ton small Type II coastal U-boats, none of which were capable of crossing the Atlantic. Eighteen of those were used for training, leaving thirty-nine to fight the British and French naval forces, which had ten times more power in their warships.

The remaining five boats were the heavier 761-ton medium Type VII submarine like the U-491, with a cruising range of 6,500 nautical miles, easily capable of crossing the Atlantic. This type U-boat was considered the workhorse and main attack submarine of the fleet. The "Type VII" U-boat was responsible for ninety percent of all Allied loses. By the time the war ended, 694 of these type boats had been constructed, but only a smattering survived intact.

When France capitulated in the late spring of 1940, the Kreigsmarine gradually relocated its submarines from the Baltic Sea in Northern Germany southward to the French ports of the Biscay Bay, thus shortening their distance to the North Atlantic, making it easier to reach the eastern coastal waters of the United States. It was this move that precipitated the Battle of the Atlantic and the voracious attacks on merchant shipping. It also was a time when Germany increased its U-boat production, constructing larger and faster boats destined for distant waters. Many of these submarines would lay mines, transport crucial material, and re-supply the U-boats already at sea with fuel, torpedoes, and provisions.

Variations of these boats were known as the "Type IX," a large ocean-going U-boat capable of operating in far distant waters such as the East Coast of the United States, the South Atlantic and Indian Oceans; the "Type XB" was a minelayer and transporter of war materials and the largest of the U-boat fleet. They had a displacement of 1,760-tons, was 295-feet long, and had an operational range of 14,500 nautical miles. The "Type XIV," was a supply U-boat designed to provide fuel and provisions to the long-range subs already on station at sea. This U-boat was affectionately known as a "Milk Cow" (*Milchkuh*).

For the German U-boat commander, attacking merchant ships crossing the vast North Atlantic in convoy took an entirely different strategy than attacking the "lonesome ducks" wallowing their way along the Eastern Seaboard. The tactics in the North Atlantic were uniquely designed such that U-boats patrolled separately across a lengthy predetermined line, where a likely convoy might travel. When a convoy was spotted, a message was sent to the commander of submarines, Admiral Karl Dönitz (*Befehlshaber der Unterseeboote*. He was referred to simply as *"BdU."* The admiral, in turn, ordered a *"Rudel,"* or mass attack.

When a sufficient number of U-boats had dutifully arrived, a call sign was made and a count of boats on station was taken. With certain exceptions, U-boat commanders could freely attack as they saw fit. But as a rule, the subs attacked as a pack. This mass gathering of submarines soon became infamously known to Allied forces as a *Wolfsrudel* or "Wolf Pack."

With the Lend-Lease Act of 11 March 1941, America was able to send millions of tons of food and equipment in large convoys across the Atlantic to the British Isles. An estimated ten tons of supplies and equipment were needed to keep one soldier in the field for one year. If the Nazi submarines had their way, that wouldn't happen, and, for the most part, that was the case up until late 1942. But it wasn't until early 1943 that Allied shipbuilding finally surpassed the amount of vessels being destroyed thus ending the U-boat threat of annihilation.

When the Germans took the war to the American Coast on 13 January 1942, only five "Type IX" submarines were available for the crossing. Though, in due course, more long-range subs would be built to replace those U-boats damaged, sunk, or returning to base for refitting and reprovisioned. Before the middle of the year, there were never less than twelve boats at any one time roaming the Eastern Sea Frontier, with each captain picking and choosing his target. In the early months of 1942, it was too easy. But, by mid-summer, German U-boat tactics had become severely challenged by a growing coastal defense force of the U.S. Navy and Coast Guard.

Because the situation on the Eastern Seaboard sharply contrasted to the campaign of the North Atlantic passageways, American inactions along the coast allowed the Germans a free hand in attacking their prey. It was unnecessary to form a Wolf Pack because a single boat could inflict serious damage in a large area by itself. Innocently traveling in the dead of night, along a lighted coastal route, a slow-going merchant ship cast a perfect silhouette from the lights of the American shoreline. To the unsuspecting cargo captain, it was a kiss of death.

In the early months of Operation Drumbeat, the U-boats were positioned from New York to Cape Fear and the Frying Pan Shoals, just off the southern tip of the North Carolina coast. Though, it wasn't long thereafter that word quickly spread the choice spot for sinking Allied shipping was off the ragged coastline and treacherous Outer Banks waters of Cape Hatteras and the Diamond Shoals. For merchant vessels to circumvent these capriciously shallow waters, they had to travel over thirty-five miles out to sea just past the continental shelf. For lurking U-boat commanders, it was an easy kill with plenty of deep water to make an escape. Many a submarine captain soon abandoned his specified quadrant to enjoy this easy prey. To the Germans, this area was known as "Quadrant CA, Section 87."

The order from Admiral Dönitz to his U-boat fleet was very clear: sink all cargo ships and fuel tankers, either full or running in ballast. But Kapitänleutnant Hans Vogel of the U-491 had a separate and more distinctive order when he arrived off the North Carolina coast on Sunday, February 15: sink highly-classified military cargo coming out of the Chesapeake Bay.

Coming from a small network of American collaborators hidden well within the small Outer Banks population, Vogel was to periodically receive a specially-coded "beacon of light" emanating from the Wright Brothers Monument atop Kill Devil Hill. These signals directed Vogel to his merchant-ship prey.

For an American citizen, these acts were treason at the highest-level only money could buy.

Chapter 6

It was late afternoon when Kapitänleutnant Hans Vogel brought his U-491 to the surface. It was cold, gray, and foggy and the seas were choppy with wind-swept whitecaps curling about a rolling black sea. Cruising at ten knots, the boat sliced through the smaller waves with the minimal of ease, but rose and fell with the larger waves. As a general rule, the German U-boats only surfaced at night when on station or traveling across the Atlantic to or from their homeports on the Bay of Biscay. But because this day held a veil of low-visibility weather surrounding his boat, Vogel felt it safe to surface. The more he could boost his batteries, the better chance for survival—as long as U-491 wasn't caught on the surface.

"It would take a stroke of luck to find a target in this soup, Herr Kapitän," remarked Oberleutnant Staats as his binoculars scanned the choppy seas.

"Ja, Ja ... that it would. Those large freighter kills last week sapped our strength. We must recharge our batteries and prepare ourselves for a new attack. I think we should have a new target tomorrow night based on my contact with *BdU*."

"But Herr Kaleun, could we not have passed that kill off to a fellow commander in the area? We had a long haul."

Nein ... it is our mission to exact these kills and not a comrade. Besides, if the Americans intercepted our radio signal, it might compromise the operation. They may get wise to our scheme and it is best to let them think otherwise. Our boats are already sending mass tonnage to the bottom. Let them think it was just their bad luck that all that hardware went to the bottom on their dumb ignorance. Our secret missions must remain secret," replied Vogel as he scanned the monochromatic seascape with his glasses.

"Ja, but we used a lot of fuel. Maybe our new target will keep us closer to the Carolina coast and the Chesapeake Bay. These last two months have seemed so easy for our fleet, and we have yet to lose a boat. I wonder why they are not defending their ships any better, Herr Kaleun?"

"I fear it won't last much longer. Our secret operatives in England have reported British trawlers will soon be crossing the Atlantic to help the Americans. These are the same vessels we were up against over a year ago in Britain's coastal waters and the Norwegian fjords. This means the British are offering their help. If the Americans take the British advice on combating our tactics with convoys, our present path of destruction will soon become a rocky one just as it did in their waters. The Americans aren't stupid ... stubborn at best, but they are not stupid. When they come to their senses, we must be ready to alter our tactics."

"Ja Kaleun, I believe you are right."

As the officers continued their visual sweep, a distant and unusual drone appeared louder and louder. Both Vogel and Staats glanced at each other and then turned sternward of the boat. The mien on their faces knew what it meant. As both men looked skyward through heavy mist and swirling fog, they vaguely recognized the outline of a bulbous gray airship. It was only by happenstance that an openly thin spot in the swirling fog allowed the blimp to spot the U-boat.

"ALARRRMMM!" Vogel yelled into the conning tower voice tube as Staats and the four watchmen already were sliding down the aluminum ladder connected to the conning tower hatch. This loud verbal warning was standard operating procedure on all U-boats and only given by an officer on the bridge alerting the crew to immediately submerge the boat. To American submariners, the term was, "DIVE! DIVE!"

Within seconds, Vogel slammed and dogged the conning tower hatch cover. The quiescent crew immediately sprung to life turning precious valves and switches to plunge themselves to safety. The non-essential crew ran to the bow of the boat, adding weight to her nose to assist in her dive.

"Chief, get her to one hundred meters ... schnell, schnell! Come to heading 2 – 4 – 0 degrees. Engage the electric motors. Make for seven knots!" Vogel firmly commanded to Stresemann.

"Aye aye, Kapitän."

To fully submerge beneath the surface, it took twenty-eight seconds assuming the boat had been properly adjusted to a variety of factors -- the ever-wavering seawater's density caused by the fluctuation in temperature, tides, and consumption of supplies. Sometimes the ocean's surface tension slowed its descent exposing the tail near the surface. With an enemy airship moving in for the kill, such moments were terrifying for a U-boat crew.

U.S. Navy Lighter-Than-Airships, commonly known as "blimps," or, as American sailors called them, "Shit Bags," were the most terrifying weapon an enemy from the sky could use against a submarine. Unlike a dirigible, which has a rigid airframe, covered with fabric and filled with gas, a blimp has no rigid inner structure. It's basically a big bag filled with gas, losing most of its shape as it deflates. Only the cockpit gondola under the dirigible and the blimp is a solid structure.

The age of the huge dirigible airship, (the Germans called them "Zepplins," came to a halt in 1937, with the burning crash of the Hindenburg. Germany filled their airships with volatile hydrogen, whereas American had discovered the less-flammable helium. When the United States refused to sell helium to Germany, the Nazis abandon its airship program.

Vogel knew depth charges (*Wasserbomben* or *Wabos*) would be dropped from the American blimp. He leaned on his chart table visibly worried. He watched the clock's second hand; then the depth meter. The sweep hand slowly reached the twenty-meter mark. It seemed to take forever. He knew his tail was still near the surface and probably visible to the blimp. If not, the phosphorescent bubbles produced by his boat would surely give him away.

"We *must* get her to one hundred meters Chief. I am afraid we left a large frothy footprint in the sea that will be impossible to miss even in this weather."

As the boat approached thirty-five meters, Vogel ordered.

"Rudder hard to port ... starboard E motor half ahead! Schnell ... schnell!"

Seconds later, the crewman monitoring the hydrophone notified Vogel.

"Kapitän ... two *Wabos* have hit the surface!"

The Kapitän remained quiet. The crew remained quiet. A few seconds later a depth charge exploded at twenty-three meters, violently shaking the interior. The boat seemingly groaned as the heavy metal interior deck plates lifted and crashed with a deafening clang. A few seconds later at twenty-five meters, another thunderous explosion. A small wooden door in Vogel's tight quarters cracked down the middle; the thick moisture laden glass covering the well-watched depth meter (*Tiefe meter*) shattered leaving shards of glass branching from the bezel.

All the crew held tightly except Erick Koehler, an engineman (*Electro Obermaschinist*) for the electric motors. The violent explosion loosened his grip from his hold sending him head-first into a thick steel bulkhead carving a gruesome gash into his forehead just above his left eye. He folded like a rag doll at the foot of the support completely knocking him cold. Just then, the cabin lights flickered off, then on; then another nervous flicker. Only a faint glow remained from the emergency batteries. The main power had been compromised.

As the boat slowly plummeted at a forty-degree angle, it seemingly stood still as it reached the thermocline. The meter sweep hand barely moved—thirty-eight – forty – forty-two meters. The situation was critical. The boat had to dive for it to survive.

"Kapitän ... two more *Wabos* in the water!"

"Ah shit!" exclaimed a crewman in the control room as he grabbed his head. Other crewmen continued holding tightly to anything solid they could grab.

A few seconds later when the boat passed forty-five meters, both charges exploded sending a massive shockwave through the water. Six glass-covered pressure gauges exploded sending shards of glass flying through the air, cutting a crewman on his neck. Gaskets and seals within the valves loosened and sent streams of cold water cascading into the bilges. It was imperative to keep the inert seawater away from the corrosive sulfuric acid in the batteries. The seemingly harmless combination of these two liquids forms deadly chlorine gas and a cruel and instant death. Aside from an ongoing depth charge barrage, this was the sailor's worst nightmare.

Unknown to the crew in the airship, their deep-sea bomb jolted the submarine through the thermocline, forcing it into frigid waters at a much-faster dive rate. Kapitänleutnant Vogel immediately noticed the change in buoyancy. At a forty degree angle, his boat sank like a rock and the depth meter showed it—forty-seven – fifty – sixty – seventy meters. It was now evident there was a problem. The boat was out of control.

"Stop blowing ... boat out of control! Bow planes up twenty degrees. Aft planes up ten degrees!" the chief of the boat yelled to the men controlling the planes.

Chief Stresemann immediately went into action, nervously adjusting the tanks, bringing the boat to an even keel. It was an experience like no other and no one liked it; they all knew it wouldn't be their last. The crew coordinated their actions bringing the U-491 under control. And none too soon—the continental shelf was fast approaching.

Upon reaching a hundred and fifty meters and very close to the bottom, Kapitän Vogel ordered a speed of two knots. He also ordered a damage control check. When all stations reported with moderate to minimal damage, he ordered a course and depth change.

"Exec ... bring her to course 2 – 3 – 0 ... rise to eighty meters ... port motor seventy revolutions ... starboard sixty."

"Aye aye, Kapitän."

The crew finally began moving about their duties and repairing the minor damage. For a few of the crewmen, it was their first experience with the *Wasserbombe*. They knew if one exploded close enough, it could rupture the pressure hull and seal their fate to a quick and agonizing death. Even though their training prepared them for escape, the chances of survival from this depth were nil.

The two wounded crewman were receiving medical attention. The neck wound was not severe; the head wound on the other sailor was another matter. Koehler remained unconscious and breathing hard. He needed serious medical attention.

Aside from the severely-wounded crewman, Kapitänleutnant Vogel considered today a lucky one. It could have been worse. Because of the foggy weather and darkness that was setting in, the United States Navy airship reluctantly retreated from the hunt. The air commander was low on fuel after a thirty-hour patrol and, because the wind had steadily increased, forcing him away from the surface of the sea, he was resigned to head for home, which was Lakehurst, New Jersey. Even though he radioed his position and dropped a yellow dye-marker to indicate the U-boat's position, it was extremely doubtful an airplane, cutter, or destroyer could rendezvous in time to track the sub. Nevertheless, Vogel took his submerged boat away from the area as fast as possible.

* * * * * * * *

American isolationism from the war in Europe was beginning to wane when President Franklin Roosevelt and Prime Minister Sir Winston Churchill acknowledged their new Lend-Lease Agreement. During this time, the American government needed to protect its water-bound borders. In July 1941, Congress authorized the construction of strategically-placed aviation facilities to accommodate an assortment of aircraft, including bombers, patrol aircraft, and lighter-than-air ships -- blimps.

With war looming on the horizon with Imperial Japan and the threat of entering the European Theater against Germany's Third Reich, priority was given to hasten the construction of these bases. By early January 1942, just after America had been forced into war with the attack on Pearl Harbor, vast quantities of American airships were being produced and deployed all along the United States coastlines to prevent attacks by Japanese submarines on the Pacific coast, and German U-boats on the eastern seaboard and southern gulf shores.

At the time of this authorization, America's only East coast blimp facility was located in Lakehurst, New Jersey. With the Lakehurst Naval Station too far north to adequately cover the entire Eastern Seaboard, an air station further south was needed. Because of its

47

proximity to Norfolk, a key harbor for the United States Navy fleet, Weeksville, North Carolina, six miles southeast of Elizabeth City, was chosen for a new base. The area was perfect as it was midway down the Eastern coastline where a squadron of blimps could easily cover the Chesapeake Bay south to Cape Hatteras, Cape Lookout, and the Frying Pan Shoals of Cape Fear. Construction began in early August 1941. The base was commissioned in early June 1942, and became known as the Weeksville Naval Air Station for Lighter-than-Air ships (WNAS – LTA). It was the first facility built on the East coast since the Lakehurst Station in 1921. When operational, the Weeksville Station was designated as Wing One, Squadron ZP-24.

Many years prior to World War II, and unbeknownst to the Nazi Third Reich, the U.S. Army and Navy, along with the Goodyear Rubber Company, initiated extensive research and development programs to improve on the World War I-era airships. After scrutinizing each others' work and combining all their practical attributes, a new blimp was born with state-of-the-art features: a woven fabric and synthetic rubber-hybrid skin to encase the helium gas cylinders in order to diminish gas diffusion; refined aerodynamics for increased airspeed and range; and, a new means of buoyancy to better control the non-rigid frame while flying.

The new and improved blimp came into service at the Lakehurst Station in January 1942 when the station was commissioned as Wing One, Squadron ZP-12. The blimps were designated as ZNP-K: Z for lighter than air; N for non-rigid frame; P for patrol; and, K for specific type airship. Truth be known, the "Z" undoubtedly stood for "Zeppelin," in honor of the German inventor and builder, Count Ferdinand von Zeppelin, who championed lighter-than-air aviation during the early 20th century. The Germans used Zeppelins as aerial bombers during World War I, and later Count Zeppelin built large passenger ships that carried travelers across the Atlantic to both North and South America. Zeppelin even built the U.S. Navy's first dirigible, the Los Angeles. There other three dirigibles the Navy had, the Macon, Akron, and Shenandoah, were built in America. Ironically, the only one to survive until it was decommissioned in 1932, was the German-built Los Angeles. The other three all crashed due to bad weather or mechanical problems. Unpredictable weather for the Americans, and the volatility of hydrogen for the Germans ended the great Zeppelin era.

The ZNP-K blimp was a well-built airship specifically designed for patrolling the seaboard and spotting enemy subs. When a submarine was detected, its technology allowed the blimp crew to see beneath the seawaters, using a device called the Magnetic Anomaly Detector (MAD). The inner workings of this equipment cancelled out the earth's magnetic field inside a thirty-foot circle, allowing this void to travel with the airship; anything metal within the circle, be it on the surface or under the sea, registered as a wide pen mark on a small revolving drum. The airship could then home in and pursue its prey. Even though the blimp had a seventy mile-per-hour airspeed, it could hover almost indefinitely over its prey and make thorough and methodical sweeps of its target. Only a crafty and intuitive U-boat commander could wiggle free from this highly-effective invisible force above him.

When an airship registered a hit on a U-boat, the blimp bombardier could drop up to four M-17 or M-47 depth charges designed to explode between seventy-five and one hundred feet (twenty-three and thirty-one meters) below the surface. The average total weight of these depth bombs was 350 pounds (159 kilograms) with an explosive charge of 240 pounds (109 kilograms). If a U-boat kill wasn't successful, the pilot dropped a yellow dye marker and called the Combat Information Center (CIC) for airplane and destroyer support. When the weather was good, this was an effective way to find and kill a submarine or bring it to the surface.

In the event a U-boat commander brazenly decided to gamble his chances on the surface, the airship was equipped to fight back. It carried a fifty-caliber aircraft machine gun in the forward section of the forty-foot control cabin and a thirty-caliber air-cooled machine gun in the cabin's rear. Along with this weaponry was a thirty-caliber Browning Automatic Rifle (BAR) for extra firepower.

* * * * * * * *

Kapitänleutnant Vogel was sixty-five miles due east off Virginia's Cape Henry lighthouse when he was spotted by the blimp. He was fortunate in the respect the waters in that part of the sea were refreshingly deep, allowing him to take the evasive action he needed to escape his predator. Had he been closer to shore, it might have spelled disaster. The depth charges could have conceivably blown his boat apart.

When rising to periscope depth, Vogel ordered the boat's speed to three knots to reduce the vibration on his periscope, so annoyingly inherent with speed. At seven knots, it was virtually impossible to observe anything because of vibration. Vogel wanted to make sure he could clearly see the sky and horizon. It was imperative after what they had just experienced.

Through his observation periscope, Vogel scanned in all directions using both the one and six power magnification. He could see no ships. But what he could see was a waning moon illuminating a calming sea. The fog and mist were gone. He ordered the boat to the surface. It was safe.

Upon reaching the surface, Vogel ordered, "Both diesels half ahead. Steer course 2 – 1 – 4. Ventilate boat. Secure from stations. Watchmen to the tower."

Kapitänleutnant Vogel and Oberleutnant Staats went to the conning tower bridge along with the Second Watch Officer Brückner and three watch crewmen. It was a beautiful crisp clear night where they seemingly could see for miles and miles. It was very peaceful—no ships, no destroyers, no airships. And because of the tranquility, Vogel allowed the crew, on a rotating basis, to venture outside to enjoy the pleasant night and to smoke a cigarette if he so desired. Because of the gases released by the batteries, and the possibility of an explosion from the simple act of lighting a match, Vogel did not allow smoking inside the tube. Besides, there were enough fumes from diesel fuel, toilet gases, and body odor to foul the U-boat's atmosphere as it was.

For the time being, it was free sailing back to the Carolina coast. As with all German boats at this stage of the war, they had no radar; only the eyes and ears of her watchmen to spot their aerial attackers. But for underwater exploits, the U-boats did possess a listening device called a "hydrophone." Fitted with many pairs of microphones positioned about the hull, the radioman could listen for the sound of ship propellers. While the device could triangulate the bearing of a ship, it could not distinguish the range, direction, or speed. For total effectiveness, the boat had to be submerged with its electric motors stopped. But a good radioman could distinguish the different kinds of propeller sounds coming from the variety of ships.

Unfortunately, loud explosion noises from depth charges could damage the hydrophones, making them useless. Regrettably for the U-491, the recent depth charges did damage some of its hydrophones and she was, for the moment, left in the dark. They would attempt to repair the device as soon as possible.

"Herr Kaleun, I believe we have just experienced the first bumps on our road to victory. Now, airships are patrolling the coast ... or so it seems. It finally looks as though the Americans are becoming a bit wiser. We can no longer throw caution to the wind. We will have to be more observant," Oberleutnant Staats said.

"Ja, ja ... I believe you are correct. We must report this back to *BdU* and alert Admiral Dönitz ... although, I'm sure he has already been contacted. Still, we must continue with our mission. As long as we stay submerged during the day, we should be all right. That fluke incident in the fog almost cost us. Next time we must be more observant."

The top two officers of the boat continued chatting as more and more of the crew began rotating to the top. The atmosphere was becoming exuberant. Vogel was glad the spirit of the crew was perking up. The last couple of weeks had put a strain on their being and they

50

were becoming lethargic. With a crew complement of forty-four enlisted men and officers, crawling over each other inside a skinny 220-foot cold and clammy metal tube with only two heads, currently was unusable, it was enough to fray anyone's nerves. Suffering through a depth charge attack was yet another matter. There was only a few times where U-boat crew could totally relax and this was one of them.

"When was the last time you were home?" Vogel asked of Staats.

Staats thought for a minute looking out beyond the stars.

"It's been at least a year," he replied.

"And you, Herr Kaleun?"

"Nearly two years. But now I don't have anything worthwhile to go home to," Vogel replied. "My wife and daughter, they were ... they were in the wrong place at the wrong time. They were killed in Berlin in one of the early daylight-bombing raids by the RAF ... September 1940. The city Hermann Göring said would never be bombed ... well, it was."

"I'm sorry, sir," Staats said solemnly.

"Nein ... it's fine ... it's fine. I'm doing okay now."

"And so Herr Staats, where do you hail from?"

"Bremerhaven, Herr Kaleun."

"Ahh, a born seaman!"

"Jawohl, Herr Kaleun. I grew up dreaming of sailing across the ocean in my own yacht ... maybe with my wife and child. Of course, my goal was to sail on top of the water and not underneath it!"

Both officers laughed though Vogel had a tear in his eye. In the back recesses of his mind, he could not shake the notion of losing his family.

But Vogel wanted to avenge their deaths. He despised the British; and because the Americans were helping their war machine, he despised them too. If sinking their vessels to stop the flow of matériel, then he was exacting his revenge. If innocent sailors were being killed in the process, so be it. It was, after all, war.

When Kapitänleutnant Hans Vogel returned to his quarters, he wrote in his log: *"8 March 1942, 2200 hours, Quadrant CA, Section 8447. New course heading 214°. Seas currently calm. Minor damage from depth charges. Two crewmen injured; one seriously."*

Chapter 7

"You think we'll catch 'Ol' Whopper' today, Grandpa?"

"Well, he's a pretty crafty fella, ya know. But I think today we just might have a good chance. I brought along some special bait, so I think we just might get lucky!"

"What'd ya bring?"

"Brought some of your grandma's famous 'chicken lips' she cooked for supper last night and some 'skeeter legs' from the lower reaches of the Dismal Swamp. Either way, one of 'em ought to do the trick!"

"Ahh Grandpa...!"

It was a bright and beautifully crisp early Monday morning and for the first time in many months, Joshua was spending quality time with his grandpa—J.R. Scoggins. Since he sold his large fishing boat three years ago and had recuperated from phlebitis, he was feeling much chipper and anxious to move about. And though J.R. had lost his desire of hitting the high seas in lure of the big catches, he still liked to putter around the sounds and rivers to fish with a rod and reel. To him it was more relaxing, and it allowed time with his only grandchild. Today, he borrowed a small twenty-four foot center console fishing boat from an old friend so they could make their way around the sounds.

After a pleasant motor through the soft waters of the Croatan Sound on the back side of Roanoke Island, they worked their way north around the southern end of Albemarle Sound. From there they went into the upper portion of the fresh water Alligator River to Briery Hall Point where the East Lake and the South Lake joined the river. It was supposed to be the perfect spot to find Ol' Whopper. When they dropped anchor in the shallow waters, J.R. baited their hooks and cast them. They waited with anticipation. It was very quiet—very serene.

"Grandpa ... this sure is fun! I hope we can do this more often."

"Oh, we will, son ... we will. As you know, your Pa has been real busy at work lately, and he just hasn't the time to get away. But he loves ya just the same, and I'll see to it I can help take up the slack. We'll fish more together. I promise."

"Yeah, I know he's been busy. I guess one day when he gets unbusy, he'll take me fishing ... and you can come along too!

"But I've been curious Grandpa. What made you want'a become a fisherman?"

"Well son ... what it all boiled down to ... well, I just got tired of looking at the ass end of a stubborn blue-nosed mule! You see, when I was about your age, I helped on the family farm raising tobacco, and it was hot, miserable work. Even though we only had about twelve acres, it was more than enough for me!"

"Where 'bouts was your farm?"

"It was over there in Beaufort County, not too far from a little town called Washington. It's near the headwaters where the Tar River becomes the Pamlico River. After spending all day in them fields on a long hot summer day ... sometimes I'd take the notion and jump in the river. Boy! I can still remember to this day how cool that water felt!"

"What kind of work did you do?"

"Well ... it all started in what we called a plant bed. In the wintertime, we'd prepare the bed by hoeing and raking ... turning the soil over so it'd be all nice and ready for the seed by the early spring. Then we'd put these real tiny seeds, that looked a bit like finely ground pepper, in the bed and cover it with cheesecloth to protect it from the stormy weather. When the seedlings got to be about six inches tall, we'd then take 'em from the bed and put 'em in the plowed field. Now this is where the fun began," Grandpa Scoggins said with a laugh.

"This small hand-setter piece of equipment we had, took two people to operate. It looked like a big funnel. One person held onto the setter to release the plant and water ... and the other person had to drop the plant down the side tube. Boy! It took forever to do those twelve acres!

"After that was done, our next job was to hoe and chop the weeds, all the time keeping the dirt up and around the neck of the plant. This was real important and it was pert-near an all day affair ... and then we'd start it all over the next day. This went on until late spring when the tobbaco plant started to get about three or four-feet tall when it began to flower out at the top. Then we'd have to whack off the blooming section ... and usually there was worms that would get on the leaf and start eat'en it. That was bad and we'd have to hand-pick all those worms off the leaf before they could cause any damage. If the worms ate the leaf, the plant was no good and that would cost us money. My Pa didn't like that at t'all, I can tell you!"

54

"How big did the plants get?" Josh asked.

"Around mid-July, they'd get 'bout six to eight feet tall with a leaf that seemed to be as big as an elephant ear! Then we'd start harvesting it during the rest of the month and all through August as the leaves turned yellow. Pa usually hired some colored folk to help out. They'd get in the field and start pulling the leaf uniformly from the stalk and place 'em on a tobacco slide pulled by a mule. When it was full, they'd take it over to the barn where a looper tied the same-size leaves together into a bundle and then tie 'em over a wooden stick. When the stick was full, they'd hang it up in the barn to keep the dirt off it.

"When the barn got full, we'd turn on the heat and start curing the leaf. It went through several stages, but it generally took a coupl'a weeks to get it cured right. Once it was cured, we'd haul it off to auction and hopefully make a bit of money. That was always an anxious moment for Pa. But he usually made enough money so he could do it all over again the next year. He seemed to like the business ... but I tired of it real quick and wanted to do something else."

"Is that when you decided to start fish'en?"

"Yep, it sure was. One day a buddy and me went down to Washington to see how the rebuilding of the town was going. They had a big fire back in 1900 that damn near destroyed the whole town and we was watching 'em rebuild it. Well anyway, we went over to the docks and started jawing with some of the old-time fishermen and one thing led to another and the next thing you know I ended up get'en a job in Wanchese working on a fishing boat. I lived in an old shack there until I met up with your Grandma. She was a first cousin of Sheriff Roscoe. We sparked awhile and ended up get'en married. By then I was able to afford something a whole lot better than a shack!

"A few years later, I reckon that'd be in 1907, we had *your* Pa and became a family ... and I stayed in the fishing business from then until my leg started acting up. When that happened I thought it was a good time to quit. Your pa worked with me for many years and I offered the boat and business to him, but he was get'en a little tired of the grind himself. By then, ol' Roscoe had been sheriff for quite some time. He'd lost a deputy and offered your Pa the replacement job. Your Pa thought it was a good idea, so he joined up with the force ... if you want'a call it that! But he's been happy ever since. It was a shame the way your Ma took off the way she did ... maybe it just wasn't meant to be. You understand that, Josh?"

"Yes sir, I think I do. I used to miss her some, but Dad told me she had other things on her mind and that maybe one day I'd understand. I reckon maybe I do ... she left without saying goodbye so I guess she just didn't love us anymore. But that's okay. You and Grandma are family and ya'll have always been good to me and I'm grateful for that. It means a lot to me!"

"And you mean a lot to us too, Josh. Hey look'y there, I believe you hooked something, reel 'er in, reel 'er in ... looks like you might have Ol' Whopper!"

That was not to be, but a 10-inch bass was pretty good for that time of day.

Josh and Grandpa Scoggins continued fishing until two o'clock that afternoon until the wind started picking up making the waters choppy. A many times in thee past, the longtime fisherman had seen these rivers and sounds start rolling with the wind. He knew if it blew too hard it could be dangerous—especially in a small fishing boat like the one they were using. If nothing else, they'd get soaked from the bow spray, and the ride home would be anything but smooth.

But the day wasn't a total loss. Even though Ol' Whopper eluded them, they each caught five bass apiece with the largest being the upper side of four pounds. Of course, Josh caught that one and couldn't wait to get home to show his Pa.

After docking the boat and gathering up their gear and fish, Grandpa and Josh drove home. Grandma thought it was a marvelous catch and, because of their size, only decided to cook two of them. Earlier in the day, R.W. called to say he and George were unexpectedly delayed and wouldn't be home until much later that evening. It'd be appreciated if they'd feed and take care of Josh for him. He also imposed on his father to run an errand for him.

"Come on Josh, let's ride to the Manteo Post Office and get your Pa's mail. Besides, I need to pick up a few things at the store for your Grandma to go along with that fine catch she's cooking for supper tonight. How's that sound?"

"Sounds good to me, Grandpa. Let's go!"

The grocery store and the post office weren't that far apart so J.R. parked his car halfway between. Grandpa went left to the store; Joshua went right to the post office. They made a bet as to who'll get back to the car first.

When Josh entered the post office, he could hear boisterous voices coming from a curtained area behind the counter. Jenny Smith, the postmistress, was upset with the intercity deliveryman, Hank Larson. He had just arrived after being eight hours late in transporting the mail from the main postal facility in Elizabeth City.

"Hank, we're in a helluva mess here! Where have you been? I've had unhappy folks in here all day long looking for their mail."

"Jenny, Jenny ... listen! The mail was backed up all the way down the line. I don't know what happened with them *sort'en* fellers. All I know is they were late get'en it to me. Hell, I didn't get loaded up and out'a there until one o'clock this afternoon. And to make matters worse ... worse mind you, I had a damn flat tire from a popped up nail crossing that damned ol' wooden Wright Memorial Bridge. Fortunately,

Billy at the Martins Point Texaco station fixed it, but it seemed to take forever! Look, I know you're hot ... but so's everybody else. You ain't the only one around here who's got a burr up their fanny!"

While Jenny was quarreling with Hank, she already had dumped on the table the large sack of letters and parcels and was quickly scanning for Mr. Winters's envelope.

"Where's Mr. Winters' envelope Hank?"

"It's in there. I put it in there myself like I always do."

"He's been in here numerous times today look'en for it. You know it's important, don't you?"

"All mail is important is what my supervisor tells me."

A few minutes later, Mr. Winters walked back into the post office and Jenny quietly handed it over to him, staring into his eyes, not saying a word. He stared back, glanced over the envelope. Without saying a word, he turned around and walked out the heavy wooden and glass door.

Alfred Winters had only lived on the Outer Banks since early 1939. He was a sixty-three year old retired political science professor from the University of North Carolina in Chapel Hill. He still had the looks and physique of an old Roman warrior. Though his gait was slow, he moved about with polished poise. While Mr. Winters rarely chatted with the townsfolk beyond the pleasantries of the weather, he usually seemed lost in thought. But he was well-liked, albeit in a strange sort of way.

Mr. Winters was well-known throughout the community as the caretaker of the Wright Brothers Monument atop the Kill Devil Hill. In many ways, it was a prestigious job. It was, after all, the birthplace of powered flight that began a new era and changed the world. To nearly everyone it nearly was a sacred place. But to Alfred, it was nothing more than a big granite edifice requiring a mundane job to pass along the time. Such work, if it could be called that, allowed him to spend more time reading and writing about his deep-seated political beliefs.

After the monument was dedicated in 1932, the United States War Department placed the memorial under the jurisdiction of the commanding general of the Fourth Corps Area. The original caretaker had died a year later and the second caretaker, a former student and friend of Alfred's, stayed at the post until late 1938, when he decided to enlist with the United States Navy. Hearing about the opening Alfred quickly applied for the job. He had retired from teaching in the spring of 1938, and was looking for something to do.

Without much fanfare, Alfred Winters was duly appointed to the post and given a small cottage to live directly behind the monument along with a meager monthly stipend. Though he pretty much stayed to himself, Alfred occasionally ventured to the nearby Nags Head Casino to drink a beer and discuss politics with anyone willing to listen. His

57

radical theories always opened an ear-provoking, heated conversation and spirited debate.

After Jenny handed the envelope to Mr. Winters, she quickly noticed Joshua off to the side of the room. When he heard the commotion behind the counter and seeing the stern look on Mr. Winters' face, he backed off and out of the way.

"Well, hello there, Josh. I guess you've done figured out we've had a little problem today. Are you here to pick up your Pa's mail?" Jenny said in a more-favorable tone of voice.

"Yes ma'am. He and George will be late coming home tonight and I'm staying with Grandpa. Since we had a school holiday, we went fish'en today out on the Alligator ... caught me a big ol' bass!" Josh said holding his palms about three feet apart.

"Now, how big Josh?" Jenny said with a grin, questioning the size.

"Well ... he's big enough so Grandma's gonna have to use her big skillet to cook him in. That's how big!"

"That's a little more like it. Look, why don't you come behind the counter here and help me find your Pa's mail. It might take us a few minutes, but we'll find it right quick like so you can get with your Grandpa and get on back home to that fresh-fish dinner."

When Josh went behind the counter, Hank pulled Jenny off to the side of the room.

"Say Jenny, you want'a go over to the Casino tonight ... knock down a few brews ... roll one or two games of duckpins? I'm staying here in Manteo tonight with my cousin, and I'm buying, ya know!"

"Well I hope to shout! Yeah, that might be fun see'en how much trouble you caused me today. Pick me up 'bout seven, but we, I mean I ... I have to be back home before twelve so I won't turn into a pumpkin," Jenny hesitantly said looking toward Joshua with a hint of a smile.

Even though Hank and Jenny quarreled a lot, they really got along fine. Joshua noticed they always seemed close. It was almost as though they were married—but not quite. He just figured they had an odd relationship—or so he thought.

* * * * * * * *

Later that night, and ever so slightly, a cold and shaky hand nervously inserted a key through the eight-inch round, serrated brass handle into the lock. It slid into the right half of the eight-paneled, stainless steel and bronze double-door at the foot of the massive granite monument. A slight turn to the right and the well-designed and properly-balanced three hundred pound door easily cracked open, barely scraping the granite floor to the first downward step.

Once inside the sixty-one-foot structure and two steps below the entrance, there was a large hexagonal, pink granite-walled foyer with a circular pink granite ceiling corbelled five courses towards the center with a ceiling light. The floor was Wisconsin black granite laid in a symmetrical pattern. On each side opposite the entrance, and protected with locked iron bar doors, there were two narrow inward spiraling granite staircases that intersected at a small landing where a single concrete staircase in the opposite direction continued to the second floor level above the foyer's corbelled ceiling.

At the top of this small staircase, and sitting on six thirty-seven-inch metal legs, which were directly over the center of the foyer ceiling, was a hexagonal metal map table of the world depicting the first twenty-five years of flight.

To the left of the table, and adjacent to the wall, a tightly wound spiral concrete staircase with polished brass handrail led to the third level and a very small landing holding the monument's electrical panel.

From this level there was a tightly-wound cast-iron spiral lighthouse-type staircase, which sharply rose to a small fourth-level landing. It continued upwards to the top-most fifth level. Here there were two twelve-inch-wide, five-foot, nine-inch-high metal doors leading to a small three-foot by two-foot triangular shaped exterior observation deck. The deck was positioned at the front of the monument facing almost due north. The thick Mount Airy, North Carolina gray-granite deck walls were less than four-feet tall, preventing any accidental fall. To access the top of the wall, there was a small six-inch-high footing adjacent to the wall. The area was just large enough for three normal-sized adults.

Inside the monument, and just above the spiral staircase, was the five-foot diameter stainless steel and curved glass canopy that housed the aviation beacon light. It was a three-sided third-order Fresnel lens with an electrical motor, revolving the beacon six times a minute.

The hum of the electric motor echoed throughout the massive obelisk. Timing for the U-boat's cryptogram was critical. For this to happen, the beacon's rotation had to be stopped for exactly one minute, with one beam shinning directly due east along the 36° 1' latitude line. Then a very thick woolen blanket was positioned over the other two lenses to block its radiant light. Because of this, it was possible for a lay person to notice the sequence of flashes was amiss. It was a cause for concern because the rotation was stopped for one full minute. Eighteen flashes became dark. Somehow, this situation had to be addressed and corrected.

Once the beam was directed, a well-engineered shuttering device, similar to an Aldis lamp, that maritime quartermasters used to flash Morse code signals between ships, was affixed to the lens where it was manually flicked to send the coded-beacon signal. During the first ten seconds a preliminary code was sent, setting in motion the special sequence to start at the overall fifteen-second mark. All codes were precisely designed so a single signal would take no longer than forty-seconds, leaving the sender only five seconds to remove the blanket, reactivate the motor, and twirl the lens for exactly one minute.

On a clear night, the beacon's beam was visible to the horizon some eighteen miles out to sea. It was imperative the submarine be in position and within this viewing range. Any mis-steps and the mission would fail. So far, there have been no slip-ups.

With eight minutes left to spare, and after performing the signal preparation work, the traitorous lit a cigarette, stood on the footing on the observation deck, and peered due east towards the direction where the submarine was stationed. With two minutes left, the dark figure tossed the cigarette over the side to the granite star base below.

At exactly 0215 hours on 10 March 1942, the sequence for killing began. There were to be three heavily-laden military freighters traveling together, leaving the northern section of the Chesapeake Bay. It was to pass by the Cape Charles lighthouse in Quadrant CA 7335, at approximately 0545 hours local, heading up the East coast several hundred miles to Halifax, Nova Scotia for the final leg across the North Atlantic. If the U-491 failed in its mission to sink this vital military cargo, the chances of reaching Liverpool, England were very good. All three ships had to be sunk.

Chapter 8

"Herr Kapitän, I have received most of the message. There was a slight atmospheric aberration that caused a break in the beam," Victor Krech quietly said as he lowered his binoculars to his chest.

"Mostly received, Herr Krech?" Kapitän Vogel questioned back.

"I am not entirely certain, sir. I feel unclear at this point. I cannot fully tell until I input the code. Once I decipher it, I can judge better. Perhaps it was nothing."

"Ja, ja ... go below, and take care of matters. Any delay can cause us problems. We must know as soon as possible ... schnell, schnell!"

"Jawohl Herr Kaleun," as Krech headed down the conning tower hatch.

Kapitän Vogel and Executive Officer Staats remained on the bridge of the conning tower talking about this atmospheric anomaly. There seemed to be some concern that future missions might be in jeopardy because of the weather. It was something they really hadn't thought about. But this was something entirely out of their control; the weather was going to do whatever it wanted regardless of what the German Kriegsmarine thought.

Ten minutes later, radioman Leutnant Brückner poked his head through the hatch saying Krech had verified a certain amount of information. Both Vogel and Staats immediately returned to the control room where Krech was standing with a piece of paper.

"Sir, I have mostly determined our target is coming out of the northern section of the Chesapeake Bay in Quadrant CA, Section 7335. The time has been determined to be 0545 hours local. Unfortunately, I am unable to decipher our target. I will keep working on it, but I felt this information sufficient for you to get started."

"Ja, keep working. It is very important," Vogel impressed upon Krech.

Upon receiving the location, Staats and Navigator Heinz looked upon the maps on the table and immediately began plotting their course. Their estimated time of arrival would be 0531; nine minutes before rendezvousing with their target—whatever that was supposed to be. The boat needed to start moving now to stay ahead of the curve.

"Steer course 3 – 4 – 5 degrees, both diesels full ahead ... schnell" Vogel commanded. The essence of time was imperative.

"Aye aye Kapitän ... bearing 3 – 4 – 5 degrees ... both diesels full ahead!"

As the U-491 headed in a northerly direction and reached its maximum speed of seventeen knots, the crew jumped to their respective positions -- all except Erick Koehler, the electric motorman. He was lying in a small lower bunk in the crew's quarters aft of the control room. He appeared to be in a coma. The large gash on his forehead had been treated and bandaged; his breathing had returned to normal, but he was in critical condition as best the boat's medical intern could tell. Koehler needed serious help if he was to survive. It was quite apparent he suffered a severe injury to the brain.

Later that early morning, Vogel and Staats returned to the conning tower bridge to observe and to have a cigarette. The half-moon was now beginning to lower in the western night sky. The shoreline, once brilliantly lit, was now just a smattering of scattered lights.

"Judging by the level of lights on the shore Herr Kapitän, I believe the American public is beginning to take our actions seriously," Staats remarked.

"Ja, ja ... but they leave enough lit so we can still observe the silhouettes of their ships running up and down the coast. Based on their mentality, I don't believe there will ever be total darkness in America like it was in England or France. Those shorelines were very dark and hard to read. I think the Americans are just too cavalier to care. They only seem to think of themselves. They have total disregard for the lives of the merchant sailors who are supplying their selfish needs. If they acted like the British, more of their brethren would still be alive.

"But if there is *one* thing they aren't so haughty about ... it's their tobacco! Their cigarettes do taste much better than these shit sticks we're smoking now!" Vogel said.

"Herr Kaleun, you realize of course, just on the other side of that barrier island, it is there where all that fine tobacco is grown!"

"North Carolina? No, I didn't know that!"

"Ja Kaleun, it is. They call it the 'sand hills region.'"

"Well, we are so close ... yet so far away. Maybe we..."

"Herr Kapitän, come quickly to the control room! Kerch has deciphered the remainder of the code. Quick!" said head radioman Leutnant Josef Brückner.

Upon entering the control room, Krech handed the message to Vogel who, in turn, questioned its veracity.

"Ja Kapitän, I am quite positive this is what the code says: there will be three heavily laden military freighters. It is critical they all be sunk."

"And you are sure this is correct?" Vogel said, asking confirmation.

"Ja Kapitän. My trouble in reading the signal was, in fact, an atmospheric aberration. I think we were too far out to sea. As you noticed yourself, the signal was low on the horizon. I think this is what caused the anomaly. If we could move closer to the shore, future signals will be higher off the horizon and easier to read without the aberrations. I think this will solve the problem."

"Thank you Krech ... that will be all."

Several hours later at 0516 and fifteen minutes ahead of estimated time of arrival, the U-491began approaching their position twenty-five miles off Cape Charles in the northern section of the Chesapeake Bay in target Quadrant CA7335. In fear of being detected, Vogel ordered the boat submerged. There was sufficient light to monitor the sea through his observation periscope. He ordered torpedo tubes one through five to be prepared. When bringing to boat thirteen and a half meters, periscope depth, he ordered the boat slowed to three knots.

"Bring to course 2 – 8 – 0 degrees."

"Aye sir ... bringing to course 2 – 8 – 0 degrees."

At 0540 Vogel was spanning the watery horizon outside the Chesapeake Bay. There were still lots of shore lights burning; there was no sign of cargo traffic. He believed his targets, if they were coming, would exit the bay without their running lights.

Several minutes later at 0547, Vogel spotted heavy black smoke puffing into a weak moonlit sky. He looked closer. It was a large freighter running without its lights. One minute later he saw a second freighter steaming directly behind. It too was spewing thick black smoke. He knew the third was shortly behind. He wasted no time.

"Target ships found! Lowering observation scope and moving to conning tower."

With that, he and Oberleutnant Staats moved into the small space above the control room. Vogel sat on his swivel stool, which resembled a bicycle seat, and raised the attack periscope. Staats prepared the torpedo computer for a firing solution.

The torpedo deflection computer, known as a *Vorhaltrechner*, was a high-speed electronic calculator located inside the conning tower. It was designed for deriving a torpedo-control solution from data on the submarine's course, speed, and the known speed of their torpedo as well as the speed and direction of their targeted ship. A computed gyro-angle, which is the angle at which the directional gyroscopic control of a torpedo is set prior to firing, is electrically transmitted to the torpedo in the tube just before firing. The angle could be set to zero, allowing the torpedo to travel in the same direction as the heading of the submarine; or it could be set at some other angle to cause it to travel left or right of the submarine after it leaves the tube.

The captain, looking through the attack scope, verbally gives to the executive officer a set of numbers relating to the enemy target's speed and direction. He, in turn, takes these numbers, and the numbers of his own boat, and inputs them into the computer. Within seconds, the computer has a solution for the torpedo. Each target has to be done separately.

As the three military freighters passed the Cape Henry Lighthouse and began running a parallel course with Fisherman and Smith Islands, Vogel ordered a change in course to better position himself for the kill.

"Rudder right ten degrees, steer course 3 – o – o, increase speed to four knots ... hold it steady! We'll hit the lead freighter first, followed by the third freighter to box in the middle freighter. We'll then hit the middle freighter with our stern tube."

"Aye sir."

After seven minutes, Vogel observed the freighters change course from 145 degrees to 162 degrees. With that, the U-boat captain adjusted his course accordingly. So far, the three merchant ships have played right into his hands. It was almost a perfect firing solution.

"Staats ... prepare these numbers. Lead freighter, 1,200 meters, fifteen knots, angle on the bow green twenty, torpedo depth two-point-five meters."

"Kapitän ... torpedo room reports tubes one, two, three, four, and five ready in all respects," relayed Staats.

After a quick sweep of the area verifying it was clear of any other intruding merchant ships or enemy destroyers, Vogel re-checked his range.

"Correct range to 1,300 meters, fifteen knots, bearing o – 6 – 5 degrees, angle on the bow green twenty-two."

"Sir, computer has plotted a solution," Staats replied a few seconds later.

"Good. Tubes one and two ready! On my command. Release torpedo one ... release torpedo two.

"Time to target?"

"One minute and six seconds, sir," replied Heinz

"Staats, third ship ... range 1,000 meters, fifteen knots, angle on the bow green eighteen, depth two-point-five."

"Heinz, time to first target?"

"Thirty seconds, sir,"

"Second target ... correct range to 1,100 meters, bearing 0 – 6 – 5 degrees, fifteen knots, angle on the bow green sixteen." Vogel was waiting for an answer.

"Staats?"

"Sir, firing solution plotted!"

"Tubes three and four ready ... on my command!

"Release torpedo three...

"Release torpedo four.

"Heinz, time to second target?"

"Sir, fifty-six seconds!"

Vogel continued looking through his scope readily observing the torpedoes' trail running towards their targets. The twenty-three foot-long Type G-7a torpedoes were driven by a gas-steam engine, which always left a trail of bubbles. Because of this, it was used only at night or on rare long shoots up to 10,000 meters. If, by happenstance, a crewman on a target ship saw the track, there was a chance the ship could maneuver away from the torpedo; though, most of the time it was too late.

Within several moments, the first torpedo plowed amidships into the first vessel with a small flash from the explosion. Seconds later the second torpedo struck the aft section where the magazines for weapons were stored. The ship immediately exploded with a thunderous roar, splitting her in half. There was a massive fireball igniting fuel and all types of ammo. It was impossible to imagine anyone surviving this humongous explosion.

Vogel hesitated looking through the lens. The glow was so bright it hurt his eyes causing a momentary loss of sight. He pulled away from the scope and gently rubbed them. He blinked numerous times; floaters were swimming within his eyeballs. It was hard to focus. He stood there; face cocked to the floor—staring. Seconds passed.

"Heinz ... time of torpedoes to second target."

"Kapitän, the time has elapsed. There were two faint explosions where the torpedo made contact with the ocean floor. We missed!"

"Nein, *impossible*! We had a good firing solution."

Vogel peered back into his periscope and was shocked with what he saw.

"Damn ... the end ship is zigzagging! It must have changed course as soon as we fired on her. We missed ... *goddamnit*, we missed! And now the middle ship has turned to port and has gone around the first. We are blocked! Chief, get this goddamn boat to the surface. We will chase the son-of-a-bitch and sink her with our deck gun ... schnell!"

A few minutes later, the boat was surfaced. Vogel, Staats, and Leutnant Brückner, along with three watchmen, went to the conning tower bridge. Three crewmen went to the flak platform (*Wintergarten*) to the rear of the conning tower bridge and prepared the 20-millimeter canon while three other crewmen went to the foredeck to prepare the big 88-millimeter cannon. [This gun was not related to the infamous 88-millimeter canon, that would later become the dreaded anti-tank weapon on the European battlefields. *Ed.*]

While several thirty-pound shells were already stored for immediate action in a watertight locker on the fore-casing just forward of the canon, the remaining shells were stored in thick-card containers beneath the steel deck plates of the radio room floor. The crew set in motion a human chain to relay the shells up through the conning tower hatch and down onto the deck near the gun just forward of the conning tower.

With the narrow wooden deck always slippery and slimy, especially right after surfacing, the layer, aimer, and loader hooked themselves into a harness tied to the deck and prepared the canon for firing. The aimer brought with him the sensitive optical sight, which he affixed to an L-shaped bracket on the port side of the gun. The layer took his station on the same side while the loader removed the tampion (watertight muzzle plug) to a storage hole on the gun pedestal. He then took his firing position at the breech.

The powerful gun was controlled and directed by Second Watchman Josef Brückner from the safety of the conning tower.

When the gun was finally prepared for firing, Kapitän Vogel ordered both diesel engines engaged at full throttle. Coordinating any surface attack was critical; coordinating one at night was harrowing and exceedingly dangerous.

The U-491 headed towards the foundering freighter. When the ship exploded, the second tanker zigzagged to the port side of the burning ship escaping what was believed to be a forthcoming torpedo. The third ship, after quickly engaging in a zigzagging course, followed the second ship around the burning freighter. Both had, for the moment, escaped disaster.

"Herr Kapitän, you realize it is doubtful we can catch those freighters. They have almost a two-kilometer lead on us. If they push to twenty knots, we will never catch them!" said First Officer Staats

"Ja, ja ... I realize that, but we must try to pursue. The shipment was classified as critical. We must try Herr Staats! Maybe something will intervene to give us another torpedo shot. Maybe one of our comrades from the north will get them."

As the boat barreled north of the Chesapeake Bay entrance, they came upon the burning freighter that was just beginning to plunge beneath the surface. There were no cries for help, only the creaking and cracking and twisting of wrought-iron steel—the gloomy sound of a ship's death. Bodies were floating in and about the flaming oil; the ever-pungent smell of burning flesh was swirling with the sea. Vogel was right—no one survived.

When the German submarine passed the burning wreckage, the image of a darkened-night sky returned and the evening glow of the sinking moon had vanished. Sunrise was vast approaching. Through their binoculars, they could barely see the escaping freighters; their noses quickly picked up the oily exhaust coming from the freighters' stacks. They had put too much distance between them and the U-boat. There was no hope of catching them.

"Kaleun, we must think about returning to our home quadrant. The morning sunlight is near. I fear the Americans are too. We have a healthy run back to our coast. We must not be caught on the surface. We must turn around!" Staats implored to his commander.

"Perhaps you are right ... depth charges are not amusing. We have been lucky to get this far without being spotted. We might be pressing our luck. Secure the deck and flak gun and store the shells. I will go below and report to *BdU*. I am afraid Admiral Dönitz will not be pleased that we have failed to sink this small armada. Though, I'm sure he will position one of our comrades in their route across the North Atlantic. Perhaps they can still be sunk before reaching England. Yes, perhaps."

Having been on the East Coast of the United States for one month, Kapitänleutnant Hans Vogel and his U-491 crew had exacted seven kills—five coded kills of special military freighters and two freelance of fully-laden oil tankers too good to pass up.

Tonight's two military freighters were the only ones to escape his wrath. While two torpedoes failed to hit their mark because of a fluky change in course, Vogel's intuition kept him from firing any more torpedoes. For now, he has enough for at least six more kills, assuming one torpedo per ship will do the job and if the torpedoes don't malfunction. That is a real problem that has surfaced with many other U-boats on patrol.

Unfortunately, unless he shoots perfectly, one per ship won't do the job. It generally takes two torpedoes per ship to guarantee a kill. For the remaining targets, he must plan his attacks wisely. Otherwise he will be forced to the surface to fire his deck gun, which always is dangerous.

By 2100 (9 p.m.) hours that evening (Outer Banks time), the U-491 had made its way safely to their home quadrant of CA79. This was twenty miles northeast of the Diamond Shoals off Cape Hatteras. Kapitän Vogel ordered the boat secured and requested the vessel be policed for trash and errant, out-of-place equipment. While this mundane chore was being performed, Vogel and Oberleutnant Staats gathered inside the commander's claustrophobic quarters and closed the curtain. They began discussing the day's activities as well as the medical condition of Erick Koehler—the electric motorman, who was in a coma.

"Sir, what do you propose we do with him? Without further medical attention, I am afraid he will die," Staats said solemnly.

"I do not fully have the answer. One possibility is we might pass him to another boat returning to France to re-arm. But that might not happen for days and even at then it is over a two-week trek back across the Atlantic. It is doubtful he would survive that long," Vogel said.

"There is no doubt this is a tough dilemma if we want to save him. But, here is a thought! Let us take him to the American shore and leave him on the beach with a note. Surely they would try to help him. They obviously have the facilities that can give him a chance."

"Peter, I think that might be our best choice. Yes, perhaps that would be his best chance for survival. If we do nothing, he *will* surely die. Yes ... that just might work. We should think of doing this tonight. The seas are as calm ... as calm as I have seen them in the last few days. Of course, that can change within minutes, but maybe tonight is our best opportunity. I think we can get close enough to shore without being detected, where a raft could get him there within a reasonable time. Who would you suggest we have transport our dear comrade, Herr Staats?"

"Maybe we could ask for volunteers, but I would hate to lose a key person if, by some chance, he is captured. You know, this is enemy territory and surely they have the beaches guarded. I think it is best we 'volunteer' someone for this duty ... someone ... someone that is..."

'dispensable?'" Vogel concluded.

"I hate to lose anybody, but maybe our interpreter Jürgen Oehrn might be our best choice. He certainly seems to know the English language with all its quirky characteristics ... and, if he is captured, maybe he could bullshit his way back to us. He seems to be a crafty individual," related Staats.

"Aye, that is true. And our Second Watch Officer Brückner can also speak and read some English. Besides, Oehrn might be able to bring us back some American cigarettes!" Vogel said with a light laugh. "But, let's not plan on him being lost to us just yet. I think he will succeed. I will go talk to him and also have our medical orderly prepare Koehler for the journey. You prepare the boat and get us to a desolate beach as close to civilization as you can. There will be no sense in dropping him off where nobody will find Koehler. That would be a wasted mission."

"Aye, aye Kaleun."

Kapitän Vogel called Jürgen Oehrn to his cramped quarters and explained the situation. Oehrn's mind clicked with trepidation but realized it was imperative to get medical help for his friend Koehler. He also realized it might be a one-way mission. But in the eyes of his fellow crewmen, it was impossible to say no. And the reality was very simple: this was not a request—it was an order.

While Koehler was being prepped for transfer, Vogel had Oehrn write a legible note in English describing the injuries that were sustained. He also had him include his name and German hometown. If by chance he died, maybe the Americans would contact his family regarding his death. Probably not—but maybe.

Oberleutnant Staats verified to Kapitänleutnant Vogel that he had found a spot on the American coast that he thought would be a reasonable choice. It was about one mile south of the latitude where they normally receive the beacon code. From their present location near Diamond Shoals, it would take about one and a half hours to be in position. Based on a sounding chart they had of the coastline, he felt he could safely get within one-half mile of the shore. This was good news for Vogel. From that distance, he could attach a light tether to the raft and pull it back to the safety of the boat. He passed this information to Oehrn. Jurgen smiled slightly, saying nothing. His mind was boggled—churning.

When the U-491 approached the vicinity of the shore, Vogel ordered the diesel engines turned off and the electric motors turned on. The less noise the better. With calming seas, numerous crewmembers clambered through the lower rear deck hatch pulling ever so gently on the injured sailor. He was tightly wrapped in a blanket with his head firmly secured so it wouldn't wobble about. Other crewmembers pulled a deflated rubber raft to the deck from a compartment between the outer non-pressure casing and the inner pressure hull and inflated it through a compression line connected to a silent air compressor within the confines of the boat. It safely filled with no leaks. Koehler was gently placed inside the raft.

Oberleutnant Staats handed Oehrn a compass and a flashlight. He was to follow a reading of 270 degrees. When he reached the shore and secured Koehler to a safe location of beach above the high tide mark, he was to signal back towards the sub three quick flashes. Later when he got the raft beyond the breakers, he was to repeat two slow flashes. The crew would then pull him seaward by the tether along with him rowing. If the tether broke, he was to signal four quick flashes and continue rowing.

"Do you understand these directions, Herr Oehrn?" Staats asked.

"Jawohl! Three quick flashes when I have Koehler on the beach and then repeat two slow flashes when I am beyond the breakers. Four quick flashes if the tether breaks."

"Gut, gut. We shall see you back within the hour. Do not dally. We cannot wait long. If we are pressed for time or we are spotted, we must leave. You realize that of course?"

As the raft was carefully lowered into the sea with Koehler already strapped in, Oehrn grabbed a line and cautiously lowered himself into the raft. The light tether line had already been attached. Once Oehrn positioned himself inside the raft and oriented himself with the shore, he began the cumbersome task of rowing. It wasn't as bad as he thought, surprising himself how quickly he was leaving the boat behind—and maybe his security.

Twenty minutes later, Oehrn heard the crashing breakwaters just beyond his shoulders; he knew he was near. Now he was concerned about getting through the barrier waves without tipping over—not only for himself but for Koehler. It would be hard to save him if he went into the water. While Oehrn was wearing a life vest, it was impractical to properly secure Koehler with a vest because he was tie-wrapped to a heavy woolen blanket. If by chance they were swamped, he would surely drown on the spot.

Surprisingly, the breakwaters were small given it was a rising tide. But just the same, the waves still crashed with convincing might. But tonight, he was lucky. The raft evenly rode the waves past the breakers well into the foamy shallow waters without turning over. When the raft hit the shifting sand, he rolled out and pulled it to shore. He was completely exhausted and thoroughly soaked to the waist. He then turned towards the ocean and gasped a sigh of relief. He had made it.

For the easefulness in moving Koehler, he pulled the raft, with him still inside, past the tidemark, and below the tallness of the windswept dunes. Oehrn fell to his knees and, as gently as he could, lifted Koehler's flaccid body from the raft. With some effort, he placed seaman comfortably on the slope of a sand dune. He then reached inside his pocket and pulled out a small-chained Saint Christopher medal with the words *Sei Uns Fuhrer* (Let us Guide) and carefully put it inside his handwritten note. He took the message and medal and placed it halfway inside the blanket making sure someone would see it. As a gesture of kindness, he lightly patted Koehler on his chest, wishing him well and for the courage he has suffered. *"Godspeed, my friend."*

With a sigh of relief, Oehrn took another deep breath. After a few seconds, he regained his composure and pulled the raft towards the sea. The tether was still attached to the raft. He hoped it was still attached to the submarine.

As ordered from Oberleutnant Staats, he faced the ocean and signaled three quick flashes. He hoped they could see it. He pushed the raft to the breakers and then beyond. He wanted to make sure for its easy return. He had made his decision.

Without hesitation, Jürgen Oehrn removed his life vest and threw it inside the raft. He then stuck a knife into its rubbery side—a slight pop and whoosh went the air. To confuse matters, he signaled only one quick flash. He then turned about and slogged to shore. His ever-lasting thought was premeditated. He knew what he was doing.

"To hell with them! If Kapitänleutnant Vogel thinks for one minute I am going back to that goddamned boat, he is crazy as hell! Now, if I can just get a shower and a shave and get my skinny little ass to my uncle's house in New Jersey, I am free as a jailbird. So long Germany ... and to hell with you Herr Hitler!"

Chapter 9

In response to Bodie Island Coast Guard Station's Lieutenant Mark Fleming's request, his sister, Navy Lieutenant Junior Grade Sandra Fleming, was able to send her brother twenty more Guardsmen. It was a welcomed relief because he could now add another duty shift and give him the relief he needed. However, this added support posed one small problem: where to put them?

Contacting his Army supply sergeant-friend in Elizabeth City, Fleming, again, bartered his way for ten field tents, which should be enough to comfortably house his new arrivals. But none of them would be too happy with the constant wind and blowing sand of the Outer Banks. Fleming instinctively knew he was going to hear a lot of moaning and groining.

"We'll get those tents down to you in a couple of days, Lieutenant. When your new recruits com'en in?" asked his Army friend.

"Ah ... they'll start arriving later in the week. We should be good to go until then. Sarge, you think you can send me a truck too?"

"Don't push your luck ol' buddy! My ass would be in a sling if'n I sent you a truck! Besides, the olive-drab Army paint might give it away."

"Now Sarge, ain't you ever heard of gray paint? Hell, by time your driver drops off those tents and takes a leak, you'd never see that truck again! Why most everything we got around here at one time or other's been olive-drab. If there's one thing we do have 'round here ... it's gray paint."

Fleming told his sergeant friend about his two chief petty officers, who have their enlisted charges will disciplined.

"If it moves, salute it! If it stands still, paint it gray!" Fleming told his Army friend.

Laughter could be heard on the other end of the phone.

"I'll make note of that and make sure my driver pisses in the ocean *after* he leaves your place! But hey, listen ... when we get low on shrimp and oysters, I'll holler at ya and we might can work something else out. But right now, things 'round here are buzz'en like a buzzard over a dead cow. We need any and everything we can get our hands on with four wheels or four hooves. The Weeksville Navy base down the road is work'en like crazy trying to get some hangers built for their new blimps. We need to get those puppies built as fast as we can. Them damn U-boats are playing havoc with our merchant shipping. Hell, they've even blown up a few of our old Navy trawlers trying to act like destroyers. They even sank a blasted YP [Yard Patrol]. Those damned Krauts are sink'en everything! If they keep it up, the only thing left will be a coupl'a rubber rafts!"

"Tell me about it," Fleming counters. "I just found out the other day I lost two good buddies sail'en on the SS *Jacob Jones* that was blown apart a few weeks ago. I wouldn't mind get'en my hands on the son-of-a-bitch who pulled that trigger."

But for the moment, Fleming had more pressing problems. Earlier that morning, just after sunrise, two of his Guardsman were combing the shoreline in their Jeep along the upper reaches of the Outer Banks near Nags Head when they found a German sailor wrapped in a woolen blanket. He was carefully propped up against a sand dune. There was a note just under the blanket written in plain English:

"Erick Koehler. Neuwied, Germany. Serious head injury. Probable concussion. Coma for two days. Please help!"

Also plainly written in small letters in the lower right hand corner of the paper was "U-491."

After finding the injured German sailor and acting on their own initiative, the two Guardsmen carefully lifted Koehler into the jeep, supported his body, promptly driving him to the small medical facility in Manteo. The doctor on call quickly admitted the young sailor into the emergency room for further testing to fully determine the extent of his injuries. Based on the commotion with the Guardsmen, he knew this patient was probably a German. Guardsmen John Allen said he would stay with the prisoner. His fellow Guardsman should return to the Coast Guard Station to report the incident to Lieutenant Fleming.

It wasn't long after that before Chief Petty Officers Bleu and Hatfield, along with another Seaman, arrived back at the hospital. There Seaman Allen gave them a verbal report and the handwritten message along with the St Christopher's medal found on the German sailor. For the moment there was nothing else to do except talk with the doctor and learn more about his condition.

In the meantime, Chief Bleu and Seaman Allen returned to the station to give Lieutenant Fleming their report. Allen returned to his patrolling and Bleu met with Fleming near the shore of the Pamlico Sound next to the station where the officer was enjoying watching a resident Great Blue Heron stalk his food along a marshy section of the sound. Fleming noticed the heron had built a large bulky stick nest atop a tall piling not too far away.

"Smoke, Chief?" said Fleming.

"No sir ... trying to give 'em up. But after this morning, I might start back again. Finding that sailor ... well, you know what this means, don't you sir?"

"Yeah ... yeah, I do. If those German sons of bitches can sneak ashore to drop off an injured comrade, they've got the capabilities of coming ashore in force. How did they get past our men on patrol, Chief?"

"Sir, it was way up there just past the Nags Head Casino. You know that we're covered pretty thin up in that area. I don't think it was because of a lack of vigalence on our part ... just dumb luck on theirs for finding a weak spot in our defense ... that is, if you want to call what we got a defense.

"But generally, the sheriff's department handles that section of the beach ... and hell, they're thinner than we are! Had that Kraut been dropped a little further south, I think we might have nabbed the sons of bitches. Then again, we don't even know what time they came ashore, or even how many there were. It may have been just one guy or a whole goddamn platoon of 'em. We don't even know if they returned back to their boat or have already infiltrated us. Until we get more evidence, hell ... it's anybody's guess."

The chief continued.

"The Kraut sailor is still knocked cold and the doctor hasn't a clue as to what's wrong with him ... yet. We showed him the note, but he had already surmised as much when he saw the guy. The doc's going to do some preliminary testing and let us know something as soon as possible. But right now, we don't know a damn thing," said Bleu.

"Look Chief ... here's what we're gonna do. Let's send a detachment of twenty men and place ten of 'em from Whalebone Junction north up to the Corolla area. Have 'em stay on the street side and poke around the buildings. You know, the cottages, the sheds ... shit, whatever. Have 'em check for demolition charges under the Wright Memorial Bridge. If that bastard blows, we'll all have to swim out'a here. Put Seaman Allen in charge of that. He recently passed his third class petty officer's exam, so he'll have a crow on his sleeve soon and this'll give him some good leadership experience. Now for the other ten troops, I want ya to split 'em up and send some to Manteo and Wanchese -- do the same thing. Let's see what turns up. Check the Wash Baum Bridge too. If they're on this goddamn island, we'll find 'em. I mean ... hell, they got'a stick out like a sore thumb, don't ya think?"

"Yeah, I would think so, sir."

"So far I haven't contacted Norfolk. I've been wait'en to get more info. But that might take awhile. It's probably best I go ahead and give 'em a call and tell 'em what we do have so far. When you going to relieve Hatfield at the hospital?" Fleming asked.

"I told 'em I'd be back after lunch. The doc thought he might have something by then. You wanna contact the sheriff's office?" Bleu asked.

"Yeah, I'll give ol' Simmons a jingle. He's probably already caught wind of what the hell's going on from Jenny Smith, the ol' 'Mouth of the South' herself ... but I'll give 'em an official notice as to what we got. Maybe he knows something."

"We got a plan Chief?"

"Yeah, we got a plan."

"Well ... let's get to it!"

When Jürgen Oehrn awoke from a much-needed three-hour nap, he heard the sound of a heavy truck moving down the small two-lane road. He knew he was probably in trouble. He surmised the Americans had found Koehler earlier that morning and had sent out a detachment of troops looking for signs of enemy infiltration. He hoped the wind had covered his fresh footsteps in the soft sand.

Jürgen cautiously peeked outside the small shed door and saw a gray deuce-and-a-half (two and a half ton) truck heading in a northerly direction with what appeared to be soldiers with rifles in the rear bed. While he was glad his shipmate had been found, Jürgen wished it had been a little later in the day, giving him more options to escape the Outer Banks' islands. For now, he had to adapt to the situation. The only thing Jürgen could think of at the moment was to sit tight and keep his eyes and ears open. He had a gut felling this was going to be a long day.

When Chief Bleu returned to the hospital, he met up with Chief Hatfield. After a few minutes of conversation, the doctor came out of the room reporting he had diagnosed the German sailor.

"I believe this fellow can count his lucky stars. He took quite a knock to the noggin, but I think he's going to be okay. Only time will let us know for sure. We cleaned his wound and dressed it, giving him some antibiotics. He also suffered a focal intracranial injury ... a cerebral contusion. His brain tissue was severely bruised when it was jostled inside his skull. This of course, caused some microhemorrhaging ... that is, he had some small blood vessels leak into his brain tissue.

The two chief petty officers shook their heads, acting as though they completely understood what they were being told. They had only the vaguest of understanding.

The doctor continued

"Our young friend does have some pressure on the brain and we're counter-acting that by trying to raise his hypotension and correct his hyponatremia."

The two chiefs were dumbfounded, each trying hard to let on like they understood completely what they were being told.

"He also has hypercapnia and we're trying to cope with that," the doctor droned on. "And, the boy is severely dehydrated, so we're pumping fluids into him."

"What'd you just say, Doc?" Chief Bleu finally asked, admitting their ignorance.

The doctor smiled slightly, in a somewhat superior manner.

"Son, we're taking care of him! We're adjusting his body chemistry ... that's to relieve the pressure on his brain. That's all we can do right now. But in the meantime, to make him more comfortable, we took his clothes off and had a nurse sponge bathe him as best she could. She also shaved his face. Those damn clothes of his reeked of diesel fumes! I've got 'em in a sack for you out back. Quite putrid, they are. I'm sure ya'll probably want'a take them back to your commander. If not, we'll burn 'em for you."

Now the physician was speaking plainly and in a southern manner.

"When you think we can move him, Doc?" Bleu asked.

"It's hard to say. First, we have to see some improvement. Assuming our diagnosis is correct, and he responds accordingly, we probably should see something in two to four days. He really needs to remain stable. Had your men not gotten to him when they did, I don't think he would've made it. If everything goes the way it's supposed to, I'd say we can probably move him in about a week to ten days.

The doctor reverted back to a higher level of diagnosis.

"And there's also the chance this young man may have suffered a stroke. We really won't know that until he awakens, and we can check his motor skills. Though right now, fellas, it's just wait and see. Look, ya'll feel free to keep a guard posted if you'd like, but he's not going anywhere... but I know ya'll have to follow orders and procedure. I guess what it all boils down to is that to you he's a prisoner, but to us, he's a patient and human being."

The doctor brought back a bit of his superior attitude to the two chiefs.

"Anything else there fellows?" he asked.

"Not right now Doc. We'll keep in touch," Hatfield replied. "And yes, we'll keep a guard by the door. How's the coffee situation 'round here?"

A boatswain's mate without a cup of joe in his fist was out of uniform.

"Around here we keep a fresh pot brewing twenty-four hours a day. By all means, help yourselves," the doctor replied.

Chiefs Bleu and Hatfield returned to the station leaving a Guardsman by the door. The young seaman was given a .45 automatic pistol to strap on his hip. The two chiefs, in turn, reported the progress on their prisoner to the lieutenant. Fleming already had earlier reported the incident to his commander in Norfolk, knowing the information was going straight up the line to the head office. How far, he didn't know.

Much later that afternoon, Fleming's detachment reported back that no evidence of infiltration had been found and none of the bridges had been compromised. Fleming also had a visit from Deputy Scoggins and his man Dawkins. They further discussed the situation, trying to work out details as to how their respective organizations could cover for each other. Word had already leaked out around the town that a German prisoner had been captured. The story had built to a fever pitch.

"The Nazis were fighting it out with thirty Coast Guardsmen down on the beach," was Jenny's last news flash to anyone she came in contact.

"Amazing how rumors can spread so quickly," R.W. remarked with a chuckle.

"Hell, I imagine by the end of the week it'll be how we captured a whole damn submarine with two men in a raft, bribing 'em out of the water with some of Bessie Pott's pork ribs and sweet 'tater pie," Fleming countering with a belly laugh.

"Well I don't know about ya'll, but I have to admit … even I'd come out of a damned sub for some of Bessie's pork ribs and pie!" added Dawkins with a chuckle.

The mood quickly became serious.

"Mark, look, I know your detachment is a good thing, but they've been running all over town turning everything upside down and the townsfolk are get'en a tad antsy," R.W. said with a somber tone. "Bob Hartsell down at the hardware store tells me he's already sold out'a shotgun shells to a goodly amount of nervous residents. If we don't do something to calm the situation, these folks are gonna end up shoot'en each other before the weeks out. Why don't you pull your people back a bit. George and me'll start try'en to ease things up some," R.W. implored.

"Yeah, I guess you're right," Fleming admitted. "If they haven't found anything by now, I doubt they will. About the only thing a German's gonna find around here is a lot'a sand and some fresh shrimp. I'll get 'em pulled back in before dark. You got my word on it."

"Well, I'm sure Roscoe will appreciate it. His phone's been ringing off the hook all day. I haven't seem him this busy since the dedication of the Wright Brothers Monument back in '32, when he believed President Hoover was gonna attend. What a mess that day was ... rain, wind, hats flying all over the place!" Scoggins reflected. "Of course, ol' Roscoe got blamed for everything, including the weather."

"We'll take care of it from here and you take care of it on your end. I believe things'll start calming down in a day or so.

"Okay now... you guys take care and we'll chat with ya later." Fleming said, standing up and shaking hands with both lawmen.

No sooner had the two deputies left, the phone rang. A Seaman sitting at a desk picked it up. He immediately straightened up in his chair, almost at attention. It was important. Covering the mouthpiece with his palm, he loudly whispered to Fleming.

"Sir ... it's Admiral Andrews! He wants to speak with you!"

Fleming knew the actions of the last ten hours would get somebody's attention, but he never figured on a call from the head man, himself. Before getting on the phone, Fleming lit a cigarette and sat down. He slowly picked up the receiver, not wanting to sound too apprehensive. He wanted to act as if it was just another phone call. It wasn't.

"Yes sir, Admiral Andrews, sir ... Lieutenant Fleming here."

"I understand you fellas had a bit of excitement down your way today. Have you got any more information for us?"

"Just a little while ago, we got updated on the injured German. Seems he's got one helluva a headache. So far, he's still out cold, but the doctor believes he's gonna make it ... says it's gonna take a few days to see if the German responds to medication and what all. Assuming he does responds, and hadn't had a stroke, the doctor thinks he might be able to be moved in about a week or ten days. Beyond that, it's just a wait-and-see game right now, sir"

"I hear he had a note on him. Anything significant in it?"

"It had his name and hometown in Germany and the extent of his injuries with a plea to get him help. But in the lower section on the note was lightly written 'U-491.' To me, the way it appears, that was slyly written ... such that, whoever wrote the note didn't want anybody else to see it'd been written. More than likely, it's the submarine he came from. I think it means something, but don't know just what as yet."

"You might be right, son. Have you taken precautions?" Andrews inquired.

"Yes sir ... sent most of my men out to scour the area to see if they could find anything. So far nothing's turned up. Though, the townsfolk are hopping around like a bunch of Mexican jumping beans, causing a bit of a stir ... but our local sheriff's office is handling that situation. I'm gonna keep a handful of guys nearby just in case something pops. Other than that, the situation seems under control."

"Okay Fleming ... good work. I'm going to send a couple of my security guys down your way tomorrow and get that note and check on the German. We'll follow the doctor's orders. When he gets better, we'll take him off your hands and transfer him to Norfolk. Hopefully, we can do all this without the FBI folks pokin' their noses into the situation.

"Well, it seems the German sons-of-bitches do have a sense of compassion for their own kind, but it pisses the hell out of me they're blowing up innocent merchant ships and killing innocent human beings in the process ... folks just doing their jobs," the Admiral continued. "That's about as calloused as it gets. But we're starting to get some better support from the Navy. You should start seeing a difference within the month.

"Now look, Lieutenant, let's try to keep the Navy and FBI out of this. I don't want them horning-in on our bailiwick. It proves what I've been saying all along. The Krauts could get an armed landing party ashore, blow up some of our key installations, and get back to sea with little or no trouble."

"Yes sir, I've been saying the same thing all along. We're doing the best we can with what we got..."

"Yes commander, I know you are and I know you're spread thin. I hear you've got some reinforcements coming your way soon. That should help you!" the admiral said in a knowing voice.

"Well ... uh, yes sir ... yes sir, we do. But how..."

"Lieutenant, look -- it's okay. I applaud your boldness and ingenuity. I like that in a leader!"

"Yes sir. Thank you, sir!"

"And by the way, lieutenant, I want you to keep me informed directly. Don't go through channels. This is important, and I want to stay fully abreast of the situation down your way as soon as it happens. And one last thing ... you think you could round me up about twenty pounds of fresh shrimp and pass 'em off to the security guys that'll be coming your way tomorrow?"

"Sir, I think we can accommodate that request ... yes sir!"

Fleming paused. "But, why twenty pounds."

"C'mon, lieutenant. You think my security men are gonna bring all twenty pounds back to me? I'll be lucky to get ten of 'em."

The two men laughed and signed off.

As darkness descended over the Outer Banks, Jürgen Oehrn escaped the small closet shed. His clothes were still damp from that early morning ocean dip, and he was cold. He would have to do something different than already has in order to survive.

"Think Jürgen ... think!"

Chapter 10

Around eleven o'clock the following morning after the German sailor had been found on the beach, Deputy Scoggins entered Ned's Drug Store for a bottle of cough syrup for his son, Josh. He chatted with a few customers regarding the hoopla that occurred the previous day. He assured them the situation was well in-hand and that the Coast Guard was soon to establish more security around the beaches. After retrieving his medication from the shelf, he glanced over to the lunch counter at the rear of the store and noticed a new face.

While heading to the cash register at the front of the store, he slowly turned his head and glanced back over his shoulder to the lunch counter not watching where he was walking and crashed into the swivel metal postcard rack standing by the cash register. It so startled him that it appeared as though he was performing the jitterbug trying to catch the rack before it crashed to the floor. He was embarrassed. Fortunately, the only person nearby was Ned Moody, the owner, who chuckled.

"I see you just noticed the new girl I got working at the lunch counter!"

"Oh, you noticed that did you, Ned. You know you ought'a move this rack or somebody's gonna get hurt," R.W. said, picking up postcards that had fallen to the floor. He felt like a fool.

"Now there ain't nothing wrong where that rack is ... but if I was you, I'd suck them eyeballs of yours back in your head. You might just go blind one day!"

"Ah Ned, there ain't noth'en wrong with my eyeballs. Tell me now, where in the *hell* did you find that purty lass?"

"I thought you'd never get 'round to asking me. She comes from Hillsville, Virginia. I hired her a few days ago, but this is her first day on the job. She drove in last week and I set her up in a small rental cottage out on the beach ... ol' Jud Wilson's place up there in Kitty Hawk. He told me to rent it if'n I had the chance, and this was the chance.

"She went ahead and paid for the whole six months upfront with cash. She told me she'd like to stick around at least through the summer and would decide later whether or not she wanted to stay longer ... also said she was looking for a job, telling me she'd worked in a pharmacy before. Well, what could I say to that? I told her she'd have to wear a lot of hats 'round here and that didn't seem to bother her none. I offered and she accepted. I reckon with the summer crowds just 'round the corner, I could use the extra help. I think it'll work out okay," Ned said, feeling good about his hire."

He continued.

"Now R.W., ain't she about as pretty as a speckled pup under a cedar tree on Christmas morning?"

"Well, I really didn't notice, Ned," the deputy mumbled, not taking his eyes off the new girl. "But, now that you mention it, she is right cute. What's her name?"

"It's Claire Belle Charboneau."

"Good gosh a' mighty, that sho' is a mouthful." R.W. said, pulling back his head with beaming wide eyes.

"Ain't it though!"

"So ... just her, huh?" R.W. asked probing the druggest.

"Yeah, as much as I can gather ... said she just wanted some new scenery ... got tired of the mountains ... wanted to see the ocean and smell the sea."

"Sounds to me like a woman running away from something," R.W. said, fathoming a guess.

"Well, maybe so. She made no mention to me about a husband or child and I didn't bring it up ... really none of my business I reckon....

"By the way, how's your deal going with Emily Mae? You got'en that mess all squared away yet?" Ned asked inquisitively concerning R.W.'s former wife.

"Yeah, she's gone for good. I guess she's found what she was looking for. Sent me some papers not too long ago. Got ol' M.A. Michael over there in Raleigh take'n care of all the legalese for me."

"That the same Michael married to that cute blonde, Casey from Shelby ... the one's got that cottage over there just above Whalebone Junction?" Ned asked.

"Yep, that's them."

"What a knock-out she is! You ever see her in a swim'en suit?"

"One time when I was out that ways patrolling last summer. They invited me in for a cocktail, but I was on duty ... did fix me up some ice tea, though."

Both men continued looking at the new girl behind the lunch counter.

"Sure looks good, don't she R.W?"

82

"Now Ned, are we talkin' 'bout Michael's wife, or your new girl? Get your mind right. Yeah, Miss Michael's purty and she's a nice lady, and all so let's just leave it at that. You keep talk'en that mess, your wife's gonna whack you upside the head. You know that don't ya?"

"Well, don't tell my wife I said anything, okay?"

"Now, why in the hell would I do that?"

"Well, I reckon it was kind'a stupid talk. I know you won't say anything."

"Look Ned, I got'a go. Let me pay for this cough syrup so's I can get it on over to Josh. He picked up a nasty cough and sore throat when he and Dad went out on the Alligator River this past Monday look'en for 'Ol' Whopper.' He's racked out on their sofa right now feeling some kind of miserable. I feel so sorry for the little feller."

After paying his tab, R.W. opened the door to leave and again quickly glanced back over his shoulder, looking to the back of the store, hoping to get another glimpse of the pretty, new lady. In doing so, he smashed his forehead on the side of the double wooden and glass door, making another loud racket. Looking sheepishly, he finally made it out to the car without breaking anything. The only impression he made this morning was on his ego.

Today, R.W. was driving Sheriff Simmons's official county patrol car. In the meantime George, using R.W.'s car, was making the long patrol trip to Duck and Corolla, checking on the Currituck lighthouse keeper as well as the family that owned the Corolla Island Hunt Club. He knew the Coast Guardsmen had been up there the day before, but thought it might be worth another trip to let the folks there know the Sheriff's Department was also on top of things. He probably wouldn't be back until late that afternoon because it was a long trek.

While George was in Corolla, the lighthouse keeper told him that the husband and wife that owned the "Hunt Club" had packed up that morning and motored back to Philadelphia. He was a very rich railroad magnet, and he and his wife became fearful of a German invasion.

The mansion was actually their second home. He built it on the shores of the Currituck Sound as a retreat back in the mid-1920s, and invited many of his friends to join him from time-to-time to hunt ducks so prevalent in that part of the Outer Banks.

It was an enormous house, which could accommodate many of his friends all at once. While George was there, he peeked in through the windows and noticed a floral motif with corduroy wall coverings and cork flooring. He also saw an elevator and an indoor swimming pool. The house, at 22,000 square feet, was by far the largest single family home he had ever seen.

After taking the medicine to his son and spending a little time with him and his parents, R.W. headed back over to the office to mind some paperwork Roscoe had turned over to him. Spending about three hours with that chore and still answering phone calls from nervous residents, R.W. thought he might take a break and head back over to the drug store for a refreshment soda and, maybe—just maybe, try to properly introduce himself to Claire Belle Charboneau. But as soon as he walked out of the courthouse, something caught his eye.

"What's up there feller? You look like you might be lost or something."

"Well sir, I *think* I know where I am but not entirely sure. You see, I hitchhiked this way sort of by accident because my ride came this way. It was getting late in the day and I really didn't want to be out thumbing in the dark. The roads around these parts look lonesome. So I decided to come into town thinking I might just get a fresh start in the morning. Yes sir ... that's what I'm doing. By the way, what charming town is this?" said the stranger.

* * * * * * * *

Unbeknownst to Deputy Scoggins, the person he was talking to was Jürgen Oehrn -- the German submarine interpreter, who had escaped the U-491 and brought Erick Koehler to shore. Realizing he was close to being captured when the Coast Guardsmen dispersed themselves throughout the Banks, Jürgen carefully hid himself inside an outdoor closet for the remainder of the day. He was lucky that a Guardsman never noticed the small shed or his fresh footprints in the sand.

That evening at dark, Jürgen broke into an empty cottage next door where he took off his cold wet clothes and shoes, grabbed a blanket from the bed, and wrapped himself for warmth. He felt hypothermic, however, a few hours under the blanket thwarted the threat. To keep from arousing suspicion, he kept the lights off using only his flashlight to move about the cottage.

Much later that night, after warming up, he looked through the closets and dresser drawers and discovered an array of clothes left behind by the cottage owner. To his surprise, most of the clothes fit, although the khaki pants were a little big in the waist and the legs drooped a tad long. Nonetheless, they fit well enough without causing suspicion. But, on the other hand, the comfortable cotton knit shirts were a perfect fit as was a nice cream-colored canvas jacket. He also found a small light brown leather suitcase. To Jürgen, he had just found his path to freedom.

Early the following morning, at 6:24 a.m., just after the sun had crested the Atlantic horizon, Jürgen opened the valve to the water supply and took a very cold shower. Unfortunate for him, the hot water-heater had been turned off and drained for the winter season. He did, however, find a well-used cake of soap, putting it to good use by purging himself of the putrid diesel smell emanating from his skin and hair.

Jürgen also found a dull razor that was painful to use when cutting away his beard, nicking himself twice, drawing drops of blood from his left cheek and from just under his nose.

In the medicine cabinet over the bathroom sink, he found an old bottle of hand lotion to soothe his sore face. After all this, he felt like a million Reichmarks -- er dollars. It had been almost two months since his body had felt this refreshed. Now if he could just find a pair of shoes because his boots were a mess and they might give him away because of the rough, European-made look.

After dressing and packing the suitcase with an array of clothes, socks, and undergarments, he set forth a plan to escape his makeshift prison. He could find no maps of the islands. While he was on the submarine, Jürgen only glanced at the charts in the control room with no real knowledge of what he was observing or where he was on the globe. As a precautionary measure, and because of the secrecy of the mission, no charts of the East Coast were made available for fear of them being captured. The charts that were used for navigation were simply marked off in quadrants and grids. Only the officers on the boat knew what they pertained to and how to use them.

But while on the boat, Jürgen did have the opportunity to get the lay of the land by unusual means. Another sailor had brought along a 1938 Knaur Pocket Atlas that had been produced in Berlin. It was this small atlas he read to visualize his location based on information he heard from the navigator. But, while looking at the atlas, his main focus was New Jersey—not North Carolina.

Of course, at the time, there was no possible chance of escaping so he really didn't pay all that much attention. All Jürgen knew was his boat was mostly positioned somewhere off the North Carolina coast and that the barrier islands ran many miles from north to south and was located only a few miles off the mainland. On the atlas, the Outer Banks were prominent and well defined.

Looking out the window towards the narrow street in front of the cottage, it appeared he only had two choices: go north or head south. He wracked his brain trying to remember the geography of the islands. Observing through the window, he noticed more cars going south than north. Yes, that seemed logical. The bridge to the mainland was to the south. That's where everybody was going. Perhaps that was the safe bet. But the one thing he did know about America: New Jersey was to the north of the Carolinas. So, to go north, first he had to go south. Somehow that seemed logical. Anyway, that was his plan—head south.

As strange as it may have seemed, Jürgen promptly straightened up the house as close to possible to the way it was when he entered.

Thereafter, he briefly left the cottage and buried his old clothes at the base of a soft sand dune using a rusty shovel he found in the small closet shed next door. When he finished, he returned it to its rightful place. Upon re-entering the cottage, Jürgen found a pencil and piece of paper. He wrote the cottage owner a note apologizing for stealing his clothes. The young German ended it by saying *"I am sorry, but also desperate."* Afterwards Jürgen sat down on a wicker chair and waited for the right time to leave -- whenever that was. Right now, everything was a guessing game, but, he knew he had to leave soon.

By early afternoon, Jürgen decided it was time to set out on his journey. He walked out the screen door that fronted the beach, down a small flight of stairs to a landing, made a u-turn down another small flight of stairs, and walked underneath the stilted house to the blacktop road. Just to be sure, he pulled out the compass Staats had given to him before leaving the boat and verified the southerly direction. Yes, he was right -- left is south. Now, beginning to feel more comfortable, he casually started walking south on Highway 12, believing sooner or later he would reach a bridge to the American mainland.

About a mile and a half down the road, just past Nags Head, a car pulled over with the driver asking him if he'd like a ride into Manteo. Without much ado, Jürgen got into the front passenger seat passing on a thoughtful greeting. Other than light chit-chat about the weather, the conversation remained cordial. *These Americans are a friendly bunch*, Jürgen thought.

When the car turned right at Whalebone Junction, making its way over the causeway and the short Melvin Daniels Bridge, the road continued across the longer wooden Wash Baum Bridge. This caused Jürgen to feel a swell of joy in his stomach. He knew he had made the right decision. Jürgen Oehrn was going to the mainland of the United States, or so he thought.

After crossing the bridge and going another mile or so, passing through a vast marshland while traveling over a raised roughly-paved asphalt roadbed, the driver turned right. He drove a short distance to the waterfront portion of Manteo, and dropped off his passenger, wishing Jürgen well on his journey. After leaving the car, Jürgen walked a few hundred feet.

This is where Deputy Scoggins noticed the youth.

* * * * * * * *

"Well son, you are in Manteo, North Carolina. Home of the Lost Colony of Roanoke Island!" said R.W. in a friendly gesture.

"I'm on an *island*?" Jürgen said with total amazement.

86

"Yep, you sure are. You seem a little more lost than you thought you were. Son, where did you think you were?" R.W asked.

"Well, I *thought* I was back on the mainland," Jürgen responded.

"Nope ... no you're not. You left the mainland when you crossed over that three-mile wooden bridge at the upper end of the Banks. The bridge you crossed to get here only brings you to another island ... Roanoke Island. There's no other exit from here to the mainland. Boy, I think you're lost!"

"I suppose I am."

"Just where *did* you come from if I might ask?" Scoggins asked more inquisitively.

"I came down from New Jersey ... Paterson to be exact. I lived with my uncle until we had a falling out and I left. He owns a textile dye manufacturing facility there. I worked with him for a while and one thing led to another and I decided to leave. You see, my parents are no longer with me, and I was forced to live with him. Things just didn't work out and I decided to leave. I was hoping to make my way to Florida."

Jürgen didn't want to delve too deep into his lie for fear he'd never remember what he said; that would throw up red flags in his ruse. But the truth was, his uncle is from Paterson, and he was a man of means, owning a textile dye facility. That much was true. The rest of the story was improvised to the point Jürgen knew he could remember.

Jürgen Oehrn's uncle was his father's brother. His German name was Johann Oehrn. In the early 1900s, he immigrated to America from Germany with the hope of a new life. He and his father, from what he was told, always quarreled about politics and that Johann always believed the American way of life was better. When he finally entered the United States, he denounced his German citizenship later becoming an American citizen, vowing never again return to the family or to Germany. To this day, that has held true.

When he became an American citizen, Uncle Johann changed his name to John O'Hearn. While it had a Scottish flair, he liked the moniker and kept it. Besides, he joined a local country club and learned to play golf. As the game itself was developed many centuries before in Scotland, he felt comfortable with it and let the name stand.

When Jürgen was in his mid-teens, he visited with his uncle at the bequest of his father to try and smooth old wounds. What he found was his uncle had become successful, and he thoroughly enjoyed his company. As the years progressed, his hardened stance against his brother had waned, but he still had no intention of ever returning to Germany. His life in America was fine, and he had become successful. If his brother ever wanted to visit, he would be welcomed with open arms. That is how it was left.

"You know son, you're quite a distance away from New Jersey and about halfway to Florida depending on where you're going."

"Yes sir, I believe I am ... but, I am in no real hurry. I guess I just got turned around a little bit hitching rides. I was trying to stay as close to the coastlines as I could, and I suppose things around North Carolina aren't as smooth as I thought. I'll straighten myself out tomorrow. Is there a YMCA nearby I could maybe get a room and a meal for the night?" Jürgen asked wanting to change the subject.

"No ... not really. You don't have much money, do you?"

"No sir ... no I don't. As a matter of fact I don't have any. Mostly I've been able to work my way along to pay my debt, but right now I am all out of dollars."

R.W. listened to his story with apprehension. Not too many folks get lost on the Outer Banks and it's even rarer somebody thumbs his way here even by mistake. But R.W. scoffed it off believing Jürgen was probably telling the truth, so he offered to help.

Jürgen had a nice smile, and he was well-mannered. He looked like he had come from a good family and was brought up to respect his elders regardless of the squabble he had with his uncle. He also looked like he hadn't eaten in a while.

"You look a bit hungry. Would you like something to eat? The drug store is just down the street and we can grab a sandwich there. I was just heading over there myself to grab a late lunch. Come on ... let's go. I'm buying. By the way ... what's your name?"

"O'Hearn, sir ... John O'Hearn." Jürgen said, having not revealed his real uncle's name. This name he could readily recognize even if called from behind.

When the two walked into the drug store, Ned was near the front door re-arranging a section of stock. Nobody else was in there. R.W. specifically looked to the rear of the store hoping to see Claire Belle.

"She left about thirty minutes ago R.W. ... said she had to run an errand. There's not much going on, so I gave her the rest of the afternoon off. Besides, it's not too far from quit'en time. What can I do for ya?"

"Well I was hop'en to grab a soda and a sandwich for me and my new found friend here ... but looks like you got the counter all closed up." R.W. said disappointedly.

"Ah hell R.W., I'll fix ya'll a sandwich. Claire Belle made up a fine batch of chicken salad for the lunch crowd today ... had a lot of compliments ... here, let me fix ya'll one. I had one for lunch myself and it sho' was tasty."

John and R.W. sat down at a small round table near the counter while Ned made each of them a sandwich. He already had given them a soda fountain drink. They continued talking but the young German kept the conversation light and away from anything personal. So far

88

his masquerade was working. Fortunately his English was sufficient enough that it didn't cause a stir; although, R.W. did mention he spoke with an interesting brogue he had never heard before, but attributed that to his own lack of travels and other peoples' dialects. John just brushed it off with a laugh.

"Say listen, John, I've got an idea. If you're willing to stick around for a few days, I *think* I can get you a job and a place to stay so you might can pad your funds a little bit and make things easier on you as you travel to Florida," R.W. offered. "I've got a buddy of mine over on the barrier island who owns a facility that usually brings in a crowd most every night, and he's always look'en for good help. Most of the kids he usually hires haven't come in for the summer season yet, so I think he might be a little short-handed right now. I understand he has a spare room on the second floor with a bed. I'm not too sure about it all right now, but tomorrow morning we'll take a drive over there and I'll talk to him. He's a real nice feller. Known 'em for about ... well, going on 'bout ten years now. Interested?"

"Well sheriff that sounds awfully nice ... and yes, let's give it a go and see what happens. But I do need a place to stay for tonight."

After finishing their sandwiches, R.W. and John got up to leave to which Ned remarked he'd tell Claire Belle about him coming by to see her.

"Now Ned, don't be do'en that. Hell, I ain't even met her yet! I'll just come by tomorrow ... okay? Now Ned, don't be say'en anything stupid now. I've already made a fool out'a myself once today. I don't want'a be mak'en a habit out of it!"

In the meantime, for today, John could spend the night in the sheriff's office in a small spare room they had where, from time-to-time, one of the deputies would stay when they had a prisoner. He would ask George, when he came back to the office, to spend the night there to keep the situation on the level. The following morning, R.W. would pick them up and everybody would go over to Bessie's Café for breakfast.

After another hour or so in the office, George returned from his rounds with nothing serious to report. He spent fifteen minutes talking about the Corolla Island beach house and the beautiful grounds around it. He also mentioned he spent awhile talking to the lighthouse keeper and the possible threat of an invasion. He told George he would keep his eyes open for anything suspicious.

R.W. left the courthouse for his parent's house to check on Josh and have dinner. He was still hungry. The sandwich didn't hold him. When he arrived, there was a surprise.

"Well, my goodness! Who do we have here?" R.W. said with a wide smile.

"Son, this is Claire Belle Charboneau from Ned's Drug Store. She heard that Josh was sick and brought over a pot of Hatteras-style clam chowder for us ... now wasn't that sweet of her dear," R.W.'s mother said pleasantly.

"Why yes ... yes it is. That was very thoughtful," R.W. said shyly.

"Have you two met before?" his mother asked.

"Well, not exactly Mom. I was over there earlier today, but didn't get the chance. I was sort of in a hurry to get the cough syrup and rushed out'a there before I had the pleasure. But now that I'm not pick'en up postcards from the floor and bang'en my head ... Miss Claire Belle, it's a pleasure to meet your acquaintance!"

Claire Belle stood with a broad, fixed smile, looking straight at R.W., making the deputy even more nervous.

"No R.W., the pleasure is all mine. I finally am glad to meet you. Ned has told me so much about you and I've had a wonderful little chat with your family here. I think Josh is making a good recovery. It won't be long before he's up and about," Claire Belle said, now with a softer smile on her face.

"Are you going to help us chow down on this clam chowder you brought?" R.W. inquired. "I'll have Ma fix us up some biscuits to go along with it."

"No, really ... I must be going. I have some things I need to take care of ... but you folks enjoy it. It's an old recipe Ned had lying about and I doctored it up a little. I hope you like it."

R.W. walked Claire Belle out to her car making boyish small talk along the way. He opened the door and thanked her for the soup. She smiled. With that she put the car in reverse and slowly backed away. With a grin from ear-to-ear, R.W. watched her disappear into the darkness. All he could do was stand there, seemingly struck by a wayward bolt of lightning—a feeling he hadn't felt since the early days of high school; he knew what it meant. As he walked back to the house, he awkwardly tripped over a long blade of grass catching himself before falling to the ground. *"Now that was stupid,"* he thought to himself.

It was understandable why R.W. was stupefied and acting so boyish for he had just met an incredibly stunning-looking woman, who had surreptitiously warmed the cockles of his thumping heart. It wasn't her silky auburn hair or her lovingly hazel eyes, but her soft lustrous cheeks adorning her pleasingly convivial smile. It was this look of wholesomeness that melted his heart.

The following early sunrise was bright and crisp and typical for a mid-month March. And for this morning, R.W. was openly joyful and whistling away as he drove to the courthouse to pick up George and John, who were anxiously awaiting a hearty breakfast at Bessie's. While driving to the restaurant, George humorously described to John what he could expect to eat. After arriving at Bessie's, they went inside to a full house of patrons already enjoying their meals.

"Morn'en there Miss Bessie. You got three hearty specials for us?" R.W. said in a chipper-like mood.

"Why you know I does sugar. Now ya'll go on and grab yo'selves a table and I'll has ya'll sump'en to eat in jes' a minute."

It didn't take long before Bessie had three big plates in front of them. While George and R.W. knew what to expect, John was overwhelmed. Three fried eggs, hominy grits, sausage and bacon so thick it looked like it was still attached to the hog, and a large separate plate filled with the softest cat head scratch biscuits he'd ever seen. There was a whole stick on a plate all to itself. To wash everything down, Bessie had plenty of black coffee.

"Hey Bessie ... don't forget the cane syrup," George lightly hollered.

"Com'en right up there Big George," Bessie hollered back.

John was mesmerized with what was on his plate, having no idea where to begin.

George started by gouging a thumb-sized hole in the middle of a biscuit, making sure not to pierce it through.

R.W. started by buttering his grits. Then George poured syrup into the hole of his biscuit; then John noticed R.W. shaking salt and pepper on his eggs. All movements synchronized. They had done this before, John reckoned.

John decided to start with the eggs. He first had a couple of bites before he put salt and pepper on them. Then he had a taste each of the sausage and bacon. Then he buttered up a biscuit and had a bite of that. He now had tasted everything on his plate except the grits.

"What's this George?" John sheepishly asked.

"You never had hominy grits before, boy?" George said humorously wrestling with a mouthful of breakfast.

"No, I can't say that I have. What are they?"

"They come from corn. You know what that is don't you?"

"Yes."

"Well hominy grits come from the heart of the corn," George said smiling.

"You know R.W., when I was working up in New York, I discovered them folks up there never heard of grits. I believe our boy here is a Yankee from the north," George remarked with a laugh.

"You know, George, he did tell me that yesterday. But no, I didn't know northerners knew noth'en about southern grits."

John laughed, quickly picking up on what it meant to be a Yankee ignorant of a southern state's ways, so he buttered his grits, and took a mouthful and liked it. Then he followed George's cue with the syrup on another fresh biscuit. The trick was to let the syrup saturate

91

throughout the biscuit before taking a bite. This usually required pouring the syrup into the hole two times to get it fully saturated. John learned quickly.

While they were enjoying their breakfast, a patron walked up to R.W. patting his hand on his shoulders making a quick humorous joke. Then it turned ugly.

"You hear anymore 'bout that German prisoner we got in the hospital?"

"Yep, I was by there yesterday and he seems to be improving. I believe he's gonna make it."

"Know what's gonna happen to him," the man asked.

"From what I hear tell, when he can be moved, the Navy's gonna take 'em up to the Norfolk Naval Hospital. But he has to improve a little more before they can do that. I guess we'll have to wait and see ... but don't worry, he's not causing any harm where he is. There's a guard on the door."

"Well, I hope the son-of-a-bitch don't make it!" the man cruelly remarked.

The remark quickly riled R.W.'s competitive spirit.

"He is a human being ... you know that don't you, sir!" R.W. retorted back.

"Yeah well, so were all them other brave men who's gotten their asses blown away from some goddamned torpedo and being burned alive screaming for their lives. You know that too, don't you Deputy!" the patron replied back to R.W., as he walked out the door hot as a firecracker. The three men's table got quiet, then whole restaurant got quiet.

"Don't worry about him, R.W." George said in a hushed tone.

"Ah hell ... I ain't worry'en about him. Let's enjoy our breakfast."

John just sat there keeping his eyes glued to the grits. He was afraid to look up. When the patron walked out the door, he finally got the nerve to raise his eyes. He was pleased to hear his shipmate was improving and probably going to live. He also was pleased he had taken part in the mission to save Erick's life. But now he had to be careful as he had just witnessed the anguish of American anxiety towards the Germans. It was imperative that, from here on out, he walk straight or he might be hanging from the end of a rope. Though, at least for the moment, he knew George and R.W. didn't feel the same way; nonetheless, he still had to be careful.

"Come on fellers, let's go get some work done," R.W. said, breaking the silence. "George, where's Roscoe and Sam today?"

"Roscoe's taking his usual Saturday off, and Sam's using the cruiser out to the islands," George replied. "I'm sitting in the office unless *you* want too? Where're you supposed to be?"

"I'm taking the morn'en off and gonna take John here over to see Rags Truscott at the Nags Head Casino and see if I can get him hired on as one of his helpers. Then I need to run an errand to Elizabeth City. When I get back and had a bite of lunch, I'll relieve you at the office, 'Big Guy,' and let you patrol in the car.

"You all filled up and ready to go there John?"

"Yes sir, I sure am. I'm ready to go!"

Chapter 11

Mid-morning on Monday, 16 March 1942, three deuce-and-a-half trucks pulled up in front of the Bodie Island Coast Guard Station with a delivery for Lieutenant Mark Fleming. It was the extra Guardsmen that his sister Navy Lieutenant Junior Grade Sandra Fleming sent to him at his request. Two of the trucks held 10 Guardsmen each, while the third carried their seabags of personal belongings. It was definitely a welcomed relief for helping fill the gaps in his sand dune defense to the far reaches of the sparse Outer Banks. It was also going to help relieve the stress on the regular Guardsmen that were already pulling double-duty.

Chief Gunners Mate Jim Bleu walked into the commander's office with this refreshing news. Lieutenant Fleming was sitting at his desk puffing on a cigarette doing busywork regarding Victor Krech. The injured, unconscious German submariner found at death's door had been carefully propped up against a beachside sand dune near Nags Head. Since receiving medical attention on Manteo, his condition had greatly improved and was scheduled to be released in one week from the medical facility. He was to be taken to the Norfolk Naval Hospital for continued rehabilitation, further interrogation, and probably end up a prisoner of war camp. The U.S. Army was beginning to plan for the possibility of POWs being held on American soil. A number of locations in the nation's interior were being investigated. Places like Iowa, Nebraska, Kansas, Oklahoma, Texas, Alabama, and other interior states were targets for isolating enemy combatants.

"What'cha got there Chief?"

"Your extra recruits have finally arrived, sir! All twenty-one of 'em."

"Twenty-one! Hell, there's only supposed to be twenty. Where'd the extra guy come from Jim?"

"I'm not sure sir, but here ... here's their '201 Files.' Everything seems to be in order, sir. I sort'a looked 'em over and all seems copasetic to me so far as the paperwork's concerned, but anyway ... here they are for your eyes. Maybe it was just a clerical error that he was sent here, but I think we ought'a try and keep him. Having an extra man around here wouldn't hurt a bit."

"Yeah, you're probably right, Jim. I'll look into it later... just put them files over there on the table. I've got'a enough shit on my desk as it is. Ever since we found that Kraut laying on the beach, my damn paperwork has doubled."

"Yes sir, I can imagine. Where you want'a encamp these guys, sir?"

"Well let me think. Let's put 'em in that large sandy field just north of the entrance. Should be enough room there for all three of those new eight-man tents. And see'en how we got that extra seaman, we can divide them up into units of seven seamen to a tent. Make sure there's a senior man in each tent if there are any available."

"Yes sir ... that'll be no problem," said Chief Bleu. "We happen to have four third-class petty officers among this bunch, so I'll make sure we have one in charge of each tent.

"The tents are in the storage building. Get the men together, pass 'em out, and have 'em start put 'em up. Weather's com'en in tonight and it's gonna be airish. If they don't get 'em put up in time, I believe the white caps in their thunder pots probably gonna be freez'en...

"We get anything else on that truck, Chief?"

"Well, as a matter of fact we did receive another 1,000 rounds of .30-6 caliber ammo and about twenty SCR-536 walkie-talkie transceivers. Now what in the hell we're gonna do with 'em is anybody's guess 'cause of the short range they transmit," Bleu fathomed.

"Headquarters sent 'em down to us because of that Kraut sailor," Fleming said with a smile. "Later today, you and me along with Chief Hatfield will sit down work out some kind'a plan where we can put 'em to good use. No sense hav'en 'em sit in that damn storage building. We'll find some way of using 'em. Did they send any extra batteries? Those things don't last very long."

"I'll check. Oh, and Lieutenant. You got another little surprise. It didn't come from headquarters though. Come on over and look-see out the window here. I think you'll like this!"

Getting up from his wooden swivel chair and lighting another cigarette, Fleming took a puff and walked over to the filmy window. Chief Bleu had a big grin on his face.

"Well I'll be ... another goddamn Jeep! Now *that* is a welcomed surprise. Hell, Jim, now we just might have enough firepower and mobility to run them damn Krauts off the beaches if'n they ever do show up," Fleming remarked satirically.

While Fleming didn't want to kick a gift horse in the mouth, he was very pleased. Apparently the case of Jim Beam bourbon he sent his sergeant friend in Elizabeth City last week paid off. Just after he and Bleu had a good chuckle, the phone rang. It was a call from the sergeant in Weeksville.

"You get my little present down there did 'ja Loo'tenant?"

"Yeah, I sure as hell did. It just arrived. I assume you got my little package, as well?"

"Yep ... sho' did. Now listen, you said you had gray paint, right? That I couldn't do for ya ... paint it that is. I highly suggest you get two *heavy* coats on that sucker as soon as possible and make *damn* sure you cover up all them numbers and letters already on it and come up with a set of your own. There's gonna be one pissed off Army Engineer captain down there at the Weeksville Naval Air Station that's really gonna be chew'en nails an' spit'en rivets when he finds out his Jeep's gone a'miss'en. He'll come up with some fool reason, saying it's vital to the construction of the base."

"We'll do Sergeant, and I do appreciate it," Fleming said. "Say, that brings up a point. Why are the Army engineers building that Navy base? What happened to the Sea Bees?"

"I guess all of 'em are out in the Pacific building stuff on the islands the Marines are takin," the Sarge surmised. "Look Loo'tenant, I got'a go now. You keep this little deal under wraps so we can keep on do'en business. I'll be back in touch with ya when things calm down a bit. And listen, ya'll wrap up tight tonight. We got word a big nor'easter's moving in and you know what in the hell that means!"

"I hear ya, Sarge! We're on top of it."

Lieutenant Fleming was beginning to feel considerably more comfortable about fortifying his coastal defenses; nonetheless, he still found it frustrating in procuring the materiel he needed. Coast Guard headquarters simply wasn't all that much help, so Fleming found himself more and more bypassing regular channels and going through the backdoor to get what he needed wherever he could. The Navy had a term for such back channel bargaining: "cumshaw." It was the art of obtaining anything of value in an unorthodox, maybe even illegal, manner. Nearly ever command officer in all of the armed forces had at least one cumshaw artist at his disposal.

Fortunately, for his bartering strategy, the seas held an abundance of shrimp and oysters from local fishermen. A first cousin on his mother's side, who works for the Beam Distillery in Clermont, Kentucky, was sympathetic to his cause and kept him well-supplied with the spirits. As long as those supply lines stayed intact, he felt he could keep his head above water with the fishermen. He wondered if Admiral Andrews felt the same way when he dealt with Admiral King in bartering for protection against the whole Eastern Sea Frontier.

Though, Fleming did find the bourbon-bartering angle a bit humorous. It was ironic the distillery's family were immigrants from Germany in the late 1700s and that their name originally was Böhm.

Shortly after settling, they changed their name to Beam to make it sound more American. *"Interesting how their liquor is now being used to fight the Boche,"* Fleming thought.

Later that afternoon, Fleming and his two chief petty officers gathered in his office and started working on a plan to adjust their beach alignment so the walkie-talkies could be of value. Ensign Hargrove seldom sat in on such meetings. His primary assignment was the running of the small base – supply, mess hall, berthing, and the like. Because this was a supply issue, the young officer was invited to sit in with the more seasoned officers. Even though he outranked the two chiefs, Fleming relied more on their judgment because of their many years of service and experience.

The extra Jeep they just received assured their communication problem would be greatly improved. But their biggest concern, as always, was keeping the Guardsmen on duty awake and alert through the night whilst they patrolled their section of beach. Such duty was terribly boring and the sound of crashing waves had a soothing effect that seemingly numbed the senses -- especially the hearing. It was always possible to find a soft, sandy dune, curl up, and fall asleep. Now, with the extra Guardsman, the line could be bunched tighter allowing for better communication with the transceivers.

To keep alert, Fleming ordered the Guardsman furthermost to the north along the upper beaches to relay a message every thirty minutes to the man just south of him and that man in turn relay a message to the next man south of him, all the way down the line to the last man in the southern reaches. In the meantime, the extra Jeep would be driven by a Guardsman up and down the beach, further checking on each man's status and bringing them coffee. It seemed to be a good plan. But first, the radio batteries had to be charged and the Jeep had to be painted. As soon as that was accomplished, the plan would take effect.

Just as the meeting was over, Dare County Deputies R.W. Scoggins and George Dawkins arrived at the Coast Guard Station, bringing two civilians with what would turn out to be an incredible story. R.W. felt the need to have them recount their tale in person to Lieutenant Fleming, who might glean important information to help matters regarding the coastline defense.

The two civilians were from Raleigh. One fellow was a slightly-aged bank president named Mr. Chalmers, and the other gentleman, Mr. Webber, was a bank customer and owner of a plumbing supply company. Because of his favored relationship, Mr. Chalmers was treating Mr. Webber to a full-day of deep-sea fishing in hopes of catching blue fin tuna. They had arrived the previous day and contracted with Joby Brown and his mate for a day of sport fishing near the Gulf Stream in a forty-three foot trunk cabin. She was a gorgeous boat with elegant lines. She was named "Dawn's Grace."

Just after a hearty breakfast at Bessie's Café, and well before sunrise, the charter headed out from the Wanchese wharf, working their way out to the main channel and then through the shoal-infested waters of the Pamlico Sound adjacent to the Oregon Inlet. The boat's two-man crew carefully maneuvered through this maze, and the inlet, then safely motored three-quarter throttle to the wide-open sea. After a speedy fifty-mile ride due east, and one hour after sunrise, the charter slowed to a putter where the mate baited the businessmen's hooks. The jubilant fishermen thenceforth cast their lines into the cold green Atlantic, just shy of the Gulf Stream, in hopes for a terrific day of fishing.

If they only knew what lurked below.

"Well, no sooner had we sat down on our aft deckchairs, when Mr. Chalmers here got what he thought was a bite and it sho' felt like a big'un. We both stood up, and he started reeling ... and reeling ... and reeling ... and before you know it, right before our eyes, this huge goddamned submarine surfaced from the bow ... and then, the whole damn thing popped out'a the water. My word, it liked to scared the shit out'a us...

"Well then, the first thing we know, ol' Joby cracks open the lid on a jug of white liquor and starts gulp'en, figuring his days were numbered. I don't mind tell'en you that me and the mate took a right big slug ourselves. Mr. Chalmers just sort of stood there wide-eyed like a turd float'en in a backwater eddy, not knowing quite what to do. Can't say's that I blame him none!" said Mr. Webber.

While the situation seemed perilous with what the gentlemen were imparting, the deputies and Coast Guard officer were holding their breaths to keep from laughing. So far, the story sounded like a joke. Mr. Webber continued telling his story, although Lieutenant Fleming did have the presence of mind to keep a straight face. He then asked Mr. Webber a question.

"Where are Joby and the mate right now?"

"Now just hang on there a minute, sonny. I'm get'en there. He and the mate are fine and back at the wharf, a little drunk but they're okay. Joby's boat's messed up a little bit but, all and all, they're all right, and the boat can be fixed.

"Well anyway, out'a this tall tower on the middle of the boat comes a man with a white cap, followed by about eight other sailors head'en in different directions carrying sub-machine guns and pistols with a two of 'em get'en behind a really powerful look'en machine gun on the backside of that there tower. I don't mind tell'en ya, at that point, things weren't look'en so good. I'm thinking we're all just about gonna be tuna bait!

"Then out'a the blue, somebody up there on that boat tower hollered down want'en to know if we had caught anything and Joby's mate hollered back, 'Yeah, we caught your goddamned submarine and our hook is caught on the bow. Ya mind unhook'en it for us?'"

Webber continued with the sea story.

"By now, our boats had drifted together because Joby cut our engines, and a couple of them German sailors came over and sort'a tied us together. Another German ol' boy went down to the bow and unhooked the lure from a drain hole and Mr. Chalmers, here, reeled her back in."

"What happened then?" Fleming asked managing to keep a straight face.

"By now we're all standing aft of our boat, looking at the Germans and they're all over the deck looking back at us with them machine guns point'en right at us. Then this English speak'en German in the tower pointed directly at me and told me to come aboard his boat and follow him down below."

"Why just you?" asked Fleming, who by now wasn't thinking this story very funny.

"I didn't have a clue, but he pointed at me and with them guys and their machine guns, I wasn't going to stand there and argue the point. So's I went...

"And I don't mind tell'en ya, it was a bit unwieldy get'en on that boat without break'en my neck, I tell ya that ... but I made it okay with the help of a few of them Nazi crewman. I had no idea what the hell was gonna happen next other than maybe I was gonna be taken a prisoner or something. I gave Mr. Chalmers my wallet and told 'em to give it to my wife if'n I don't come back.

"Well anyway, I got escorted down below and I want'a tell ya'll the whole inside of that boat stunk so bad it would'a knocked a healthy buzzard right off a gut wagon. I ain't never in my dear-born days smelled anything so rank or as rotten as the inside of that boat. It was like being inside a giant hollowed-out bobb'en turd cockleshell, bouncing up and down ... up and down ... and I'm turning all shades of blue, green, and purple. I mean, it was awful. I thought for a moment there I was gonna put Bessie's breakfast right there at the foot of the captain ...Whew'ee! Don't know which was worse, the smell or the bobbin' up and down.

"Anyway, here I am, down on the inside of this tub in some small-ass room a sailor called the 'Zentrale,' or something like that. I later learned it was their control room. They motioned me to sit down, and then the guy in the white hat head-motions to the English-speaking German, who starts asking me all sorts of questions ... like where was I from, where did we sail out of, what we had on the boat ... just a bunch of questions like that. Then he asked me what kind of work I performed ... in my job that is. That might have been a mistake but, what the hell did I know!"

"What'a you mean?" asked Fleming.

"Well, I told 'em I owned a plumbing supply business back in Raleigh and that got their attention because the next thing you know they got me further down in the boat with my head stuck in their filthy toilet, want'en to know if I can fix it!

"Hell, I told 'em all I do is *sell* the supplies to fix toilets, not repair 'em! But that didn't seem to satisfy them. So, I took a look-see just out'a curiosities sake – you know, to see how their flushers worked. Ya'll cannot believe the levers and valves ya have to operate just to take shit in those contraptions. I mean, it's a *big ass* deal just to crap and pee on that there boat. Damn'dest thing I've ever seen, I can tell ya!"

Webber kept on telling his story like he was in a bar mesmerizing fellow drinkers.

"But what was kind'a funny about the whole mess was this clipboard they had hang'en by the entrance to the head. It seems that every time a crewman finished doing is business, so to speak, he had to sign his name on that clipboard and the date and the time he did it! This, they told me, was mandatory in case the next guy found a mess. Then they'd know who to find to clean it up. Ya know, I think I'll do something like that back at my warehouse," Mr. Webber said with a straight face looking up at the ceiling rubbing his neck with his hand, wondering how his employees would react.

"Get on with it, sir," Fleming growled, becoming impatient with Webber making a short story very, very long.

"Well, anyway, I got down on my hands and knees and stuck my head underneath the wall pedestal and did notice something amiss. Seems some kind'a small hose was loose from a valve. Hell, you would've never noticed it unless you stuck your head down there. So, I just sort'a hand tightened 'er up and asked how to flush it. The English-speakin' feller thought it was best to let him do it, saying it had to be correctly manipulated or it could be 'back-flushed' causing a big mess. Well, I can tell ya, I wasn't gonna argue with that. So I got up off the floor and sort'a backed away a few feet and held my nose. Then the ol' boy flushed her and the whole damn thing nearly exploded 'cause it was so clogged up. It started gurgling and gargling and mak'en all sorts of racket and then there was a couple of loud thumpa, thumpas. It then must've re-pressurized 'cause when he flushed her again, you could feel the suction of that puppy pulled in! Whoosh....

"I mean, you should've seen them kraut bastards. They was all like a bunch of clams at high tide, smiling and slapping me on the back and the like. For that moment, I was their hero. Well, the guy in the white cap took me forward again, which was good 'cause I wanted to get the hell out'a there. Now I don't want'a say I was get'en used to the smell, but it *had* gotten better 'cause they had two of them hatches open and the boat was airing out a bit. I'm sure the smell came out through the hatches."

Mr. Chalmers was sitting there intently listening, affirmatively nodding his head lightly holding his nose and rolling his eyes to the back of his head. Dawkins let out a chuckle, observing Mr. Chalmers' humorous expression.

"Anyways, he gave me two bottles of cognac and a carton of German cigarettes and then asked me if we had any American cigarettes on our boat. I told 'em I didn't know, but we had some sandwiches and a cooler of Schlitz beer.

"As it was, when I got back to our boat, a couple of them German fellers jumped on board too and took all our beer and sandwiches and a half carton of Pall Mall cigarettes that Joby had hidden in a small nook behind the helm. He was pretty ticked off about that ... but what *really* pissed him off was when they took our sack of country ham biscuits we had gotten that morning from Bessie's. I reckon there really wasn't too much he could do about that other than give 'em the universal sign language with his middle finger to which Mr. Chalmers quickly threw a towel over it so's they wouldn't take notice. It might've pissed 'em off and they could've started fill'en us with lead ... who knows.

"Anyhow, shortly after that, I heard their captain, he was the feller in the white cap, give what sounded like some kind of order and the next thing we knew they threw our lines back to us and told us to be on our way. But just before Joby fired up the engines, I heard the English-speakin' feller holler back that this was '*Kapitän Hans Vogel's U-491 and tell Roosevelt to kiss his ass. This was war!*' Yep, that's what he said. '*Tell Roosevelt to kiss his ass*'!"

"So, what happened to Joby's boat?' Fleming asked.

"Ah hell, when I got back to the boat, he was well into the cups with that white liquor. He fired the boat up, but when he put it in gear he accidentally backed the sumbitch into the sub damaging a rudder and a prop. It took us all day to get back to the wharf. He's back there now, nurse-maiden the damn thing, trying to get her fixed."

"Mr. Webber, is there *anything* else you can remember or think of that might help us out ... anything at all that comes to mind you may have forgotten?" Fleming asked trying to jog the man's memory.

"Well, as a matter of fact, there was one kind'a interesting off-the-wall question they asked me that just sort'a flew right over my head at the time. I forget all about it 'til you just jogged my memory. But the English-speakin' feller did ask me if'n I'd ever seen the Wright Brothers Monument ... wanted to know if I'd ever been to it and what it was like.

I told 'em I'd never even seen it and didn't even know where it was. It just seemed like an off-the-wall question considering all the other type questions they asked me ... or at least that's what I thought.

"Is that enough there fellers? It's get'en late and I'd like to get Mr. Chalmers here back to our hotel room so's I can fix us up a little shooter. It's been a long worrisome day and we need to relax so we can get a fresh start in the morrow and head on back home. Hell, ain't nobody gonna believe us anyhow, but that's what happened there fellers. I hope you guys believe us because our wives sure as hell ain't gonna!"

"Yes sir we do ... uh, Mr. Webber ... Mr. Chalmers. And I think it would be wise not to mention this to anybody else outside this room -- even to your wives. What you have told me is certainly interesting, no doubt. But yes, I do believe you. You've heard the ol' expression, 'Loose lips sink ships'? Well, this is a prime example of what that saying means. So it's best we all keep this matter under wraps until we can sort it all out. Lot's going on out there on the coastal seas right now and a lot of men are being killed. I think this is something important enough that needs to be kept quiet! Everybody agree to that?"

"Hell, son, ain't no one gonna believe that fish story, no how," Webber concluded.

Everybody in the room gave a slight chuckle, then shook their heads in agreement.

"And Mr. Webber, I will pass on to Mr. Roosevelt Kapitän Vogel's request!"

"Well, that's what he said," Webber replied. "He sho' as hell did!"

"Look, before ya'll go, let me give you something for your troubles for com'en all the way out here."

Fleming went to his office closet and retrieved two bottles of Jim Beam bourbon and handed them to Mr. Webber.

"Here, ya'll use this for fix'en them shooters tonight!"

Both men looked at each other and smiled at their prize.

"This ain't been a bad day of fishin' afterall," Mr. Chalmers replied.

From this story, Lieutenant Fleming did gain some useful information he could pass on to Admiral Andrews. It was, by all means, an incredible story—almost unbelievable except for one small fact: Webber's clothes did emanate a foul, almost indescribable odor he knew could only have come from that submarine. When you confine men together for long periods of time without benefit of wash water, they can stink to high heaven. And a backed-up toilet in a cramped area can be quite unpleasant. Fleming knew this. He had, himself, smelled it before on long training voyages.

As they all stood up, Lieutenant Fleming asked Deputy Scoggins to stay behind. He had something he wanted to share. Fleming would have one of his men take R.W. back to Manteo in the short while after their meeting. In the meantime, R.W. asked George to take the two gentlemen back to their hotel room, and he would catch up with him later. He also asked George to drive over to the wharf and tell Joby and his mate to keep this adventure under their hats if they haven't already told their story. Revealing this incident might compromise the beach security. It wasn't necessary to let any of the townsfolk know the details—especially the part about the U-boat number.

"Mark, is that not a whopper of a story or what?" R.W. said, chuckling after the men had left the room.

"Well, I tell ya, R.W., aside from the awful smell on his clothes, which certainly was revealing, the real kicker was the U-boat number he mentioned ... the U-491. That's what I wanted to tell ya. What you probably don't know is that's the same number written on the note we found on the German sailor down on the beach. I kept it quiet around here ... only Bleu and Hatfield know plus Seaman Allen, who found him. I've told them all to keep a lid on it.

Fleming sat down and lit a cigarette.

"After finding the sailor, the following day Admiral Andrews sent a couple of his security guys down here and retrieved that note, but I did secretly hand-copy it ... or I should say I traced over it. It's purty close to what the original looks like except for the paper itself. I just felt like I needed to have an near copy here at the station. Here, take a look at it."

Fleming reached into his top desk drawer and handed it to Scoggins.

"I've been nosing around by phone to headquarters lately try'en to find out a little more on what's happening out there off shore. So far, about the only info I can get is that the big kill'en zone for our merchant shipping on the Eastern Seaboard is happening right here in our own backyard ... off Cape Hatteras in the Diamond Shoals area. There doesn't appear to be that many subs out there, but what boats are out there are doing one hell'uva lot'a damage." Fleming lit another cigarette.

"By connecting this information, there's no doubt the U-491 is one of those boats and Vogel is certainly doing his part," Fleming continued. "How long he's actually been out there and how much damage he's done, I haven't the faintest of clues. But what I do know is that he's been out there at least eight days. From what I hear, when these guys use up all their torpedoes, they head for home and another one, or two, replaces him with a fresh load. It almost seems endless. But intuition tells me this guy is different, and I can't quite put my finger on why."

"Damn! That's scary. Our forces ... our defenses that weak?" R.W. remarked.

"Well, there seems to be a struggle right among the various commands now try'en to get organized ... get'en the defenses built up to the point where we can go on the offensive," Fleming went on. "But, right now, it's purty pathetic. I just hope them Flag Officers up north get their pettiness out of the way so we can get back to the business at hand ... take'en back our waters and keep'en our supplies from going to the bottom. If you think rationing is bad now, you just wait and see. It's gonna get worse!"

* * * * * * * *

Lieutenant Fleming was right. Things were going to get worse. Not only for the Americans, but also for the British, who been rationing nearly everything since early 1940. But that wasn't Fleming's problem. His problem was building a stronger shoreline defense and his own resourcefulness was partly the key. Fleming was determined to do the best he could with what he had. It was bad enough that many lives were needlessly being lost. He just didn't want that to happen on his beach.

"Robbing Peter to pay Paul" was pretty much how Admiral Andrews sized up the defense of the Eastern Sea Frontier by the middle of March 1942. Because so many ships were sinking to the bottom, he knew in the long run the tide would have to change. He continued his pleas for help.

In the first three months of 1942, there was a never-ending tug-of-war within the upper Navy echelon, and Admiral Andrews was losing this war. All of his requests for ships and planes were continuously being denied. He was ordered to deal with what he had, but the arsenal of equipment and manpower had neither the might nor the main to confront the preying wolves clandestinely sinking the hordes of ships off the Outer Banks of North Carolina.

In 1940, fifty of the U.S. Navy's oldest destroyers from the First World War, were transferred to England. This maneuver was a bargain between President Roosevelt and Prime Minister Churchill. It was a pact that gave the United States use of Caribbean bases to facilitate their merchant fleet in exchange for the sorely needed destroyers so the Royal Navy could use them against the Germans for control of the North Atlantic.

Ninety of the remaining 170 Navy ships stationed in the Hampton Roads harbors were pressed into action for the North Atlantic escort service. It was understandable that Admiral King resolved the power to preserve the fleet and avoid the risk of destruction by enemy U-boats in the undersea war. Nevertheless, most of the ships were destined to sail sooner than later --eastward towards the cold gray waters of the belligerent Third Reich or westward towards the aggressive "Rising Sun" in the bloody blue Pacific. But, as circumstances evolved, King's decision was clear. The Royal Navy soon took control in their vast North Sea whilst the Japanese took control of the valuable West Pacific.

What was not acceptable was King's cantankerous attitude in protecting his very own coast. He didn't seem to grasp, or, rather failed to grasp, the raging war already exploding in his own front yard along the Eastern seaboard. While his distinguished officers were a mindful set, King's fortitude was questioned when he failed to heed their warnings. His confounded arrogance created a stir, as well as a cry for help. Eventually a call from the President would settle the stew.

Admiral Andrews relegated his Coast Guard cutters to patrolling the gravest of harbors, and, with outright conviction and the humblest of pleas, finally swayed the Army Air Corps to send patrol aircraft from Mitchell and Langley Fields for twice-daily sweeps along the coast. Then, as implausible as it may have seemed, Admiral King honored two simple requests: he reluctantly allowed the coastal merchantman corridor to be moved sixty miles from shore, and he ordered the approaches to the harbors of New York, Boston, and Portland, Maine, as well as the vast opening of the Chesapeake Bay, to be mined -- a weak defense at best.

But Admiral Andrews wasn't totally in the dark. He did have, as part of the regular Coast Guard fleet, the 165-foot *Dione* (WPC-107), a World War I cutter, patrolling from the Chesapeake Bay south to Morehead City, North Carolina. It was well-equipped with depth charges, three-inch cannons, and fifty-caliber machine guns. Originally designed to tackle the smugglers of illicit alcohol running the coast during the '20s and '30s, it was now forced into service to battle an unknown and darker enemy—German U-boats.

Somewhat later, and to his credit, Admiral King did make changes to other defense areas of the coast, mostly in the Third, Fourth, and Fifth Naval Districts. Eleven destroyers from the regular Navy fleet were deployed, though not all at once. While the extra ships were a welcomed relief, it proved a worthless cause. Because the ships were considered temporary, there was constant confusion of orders, and, along with coastal indoctrination and a need for special information. There also was the problem of a never-ending demand for fuel, repairs, stores and provisions. The "temporary" fix ultimately proved a waste of time. What Andrews needed was a permanently assigned flotilla -- not a ragtag task force. Unfortunately, the one destroyer King did assign full-time to the Eastern sea frontier met an untimely demise. On its first day of patrol out of the New York harbor, the Wickes-class destroyer, *USS Jacob Jones* (DD-130), commanded by Lieutenant Commander H.P. Black, was blown apart on 28 February 1942, by the U-578 commanded by Korvettenkapitän Ernst-August Rehwinkle. She sank within minutes and only eleven of her Navy crew survived.

To the British, it was clearly evident the only way to fight the threat and to preserve the fleet was to convoy ships with a heavily-armed armada. This the British learned the hard way when posting the subs in their waters. To urge Admiral King in a meaningful way, the Admiralty in London (Royal Navy) deftly expressed their views. Because of his sneering antipathy towards the Brits, he coldly responded to their views. King felt the British haughty and arrogant and not to be trusted. As far as the British were concerned, that was nothing more than the "pot calling the kettle black."

Not only were the Americans suffering heavy losses, so were the British. With critical supplies bound for the British Isles plummeting to the bottom faster than a sack full of concrete, the Royal Navy was resigned to offer their help to their cousins across the pond. In an effort to prod the Americans, and with President Roosevelt's approval, the British sent twenty-four anti-submarine coal-burning trawlers. Also sent to the United States were ten corvettes, a fast and highly-armed maneuverable ship that is smaller than a destroyer. Though the trawlers sailed from Britain in the middle of February 1942, it wouldn't be until the first of April before they could be of service. It appeared their lack of maintenance required a profusion of repairs by the Americans to keep them running.

While the convoy system was working well in the vast North Atlantic, surprisingly, Admiral Andrews said such a system would not work for coastline runs. At first he was cool to the British idea and rebuffed their convoy notions. It was, at present, the only time Andrews and King agreed. But with current tactics simply not working -- randomly stalking submarines with only a smattering of ships, Andrews subsequently altered his beliefs and resolved that convoys *were*, indeed, the answer. Andrews pleaded with King without success. It was the phone call from President Roosevelt that changed King's mind. Roosevelt was being pressured from within his administration, as well as abroad, meaning Winston Churchill.

Roosevelt was the only man King would listen.

A private group of influential oilmen, better known as The Petroleum Industry War Council Committee, determined that, at the present rate that oil tankers were being sunk, there would not be enough available oil to continue the war past the end of the 1942. The committee took their concerns to the President, who in turn prevailed upon Admiral King. It took this kind of political pressure to change King's mind. Unfortunately for Admiral Andrews, King pitched the convoy idea as his own to the President and the Joint Chiefs of Staff, impressing Roosevelt. Andrews could have cared less. The convoy plan was being implemented and that's all that really mattered. Nevertheless, it would still take several more anxious months of hard-fought lobbying and finagling before the convoy system became a reality and demonstrate success.

Sadly enough, the attacks continued with a presence of malice. In the first three months of the year, forty-two different German U-boats leveled a reign of terror so vile it seemed as though it would never stop. To the Germans, it was known as the "Second Happy Times" [The "First Happy Time" was against the British before the installation of their convoy system. *Ed.*] where virtually every torpedo struck its mark, day or night, with the greatest of ease. But, Americans were wondering, *"Damn the torpedoes! What are we doing to stop this madness?"*

By the end of March 1942, German U-boats had attacked and sunk 122 merchant ships killing scores of sailors. In return, only two German subs had met their fate: the U-656 was targeted on March 1, and two weeks later, on March 15, 1942, the U-503 was besieged. Both U-boats were spotted off the Newfoundland coast and were bombed to the bottom by Hudson PBO-1s on their aerial tour of convoys that had departed from Halifax, Nova Scotia destined for Liverpool, England. Ninety-six German crewmembers were drowned, but it was a drop in the bucket to what they had caused in sinking Allied shipping. It wasn't, by any means, a fair exchange. It would take many more months before the score would be settled.

In the meantime, the U-491 continued to target her high-grade military cargo chugging from the Chesapeake Bay as directed from the mysterious messages coming from Kill Devil Hill. These weren't ships loaded with bauxite or the boat loads of bananas, rather they were laden with fighter planes, tanks, Jeeps, and ammunition. The fewer ships that reached England, the better for Germany.

* * * * * * * *

Deep within the confines of the old New York City Federal Building at 90 Church Street, Admiral Andrews was in his fifteenth-floor office, quietly pondering his foray against his enemy, the renowned Admiral Karl Dönitz, the author of Operation Drumbeat. And while not considered a foe, he pondered his strategy with Admiral King. Andrews' mission was saving the merchant fleet and its valuable freight. It was a life and death struggle -- the outcome of the war depended on it.

Admiral Andrews chose the downtown New York City location for his headquarters before the start of the war. He packed it generously with an assortment of communication gear and established an enormous room to plot his coastal defense. The room held a massive board measuring more than sixteen-feet tall and thirty-feet long. Every piece of information regarding the sights or sounds of enemy U-boats, or even the likely presence of one, was collected and plotted on this huge map, and it took dozens of analysts to sort it through.

Admiral Andrews had hand-selected his headquarters staff, which contained a large intelligence section responsible for sifting through the vast quantities of collected data.

Admiral Donitz's tactics changed little since his fleet's arrival along the Eastern seaboard -- attacking at night and hiding during the day. In hours of darkness, his U-boats surfaced and began their attacks. It soon was determined the U-boats were attacking alone, not using the formable Wolf pack formations used later against convoys in the middle North Atlantic. In the early part of 1942, such tactics weren't necessary because Allied merchant ships were easy prey. Naval defenses, both on the sea and in the air were mostly absent.

After ship sinkings, many unwary sailors were mercilessly killed when thrashing about the sinking decks looking for safety. However, when lucky sailors did make it to the lifeboats, there had been no reports of maliciously killing of survivors -- at least so far.

On the afternoon of March 16, the 11,628-ton American oil tanker *Australia* was hit with a torpedo off the Diamond Shoals by the U-332, commanded by Kapitänleutnant Johannes Liebe, but she failed to sink. Its cry for help was quickly received by the U.S. Coast Guard cutter *Dione,* who responded within thirty minutes before the U-boat could do any more damage. After discharging a volley of depth charges in the nearby vicinity, the *Dione* circled the tanker looking for survivors. None could be found. They later learned all survived and were picked up by a nearby passing freighter. The U-332 escaped.

Around sunset that same day, Admiral Andrews was in his office when his submarine tracker, Lieutenant Commander Harry Hess, entered his office with an array of reports, which included something of interest. His team of analysts had deciphered an enemy message out of the ordinary. Hess wanted to personally present it to the Admiral. While it wasn't thought to be terribly important, it was unusual.

"Sir, I don't know if this means anything, but I believe we have something of interest. After tracking and plotting all the ships that have been sunk since mid-January, there *seems* to be a bit of an anomaly in one area that re-occurs periodically at just about the same time of day. We traced it back to the middle of February when the sinkings began en mass. So far, things are still sketchy, and we haven't quite been able to put our fingers on it ... "

"And, where's the area you are talking of, Commander?" Andrews inquired as he sat sifting through various dispatches and reports.

"It's the mouth of the Chesapeake, sir ... about twenty miles out."

This caught the attention of the Admiral, causing him to look up from the paperwork.

"And what's the anomaly?" he asked.

"The time frame and the cargo, but it all could be just a coincidence. Time and data will make it more precise now that we know what to look for."

"What's the cargo?"

"Military ... high-grade military equipment and munitions. Although, there was one particular sinking that fits our schematic, which wasn't military. While all cargo is important, this one was a middle-of-the-road shipment. Traveling very close in the same group of ships were several high-grade military freighters. It almost looks as though the U-boat knew what he was after, but just plain missed ... but that's just a guess on our part."

After ten more minutes discussing the matter, Commander Hess left the room as Admiral Andrews received a call from Lieutenant Fleming at the Bodie Island Coast Guard Station.

Fleming wanted to report directly to Admiral Andrews, as directed, about what he had gathered from a civilian interview earlier in the day. Fleming explained that thought this was important enough to break the chain-of-command.

"Yes, Lieutenant ... good to hear from you. What have you got for me?"

"Well sir, you ain't gonna believe this shit, but earlier today...."

After the report, Andrews hung up, sat back in his chair and smiled. Things were beginning to reveal themselves.

* * * * * * * *

Later that cold and very windy night off a boiling Cape Hatteras, two more ships were blasted into oblivion. Northwest of Cape Charles, Virginia, the 8,073-ton tanker *San Demetrio* quickly went to the bottom when the U-404, commanded by Kapitänleutnant Otto von Bülow, savagely sent two torpedoes into her. Nineteen crewmen were killed outright and thirty-two barely escaped into lifeboats. These crewmembers were picked up two days later. That wasn't the case thirty minutes later, when the U-124 blew up the Honduras banana boat *Ceiba* heading for New York.

All crewmembers, many with their wives and children, safely made it to the lifeboats and rafts. Shortly thereafter, the sub surfaced where Kapitänleutnant Johann Mohr questioned the banana boat's captain as to her size. Believing it was a freighter of significant bulk, Mohr became visibly annoyed to learn that he had wasted a torpedo on a ridiculously small 1,500-ton boat—as reported by her captain.

Still not believing the banana boat's captain, Mohr called below for his information officer to verify its tonnage with the Lloyd's Registry of Shipping book. He discovered the weight to be exactly 1,698 tons. He curtly corrected the banana boat captain, who, at the moment, could have cared less for such useless information. Leaving in a huff, Mohr swiftly submerged leaving a trail of phosphorescent bubbles.

With the nor'easter now gusting at fifty-plus miles per hour, some of the *Ceiba's* lifeboats quickly tore apart. After spending two full days tossing and in the choppy seas, only one lifeboat with six crewmembers was ever found. It was rescued by the 347-foot *USS Hambleton* (DD-455). The remaining three lifeboats, carrying an assortment of forty-four men, women, and children, were presumed lost. All sinking's are tragic, but this one was pointless and arrogant because Spanish Honduras was neutral a neutral nation. (British Honduras, known today as Belize, was a separate country).

At 0155 hours on March 17, Kapitänleutnant Vogel was a few miles south of his rendezvous point at latitude 36° 01' north. He was preparing a closer approach to shore so Victor Kerch, the decoder, could better read the signal from Kill Devil Hill. He previously station had been fifteen miles from shore, but tonight he was going five miles closer. Kerch recommended this because of the atmospheric anomaly caused from the signal being so close to the horizon.

It was a crystal clear night and a new moon, which meant it was extra dark and good conditions for observing the signal. The only problem was there blew savage nor'easter, creating huge rolling waves that crashed over the bow, spraying the bridge of the conning tower. With the U-boat twisting and rolling in all directions, it was nearly impossible to stand still and stare through a pair of binoculars.

Earlier that night, when the boat was submerged and running smoothly beneath the waves, Vogel experimented by using the observation periscope in hopes of retrieving the signal from within. Unfortunately, Krech felt the water-drenched lens would scatter the beacon's ray, making it more difficult for a proper reading. There was no other choice but to surface and try from there.

At 0212 hours the boat was moving into position on the surface and Vogel knew it was going to be impossible to keep her steady as the sea was already sending gobs of spray whistling into their faces. It was neck-wrenching at best and there was nothing he could do. At this point, it was all up to Krech. He seemed prepared and was securely strapped into his harness, ready to go. While preparing to receive the signal, a large wave crashed aft. A watchman screamed out.

"MAN OVERBOARD ... STARBOARD SIDE!"

"Ah shit...!

Chapter 12

By the first week of April, life on the Outer Banks had mostly returned to normal. The Coast Guard continued their nightly patrols, the dark and oily plumes of smoke continued rising on the eastern horizon, and Claire Belle Charboneau continued making her specially-spiced chicken salad at the now-popular lunch counter at Ned's Pharmacy. In the short time since her arrival, Claire quickly gained acceptance as her friendly and sociable manner always made her customers smile.

To all the folks on the islands, Claire Belle Charboneau was a curious enigma. She had arrived on the Outer Banks from Hillsville, Virginia seemingly to start a new life. Even though she possessed a wonderful gift for gab, she rarely, if ever, talked about herself and left many a folk to wondering. But for Claire Belle, it was nothing more than superfluous hearsay where she jokingly played to the whims that made its rounds. Nothing seemed to bother her.

Nevertheless, to the local folk, her mystery was furtive. As most of the natives were descendants of descendants who had settled years before, the rest of the folk were well-fixed summertime residents who fashioned themselves with fanciful cottages for relaxing vacations -- or discreet affaires de coeur. But still, the local people wanted to know -- and to gossip. To them, it was just their way of talking.

Since Claire Belle had arrived and began working the counter, R.W. subtly began taking his lunches after the crowd had finished. This he devised himself, for the likelihood of chatting with the pretty lady that caused his heart to flutter. Though, if he didn't know any better, he believed her heart fluttered as well. But it was hard to tell. He had yet to embellish his verve to ask for a date.

If there was a subject that peaked Claire Belle's interest, it was the calamity unfolding beyond her door -- literally. The cottage she rented was beach side of the road going north one mile past the Nags Head Casino. More often than not, she would witness an ominous thick cloud of smoke emanating from a forlorn freighter that had just been blown out of the water. On some occasions, small debris would wash ashore. So far there hadn't been any bodies.

"Was that an oil tanker that blew up Saturday night?," Claire asked of R.W. "I heard the explosion around quarter to ten. I went outside on my front porch and could see to the north of us on the horizon the bright reds and oranges. It must have been awful!"

"Yes, it was a tanker," he replied. 'And yes, it had to have been awful. The reports I heard this morning said it was the oil tanker *Bryon D. Benson.* It was about eight miles offshore, north of the Currituck Lighthouse. I hear tell there were around twenty-eight who survived. I've yet to hear how many who didn't. But what bodies the Coast Guard did find and pulled aboard were all burnt to a crisp. I can't think of a more horrifying way to die. Yes, I think it was purty damn awful."

"Think it was the U-boat that's been hanging 'round these parts?"

"Now what makes you think that?" R.W. asked with a certain amount of curiousity.

"Well, I've been talk'en to Jenny..."

R.W.'s face dropped, then smiled.

"Claire, you don't need to say anymore. The ol' 'Mouth of the South' herself seems to have a sixth sense 'bout these matters ... so I see you know about as much as I do. We've been trying to keep a lid on that, but I reckon we're not doing a good job."

"I'm sorry R.W. I didn't know..."

"Well of course you didn't know. You ain't been 'round these parts long enough to know," he said. "Listen, don't worry 'bout ol' Jenny. She's just somebody who doesn't know when to shut up. After she gnaws at you awhile, ya end up just get'en used to her, but sometimes it just frustrates the hell out'a us in the Sheriff's Department the way she runs her mouth. Hell, maybe we ought'a just move her from the Postmistress job to the 'Deputy-of-Information mistress' job. Maybe she'll understand better then!"

Claire had no inkling she had rubbed a sore spot with R.W. about Jenny's abhorrent idiosyncrasies. She seriously apologized to him for her ignorance. And R.W. realized the hairs on the back of his neck stood on end, and he meekly apologized for his subtle outburst. It was stupid. Within seconds each looked at the other and broke out laughing. The thick air between them quickly cleared. R.W. grinned and gestured.

"I smell some *fresh* apple pie back there. Is there any left for a 'mean ol' deputy sheriff'?"

"R.W., I especially saved the last wedge for you! Would you like it 'a la mode'?"

"No, I'll have it right here at the counter. I've already been to the commode."

"Now R.W., it means 'with ice cream!' Do you want ice cream with your pie?"

"Oh...."

"Well ... do you?" Claire said with a slight chuckle.

"Yeah sure, why not. A little ice cream with fresh apple pie sure sounds good."

After ten more minutes of lighter conversation and finishing the delicious dessert, R.W. thought it best to head back to the office and finish up paperwork that had accumulated throughout last week. He was going to work on it yesterday, but that was Easter Sunday, so he spent the day with Josh and his mom and dad.

When leaving the counter and saying goodbye, R.W. inadvertently backed into one of the small wooden round table and chairs near the counter, lost his balance, and stumbled into the magazine rack, knocking numerous issues to the floor. For some reason, every time he was around Claire Belle, he had a knack for tripping and causing a commotion. Claire noticed R.W.'s awkwardness. She thought it was cute and giggled. R.W. thought it was embarrassing. He wished to himself he would stop doing it.

Before R.W. reached the courthouse, George walked out catching him just before walking in. They had received a call from the Coast Guard Station.

"I was just heading over your way to get you. Lieutenant Fleming called and wants to see us at the station right away ... says it's important."

"Any clue as to what it is?"

"No, not really. He didn't want to tell Roscoe over the phone being afraid somebody might be listening in on the conversation."

"Well, let's head on over there and see what he's got."

After reaching the station and entering the commanding officer's office, Lieutenant Fleming was there with his two chief petty officers. He hustled them into his office.

"R.W. ... George, one of my Guardsmen early this morning found a body washed ashore. They just got him here to the station a little while ago."

"And...."

"He's not a civilian fisherman or sailor from any of the blown up merchant ships. He's a German sailor from our U-boat friend ... the U-491!"

"And you surmised this how?"

"We believed he was a watchman that somehow got washed overboard ... probably during bad weather. He still had a pair of binoculars strapped to him. How those damn things stayed with him is beyond me. He was chewed up pretty bad, but somehow they stayed strapped to him ... kind of remarkable, actually."

"How do you know he's from the U-491?" asked R.W.

"He was wearing a yellow life vest and we could barely make out the markings of 'U-491' written on the back of it," said Fleming.

"Where 'bouts was he found, Mark?"

"Down south of us on Hatteras Island 'bout halfway between Rodanthe and Avon. That area is purty dissolute. How long he's been down there is anybody's guess, but I reckon we're the first to get to him before any fishermen or other civilians. The fellers tightly wrapped 'em up in a blanket in the Jeep so's the ferry tender over the Oregon Inlet wouldn't be none the wiser. As best I can tell, we're the only ones who know. That's why I called you guys. We got'a keep this shit quiet. I'm not ready for another incident like we had with the other German sailor we found on the beach awhile back. You know what a mess that caused!"

"Yeah, we sure as hell do, don't we!" R.W. said, looking at George, then at Fleming. "But I can assure you it ain't go'en any further with us. What ya'll gonna do with him? You're not think'en 'bouts taking him to the medical building in Manteo are you?" R.W. asked.

"No, hell no! I got'a truck coming down from Norfolk ... should be here first thing in the morn'en. We're haul'en his ass up there. I've instructed all my guys to keep their months shut or I'll have 'em court marshaled."

"Well, maybe the guys up in Norfolk can put their forensic minds together and determine how long he's been in the water. What good it'll do, I don't know, but something might come of it. But the biggest key was finding out that same damn U-boat is still hang'en around. Looks like he's determined to keep causing mayhem to our merchant fleet," R.W. reckoned.

"You know R.W., I was just think'en. The only real bad weather we've had lately was that big nor'easter 'bout three weeks ago that caused so much havoc. You remember that! If he was to get blown off a boat, that would've been a perfectly good time for it to happen."

"Mark, I think you're probably right. Look, George and me need to head on back. We'll keep a lid on it and somehow make damn sure Jenny won't find out 'bout it. I might have to kick her little butt if she does. How that woman finds shit out is beyond me!

"Anyway, thanks for keeping us abreast of the situation ...."

* * * * * * *

When R.W. and George returned to the office, they told Roscoe the news. About all they could do for the moment was keep their eyes and ears peeled for any unusual activity. But in the meantime, all R.W. wanted to do was finish his paperwork. He knew it was going to take awhile, so he asked George to bring him back a takeout supper plate from Bessie's along with a glass of iced tea. He also made it a point to tell George to be sure to bring back a wedge of her sweet potato pie. He thought it was going to be a long night, and he could eat it later in the evening as a snack.

Tuesday morning turned out to be a beautiful early spring day with a slight chill in the air. What was not so beautiful was the appalling cloud of oily choking smoke stifling the air over the Banks. The tanker *Bryon D. Benson* was still aflame and had been drifting for the last three days reminding everybody on the coast that war was very close. R.W. continued to wonder if the U-491 was the boat that caused this tragedy. He really had no way of knowing.

[The U-552, commanded by Korvettenkapitän Erich Topp, was the culprit. In his two weeks on the American coast, Topp sank eight ships. He survived the war and actually came to the United States and served four years as a German staff member of the Military Committee of NATO. He died in 2005. *Ed.*]

R.W. picked up George at his new residence. He seemed to have found a nice lady several months ago who corralled him into moving in with her. The new accommodations suited George. R.W. noticed his friend smiled more than he used to.

The two deputies went to breakfast at Bessie's and then headed to the office. Roscoe was already there pacing the floor with his usual cup of strong black coffee. Sam was out on foot patrol around town.

"Roscoe, you tell Sam 'bout that dead German sailor wash'en up on the beach?"

"Yeah, I sure did. Hell I can't keep everything from him. But I specifically told 'em to keep it under wraps. I think he believes me this time because he remembered how busy he was when the townsfolk found out 'bout that other sailor. I think he'll keep quiet."

"Well, I hope so. I think me and George will head on over to the islands and patrol there awhile and nose 'round a bit and talk to some of those city folk com'en in to get their cottages ready for the summer. I noticed this past week a few of 'em have already started arriving. I'm sure they'll have some questions for us 'bout the ships we been see'en going to the bottom. I hear tell the newspaper folks are sort of keeping mum about how bad it is."

"Well, don't give 'em too much info. You know, just the basic stuff. We don't want'a scare 'em. The merchants here in town are count'en on their fresh bucks for the summer season ... war or no war," Roscoe cautioned.

By mid-morning, the two deputies had worked their way up Bodie Island, just past Nags Head to Kill Devil Hill. They were driving slowly along the narrow two-lane road when one of the regular summertime residents noticed R.W. and motioned him to pull over. It was Ben Johnson from Durham, North Carolina. He wanted to make a report.

"Well hello there, Mr. Johnson. Glad to see ya back for the season. How's everything back on the mainland?"

"Everything's fine ... tobacco business doing real well and the little lady's doing fine too. She'll be coming down in the next month or so with the kids after they get out'a school. But what I pulled ya over for, well ... our cottage got broken into and don't know when it happened. After unpacking, I was gonna come on into town and report it. But see'en how I saw you driving by..."

"No problem there Ben. Any damage ... anything taken?" R.W. asked.

"Well, no real damage other than some marks on the door jamb where they jimmied the door open. Other than that, it's purty clean, although, they did steal some clothes and a small brown leather suitcase along with my favorite cream-colored canvas jacket."

"Well, that's the pits!" R.W. sympathized. "Let's go inside and take a look around and see what else we might find out. First break-in of the season so far as I know."

"Yeah, okay ... ya'll go right on in. Oh, and by the way ... there is one other tidbit of evidence I found what I believe ya'll might find interesting. The sumbitch left a note. It's in the house on the counter where I left it."

"You're kidd'en!" R.W. said, looking at George with a puzzled expression.

"Nope, I'm not! He left a damn note saying he was sorry. Can you believe that?"

Sure enough, lying there on the kitchen counter was the note. In all the while R.W. had been a deputy, he'd never seen or heard of such a happening. It certainly was a first for him. He told Mr. Johnson he was going to take the note with him.

After he and George spent the better part of an hour combing through Mr. Johnson's cottage and getting a description of the stolen clothes, they determined someone probably had spent at least one night there. While the thief cleaned up well, he failed to fully cover his tracks. Why he went to this much trouble was certainly a mystery to them.

"Ben, we'll look into it further. Though, I can't promise you anything."

"Well I appreciate it fellows. I know it wasn't much and I'm not too disturbed about the clothes or even the suitcase, but I did happen to like that old canvas jacket ... had it for years, don't ya know."

"I hear ya, Ben. George and me'll let you know if'n we find anything. You down to stay for the summer already?"

"Naw, just wanted to make a quick trip to clean up a bit. You know, turn on the hot water. Might do a little shore fish'en before head'en back on Thursday. I'll probably be back in a week or two and fiddle-fart around some more. I hear tell the government might be implementing gas rationing, so we'll have to see how that goes. Might be tougher get'en back down here if it gets too stringent. You know?"

"Yeah, so I'm hear'en. Seems these Germans got a keen eye on our oil and gas tankers. You know 'bout the one that got blasted up there off Currituck Beach don't ya?"

"Is that where all that smoke coming from?"

"Sho' is. I think George and me'll drive on up there and see what we can see. I sw're it's been burn'en now for 'bout, let's see ... go'en on three days now, I believe."

"Okay fellas, ya'll take care an' be see'en ya 'round."

And with that, George and R.W. motored up the coastal road towards the small hamlet of Duck. George heard a report from Roscoe that the tanker was drifting south. He also heard that ten sailors had died when the tanker exploded.

Having reached the tiny township, George and R.W. left the car and high-stepped it through the fine white powdery sand to the top of a large gently sloping dune. From there they could easily see the pitch-black rolling-clouds of boiling smoke curling about the sky. Using his binoculars, R.W. zoomed in on the wave-less sea that was finally laying its dark green cover gently over the burning hulk. The ship's death was imminent. In the hours to come, the wind and the current would probably smother the slick and quash the smoke. It had been unbearable.

Sticking around, he and George walked to the foamy waters of a rising tide where flotsam had washed ashore. Most of what they found was charred and impossible to recognize. It made them angry this tragedy was happening. They quietly cursed the Germans.

"Come on George, let's get the hell out'a here. This shit's mak'en me sick. Let's ride on down to the Casino and have a beer. It's get'en late in the afternoon. Besides, I want'a see how our new buddy John O'Hearn's do'en these days."

Chapter 13

While driving back south down the Virginia Dare Trail towards the Casino, George and R.W. tossed around ideas about the theft at Ben Johnson's cottage. It was interesting that someone would go to the trouble to leave a note. Given the time frame, it was, for the moment, hard to tell when the break-in could have occurred. It would have been nice if the thief had scribbled a date. But then again, that would have been too easy.

They pulled into the parking lot adjacent to the large elongated two-story wooden structure. It was, by and far. the largest building on the islands, capable of holding a thousand people when the big swing bands were in town. That usually happened on a Friday or Saturday night. But for a lazy Tuesday afternoon, there were just a dozen or so cars in the parking lot where the patrons were probably bowling duckpins on the lanes or shooting nine-ball on the green felt tables.

Upon entering the large front doors, they walked through the small foyer into the lower cavernous room where the alleys and game tables were located. After glancing around, R.W. saw owner Rags Truscott behind the long snack counter kibitzing with an elderly gentleman who was having a beer. It looked as though they were both in high spirits and belly laughing from a joke. After retrieving a fresh Pabst Blue Ribbon beer for his patron, Rags noticed R.W. and big George. He walked over, greeting them while still laughing from the yarn he'd just heard.

"Well hello there fellers. What can I do for ya?"

"Howdy Rags. We just thought we'd stop in for a nice cold beer and wash down some of that oily smoke that's caught in our throats. Ya got'a coupl'a cool ones for a coupl'a thirsty flatfoots?"

"Yeah, I sure do. Ya'll come on over to the counter here and I'll fix ya right up. Taking the rest of the day off are ya?"

"Naw, not really. George and me just got back from Duck where that burn'en tanker drifted. What a mess."

"Wasn't that awful! All of us here Saturday night saw the flames when she went up. That's the first one I've seen in this neck of the woods. Most all them others been down south of us. Looked like a bad one."

"Yeah, it sho' was. George here says ten sailors were killed, but fortunately twenty-eight or so survived. With all those flames, it could've been a helluva lot worse."

"I reckon you're right. But hasn't that smoke been awful?"

"That it has. But I think it'll all be gone purty soon. Whilst we were up there, I saw her finally get'en ready to go under. Give it a coupl'a more hours and I think the smoke'll probably clear out.

"Well, how's business there Rags?" R.W. asked.

"Been a little slow lately, mainly 'cause I hadn't had any big groups in here this year. Though, this weekend, we got Johnny Long's sweet band coming down for the weekend, so we ought'a have a good crowd. But so far as Saturday night went, we had a good crowd in here from the Weeksville Air Station. Those swabbies drank their fair share of beer."

"Any trouble?" asked George.

"Nothing I couldn't handle. Did have a couple of guys get into a piss'en contest over a game of pool, but I got it squared away before it got out'a hand. So far, hadn't had to replace any cue sticks!"

"How's our young friend John work'en out for you these days Rags? Do'en a good job for you is he?"

"Oh yeah, he sure is ... glad you hooked me up with him. He's been working out just fine and working his little butt off. Right now he's upstairs polishing up my dance floor for the weekend."

"Well I'm glad to hear it. Think we can go up and say hello to him?"

"Sure fellas ... ya'll just go on up. I'll catch up with ya when you come back down."

Up the stairs they went and sure enough John was down on his hands and knees swirling a large white rag and working up a sweat. The deputies purposely made a little light racket so John would look up. When he noticed his friends, John grinned from ear to ear, quickly getting to his feet and sliding his way over to greet his buddies.

"Looks like ya got that floor slicker 'an owl shit there John," R.W. remarked.

"Yes, I believe I do. Mr. Truscott said he wanted it smooth as a baby's butt. Said the kids love it when they go to dancing with just their sock feet. We got our first band coming in this weekend, you know."

"Yeah, so I've heard. And how are you do'en these days?"

John went on to explain how he really liked working for Rags and how much he appreciated R.W. for helping him get the job. After about three weeks, he's built up a little pocket change so now he doesn't feel so poor. He's also met an array of the local folk, who've treated him kindly. He's even met a few cute girls his own age.

"Where ya staying now John," George asked.

"I've got a little room up in Kill Devil Hills overlooking the Kitty Hawk Bay. It's about three and a half miles from here. The house is owned by a friend of Mr. Truscott's ... a fellow by the name of Wally Palmer. It's very nice and he treats me well. From my bedroom window, I can see the beacon light flash from the Wright Brothers Monument. Many nights I just lay there in bed and watch it go round and round ... puts me to sleep a lot. Of course the soft bed helps too!"

"You walk to work do you John?" R.W. asked.

"At first I did. But then Mr. Truscott got me an old bicycle. So now I can get to and from work a little quicker. Keeps the ol' legs and heart in shape!"

"You been eat'en okay, I gather?" George asked.

"Oh, I never go hungry. I eat lunch with Mr. Truscott some, and I have leftovers at the house when I get in late. And every now and then I get invited to a patron's house for a fresh fish supper. But you know, one day I'd like to go back over to Bessie's and try one of her supper plates! I've only had the one breakfast when you fellows treated me, but haven't had a supper yet. I hear they're quite tasty!"

"Well John, tonight's your lucky night. George and me are head'en over that way in a bit. Why don't you finish up with what you're doing and we'll see 'bout get'en you off work a little early. We'll take ya over there and fill ya up! How's that sound?"

"That sounds great! But it'll take me a few more days working on this floor. As you can see, it's pretty big. But I'll be down in about twenty minutes if that's okay?"

"Sure, that'll be fine. It'll give George and me a chance to have another beer."

After finishing a small section of the floor, John tidied himself up, grabbed his coat, and met his friends down below. R.W. and George were just swigging the last drops of their second beer. Rags told John he could have the rest of the night off, but wanted him to come in first thing in the morning to start back working on the dance floor. There was still a lot left to polish, and the weekend was coming up fast.

By the time the boys made it to Bessie's, the smoky air had virtually dissipated and the spring freshness had begun to return. It was a welcomed relief but everybody had a feeling that sooner or later another blown-up ship would cause it again. But for the time being, it was nice to have the clean fresh air return.

After a filling supper that nearly caused John to explode, they all slowly got into the car to where R.W. dropped George off at the courthouse to relieve Sam. Roscoe had left earlier in the evening to attend a church function with his wife. In the meantime, R.W. drove John back to the Casino. Instead of having him peddle his way back to the house, R.W. put his bicycle in the backseat of his Pontiac and drove him home. John thanked him for the dinner and hospitality and went inside. He was so tired and full that he went straight to his room and sacked out. There would be no beacon watching tonight.

After unloading the bicycle from the backseat and wishing John a good night, R.W. returned to his car, slowly turning it around. He stopped before entering the dark coastal highway to ponder a few thoughts.

"If I don't ever get around to asking Claire Belle out for a date, then somebody else will and all I'll be left with is gnawing on chicken salad sandwiches and Dutch apple pie talk'en 'bout the weather.

Since Emily Mae left, I hadn't had much notion to go out with anybody. But then again, there ain't exactly been nobody that's peaked my interest. Now, this gal Claire Belle sho' has put a little extra 'hip' in my 'hop' and I reckon it's time for me to get off the pot and go a knockin' on her door. Hell ... she only lives about a mile down the street here and I know she's home. I saw her car when I drove by. Buddy ... it's time for you to step up to the plate and go for broke!"

When finally pulling out onto the highway, he slowly drove south the one mile and pulled left into her short sandy driveway. Her 1940 Model 41 yellow Buick, with black convertible top, was parked underneath the stilted three-bedroom cottage that was so common along the beach. It was a typical frame constructed house designed so the waters that breached the dunes during a heavy storm would wash underneath the house instead of washing it away. As a rule, the front door faced the ocean, but numerous cottages had steps and an entrance from the driveway. Claire Belle's cottage did not.

After gathering his nerves, R.W. walked underneath Claire's house to a wide staircase, which led to a small open deck. It adjoined a screened-in porch that enclosed the front door. From there, looking through the screen, he could see Claire Belle sitting in a comfortable chair reading a book. He gently opened the screen door. As with most old screen doors, it had sagged on one side, causing it to scrape along the deck. The jarring action clanged a small rusty brass bell alerting Claire, and the cottages nearby, that somebody was at her house. Not appearing alarmed, she casually closed her book and opened the door. She looked out.

"R.W.? Is that you?"

"Did I make enough racket for ya?"

"Well, that old door causes me the same problem. I guess one of these days I'll get around to fix'en it," Claire Belle said. "What brings you over here?"

"Ah. I was on patrol duty ... saw your lights on and just wanted to stop by and make sure you're do'en okay. Well, it looks like you're okay."

"Would you like to come in R.W.? It's a little chilly out here, and I don't want to lose what heat I've already built up in the house."

"Well, I reckon. It is a'might nippy one tonight."

After walking inside and closing the door, R.W. casually looked around the room noticing she had it nicely arranged. Even though the place was already furnished when she rented it, Claire had added small touches, making it feel comfortable and homey.

"So, how was the fried white catfish at Bessie's tonight?" Claire asked.

"Now how did you know I was at Bessie's tonight and had the fried catfish? You been talk'en to Jenny lately?"

"No I haven't R.W.! I can smell it on your clothes. Every time you come to the lunch counter, I can smell what Bessie's been cooking that morning. Haven't you ever noticed that before?"

"Well, I can't say that I have. I reckon George and me eat there so much we're just plum used to it. You can smell it that much ... huh?"

"Oh R.W. ... don't take offense. Most everybody else that comes into the pharmacy that's eaten there, has Bessie's cookin' on their clothes too! It's no big deal. I haven't eaten there yet, but I hear the folks brag about her cooking."

"Would you like to go there sometime and try it out? I can get us a good table by the window overlooking the wharf and all the fish'en boats!" R.W. said with a little smile.

"Now wouldn't that be romantic! But no, I don't think so. Personally, I don't care too much for that kind of food. It's way too greasy for me, and I don't like smelling like turnip greens when I come out. But I know it's a popular place to eat!"

Claire Belle had a sixth sense that R.W. just didn't happen by to check on her well-being. She perceived he had another notion -- to ask her out. For the last several weeks, she had purposely played coy with R.W., not really giving him a chance. But she had gotten to know him better and believed he was a good man with good intentions. She knew this by the way the townsfolk talked about him while they were in the pharmacy. She also knew a few underlining secrets about him from Jenny. But coming from the town gossip, Claire Belle figured she could take most of that talk with a grain of salt. R.W.'s problems were really no different than anybody else's.

She thought she might turn the tables on R.W.

"Say listen, R.W., I understand the Casino has a band coming in this weekend. I'd love to go, but I don't really want to go by myself. Would you like to escort me?"

R.W. was dumbfounded with this revelation. It was the first time in his whole life he'd ever had a woman ask him out for a date. But then again, he'd been hawing around to the point she must have noticed. R.W. was a proud man, but in this situation, he thought, *"What the heck."*

"Well ... I uh ... well heck. Sure, why not! You sort of caught me off guard there. I wasn't expect'en that!"

"I didn't mean to catch you off guard, but I didn't think you were *ever* going to get around to asking me out! You were gonna ask me out weren't you?"

"I was building up to it. But yeah, I reckon I was! Sort of funny the way I asked you though."

"Well, I knew you were. I just gave you a bit of a push, that's all! So, how's about Saturday night? Pick me up around seven o'clock -- that sound okay to you?"

"Yes 'um. That sounds okay to me. I'll see ya 'round seven o'clock then!"

Without further ado, R.W. excused himself saying he needed to get back to the office. They each bid farewell with a smile. Claire went back to her book and R.W. headed to his car feeling overly-thrilled about finally getting a date even though she asked him first.

After reaching the foot of the staircase facing underneath the cottage, and not watching where he was going, he stumbled into Claire's trash can, knocking it over and making one helluva racket. When he reached down to pick it up, he whacked his head on a cross support, causing him to fall into the can and crush it. Claire, hearing the loud racket and muffled mumbling coming from underneath her house, just shook her head, chuckled and went back to reading her book.

When R.W. got back to the office, Sam told him that George was taking care of a disturbance in his own neck of the woods. It seemed the Silver brothers had gotten liquored up and were having a fight. It's not the first time George has had to pull these fellows apart. R.W. felt George could handle the situation, but thought he'd drive over there to make sure it was no worse than just a fistfight. When he arrived, George had everything under control and was giving the brothers a chewing-out, telling them the next time he had to break them apart he was going to haul their asses to jail. This time when he told them, he was serious.

When the deputies walked out of the house, R.W. mentioned to George he had something on his mind and told him he'd pick him up first thing in the morning. He wanted to head back over to the Coast Guard Station. George could read R.W.'s mind.

"You thinking about that jacket John was wearing tonight?" George asked.

"Yeah, I am ... looked familiar didn't it?"

"From the description Mr. Johnson gave, yeah ... I think so."

"Ain't nothing we can do 'bout it right now though. When you get back to the office, tell Sam to tell Roscoe we'll be in 'bout mid-

126

morning. Don't tell 'em where we're go'en just yet. I got an angle I want to pursue first. We might be on to something."

* * * * * * * *

At seven o'clock the following morning, the boys headed over to the Coast Guard Station. When they arrived, there was a swarm of activity as most of the seaman on night beach patrol were coming in from duty and heading to the mess tent for breakfast. Lieutenant Fleming was on the front porch of his office building smoking a cigarette and talking to Chief Bleu.

"Well, well ... what do we owe the pleasure from Dare County's finest this bright and sun-shiny early morning?"

"Howdy there, Mark. Got'a fresh cup of hot joe for us?"

"Ah shit fella's, we can do better than that. Let's head on over to the mess tent and grab some breakfast. Ya'll look like ya missed out on Bessie's this morning."

"Well, we did at that. Got something on our minds but, first we'll grab a bite to eat with you and afterwards tell ya why we're here."

"Ya'll want'a talk first?"

"Naw, we'll eat first. I hear George's belly gurgling!"

After a big breakfast of scrambled eggs, oatmeal, and several cups of strong black coffee, the boys headed back over to the headquarters building. Mark had a curious tone in his voice.

"What'cha all got on your minds there, R.W.?"

"You still have that copy you made from the note of that injured sailor found on the beach? The one you showed me the other day?"

"Yeah, I got it right here," Lieutenant Fleming said reaching into his desk drawer and pulling it out.

"Mark, you think you could loan it to me for the day or so. I'm on to something."

"Well sure, I can do that. You find something of interest I need to know about?"

"I'm not sure just yet. Until I can make heads or tails with what I got, I won't know."

"But, you *are* going to let me know ... right! That note was written by a Kraut and that's my territory!"

"I'm perfectly aware of that. But in this case, you just have to trust me. I'll let you know what I find. I promise you that."

"Well here, let's put this thing in a brown envelope so's it want get messed up. I know you'll take care of it. It's important to me too you know."

On the way back to the office, George asked R.W. about the copied note from Lieutenant Fleming's office. He had been unaware of it. R.W. explained that Mark first showed it to him when the civilian fisherman came by to tell their story about the German submarine they had encountered. The original was given to Admiral Andrews' security team that made a special trip to retrieve it just after it was found. Before they picked it up, Mark made an exact replica from the original by tracing it onto another piece of paper. At the time, he saw no need to tell George because it didn't mean much. But now it did.

After crossing the Wash Baum Bridge, R.W. had second thoughts about going to the office to make the comparison. He felt it might cause a stir and decided instead to go over to his house where they could sit and not have any distractions. Josh was at school.

Inside the house, he and George sat at the kitchen table and compared the notes. There was strong indication that both notes were written by the same hand: the German sailor who came ashore to save his injured shipmate and the thief who stole the clothes. R.W. surmised it was John O'Hearn, or whatever his name was.

In talking the matter over with George, R.W. rehashed events that made him believe this was their man. The day after the injured German sailor was found on the beach, a young stranger walked into town seemingly lost claiming he had been hitchhiking from New Jersey. He was, as R.W. remembered, wearing a cream-colored canvas jacket and carrying a small light brown leather suitcase. But that would seem normal.

While chatting with the young man that afternoon, R.W. noticed he was unusually clean and freshly shaven. Someone who had been on the road thumbing for several days should have appeared slightly more disheveled. R.W. listened to his story with reserved skepticism but eventually scoffed it off because of his friendly and well-mannered behavior. As he remembered, he took him to the pharmacy lunch counter and bought him a sandwich and a soda. The young man was totally broke.

On the day the sailor was found, the Coast Guardsmen went to full alert and canvassed the entire Bodie and Roanoke Islands. It was quite reasonable to believe that someone being hunted would gamble his best to escape pursuers. Breaking into a vacant cottage seemed logical. Breaking into a vacant cottage containing a closet full of clothea that fit was sheer luck. But as mundane as it may have seemed, the key to it all was a very simple and plain cream-colored canvas jacket.

"Now what?"

"I'm not sure, George. I'm gonna smoke it over a little bit. I think I've got an angle. But I *believe* this afternoon I'm gonna go back over to the Casino and have another little chat with our young friend.

"Why don't I drop you back over to the office and you make up some kind'a bullshit story as to where we've been. If we tell Roscoe right now, he'll be walk'en 'round like a chicken with his head cut off.

128

It's best we don't tell him now. In the meantime, I'm gonna take Mark his note back so's to keep him from worrying about it. That a plan?"

"Yeah, that's a plan."

Lieutenant Fleming was still in his office when R.W. returned. He was stunned to see him back so quickly. He immediately started questioning his lawman friend.

"Well hell, that was awful sudden. You figure it out that fast?"

"Mark ... I think I found our man."

"You mean to tell me the son-of-a-bitch is still here on the islands?"

"Yeah, I think so."

"Well, where the hell is he?"

"I don't want to say just yet. I want'a talk to him alone and verify what I think. Besides, I want'a believe he's on our side and that could be helpful. If you guys go barrel rolling in there with guns flailing away and put the cuffs on 'em, you won't get anything. Besides, you know damn good and well word'll leak out and we'll have another crisis on our hands, and we don't want that now ... do we? Look, I know this guy and he trusts me. Believe me!"

"You mean to tell me you *know* this guy?"

"Mark, it's a *long* story, and I know you got the rights to him. But at the moment, I think it's best you let me handle this as I see fit. I know what I'm do'en here."

"What makes you think he's on our side?"

"It's just a gut feeling I have. Hell, you've had gut feelings before! Look damnit, I came in here with good intentions keep'en you abreast. I just can't tell ya everything I know right now. But I very well could've walked in here and lied to you saying I didn't have shit and gone on 'bout my business and everything would've been just hunky-dory. But I felt obligated to say something."

"Well, I guess I do owe you that much. Hell, you're the one who did all the investigative work in the first place to find the SOB. Okay, okay ... I'll hold off an' keep a lid on it. But don't stay gone too long ... and you *will* tell me that *long* story someday?"

"Mark, I always knew you were a peach of a guy!"

It was closing in on the lunch hour and R.W. wasn't much in the mood to heading back over to Manteo to grab something to eat. So, he just decided to drive over to Whalebone Junction and grab a ready-made sandwich and a bottled soda at the Midget Market. It would give him the extra time to think about what he was going to say to John—or whatever his name was. Though, the only thing that kept running through his mind was how nice and polite the kid was and how appreciative he was in getting a job. He really seemed sincere. But in reality, the situation was becoming more tense because of the way German submarines were continually devastating the American merchant shipping running up and down the coast. Each day it was getting worse. Was it possible John was a spy in sheep's clothing?

After grabbing a sandwich and a cold bottle of Royal Crown Cola out of the ice tub inside the Midget Market, R.W. went outside to a small table in front of the store and peeled back the wrapper of his sandwich. Just as he bit into the ham salad, Jenny pulled up in her small mail truck.

"Well, howdy there deputy!"

"Oh Jenny, it's you ... and how art thou today?"

"Aw R.W. ... you don't need to be sarcastic. I'm doing fine. I hear tell you're do'en purty well yourself!"

"And how might that be?"

"I hear tell you're tak'en Miss Claire Belle to the Casino Saturday night!"

"Well as a matter of fact I am. Another little angel tell ya this time?"

"No, actually I saw her earlier this morning go'en to work and she said you stopped by her place last night to ask her out. Wasn't that sweet of you!"

"Ah Jenny, why don't you just shut up. It ain't no big deal."

"Well, I'll be glad to tell her you said that!"

"Why don't you just mind your own bees wax. You know what I meant."

"Of course I do. I just like see'en you get riled up."

"Well ... are you going to the dance?" R.W. asked Jenny in a more pleasant tone.

"You know I am. Wouldn't miss the first dance of the season. Going with Hank Larson. You know him don't you?"

"Yeah, I sure do. When ya'll get'en married?"

"Married! Hell I ain't get'en married. Where'd you get that notion?"

"The way ya'll cuddle up to each either, I just figured..."

"Cuddle ... yes. Marriage ... no! Hell no! It just ain't gonna happen. Got too much going on right now ... just don't have the time nor the inkling. But I don't mind cuddling."

"Well, I reckon I was wrong then."

"Well, I reckon you were," Jenny concluded. "How's the ham salad?"

"Right good. Come to think of it, it's real good."

"You know Claire Belle made that?" Jenny said, smiling coyly.

"Ya don't say!"

"Yep, she makes 'em on the side here for the Midget Market to pick up a few extra bucks. I reckon you've had her chicken salad?"

"Yeah, I've had the chicken salad and no, I didn't know she made the ham salad. But I'll mention it to her when I see her again."

130

"Yeah, you do that. Think I'll go in and grab one for myself."

After finishing off the ham salad, R.W. lit up a Chesterfield cigarette. He was a light smoker, usually lighting up when something weighed-in on his mind. Right now he had a lot on his mind. He thought a little fresh tobacco might help smooth out his thoughts.

After smoking his cigarette and stomping it out on the concrete front entrance, he decided it was time to head over to the Casino and talk to his little buddy. R.W. thought he had it worked out in his mind how he was going to handle the situation, but wouldn't make any rash decisions until talking to him. It's always good to know first what the other man is thinking. But most of the time the fellows he's hauled to jail were drunks and not very cohesive in their thinking. In John's case, he thought otherwise. Then again, this was a highly unusual situation and he had to be careful lest he end up dead or injured.

Upon arriving at the Casino, he went in through the foyer and saw his buddy Rags behind the snack bar. This time he was restocking the shelves with sundries he was low on. He casually walked over greeting Rags in a humorous way. He turned around.

"John says you boys filled his ass up purty good last night over at Bessie's."

"Yeah, the boy ate like it was his last meal. He make it in to work okay this morning?"

"Aw, he was a little late ... no big deal. He wasn't that late. Right now he's upstairs working off all the grease he ate last night. Doing a right fine job on that floor, he is. Outta be finished later this afternoon. You need to talk to him again?"

"If'n ya don't mind. Care if'n I go up and bother him for a minute or two?" R.W. asked.

"Naw, go right ahead. He's probably 'bout ready for a break now anyway."

When R.W. walked into the large dance hall, John had just cracked open one of the many windows in the hall and was prepared to sit down. Upon seeing R.W., John greeted him, motioning him over to have a glass of water with him.

John O'Hearn, a.k.a. Jürgen Oehrn, was small in stature and appeared younger than his twenty-four years of age. This was due to his ever-present boyish grin and smile. With dirty-blonde hair and bright blue eyes, John projected the good looks so prevalent with his Germanic race and caught the looks of many of the island's young ladies coming to the Casino.

In order to keep his ruse from detection, John rarely ventured beyond his work, but did travel into Manteo with Claire Belle and R.W. a few times when they invited him to the movies at the Pioneer Movie Theater. Claire Belle, not really knowing his true identity, thought he was the perfect gentleman.

131

"I should be done in about an hour or so. I was getting a little tired and thought I'd take a short break to get my second wind. This sure is a big floor."

"It is at that and you've done a nice job shinning 'er up. I'll be here Saturday night, so I'll be test'en 'er out for you."

"Well don't break-a-leg. It is mighty slick!"

"Oh, I'll be careful."

John could sense R.W. had something on his mind. He could tell by his voice and facial expressions when he asked John to have a seat.

"John, I'll get right to the point."

Reaching into his coat pocket, R.W. pulled out the note that had been written at Ben Johnson's cottage. He laid it on the table.

"You recognize this?"

There was a moment of silence. With just a slight hesitation, John looked out the window and then back at R.W. and then at the note. He picked it up and put it back down.

"Yes sir. I recognize it. It's the note I left in a cottage when I broke in and took some clothes. I felt bad for doing that, but I was cold and desperate. I knew sooner or later somebody would find it. That's why I left it. But how did you know it was me?"

"The handwriting on this note is the same handwriting on the note we found on that injured German sailor on the beach. You're the one who wrote that note too, aren't you. You're the one who brought him to shore, isn't that right?"

"Yes sir. That was me."

"John, the key to this whole matter is that canvas jacket you've been wearing. If you notice on the inside underneath the label, you'll find the initials BJ. That stands for Ben Johnson, the fellow you stole it from. Shall we look?"

"No sir ... no, I don't think that will be necessary. Are you going to turn me over to the authorities?"

R.W. looked sternly at the young man.

"Son, I am the authorities," he said, firmly. "First off ... I want to know what your real name is."

"Jürgen Oehrn, sir. The name I gave you is my uncle's name. His German name was Johann Oehrn. Like I told you a while back, he immigrated to the United States in the early 1900s and denounced his German citizenship. He later became an American citizen and changed his name to John O'Hearn. So you can see why I used that name."

"And the story you told me about your family?"

"It was all mostly true. I, of course, fabricated that I was an American living with my uncle because my parents were no longer around. In truth, and as far as I know, when I left Germany for my sea duty, my parents were still alive unless the Gestapo has done something with them. My father was strongly opposed to Hitler and the Nazis Party.

"But as far as my uncle was concerned, all that was quite true except, as you know, I was not exactly living with him. Some years back, I did visit with him for a summer and we got along very well. He is a business owner and very wealthy. As implausible as it may have seemed, my goal was to somehow escape from our boat and join him. I loathe Adolf Hitler and the Nazis. I will take pleasure in celebrating his death. The sooner, the better for all of Germany!"

"And your chance came when you brought your injured comrade ashore?" R.W. asked.

"It was purely by happenstance. I was chosen for that duty because I was dispensable. But had they asked the rest of the crew, I would have been the first to raise my hand. But yes, I was chosen and it truly was a godsend. I haven't looked back since. By the way, how is he ... my friend, Erick Koehler?"

"The last I am aware of he had recuperated well enough to be moved to the Norfolk Naval Hospital in the Chesapeake Bay area. I haven't heard any more since."

"That's good. I am glad he has made it. I feel very good he has survived."

"Well, what caused the accident in the first place?"

"As I remember we were running on the surface during a daytime fog when we were spotted by one of our airships. The Kapitän crash-dived our boat. Our angle of descent was forty degrees. When the first *Wasserbombe,* exploded, I you call them 'depth-charges,' it violently shook the boat and Erick lost his grip, going head first into a bulkhead. He was a motorman for the electric engines and stationed in the rear of the boat."

"And your captain's name is Vogel?"

"Yes! But how do you know that?"

"Suffice it to say his name has become rather popular around here," R.W. replied. "Let's just say that he has invited our President Roosevelt to get close and personal.

"Kapitän Vogel is a strong individual who is a good and fair leader," John defended. "Though, he does have a hatred for the British. Their bombers killed his family in Berlin. And, with the Americans helping the British, he also dislikes you Americans, who are supplying them. But I guess he has forgotten who really started the war."

"A lot of hatred, huh?"

"Very much so! But, you must understand," John pleaded. "The hatred goes back to World War I and the Versailles Treaty. So many restrictions were put upon our country that it began choking us, and we went into a deep depression."

John continued, trying to give R.W. a history lesson of why Herr Hitler and his National Socialist Party, the Nazis, came to power.

"He promised the people all sorts of things," John went on. "But he said all he wanted was equality for Germany with the other powers. To gain that power, Hitler gradually started dismantling the Treaty and both the British and the French did nothing to stop him. Hitler knew he had gained the upper hand. He felt as though he could do just as he pleased without retribution, and he did so by enlarging our *Heer, Kriegsmarine, and the Luftwaffe.*"

"The what?" R.W. asked with a puzzled look.

"Our *Wehrmacht,* our armed forces. The Army, the Navy, and the Air Force."

"Oh...."

"Yes ... and at first, our *Unterseebootes,* our submarine force, was given a back seat. Our *Befehlshaber,* our commander, Admiral Dönitz, in his quest to build its force, wanted a strong U-boat presence. Herr Hitler and Grossadmiral Raeder, who is the commander of our Navy, believed the sea battles were to be won on the surface using battleships, so they got priority over U-boats."

John continued telling R.W. how Admiral Dönitz believed that for Germany to win the war, it would have to be done by attrition by keeping the Allied supply ships at bay -- keeping them from crossing the Atlantic. It wasn't until he authorized a daring mission to show just how stealth submarines could be.

"Admiral Dönitz called upon one of our top U-boat commanders, Oberleutnant Günther Prien of the U-47, to sneak into the heart of the Royal Navy's harbor-basin in Scapa Flow of the Orkney Islands north of Scotland, and sink their battleships and then escape."

"And...?"

"He did, but he actually only sank one," John replied.

On 14 October 1939 Prien and U-47 secretly entered the basin and blew-up the highly-decorated World War I battleship. *HMS Royal Oak.* The mighty battleship was destroyed with four torpedoes, killing more than 830 officers and men.

"And you remember all this?" R.W. asked the young man.

"How could we not! It was monumental!" John replied. "But what else I remember was when I heard Prien's U-boat was lost in the North Atlantic the first week of March 1941. There was no word as to what happened to him. He just disappeared, never returning. Nobody knows. He must have hit a mine."

"That's interesting," R.W. pondered. "Maybe there's something you ought'a know. We recently found another one of your comrades on the beach. He was not as fortunate as your other friend. It looked as though he'd been float'en in the sea for quite sometime."

"Do you know who he was?"

"He had no tags to identify him. The only evidence we have was he had a pair of binoculars that somehow stayed wrapped around his neck. On his life vest were the markings of U-491. The Coast Guard thinks he somehow got washed overboard."

"Yes ... that is very possible," John replied. "Being on watch on the bridge of the conning tower, the rear flake platform or even the lower platform during bad weather and rough seas is quite hazardous. The first thing one does is strap into a belt harness to keep from falling or being washed overboard. Maybe he either didn't strap in quick enough or he improperly strapped himself in ... I really don't know. I had done numerous four-hour watches myself, but the weather was mostly good. As a matter of fact it was pleasurable to get away from the stench inside the tube. It was awful!"

"So I've heard ... so I've heard," R.W. said, reminiscing in his mind the story Mr. Webber told to him and Lieutenant Fleming.

Jürgen/John looked at R.W. as though he knew more than he was letting on.

"You say that you were dispensable. How's that?" R.W. asked. "I would think everybody on a boat like yours would have a specific job ... that nobody would be dispensable."

"Yes, that is actually true so far as the operating of the boat. But many boats had some non-essential personnel such as a propaganda photographer, a war correspondent, and intelligence personnel. Because of our special mission so close the American coast, our Command felt our boat needed someone fluent in English. That is how I came to be on board."

"Secret mission?"

"I was not privy to that information. Only the officers and a few other key personnel knew the specifics. The rest of us only knew that we were going to the American east coast and sink merchant ships and disrupt your economy."

"But, your secret mission ... did you know *anything* about that at all?"

"All I knew was that at certain times, the boat surfaced to receive a specially-coded message from the shore. It was then decoded by a specialist named Victor Krech, who gave the information to the Kapitän. He would then direct the boat to a certain area where our target was located, and we would destroy it."

"Where was the location ... do you remember that?"

"I really can't remember right now. My mind is foggy of what I heard because it made no sense to me at the time."

"Well do your best to remember. Why do you think you were dispensable?"

"I didn't have a specific job other than being an interpreter if called upon ... and I filled in at certain positions or helping out with certain

135

duties. I worked all over the boat from helping the mixers [torpedo mechanics] in the bow torpedo room, to making soup in the galley. I guess you could say I was a swingman. I did help out, but I could see that my over-all position was tentative. Besides, I later found out our radioman, Leutnant Brückner, could speak English fairly well ... not as good as me, but well enough to get by. I suspect they could have used him if they had to."

"Did anyone on the boat know you wanted to defect?"

"No sir ... no one! I kept that strictly to myself. It certainly would not have done me any good had I talked of such things. No one that I knew on the boat ever talked of such."

"Now that you've had a taste of life here, would you want to go back?"

"Oh, no sir! I like it here quite well! For a few days after you hooked me up with Mr. Truscott, I had thoughts of trying to work my way north to New Jersey and to my uncle's home. But almost immediately, everybody was very nice to me and made me feel welcomed. I hate that now I am going to lose that ... and I am sorry for deceiving you, but I think it is obvious to you now as to why I did it."

"Yes ... obviously, based on what you've said," R.W. said with a slight chuckle.

"Are you taking me to jail?" Jürgen asked nervously.

"No, John ... no I'm not. I don't know why I'm not, but no ... I'm not gonna haul you in – at least just now," R.W. replied with a solemn, almost relieved tone in his voice. "I think right now I'm gonna let you finish up that floor and satisfy Rags and everybody else that'll be dancin' on it Saturday night, include'en myself ... and you *will* continue using the name everybody knows you by ... John O'Hearn. Do you understand that?"

"Then I am free to go?"

"You'll continue doing just what you've been doing and stay'en out'a trouble," R.W. continued. "For now, I think it's best you not leave the islands. If you do and you're caught, chances are you'll find yourself behind a barbwire fence or worse until the war is over ... and then maybe some more."

"I guess you are right. Who else knows about me?"

"Other than me, George and Lieutenant Fleming, commander of our local Coast Guard Station, and he wants his paws on you something fierce, no one knows about you. Let's keep it that way. Say nothing to no one. Lieutenant Fleming doesn't have much love for you Germans right now, especially since he's lost some of his buddies on a destroyer ya'll blew up at the end of February. But don't you worry 'bout him right now. I'll take care of him. You just worry about me and George and Sheriff Simmons. I'll be tell'en him.

136

"In the meantime, you stay out'a trouble. And I mean, no matter what it is, you walk away from it. You keep your nose clean. You got that? If you do try to escape the islands, I'll give your description to Lieutenant Fleming, and I can promise you ... he'll hunt you down like a blood-thirsty hound dog. I think you understand that. In the meantime, you act like you have been. You and I will talk further sometime soon. And, try to remember more about that special mission you were tellin' me about. That can go a long way towards your safety!"

"Yes sir, I will."

"And there is one more thing," R.W. said as he was walking away. "I want you to give me back that canvas jacket so's I can return it to Mr. Johnson. He had a real lik'en for that coat. It'll tickle his innards to get it back. Meanwhile, walk with me out to the car. I've got a spare jacket in the trunk I'll give you that'll fit you just fine."

"Yes sir...."

Chapter 14

After interrogating John and making the heady decision to let him remain free, R.W. realized his actions were probably going to cause trouble with his superiors. He knew that sooner or later he was going to have to tell Sheriff Simmons what he had done and then explain his long story to Lieutenant Fleming. He dreaded this; nevertheless, he knew he had made the right decision. His gut told him so.

But for the moment, the first thing R.W. wanted to do was return Ben Johnson's favorite canvas jacket. He knew he'd be leaving on the morrow, and he thought it'd be a nice surprise. Pulling out of the Casino parking lot, R.W. turned right and headed up the coastal road towards Kill Devil Hills and his cottage on the beach. When he pulled into the driveway, Ben was just coming over a sand dune with a cooler full of flounder. He'd been surf fishing in front of his house.

"Ben, I see by the weight of that cooler and the way you're all bent over, looks like you had a purty good day down on the beach!"

"Yeah, it was. Had a better than average day ya might say. Now if'n I can get some ice on these babies, they ought'a stay fresh until Friday night. Got some guest coming over for dinner ... can't wait to get these puppies seasoned up and frying in the pan!"

"Ben, I got a little surprise for you!" R.W. reached inside his passenger window and pulled out the canvas jacket.

"Well, I'll be dog! You found my jacket! Where'd you find the sumbitch?"

"It was in the lost and found bin down at the Nags Head Casino. I happen to be in there today talk'en to Rags when I got the notion to ask him what he did with clothes and other items he finds left over after the weekend. And well ... here it is. Can't say that I found anything else though ... this was it."

"Ah, I ain't worrying 'bout that other mess, but I sho' am glad to get this back!"

"Well, I figured you might. That's why I brought it on over to you before ya head home. I reckon whoever stole it must've stopped in for a few beers before head'en out'a town and left it there. Him being a thief and all, I don't reckon he wanted to come back and get it. Who really knows ... but ya got it back."

"Look, why don't you let me give you some of these flounders to take back for a fresh meal. I'd like to repay you."

"Aw Ben, you don't need to do that. This is what we do for a living. Besides, I'm so busy right now I wouldn't know when I'd get a chance to cook 'em. I appreciate the offer though, but it's not necessary."

R.W. knew he'd bent the truth a bit with ol' Ben, but he didn't think it was necessary for him to know the whole truth. He was just glad to get his jacket back. Nothing more.

It was getting late in the afternoon and R.W. thought it was best to head back to the office. On the highway south past Nags Head, R.W. and George passed each other. R.W pulled off to the side of the road and George turned around pulling up and stopping behind him. They each got out of their cars.

"Well ... how'd it go today?" George asked.

"Aw, I guess it went okay. We had a good talk. There's no doubt he's our man. He told me, and I believed him, he had intentions of defecting all along. When the opportunity arose, he took it. That's how he ended up here. He'd planned on mov'en his way north to see his uncle but after I hooked him up with Rags, he decided to stay. I will say he was quite surprised we discovered him."

"What did you do with him?"

"Hell, George ... nothing! I told 'em to get on back to polishing the floor."

"You're kidding?"

"Naw I'm not! But me and him got an understanding though. He ain't going nowheres. I thought it best he stay put. If we decided to make a big deal out'a all of this, these islands would erupt into frenzy and nobody wants to go through that mess again. Besides, he passed on some decent information I can give to Fleming."

"What about Fleming?"

"He wants his hands on 'em purty bad, but I was able to slow him down for awhile. I think with what I can pass on to him, Mark'll hold off. I'll go talk to him tomorrow."

"What'd you tell Roscoe?" R.W. asked.

"I told him you were 'see'en a lady about a dog' and you'd be in this afternoon. That seemed to satisfy him. You gonna tell him about this revelation?"

"Hell, George, I got'a. I don't see's I got much choice in the matter. Besides, I think he'll agree with what I done. You know how bad he hates those damn government guys. Remember when the FBI showed up a coupl'a months ago? Last thing he wants is get'en them involved!"

"Yeah, I see what you mean. Well, he's back at the office now. Go have fun!"

"I reckon now's about a good a time as any. Wish me luck!"

Without further ado, R.W. headed back to the office. Because of the way Roscoe felt about the federal bureaucracy, he believed he'd probably be okay with the way he handled the situation; though, he felt Roscoe might be hacked off he wasn't told sooner. But the way the situation unfolded, R.W. felt there wasn't much time to stop to explain. At least that was the story he was going to use and stick to it.

"Roscoe, ya got a minute?"

"Sure, sure ... come on in."

And with that, R.W. went in to explain to his boss in detail about the German sailor who had escaped his submarine and settled into the languid living of the Outer Banks. Roscoe listened intently. At first he was perturbed he wasn't told earlier but got over it fairly quickly. He understood the seriousness of the matter and the direction his deputy had taken. He was behind him all the way. But there was still one matter at hand that needed attention.

"You want me to go over with you to see Lieutenant Fleming?"

"Well, if'n ya don't mind. I think it'll be a good idea. I've got a good handle on Mark, but a little backup wouldn't hurt."

"You want'a call on him in the morning."

"Yeah, that'll be a good time."

With it already being early evening, R.W. decided he would head over to his parent's house and pick up Josh. If his timing was right, he just might catch something to eat. But it really didn't matter. He knew there'd be leftovers.

The following morning, R.W. met Roscoe at the office. George would handle the phones while Sam would patrol in the car. They told the boys they'd be back after lunch. George winked at R.W. as he and Roscoe headed out the door.

Deputy Scoggins and Sheriff Simmons arrived at the Coast Guard Station around eight-thirty. Lieutenant Fleming was there in his office taking care of the morning reports. He noticed the officers as they came to the office front door and cordially greeted them as they walked through. They immediately went into the office.

"Well R.W., I see ya brought in the 'Big Gun' this morning."

"Mark ... have you met Sheriff Simmons before?"

"Can't say's that I've had the pleasure, but we've talked on the phone a few times. Sheriff, good to finally met you!"

"The pleasure is all mine, Lieutenant."

After a few short pleasantries, R.W. went on and explained to Fleming his account of discovering the sailor but purposely left out portions of the story as to where the man could presently be found. While Fleming believed the yarn, he was hostile to Scoggins for not revealing his whereabouts. At one point, he threatened both officers that he could have them arrested for harboring a foreign combatant whose country was hostile to theirs. But he quickly backed off that stance realizing he was barking up the wrong tree. His temper was getting to the best of him. After lighting a cigarette and returning to his desk, he exhaled a long stream of smoke and apologized for his outburst. He was frustrated.

After a few moments of calm, R.W. spoke reiterating his philosophical stance to Fleming that he fully believed the German was not a belligerent, and he felt he had no intentions of causing any harm to the United States. He truly believed he was a good kid simply stuck on the wrong side of the ocean when war broke out. As a matter of fact, as revealed earlier in the conversation, the sailor had possessed certain information that might be useful. "Would a belligerent do that?"

"To save his ass, yeah, I believe he would!" Fleming retorted.

"But in this case, I don't think so Mark."

"Why are you trying to protect this guy R.W.?"

"Because of every bit of what I just said. He doesn't need to be locked up. Besides, the folks 'round here'll get into another tizzy if they knew otherwise. Right now, the only people who really know who he is are the three of us and George and by god that's all that need to know! Mark, you yourself told me you had a gut feeling something was in the wind with this U-boat patrolling the waters. How *good* is it that we now have one of their own amongst us that might provide useful information? Don't you think for one-minute we should take advantage of this?"

"Well, if ya get right down to it, I don't think I can argue with you on that. It looks like you've already set the tone and maybe that's the way we ought'a go. I guess there's no sense in me rock'en the boat. Well, is there anyway I can meet up with this kid and make my own judgment?"

"Yeah well, I guess I owe *you* that much. You like barbecue pork ribs?"

"Just like everybody else 'round here. Why?"

"I'll meet you at Bessie's tomorrow for lunch. It's her Friday special. I'll bring the boy with me and you can meet him. Don't bring anybody else. I'll have George with me so's it won't look too suspicious. We've eaten there before so I don't think anybody will pay us much mind. But they'll probably be staring at you!"

"I hear tell the ribs are purty good!"

"Absolutely the best."

Just as Lieutenant Fleming opened his office door to see the gentlemen out, an office clerk handed him a memo with more bad news. Two ships were torpedoed earlier that morning off Cape Lookout. Fleming passed on the information to local officers.

"Goddamn it ... goddamn it! Somehow all this shit has got to stop! This morning at 0250 the gasoline tanker *Atlas* was blown up within sight of the Cape Lookout Lighthouse. Two sailors were burned to death when their lifeboat drifted into flaming gasoline. It seems the rest of the crew survived and was rescued. The other ship, the American freighter *Malchace*, carrying a load of soda ash, was struck ten minutes later further off the same cape. So far they haven't found any survivors.

"R.W., I sure as hell hope you know what you're doing!"

The two police officers turned about and headed to their car and then motored up the sandy road to Whalebone Junction. From there they were going to head to the Casino. On their trip to the Coast Guard Station earlier that morning, R.W. told Roscoe that, after their meeting with Fleming, he was going to take him to meet John. He had no qualms in telling Roscoe where the boy was located. He did have doubts about telling Fleming. That's why he suggested meeting in a neutral place. Bessie's was as good as any.

When they arrived at the Casino around eleven o'clock, an employee told the officers that John was in the lower level lavatory repairing a small leak in one of the toilets. He offered to go get him but R.W. said they would walk back to see him. Rags was not there this morning. In a sense, that was good. John had lately become popular with the law officers and it may have aroused suspicion. At the moment, R.W. wasn't in the mood to explain himself.

Roscoe finally had the chance to meet the person that had caused so much commotion. They walked outside to the back of the Casino, where the entrance to the upstairs dance floor was located, and sat at one of the many picnic tables overlooking the beach and the crashing waves. The roar was not obtrusive, but it did drown out their voices for any prying ears that wanted to listen in on their conversation from one of the back windows.

"Nice to meet you Sheriff Simmons. R.W. has told me that you probably wanted to meet with me. I'm sure he has explained all there is and my exploits. I am sorry to have caused so much internal strife here on the islands with my attempt to escape Hitler's wrath. But you must understand, Germany is on a path of self-destruction, and it will not end until the maniac is dead. By then, I am afraid Germany will be nothing more than a burned out wasteland full of starving people. If you know or have read *anything* about our country under his leadership, I think you will understand why I did what I did."

"Yes John ... Deputy Scoggins and I have already had a lengthy conversation regarding that. No doubt it's a shame with what's happened. Nevertheless, your country has declared war on ours. Right now your status here in America is not very worthy. You're really walking on thin ice.

"But John, you must understand it from our side. We've put ourselves in a helluva predicament, and we have to handle this very carefully. Any missteps on either side and we're all gonna end up in jail. You as a prisoner of war and us for harboring a fugitive. You'll eventually be released ... we'll probably be shot! So, I think you can see the gamble we're taking.

"So far it seems you've been truthful and the information you've passed on has gone to our intelligence people to see what they can make of it. That's certainly a plus that'll go a long way. But if there's *anything* else you can pass on, well ... it's just that much more better for you. You do understand that, don't you?"

"Yes sir, I do. But I really don't know any more than what I've already said about our mission. If by some chance I can think of something else, I'll pass it on ... I promise!"

"John, there is one other item we have to take care of," R.W. interjected.

"Yes sir."

"I've set up a meeting tomorrow with the commander of the Coast Guard Station, Lieutenant Fleming. As you know, I had no choice but to tell him about your presence. He has some understanding of why I'm keeping you under wraps, but he's not very happy about it. He put up a purty big stink. But to keep the peace, I told him we'd meet with him."

"Is he coming here?"

"No ... no he's not. I'll have George pick you up around eleven-fifteen tomorrow morning. We're going to meet with him over at Bessie's."

"Well, that's good. What's the special?"

"Barbecue pork ribs. Ever had any before?"

"No, I can't say that I have."

There was about fifteen more minutes of conversation related to the situation and how they hoped everything would unfold. Sheriff Simmons was slightly perturbed he had gotten himself into this situation, but not to the point he was ready to pull the plug. He had to admit he believed the lad and had sympathy for his plight. And R.W. was right about one thing: he was a pleasant and well-spoken young person who would, if need be, take his punishment standing up—and hopefully not in front of a firing squad. But deep down, he hoped it wouldn't get to that point.

As the officers got back into the car, Roscoe was curious about something.

"You know R.W., I've been meaning to ask you this. Why are we driving around with a brand new trashcan in the back seat of your car?"

"Well, I need to replace one that accidently got smashed up. I figured while we were up this way this morning, I'd replace it."

"You talk'en about the one at Claire Belle's house you *accidently* fell on the other night when you were up here asking her out for the dance this weekend?"

"Ah shit Roscoe! You been talk'en to Jenny?"

"Nope ... heard it from my wife. Hell, it's all over town you're tak'en her to the dance!"

"You know Roscoe, the only person on this whole damn island that ain't been running his mouth is that German. Everybody else 'round here just don't know when to shut up!"

"Aw R.W., don't worry 'bout it. What'cha want'a do 'bout lunch."

"Well ... on the way back, I'm gonna stop off there at the Midget Market and buy you a box of cotton balls and then stuff 'em in your mouth whilst I eat one of Claire Belle's ham salad sandwiches and drink an RC Cola. That's what I'm gonna do for lunch!"

After getting back to the office, Roscoe had numerous messages to take care of and George had gotten several house calls that needed attention. He and R.W. returned to the patrol car and went about doing police business. While driving around to the various calls, R.W. filled George in on the morning happenings and asked him to pick John up at the Casino for tomorrow's lunch meeting with Lieutenant Fleming. It wasn't something he was looking forward to, but he figured sooner or later they were going to have to get together. He thought by now Fleming had cooled down and wouldn't do anything drastic. At least that was what he was hoping.

The following early morning broke with a sky full of light gray clouds moving in from the southwest. This usually meant rain was on its way and would probably stick around for at least a day.

After taking Josh to school, R.W. stopped by the pharmacy to see Claire Belle and grab a quick cup of coffee. Because he had been so busy the last couple of days, he had not had a chance to see her.

"Well good morning there R.W.! Haven't seen you in a few days. Care for a cup of coffee?"

"Sure! That'd be good. Looks like rain today."

"So it does. You been busy I see."

"Yeah, just the way it goes sometimes."

"Anything important going on we need to know about?"

"Aw ... nothing serious. Just the usual stuff that happens this time of year when the city folk start com'en in get'en their cottages ready for the summer."

"Yeah, I've been noticing more cars lately. By the way, thanks for the new trash can! But you didn't have to do that. I could've straightened the old one out."

"Aw hell ... everybody an' his aunt and uncle already knows 'bout it. Might as well keep 'em talking. Look, the next coupl'a days I'm gonna be purty busy so's it's doubtful I'll be see'en ya much during the day, but I'll a picking you up 'round seven Saturday. You still on?"

"I wouldn't miss it for the world! Even got a nice clean pair of white socks for the dance floor. I hear it's slick."

"That it is! We need to be careful ... ain't neither one of us as young as we used to be. We don't need any broken bones ya know."

"Oh, I think we'll be careful."

After finishing two quick cups of coffee, R.W headed to the office to work on the reports from yesterday's calls. He thought he would have it all finished before his lunch meeting with John and Lieutenant Fleming. Though, it really didn't matter. The meeting was too important. Any unfinished paperwork would have to wait.

About mid-morning it started raining and it looked as though it was socked in for a while. In a sense it was good because most people stayed inside and the calls to the office slowed to a trickle. It was a good chance to catch a breather. About forty minutes before noon, George went to pick John up at the Casino.

George, John, and R.W. arrived at Bessie's first and were standing under the tin roof of the front porch waiting for Lieutenant Fleming. At ten after twelve, he arrived in his Jeep with a canvas top. Unfortunately, there were no side flaps, and his left shoulder was soaked from the rain and splashing water-filled holes. Upon reaching the porch, he casually greeted the trio and shook hands. He noticed that John looked him squarely in the eye with a firm grip. For Lieutenant Fleming that was a plus.

After grabbing a table in the far corner of the room, they all ordered agreeing upon the pork rib special with plenty of extra napkins. Bessie brought over a large pitcher of sweet iced tea. The atmosphere in the restaurant was about usual except many patrons kept glancing in there direction most likely because it wasn't very often a Coast Guard Lieutenant went to the trouble of coming this far inland for a bite to eat. Then again, they figured word leaked out about today's special. Lieutenant Fleming got right to the point.

"John, I know R.W. has already told you I haven't been too pleased about this whole situation and how it's panned out. On the other hand, I've had a long night to mull it over, and I believe we ought'a let a sleep'en dog lie. You might also want'a count your lucky stars you met up with him first instead of me. Had you met up with me, you'd be in some dank prison compound eat'en baked beans and drink'en dishwater instead of barbecue pork ribs and iced tea.

146

"But on the other hand, something might just come of this. The information you gave us, I passed on to our intelligence people and they've told me it's positive information. Not much, but positive. They didn't tell me anymore than that but would like some more to see if'n they can piece it together."

"Would it mean my freedom is over?" John nervously asked.

"No, I'm afraid not. I'm agreeing to R.W.'s plan as long as you don't do anything stupid like running away and mak'en me come look'en for ya. That would be stupid."

"Well, I have been researching my mind. I think the signal we received came from some location along the North Carolina Coast just from hearing the scuttlebutt around the boat ... and it seemed like every time after receiving it, we headed in a northerly direction for several hours. I just don't recall any name of a location as to where we went. Everything was in codes, and I did not know the code names. Even the maps were in codes I did not understand."

Lieutenant Fleming was listening to John leaning forward with his arms folded on the table. John had the presence of mind to speak softly so none of the other patrons could listen in to what he was saying. He knew this might conceivably be good information that needn't be blared out. John did give a quick glance around the room and noticed everybody was more interested in the ribs than him.

From the corner of his eye, Fleming noticed Bessie bringing a large tray with their food. He leaned back in his chair, as did everybody else, and was served. Along with the ribs, there were red boiled taters, cold slaw, and a large basket of corndodgers. It didn't take long before the conversation turned to the weather and how delicious everything tasted. Lieutenant Fleming poked a little fun at John.

"This the first time you ever had barbecue spare ribs John?"

"Yes sir ... yes it is. Now I know why you asked for the extra napkins. I feel like afterwards I'll need to take a bath!"

"Hell, just ride with me back to the station ... that'll wash ya off!"

The rest of the lunch was cordial with each one telling some sort of humorous story bringing small bits of laughter. To R.W. the lunch turned out much better than he expected. He was pleased that Mark had the mindset not to go crazy. His opening statement set the tone. Letting John know where he stood was a good thing. If there was any internal strife between the Sheriff's Office and the Coast Guard Station, it was now gone. It was time to work together; but the information John possessed and passed on, was out of their hands. About all they could do now was keep their eyes and ears open for anything that looked unusual.

After the meal, George took John back to the Casino. Mark and R.W. stood on the front porch talking about John. The rain began pelting hard against the tin roof.

"R.W., I got'a tell ya. You were right about that young fellow; he's a good kid. The first thing that impressed me about him was the way he shook my hand and looked me square in the eyes. To a lot of people, that might not mean much, but to me ... it showed a strong, self-confident person who's got a good head on his shoulders. I might be wrong, but I don't think so. You know, after all that's been said and done about all this crap, I think you probably done all right. But if it doesn't, my ass is grassed. You know that don't you?"

"And I reckon mine too." R.W. said agreeing with Fleming.

"Ya gonna tell me where he's working now?" Fleming asked directly.

"Aw hell Mark, sooner or later you'll probably find out anyway. He's working for Rags Truscott over at the Nags Head Casino. I helped him get work there when he first walked into town. He's doing a good job and gotten to know some of the folks ... seems to fit right in. As far as I can gather, nobody's to the wiser. You know, it's just the four of us who know. We need to keep it that way."

"Jenny?" Mark asked.

"Oh god forbid ... but no, I don't think so." R.W. answered back.

"Well, that's good. But ya never know. Though, I think in our case, hiding him in plain sight's probably a good thing. Sure cuts down on the man effort's in keep'en 'em locked up. And don't worry 'bout it R.W., I ain't gonna cause him any problems. Besides, right now he's an asset and the best I can figure from my early schooling days, you protect your assets. So, keep an eye on him!"

"Yeah, I reckon you're right."

Later that afternoon back at the Sheriff's Office, Roscoe, George, and R.W further discussed the events over the last few days. To some degree, there was relief the pressure had eased and life could return to semi-normal. But with the continuation of freighters and tankers being blown to bits and the constant calls of submarine sightings, it was doubtful life would ever return to the normalcy they once knew. But Lieutenant Fleming did bring up one subject that was cause for concern.

"Jenny! How in the hell she seems to know so much is beyond me!"

"R.W.'s right, Roscoe. We used to make jokes about how she always seemed to know things before anybody else does ... and how she always seemed to know what went on here in the department! But now I think we need to pay a little closer attention to her. I think she can be dangerous. I don't think this is a joke anymore. If she finds out about John, were screwed," added George.

"Well, this is a right small county and people do seem to know what other people are doing, but I think you're right. And some of the things she knows about the going-on's 'round here really ain't all that good for her to know. There's gotta be a snitch 'round here somewhere. Ya'll think?" said Roscoe.

"There's got'a be somebody. I just don't believe she's clairvoyant. I don't believe in clairvoyance. You believe in clairvoyance George?"

"Well R.W., I am Indian you know. And well, our culture does. But me personally, no ... I really don't. Now on my mother's side...."

"Ah, George...."

"No really guys, what we ought'a do is plant some info and see who takes the bait. Maybe we can find out who the culprit is. Let's think about it overnight. We'll talk about it further in the morning. I got'a get home. The wife's got some folks com'en over for dinner and I got's to get!" Roscoe said standing up and grabbing his hat and coat.

And with that, Roscoe left for the evening. The other two sat there pondering what Roscoe envisioned. He was probably right. They'd think about it.

"You go'en to the dance tomorrow night, George?"

"I'm going as a bouncer. Rags hired me today when I took John back. He thinks he's going to have a good crowd with the first band of the season ... you know the regular Weeksville Air Station guys ... the Norfolk Naval Air Auxiliary fellows from Elizabeth City, and probably some of Mark's boys. When you get them all together, you just never know. Besides, I could use the extra bucks."

"I hear tell you're taking Miss Claire Belle."

"Well just who in the hell hasn't heard!"

* * * * * * * *

Saturday arrived and it was still raining and it didn't look like it was going to let up anytime soon. The low-hanging clouds touched the horizon all around as far as the eye could see. More than likely this meant a tropical storm was moving up the coast. When R.W. reached the office, he would check the forecast.

"What's the word, Roscoe, you get a weather report yet?"

"Yeah, seems a slow moving storm's a brewing along the Georgia coast and head'en our way. I don't think it's reached hurricane status yet ... so far winds have remained steady at 'round forty miles per hour. As the day goes along though, it should pick up. Then on the other hand, it might move on out to sea and spare us. We'll know better this afternoon. I'll keep my ears pealed to the radio."

"Look's like it's gonna be a messy night for the dance."

"Yeah, I believe you're right."

For the remainder of the day, the weather was the news. In as much as police work was concerned, the only calls were for assistance of cars bogging down in the soft wet sand where the drivers pulled off the side of the asphalt. There really wasn't much they could do except pass the calls to the local gas stations and give them directions to the stuck cars. What few filling stations that were on the islands, all had wreckers mainly for this purpose. This was something that had been ongoing for years. To these guys, soft wet sand always meant cold hard cash.

Later in the day, R.W. was called to a fender-bender at Whalebone Junction where one car hit a pooled area of water on the road and hydroplaned into a telephone pole, knocking it down and blocking the road. The driver got a bloody nose from hitting the steering wheel. It took several hours before the county maintenance crew could get there and remove the broken pole. It wouldn't be until Monday before power would be restored to that section of beach. Fortunately, many out of town residents hadn't moved in for the summer so the complaints were light.

By late afternoon, the storm took a turn to the east and headed out to sea. The wind calmed but the rain continued. More than likely it would be gone by the morning sunrise. With little left to do, Roscoe gave R.W. the rest of the late afternoon off to get ready for the dance. He and Sam would finish off the late shift. While R.W. never showed much outwardly emotion, he knew he was excited about taking Claire Belle to the dance.

* * * * * * * *

As R.W. drove to Claire Belle's cottage to pick her up for the dance, he passed by the Casino and could see the place filling up. He saw a lot of men in blues and khakis meaning the local Navy air stations were well represented – and the sailors probably well-oiled. He hoped there wouldn't be any fights. But as long as George was there, that possibility was doubtful.

Claire was at the door and ready to go. They hopped into the car for the three-mile trip. The parking lot at the Casino was already full so R.W. parked in an access area across the street at the base of a very tall sand dune called Jockey's Ridge. Fortunately, the lot had been packed down so cars wouldn't mire in the sand. Though, it was still soft.

Usually when a jazz band was the showcase, a fifty-cent fee was charged for the men but the ladies got in for free. Though for R.W., he never had to pay; he always offered and Rags always refused. After entering and passing through the small foyer, they looked around the game room where the alleyways and the pool tables were all under siege by the military. George was standing nearby in case a cue stick got higher than waist level.

"Let's go upstairs and grab a beer and a table and listen to the band ... okay?"

"Sure, that's what we're here for," said Claire.

The upstairs dance floor was full of kids rhythmically dancing to the beat of the band doing swirls and curls and crashing to the floor.

150

Everybody was having a grand old time. Claire herself quickly embellished the mood and started tapping her feet and moving her hips. She was ready to go.

But, first things first. R.W. wanted to grab a table but all seemed taken. While looking about and not really noticing, John, and another worker, walked from behind the stage carrying a small square table and two wooden folding chairs. He placed them in the back of the room underneath one of the large double windows on the side that would help provide fresh air in a smoky filled room. Finally catching R.W.'s attention, he motioned him over.

"This table is for you and Miss Claire Belle. We stashed it in the back until you arrived. We didn't want anybody else to take it before you got here. Is this okay for you?"

"John, it's perfect. Thanks!"

"Would *ya'll* like a couple of brews?" John asked, humorously picking up on the Southern lingo.

"Sure ... bring us two."

Claire was impressed. To get this kind of attention, she almost felt as though she was out with a big-time celebrity. In a sense, she was, and she was ready to frolic.

R.W. helped Claire off with her raincoat and placed it on a hook on the wall not far from the table. She was wearing a black with white polka dot swing dress with red accent trim along the neckline and a small bow tie between her breasts. To even out the match, she was wearing black and white buckled-strapped leather-healed wingtips.

As far as R.W. was dressed, he wore a clean pair of freshly creased khaki slacks with a lightly pressed white short-sleeved shirt rolled twice at the end. His mother had ironed it that afternoon. And while he didn't wear them often, he put on his black and white saddle oxford shoes that were neatly polished by his son Josh. After a hot shower, a shave, and a splash of Old Spice shave lotion, it was the first in a long time he hadn't been out in public where he smelled like a fried hoecake from Bessie's Café. He felt sure Claire would notice.

John quickly returned to the table with two ice-cold Pabst Blue Ribbon beers and a clean glass ashtray. He knew R.W. smoked but wasn't sure about his lady-friend. Though, it really didn't matter. Rags required an ashtray on every table as it was to help keep the burn marks off the floor.

"Well, I see you're a popular fellow around here. You come here often?"

"Aw, not really ... just every now and then I have a beer at the snack bar. Rags and me go back 'bout ten years. We help each other out. Just like that young feller, John, who brought us the table. I helped him get work here 'bout a month ago. He's just being nice."

"John's a pleasant fellow. He's got good manners."

"Yeah, he does. Have you been here before?" R.W. asked Claire.

151

"Oh ... I've met Jenny down here a few times to drink a beer and play some pinball ... that's about it."

"She's a pistol she is," R.W. remarked trying to be kind.

"Jenny's a little spicy at that, but she likes to have a good time."

"Nosey is what she is." R.W. contended.

"Well, she is the Postmistress of a small county. I guess in a sense she'd know a little bit about everybody and what they're doing ... you think?"

"I suppose it does come with the territory. I reckon you're right. But let's don't talk about Jenny ... how 'bout you. About all I know is you're from Hillsville, Virginia. Is that your hometown?"

"Well ... not really. I was born in Greenville County, South Carolina in 1907. My father worked in textiles. He was a supervisor in an area where they dyed the fabric and yarn. That whole area in Greenville was full of textile mills. One day an opportunity arose for a position in a hosiery mill in Hillsville and he took it. It was owned by a rich Frenchman and he promised my father a lot of things and we moved there. I was still very young ... so really, I consider that my hometown. So, how about yourself? Are you an island native?"

"As a matter of fact, I am. I was also born in 1907. My dad originally worked on the family tobacco farm on the mainland but he tired of it. Somehow he ended up get'en hired on as a fisherman and mov'en to Wanchese over on Roanoke Island. He settled there, met my mom, and the rest is history."

"Did you follow in your father's footsteps?"

"Yeah, I did. Dad ended up owning his own boat, and I worked for him. The sea finally took its toll on him and he had to quit for awhile. He then decided to get out of the business altogether and offered me his boat to continue. But I lost my enthusiasm for fishing. I think I was ready to do something else. Then one thing led to another and the next thing ya know Sheriff Simmons offered me a job as a Deputy Sheriff, and I decided to take it. Can't say as I regret it."

"And, how long has that been ... being a deputy and all?"

"Actually, not all that long ago ... since I think 'round 1938."

"Have you had any worthy cases?"

"Oh, no ... nothing to really speak of. In the wintertime it's purty slow but in the summer months, the out-of-towners come in with their kids and sometimes it can get purty rowdy ... especially on the weekends when Rags brings in the bands ... kind of like tonight you might say. Except, tonight there's more military fellas here than local kids. Usually we expect a little trouble when the sailors' are in town. But Rags does a good job keep'en it under control, plus George is here tonight. As big as he is, well ... nobody wants to be mess'en with him except somebody who's had a snoot full and thinks he can go toe-to-toe with 'King Kong.' That doesn't happen very often, though."

While they continued talking and sipping on their beers, the band was playing some of the great hits of the day and the dance floor was swinging from wall to wall. Claire asked R.W. if he wanted to dance.

"Maybe I ought to've mentioned to ya earlier I'm not very adept to 'jitterbugg'en' ... just can't seem to get my feet going with the beat. But I am much better at slow danc'en."

"Well, to be perfectly honest with you, I'm not very good myself. We'll wait for a slow one to come along," Claire said.

It wasn't much longer after that when the band slowed the pace with the hit *Green Eyes* and then followed that with *Dancing in the Dark*. It was a pace more suitable and enjoyable. After the two songs, the band took a break and Claire Belle and R.W. walked outside and around to the front of the building to get a bit of fresh air. By now the rain had stopped.

Looking out across the street, Claire asked a curious question.

"That's about one of the biggest sand dunes I've ever seen. How tall is it?"

"It depends on the time of season, actually. In the wintertime, it's about eighty feet. In the summertime it's about a hundred feet."

"How's that?"

"Kind of a phenomenon, actually. It depends on the winds. In the wintertime, our prevailing winds come from the northeast and it lowers the sand. Then, in the summertime, the wind changes from the southwest and puts it most of it back."

"No kidding!"

"Interesting isn't it."

"How long has it been there?"

"As long as anybody can remember. I imagine big storms from the past probably picked up the sands from shallow shoals and put it there. They're all up and down the islands. I guess you've noticed ... this is just the biggest one."

"You ever go up there"

"Aw as a kid I did ... not much need go'en up there now. In the summertime I bring Josh and some of the other kids over to play on it. They spend hours up there flying kites and rolling down. I usually have to hose him off before I let him in the house though ... damn sand gets everywhere."

"Doesn't it though! It's hard to keep it out of the cottage."

"Yeah, it's a mess. No doubt about it!"

R.W. took the notion to light up a cigarette. He noticed the clouds had moved out and could see the stars. They continued talking about various subjects trying to get to know each other a little better. For the most part, Claire didn't reveal much about herself, but did open up to one question he asked.

"The owner of the mill my dad worked for had a son the same age as me. We went to the same school and became close friends. After

153

college, we started dating and at some point decided to get married. So that's how I ended up with a French last name."

"What happened to him? Ya'll get divorced?"

"The first few years everything went well. He went to work for his dad, and I taught high school math. We lived in a nice house and had a lot of nice things. But somewhere along the line he got into the booze and became abusive. After that, I wasn't long for leaving him. Then he was killed."

"How's that?" R.W. asked, giving her his full attention.

"He'd been out late one night drinking and playing cards with his buddies as he usually did most nights. On the way home from a card game, he lost it on a curve and plummeted down the mountain. The car blew up. There wasn't much left."

"Well, I'm sorry to hear that. I know it must've been hard."

"I stayed around Hillsville for a few more years teaching. He had a nice insurance policy that paid off well. Then one day, I just decided to leave. Looked on the map and saw this place and thought it'd be a good place to get away to. So far, I've really enjoyed it. The people have all been very nice. I like it here, I really do!"

"Glad you made the choice," R.W. said with a nice smile.

"Thank you! Now, let's go back inside and listen to the band and wait for another slow song. I think we do well with those!"

On the way back inside, R.W. noticed George still standing by the pool tables talking to a couple of the Navy guys drinking beer. They all seemed to be in good spirits and kidding around bringing laughter to the big man.

On the other side of the room near the snack bar, Jenny and her boyfriend Hank Larson were talking to Alfred Winters, the caretaker of the Wright Brothers Monument, and a couple R.W. had never seen before. But for some reason, they looked familiar. He was a tall handsome well-dressed blond fellow with a very pretty lady by his side. They were all drinking beer and seemed engrossed in deep conversation. It was unusual to see Mr. Winters in the Casino at night when there were a lot of people around. He usually just stopped in during the afternoon when it was quieter. But tonight he was there talking and seemingly having a good time. R.W. thought, *"I guess the ol' boy has finally loosened up."*

Claire Belle and R.W. took to their table. John was near and brought each another beer. Tonight he was on top of his game making sure they were comfortable. For something to nibble on, he brought them a large bowl of shelled peanuts. Many of the local folk, who knew R.W. well, stopped by for friendly chatter and introduced themselves to Claire.

After the band played the popular tunes of *Tuxedo Junction, Chattanooga Choo-Choo*, and *Beer Barrel Polka*, Claire and R.W. hit the dance floor when they played *I'm in the Mood for Love, Moon*

154

Glow, and their theme songs *White Star of Sigma Nu* and *Shanty Town* all sung by their female vocalist Helen Young. This time they embraced a little tighter. But it didn't last long. Somehow R.W. slipped and fell on the icy slick floor. With Claire gazing down upon her sprawled out date, all R.W. could do was glance up and laugh.

* * * * * * * *

Later that night in the choppy seas of Quadrant CA79, the Executive Officer, Oberleutnant Peter Staats, went to Kapitänleutnant Hans Vogel's tight quarters.

"Kaleun, it's time we start moving north to our rendezvous point. The weather has calmed and the clouds are gone. We should have a good sighting tonight."

"So we should. How are the seas?"

"They are mildly choppy and there is only a light wind with no spray."

"Gut, gut ... very gut. Tonight we will get a good target. Ja ... I can feel it!"

Chapter 15

With a light swirling northeast wind gently cutting across the undulating island ridges, two nefarious creatures trudged upwards through the brush and grass-covered Kill Devil Hill, on up towards the higher reaches of the Wright Brothers Monument. Carrying with them were two thick heavy woolen pieces of blanket and a small leather case containing the inner workings of the signaling device to message their awaiting target. Tonight's code was of grave importance.

After reconnoitering the area making sure it was clear, they guardedly approached the double metal door. Tonight was moonless and, with acres and acres of white sand, there was still some reflection. Their flashlight was weak. It barely lit the lock.

"You did bring the key with you didn't you?"

"Why would I have the key? Hell, it's only my second time up here. I thought you had it. You had it the last time we were up here!"

"Yeah, and I gave it to you and told ya not to lose it. Remember? Well, where the hell is it?"

"Damned if I know. Maybe I left it in the car's ashtray. I don't remember where I put it. I think I drank too much beer tonight."

"You idiot! Well, go back and look for it! Times awast'en. We ain't got all night."

"Aw stop being so tetchy. I'm tired of it. It's 'round here somewhere....

"Well I'll be ... here it is! I put it in my coat pocket. I guess I just forgot."

"Well then ... open the door!"

"Okay, okay ... here ... it's open, now go on in. I'll be there in a second."

"Where the hell you going?"

"I'm going 'round the corner here an' see a 'lady 'bout a dog.' Just go on in. I'll lock the door when I come back in … all right?"

"All right … all right. Hurry it up! I'd hate like hell to lose this signal 'cause you had'a take a damn leak!"

"Aw keep your britches on. We got time."

Upon reaching the top of the monument, they unloaded the case and began setting their equipment in place. Tonight there was to be a slight change in protocol when sending the coded signal. A second person was required. In the confines of their little island house, they had practiced the sequence. But tonight was the real deal.

"What gave you the notion we needed to do this … to beef up the process?"

"I'm uneasy about the other two beacon lights being shut down for a full minute. There are eighteen flashes that mysteriously go dark and that's enough to cause concern. Besides, I just have an uneasy feeling there's something in the wind and we need to be cautious."

"What's in the wind?"

"Things are just too damned quiet. My usual informant in town has clamed up … says she doesn't know what's going on 'cause everybody's being so quiet around her."

"And your go-to is a she?"

"Yeah, Roscoe's secretary, Rose Ellen. All she's said so far is there seems to be a lot of unusual trips down to the Coast Guard Station, but she doesn't know what the hell it's all about. She's still keeping her eyes and ears peeled to the grapevine while still being careful. She overheard one of the officers' talk'en 'bout a leak and it spooked her."

"You're kidd'en. Rose Ellen! I'll be damned! Hell, I didn't realize she was recruited for this work."

"She wasn't! She knows absolutely *nothing* of what's go'en on or what we're do'en. She's just a sweet little old innocent lady I boned up with to keep an eye on things down at the sheriff's office. She loves to gossip, so she feels like she in on the local action. Nothing more … so you keep it that way."

"Well what about that Guardsman you bribed to keep us informed on the situation down there? Has he paid off yet with any information?"

"Not really. All he's told me so far was they found a dead German sailor float'en up on the beach last week. I don't think he's gonna be much help no how."

"Did ya'll think about trying to bring him into the organization?" Hank asked.

"Aw, we talked about it, but it wasn't going to work. Them Guardsmen down there are thicker than flies hovering horseshit at dinnertime. It would've never worked. But, that's all he's told me so far. I ain't gonna hold my breath for anything exciting."

"You want'a cigarette, Jenny?"

"Hank, I thought you'd never ask ... sure. We're 'bout set up. Let's smoke out on the observation deck here and then we'll go over the procedure one more time whilst we got the chance. We got about twenty more minutes."

The original process for sending the coded signal called for Jenny to stop the beacon rotation at a specified time where the beam of light was pointed directly due east towards its target -- the U-491. She would then quickly and totally black out, with a dark woolen blanket, the two non-essential beacons and then use the manufactured mechanism to flash the code. The signal was so designed and calibrated that all messages could be sent within a forty-second period with the first ten seconds designated as a preparation signal. The remaining five seconds was designed to remove the flapper mechanism, the blankets, and then restart the beacon drum's rotation. It required speed and agility to perform this task in a very short period of time.

This prearranged setup meant that the two nonessential beacons would remain totally dark for the entire one-minute span when in fact they should be flashing eighteen times a minute. To some degree, this was a dangerous proposition because someone beyond the monument with an overtly keen eye might notice the beacon amiss. But because of the location and a lack of populace, it was doubtful that folks were out-and-about at two-fifteen in the morning. With the advent of spring and the summer fast approaching, more and more people were bound for the beach—and possible detection.

Tonight's change in plans had nothing to do with the coded beacon itself but to as accurately as possible time the remaining two beacons to flash at the proper time. This required a second person with the agility to lift the blanket on each light for one second every three seconds to replicate the motion of a flash. This required split second timing with much concentration. At the one-minute mark, the blankets would be removed and Jenny would activate the beacon's rotation mechanism where it would then run at its normal pace. If everything went according to plan, no one would be the wiser.

But one problem still existed—the actual beacon itself. Except for the break in light similar to a flashing Morse code, the light was constantly lit. Because this was the key to sending the message, there wasn't anything that could be done to prevent this from happening; although, to the credit of the German designer, he did have the presence of mind to taper the beam and reduce the spread of light. To allow a suitable amount of luminance from a clear 1000-watt T-20 bulb inside the four-degree Fresnel lens to reach the far away submarine, it was calculated the spread of light could be safely reduced by two-degrees to a two-degree arc. This precise measurement was carefully built into the manual flapper device.

159

The purpose of this function was to reduce the shoreline spread of light that one could see. It was calculated that the Wright Brothers Monument was 3,830 feet to the low tide mark of the Atlantic; and with design information from the current Fresnel lens, it was known to have a four-degree arc of luminance that encompassed 266-feet of shoreline. With a two-degree arc beaming from the top, it was reckoned that only 134-feet of shoreline was openly exposed for detection.

But the more important figure was the distance to Highway 12, the coastal road, and the houses adjacent to the road within that arc. From that distance of 3,096-feet, the two-degree arc was calculated to spread 108-feet of light; a vast reduction from 216-feet. This spread of light only flashed over one fairly large cottage. It was much more likely that someone from this cottage could easily observe the flashes. Fortunately, at this time of year, no one was living there. But there was a cause for concern when the weather warmed and the owners showed up.

"So Hank, have you met your contact yet … the one who gives you the envelope?"

"Yeah, I finally met him. Fellow name of Dale Conner. After finishing work at the terminal one evening, we met up with each other and decided to go for a beer. We're 'bout the same age. He told me his girlfriend, Joy Lund, works in the main shipping office who gathers the information."

"Yeah, I know Joy. I'm the one who got her hooked up with us."

"No kidd'en! Well anyway, she passes the info to Dale in the special envelope and he then gives it to me. Of course, I then pass it on to you with the regular mail. Hell, that's all there is to it! He did say he liked the extra money. Can't says that I blame him."

"Well, the money is good. You know that. One of these days this war's gonna be over and I want'a nice nest egg to fall back on and I ain't gonna get that nest egg retiring on a measly Postmaster salary. I can tell ya that right now!"

"How long you think it'll be 'fore the Americans sue for peace? Six more months?"

"Aw shit Hank, the Americans will *never* sue for peace. Where the hell have you been? You don't remember read'en 'bout the Great War? Uncle Sam's in this for the long haul. Before it's over, ain't one single Jap or heinie gonna be left standing. They're all gonna be dead. Nope, it's gonna take a few more years; but once ol' Uncle Sugar starts get'en his act together, watch out brother! From there on out, it's gonna be a blood bath!"

"You don't take shame for what we're doing?"

"No, hell no! Not me. Look Hank, ya got'a understand. What we're doing is just a drop in the bucket compared to what's already happening out there on the high seas. It's noth'en I tell ya! And besides, the money's just too damn good to pass up. I don't have any shame or guilt. And as far as I'm concerned, the United States brought this whole damn mess on themselves in the first place."

"How you figure that? The Japs bombed us first and then the Germans took notion to jump in our britches. What the hell did America do to deserve that?"

"Hank, you don't get it. First off, the Japs were in a war with the Chinese go'en back into the '30s. Then the Americans sided with the Chinese and lent their support. Following that, we put an embargo against the Japs with oil and scrap metal and such that started hurt'en their economy and shipbuilding. The Japs got pissed-off and bombed Pearl and everywhere else out there in the South Pacific. They probably thought with that little surprise attack, *they* could sue for peace and soon be back to trading again. Boy did they screw up on that one. But so far as Germany was concerned, the US messed up big time by hiding under the pretense of isolationism."

"Iso ... what?"

"Isolationism ... meaning they believed national interest was best served by avoid'en any and all economic and political alliances with other countries. What it amounted to was Uncle Sam stuck his damn head up his damn fanny knowing a problem was a'com'en and didn't want any part of it. When France and Britain failed to stop Hitler in the early days when he was tak'en back the territory that was taken away from Germany in accordance with the Versailles Treaty, they got on a roll for new world dominance. The United States, along with France and Britain, *should've* held Germany's hand to the fire and forced 'em back. But *nooo* ... they didn't want'a get involved! What they didn't know, or just plain ass didn't want'a know, was just how sneaky and whacky that son-of-a-bitch Hitler was.

"When Hitler invaded Poland, it was doomsday for everybody. Both France and England had already avowed support for Poland and when that happened, they had no choice but to declare war on Germany. It took ol' Uncle Sammy 'bout a year to finally pull his head out'a his ass and realize there really was a serious problem a'coming. They knew England could *never* survive a German onslaught and started helping 'em out. Hitler already knew he was gonna fight the Americans sooner or later so he just went on and declared war to get on with it. And that my friend is why we are sett'en up here tonight!"

"Hell ... where'd you learn all that?"

"I kept up with current affairs and tried to figure a way of mak'en a buck doing it. Come on, let's get on back in there and get ready. We got'a go earn a paycheck."

"Damn ... you sure are taking this serious!"

"As well as you should. You keep one thing in mind Hank Larson. The minute you took that money, you became a traitor, a collaborator, and an enemy combatant to the United States of America. No matter how you look at it, from here on out, you ain't never go'en back to the way it was ... and if'n you are ever caught, you're a dead man. Nope, you ain't gonna go to prison and get out later. You're ass is gonna be grassed and put in front of a firing squad. So you better get your butt used to it!"

With the time of reckoning just minutes away, the duo prepared for broadcasting the signal. As practiced before, their harmonized motions were performed to perfection. Upon completion of their act, they carefully replaced the equipment back into the case. Before leaving, they went back to the tiny observation deck and leaned against the retaining wall looking due east towards the U-491. It was too far out for them to actually see it. They lit another cigarette.

"That was purty damn impressive Jenny ... think they received it okay?"

"As long as they were out there and had their glasses peeled this way ... yeah, they should've seen it. At any rate, I *hope* they got it. From what I was told, it was a real important message and to make damn sure there were no screw-ups in get'en to 'em."

"How'd you know it was an important message?"

"Well, let's just say that I know and you don't and leave it at that. There're some things you just ain't privy to."

"You ain't gonna tell me?"

"Nope. None of your business. But I'll tell you this. It's our last message for six days."

"How's that?"

"They're ahead'en out to sea to refuel and take on provisions ... get more torpedoes. I'm sure by now they're just 'bout out'a everything."

"Another sub gonna take their place?"

"Nope. Not unless I hear otherwise."

"Hmmm ... interesting."

"Come on you ol' stud-muffin you. Let's get the hell out'a here. I don't want'a hang around this place anymore. Some idiot might be out and about walk'en his stupid dog and wondering what the hell we're doing up here. Let's get back to my place and drink some beer. I'm still wound-up and ready to go. I got a real hanker'en to loosen your eyeballs! Come Monday though, we'll find out how good we did. Here, let me take hold of them keys. You make me nervous hang'en on to 'em!"

* * * * * * * *

Later the following morning and on a heading of 140 degrees, the U-491 embarked on a thirty-one hour journey far into the Atlantic swells to replenish their exhausted stock on a very empty boat. It was a welcomed relief especially after escaping a near death experience. Both officers and crew were ready for a break. They had been on station for sixty-some days and their nerves were wearing thin.

162

Earlier that morning, after sinking a trio of large and costly military freighters thirty miles east of the Chesapeake Bay, the U-491 was viciously attacked and nearly blown apart by two U.S. Coast Guard cutters that were determined to sink their enemy. Having played cat-and-mouse for nearly six anxious hours, Kapitänleutnant Vogel miraculously escaped the storm. Though, there was serious damage in need of attention. The fifty-some depth charge barrage damaged the port side diesel motor mount causing a wicked vibration; and while there was little concern of structural damage, much of the boat's upper teakwood decking was torn asunder and floated to the surface. It was by far their most harrowing experience of the war.

After Vogel confirmed his kills to *BdU*, the headquarters of the German submarine fleet, which currently was stationed in Lorient, France at the gaudy Kernével Château, they sent him to Quadrant DC6952 to rendezvous with the U-459 supply boat. He was to arrive by 1800 on April 13. It was 548 miles from the mouth of the Chesapeake Bay.

The U-459 was a Type XIV submarine and was specially designed for the purpose of refueling and resupplying the frontline fighting Type VII and IX submarines operating on the East Coast. The idea was to keep them from returning to France and losing precious time. This transporter was commonly referred as a Milk Cow (*Milchkuh*). Aside from carrying two defensive 37-millimeter anti-aircraft (*Flak*) canons positioned on the forward and aft deck of the conning tower and a single 20-millimeter gun on the anti-aircraft platform just behind the tower (known as the *Wintergarten*), it carried no other offensive weapons. After four and a half months of training in the Baltic Sea, this was the U-459's first patrol. It had a company of fifty-three crewmen.

In the built-in bulbous storage tanks, the Milk Cow was capable of refueling eight frontline boats each with fifty-tons of fuel. This was certainly enough to keep them plowing and sinking ships for another forty days. But the real welcomed relief to all the hardened crews was the supply boat's capability to provide them with large baskets of freshly baked bread from a full-blown onboard galley. This was certainly a relief from the stale and moldy bread they had been eating in the past.

The U-459 was commanded by forty-eight year old Kapitänleutnant Georg von Wilamowitz-Möllendorf and was the fifth oldest commander in the active fleet. Because of this, he was specifically transferred from the old warrior U-2, a Type IIA coastal boat, and the second oldest submarine in the fleet, and given the command of this brand new boat. His character as a good and descent leader preceded his reputation and he was summarily promoted to Commander (*Korvettenkapitän*) by the forthcoming June.

Upon arriving in the specified quadrant one hour later than expected, the two boat commanders promptly coordinated their efforts

163

to transfer the fuel, wares, and foodstuffs. Fortunately the seas were calm making the chores less cumbersome; but with portions of missing deck from the *Wasserbombe* explosions, one had to be careful while walking about. Nevertheless, the situation could change at the blink of an eye and Vogel ordered his crew to move with agility.

For the transfer process to occur, the U-459 moved into a position twenty-five meters directly ahead of the U-491 where a towline was then attached to the bow of Vogel's boat. A fuel hose was then floated back to where the crew fished it out of the water and secured it to the fuel inlet pipe on the foredeck. When the diesel fuel entered the submarine, it went directly into a specially designed tank on the outside of the pressure hull that had perforated holes in the bottom allowing seawater to enter. As diesel fuel, which was lighter than water, displaced the seawater thus filling the tank with fuel. When fuel was siphoned off to run the engines, seawater would displace the fuel. This ingenious method was designed to help compensate the ballast when the boat was diving and surfacing.

Once the boats began moving and the transfer of fuel began, the Milk Cow then passed a Manila hemp line back to the other boat using a flair pistol. It was then attached to the conning tower where mesh nets filled with provisions were hooked and dragged back to the boat using a separate line. Because the boat's foredeck was in such poor condition, all provisions had to be moved below deck through the conning tower hatch. This method took longer than expected, but it kept any seaman from dire injury on the ragged deck. For both processes to be completed, it took just over four hours.

While the Milk Cows had the means to carry additional torpedoes, this shipment had none. To receive a full complement of fourteen, Vogel was forced to rendezvous at 1330 the following day with the U-1059 Torpedo Carrier; a Type VIIF submarine that was specially designed just for this purpose. Aside from carrying torpedoes, it also carried provisions but did not have the capabilities of making fresh bread.

The boat was similar in design to Vogel's Type VIIC, but a new section was inserted forward of the control room which contained an extra twenty-four torpedoes arranged in four layers. An additional hatch, with a system of pulleys, was fitted in such a manner to enable the torpedoes to be transferred while at sea. To help accommodate this task, the deck was widened for better footing and control during transfer. On paper, the concept worked well. This transfer was the first to be tried at sea.

No doubt, transferring torpedoes was much more difficult and hazardous than transferring fuel or provisions. Depending on the type torpedo depended on how the torpedo was transferred. The G7a, the compressed air torpedo, had to be wrapped in eighteen lifejackets, and the G7e, the electric torpedo, was laid on top of a life raft. In both cases the torpedo was then floated across to the receiving boat with the help of sailors in the water in protective gear to help keep them from getting injured.

To receive the torpedoes, the collecting boat would lower its bow to whence the torpedoes were floated on top of the deck between the life rails. When correctly positioned, the boat would blow its tanks and rise above the waves. At this point, a system of pulleys and winches would raise the torpedo for entry into the torpedo hatch to its proper position inside the boat. Two torpedoes at a time could be transferred. To say the least, it was a dangerous and very time-consuming process. Performing this procedure at night was, at best, very difficult.

But the biggest key in accomplishing this task was a calm and silky sea. The biggest worry was being detected by an overhead enemy warrior. This was surely the kiss of death because both subs would not have the proper time to submerge for cover. However, with the new rendezvous quadrant just 124 miles south-southwest of their present location and 626 miles due east of the Georgia-Florida line, it was improbable they would be detected.

"Herr Kaleun, what time do you plan on leaving tonight for our rendezvous with the U-1059?" First Officer Staats asked.

"First we need to continue working on our port diesel motor mount and have it stabilized. Fortunately, the spare parts we needed were on the transport and the motormen are working on that now. The Chief has told me they should be finished by 0400. Assuming everything works properly, and is in good working order, we should leave by 0500. It will take us seven and a half hours to reach the quadrant. We should be there with time to spare."

"How long do you think it will take to transfer the torpedoes?"

"I have no idea. This is a new concept altogether and it hasn't been tested at sea, and I've never seen it done. I just don't know how long it will take. If the seas are calm and we are successful, we can return to our mission. If not, we will be forced back to France. But we must give it all we've got. *BdU* will not be pleased if we fail in this transfer. We must make it work ... we must!"

"Aye Kaleun, I have no doubt we will succeed."

The repair of the motor mount was completed by 0330. Having policed the boat of excess trash and then mopped cleaned, all the new provisions were stored. And with the boat being surfaced for hours on end with wide-open hatches, the acrid stench from deep within had virtually dissipated the unpleasant odor and was now relatively fresh to smell.

But with sailors living in and around the pungent odors for months on end, the scent had leached into their clothing and skin causing a hint of the stink to remain. Nonetheless, the situation was better. Now if they could just rid themselves of the baneful smell of diesel-infused air, life in the tube would be just hat more worthy.

165

By 0500, Kapitän Vogel restarted his engines and headed south on a 200-degree heading for Quadrant DC9641 to rendezvous with torpedo carrier U-1059. His engines were nicely purring with no noticeable vibrations. It was a job well performed.

But what couldn't be performed was repairing his deck. Much of the wood around his 88-millimeter canon was ripped from the boat. It would be very difficult to now fire this gun because the gunners had little or no footing. Underneath the planking was a vast array of piping relevant for the operation of the boat whilst it was submerged. With the decking gone, these pipes were exposed as well as the inner pressure hull. While the wood offered little protection, it did offer enough to shield it against the undersea elements. To be properly fixed, the boat would have to return to its U-boat pen in La Pallice. For the moment, that wasn't going to happen.

On April 14 at 1230 hours, the U-491 arrived one-hour ahead of schedule at Quadrant DC9641; the U-1059 was nowhere to be seen. Kapitän Vogel ordered the navigator, Obersteuermann Kurt Heinz, to the bridge, with his sextant, to recheck their sea position. With a clear and pleasantly bright sun, his readings should be true.

After observing his bearings and recording the numbers, his chart book accurately defined his location; he calculated they were at the middle top portion of their quadrant. This meant from there, it was six-miles to the bottom end of the quadrant as each quadrant was a six-mile square.

To some degree, this was purposely designed by Admiral Dönitz when he had his navigators and mathematicians devise the grid. Assuming perfect conditions, it was a mathematical fact that a person's eyes fixed five-feet eight-inches directly above the level of the sea could see three nautical miles to the horizon without atmospheric refraction from thermal deviations imposed by the temperature differences between the air and seawater.

Given this information, a person standing on the bridge of an average U-boat conning tower bridge, approximately twenty feet above the level of the sea, could see the horizon out to six and a half nautical miles. Therefore, if the boat was at the top or side of a specified grid, he could theoretically see to the opposite end of the grid. If the boat was in the center of his grid, he could see three nautical miles to the edges and four and a half nautical miles to the corners. With a good pair of binoculars, there would be no problem sighting a moving boat inside the grid—including the conning tower of a U-boat.

After moving his boat to the center of the grid, Kapitän Vogel had First Watch Officer, Oberleutnant Staats, and the four other on duty watchmen scour the horizon for the U-1059. After thirty minutes of observing and no real sightings, Vogel had his Second Watch Officer, Oberleutnant Josef Brückner, his head radioman, send out a signal and raise the U-1059. Within five minutes, a signal was returned. Oberleutnant Herbert Brüninghaus, the boat's commander, reported he had engine trouble earlier in the day, and he would be delayed. He would arrive by 1745. When arriving, he would immediately set into motion for the transfer of torpedoes. He estimated it would take ten hours as long as the seas remained calm and there were no unforeseen glitches.

"Herr Kaleun, that is not good news. Trying to transfer fourteen 1,400 pound, twenty-three-foot torpedoes at night is not going to be easy," said Staats.

"Ja ... ja, I agree. And with our deck all chewed-up, it will be more dangerous. I'm afraid we might end up with injuries. We've already lost three crewmen. We don't need to lose any more," replied Vogel.

"Ja, that is true. I am sure the watchman that was washed overboard drowned. I'm sorry we didn't have the chance to save him."

"As I recall, it happened during a savage nor'easter just when we were about to receive the coded signal. If we attempted to save him, we would have lost the signal. Ja, it was a shame but the signal was way too important."

"But it was another good kill for the Fatherland. Admiral Dönitz was very pleased! And he was also very pleased with Sunday's kill ... over 32,000 tons of important shipping that did not make it to the England," Staats verified.

"Ja ... pleased. But Staats, I still wonder about our interpreter who took the motorman to shore?"

"Jürgen Oehrn?"

"Ja ... but there is still something unusual about how his raft was returned. As you remember, it was deflated and his life vest was still attached. Something tells me there's more to this. I don't think he was captured."

"But there were indications from shore when he flashed his signal. It looked as though he was apprehended. We talked about that, Herr Kaleun. Do you not remember?"

"Ja, ja, I remember. But he also may have defected. Let us do this. Contact *BdU* and have them follow channels to get a message to our land based SD operative. With what knowledge Herr Oehrn possesses, he may cause us a problem if he has in fact defected. Maybe our operative in America can locate him."

Chapter 16

Fritz Lötz escaped the wrath from the FBI when, on 2 January 1942, thirty-three members of a Nazi espionage spy ring, working inside the United States, were brought to justice and sentenced to 300 years in prison after a lengthy and covert investigation. Fortunately, Lötz had no direct dealings with the man, William Sebold, who was responsible for their capture. He did have some dealings with one of the captured moles, but it had no effect on his own network at the Outer Banks and on the Chesapeake Bay.

After serving in World War I as a machine-gunner on the Western Front, William Sebold left Germany in 1921 to work in industrial and aircraft plants in the United States. Gaining much knowledge and enjoying the culture, he decided upon Americanization and became naturalized in 1936.

Three years later, and before Germany invaded Poland to start World War II, he returned to Germany to visit his mother. Shortly after arriving, he was contacted by the Gestapo, the Secret State Police, regarding his work in the United States. Within days, he was contacted by the Air Division of the Foreign Intelligence Ministry of the Abwehr, a secret German intelligence organization, to further discuss his work. After a lengthy period of questioning, and the fear of reprisals against his family from the Gestapo, he was persuaded to return to America as an espionage agent for the Fatherland. He was then cast into an intense training program whereupon he was instructed on how to prepare coded messages and microphotographs.

Prior to completing the program, Sebold discovered his passport had been stolen. He went to the American Consulate in Cologne, Germany to obtain a new one. While there, he quietly told officials of his forced inducement by the Abwehr to act as a German espionage agent within the United States. He expressed his reluctance to follow their demands and said he would cooperate with the FBI when he returned to America. Upon hearing this, the consulate recommended Sebold complete his training and bring them any information regarding his mission. The consul, in turn, notified the FBI of Sebold's impending arrival and set in motion a plan.

By January 1940, Sebold had completed his training and brought to the consulate various important documents as well as microphotographs containing instructions for preparing codes and detailing the type of information he was to transmit back to Germany. He was then given the name of Josef Klein, a German living in New York City, who was a photographer and lithographer and had the knowledge in building and operating shortwave radio transmitters. It was this man who Fritz Lötz had contacted.

Fritz Lötz was a sales representative with a firm that sold high-end cameras and equipment and traveled all over Europe as well as across the Atlantic to the United States and Canada. Within his industry, he was a well-known experienced salesman with a good head on his shoulders; and because of his out-going personality and friendly disposition, he was well liked amongst his customers. Because of those qualities, he made a good living and had many worldwide contacts.

One day after returning from a trip to the United States in early 1936, he was approached by an operative from the Economics Division of the Foreign Intelligence Ministry of the Abwehr. As all oversea businessmen were obligated to register with the Foreign Trade Office, he was now required to report any interesting subjects he may have observed.

It was at this time that Germany was in a period of rearmament and it became necessary to seek a variety of outside information that could be of interest. Because much of the information already on file with the United States was old and obsolete, it became necessary to amass a new and updated database.

One method of obtaining such information was to seek overseas businessmen to observe the country's infrastructure and any military movements that might include an array of weapons. And while the voyagers were traveling through the many major harbors, they were asked to observe the type of ships, military and civilian, that were coming and going. It was this type of information from businessmen that would help rebuild their overseas database.

At the time of his inquiry, Lötz had no explicit observations to report because he had not been looking for these types of things. But because this was to be an ongoing state of affairs every time he returned to Germany, he planned to be attentive.

Judging by German standards, Fritz Lötz embellished the Nordic features quintessence of the hypothetical master race embodied by the Nazis—Aryan. Standing six-foot-two with sky-blue-eyes and straight combed-back blond hair, he was the epitome of Nazi idealism. While his physical appearance was symbolic of the future German ethnicity, he was not anti-Semitic and did not condone the derogation of Jews. As were many Germans, he was mostly sympathetic and helpless in their plight; but he was afraid to get involved fearful the Gestapo would plunge his pleasureful life into a somber world of misery. He had reckoned himself well in the world of business, and he did not want to lose that standing.

With Adolf Hitler in full control and striving to revive a depressed economy engendered by the Treat of Versailles, the Führer decreed in late September 1936 a "Four Year Plan" to enhance the Fatherland's economy by instituting a program of rebuilding their broken infrastructure and reestablishing their country's resources weaning themselves from the outside dependence of raw materials. This program would put the populace back to work and regain their bygone confidence.

With opened arms and welcomed relief, the public embraced their Nazi leader for guidance back to prosperity. But with hidden truths and well-placed lies, Hitler's Four-Year Plan was nothing more than wily subterfuge to establish self-reliance while he exacted his revenge on the western allied nations that would eventually lead to another destructive war.

The average German citizen envisioned nothing more than a robust plan for recovery. While on the surface, all seemed well. Fritz Lötz had misdoubts as to the practicality of such a plan entrusted to Hermann Göring, a man with nary a sliver of economics background. Göring was Hitler's heir apparent and head of the Luftwaffe.

It was obvious from the git-go that Göring was no match with Hjalmar Schacht, the president of the Reichsbank and minister of economics, whose reputation preceded himself as the foremost expert on economic stability. But because of his constant conflicts with the rotund Reichsmarshal, in 1939, Hitler removed Schacht from those posts. Schacht, knowing Hitler was hell-bent on war, eventually turned to the German Resistance, being careful not to imperil his own life or the well-being of his family.

Fritz Lötz felt the same, but rejected involvement with the Resistance. At thirty-seven years old, he wanted no part of war and was looking for ways to avoid it; yet, still perform some worthy task for the Fatherland to avow his fidelity. While certainly not a man of means, Lötz lived comfortably and wanted that to continue as long as there were ways to make it happen.

171

Having built a pleasant relationship with the Abwehr operative from his many overseas excursions, Lötz contacted him by telephone with an idea he wanted to pursue. He asked for a private meeting to discuss the matter. The agent was a retired World War I submarine captain named Otto Pfeifer living in Bremen. As Lötz lived in Hamburg, just sixty-miles away, it would be an easy commute to the meeting.

Several days later, Lötz made his way to Bremen where he met for lunch the former U-boat Kapitän at his favorite downtown restaurant. After downing a few frothy cold draft beers and discussing the present economy, Lötz proposed his idea.

His plan was to position himself somewhere along the East Coast of the United States where a number of key harbors were vital to overseas shipping. He would, if feasible, invest in a small network of underground operatives who would infiltrate the piers and harbors and collect information on the material being shipped to Europe.

After several more beers, both men perceived that war was probably imminent within the next twelve months and that America would probably help the country at odds with theirs. But because of America's isolationist attitude, as understood by Lötz on his most recent tour, it was doubtful, in his opinion, they would join the fracas.

The meeting ended well without Otto promising Fritz anything more than a follow-up call regarding his plan. He would promote the idea further up the ladder so the powers-to-be could determine the feasibility.

For the remainder of the month and halfway through February, Lötz kept his business travels close to home only traveling to Denmark, Holland, and as far south as Brussels in Belgium. He made no travel plans to any parts of Germany, Southern France, or Switzerland. He didn't want to be far from home when his important call came through—if it was to come at all; but he felt confident.

The looming threat of war was closer and closer. The previous spring, Germany marched on Austria forcibly annexing the state. Later that fall, they occupied the Sudetenland province of Czechoslovakia that included the territories of Bohemia and Moravia that were largely inhabited by ethnic Germans. Up through the end of World War I, it was part of Austria. But rumors swirled. Hitler was now preparing to invade the remainder. Predicting war was a year away was erroneous at best; it now appeared much closer.

On Friday afternoon 24 February 1939, Fritz and his wife, Traudl, were enjoying a pleasant bottle of Armagnac, a French brandy from the Pyrenees foothills, when Otto Pfeifer finally called. He had what he thought was good news. He passed forward Fritz's plan to the head of the Abwehr, Admiral Wilhelm Canaris, who himself had plans of implementing such an operation; but, it was out of his realm of control. Believing it was a workable plan to plant such an operative inside the United States, he passed the idea to a parallel intelligence agency that could make the final call.

[Admiral Canaris took charge of the *Abwehr* (Military Intelligence) in 1935. Later in 1938 the name was changed to *Amt Ausland/Abwehr im Oberkommando der Wehrmacht* (Foreign Affairs/Defense Office of the Armed Forces High Command). Eventually becoming distraught with Hitler and his policies, Canaris secretly joined the Resistance. He was relieved of the Abwehr command in February 1944 to which it was later absorbed into the Ausland SD Department VI. Later, he was implicated in the plot to assassinate Hitler and was hanged on 9 April 1945. *Ed.*]

That parallel organization was called the *Sicherheitsdienst* (SD, Security Service) and was the intelligence service for the *Schutzstaffel* (SS, Protective Squadron) and the *Nationalsozialistische Deutsche Arbeiterpartei* (NSDAP, Nazi Party). The SD was also considered a sister organization of the *Geheime Staatspolizei* (Gestapo, Secret State Police).

There was a multitude of police and intelligence organizations established for the security of Germany. Because the organizations were so spread out, it was determined in 1939 to group them under the auspice of the *Reichssicherheitshauptamt* (RSHA, Reich Central Security Office). Each individual organization became a department within the RSHA and then partitioned further into sections. The SD was positioned under Department VI (Foreign Intelligence and Espionage) and further segmented to a branch called *Ausland* SD. Under this branch there was Section D (American Espionage). The Ausland SD was the civilian foreign intelligence of the Third Reich. Fritz Lötz would deal directly with Department VI, Ausland SD, and Section D.

[The organization mostly responsible for the annihilation of Jews in Europe was the Gestapo of Department IV, Section B, Subpart 4 and headed by Adolf Eichmann. After the war, he was captured and later escaped unrecognized from an American internment camp to Argentina. The Israeli Secret Service later found him in South America and returned him to Israel where he was placed on trial, found guilty, and hanged on 31 May 1962. *Ed.*]

Burckhard Heckler, the operative of Section D, wanted to personally meet with Lötz in Berlin on Monday morning February 27. Otto, attending as the Liaison Officer with the Abwehr, agreed to meet with Fritz on Sunday in Hamberg where they could drive together the 156 miles to Berlin. They would rent a hotel room for that Sunday night so both would be fresh for the early morning meeting.

The SD was largely manned by professionals who did their jobs mechanically and methodically and rarely knew the identities of other SD agents in the field. This was purposely designed so collaboration could be kept to a minimum in case an operative was identified and captured. If one was captured, it wouldn't necessarily compromise the whole group.

Once a person was chosen to be an operative in the field, after having their background fully investigated, their individual status was then divided into five classes: V-men (*Vertrauenslente*) who were considered to be confidents; A-men (*Agenten*) were to be trusted; Z-men (*Zubringer*) were considered informants; H-men (*Helfershelfer*) were secondary informants acting for selfish motives; and U-men (*Unzuverlässige*) who were considered corrupt and unreliable and had to be watched.

At the Berlin meeting, Heckler was duly impressed with the camera salesman and his background. Through a previous investigation, it was determined he was an exemplary citizen of the German State even though he had not joined the Nazi Party. That was a cause for concern. For Fritz to advance within the ranks, he was required to join. Secretly he did not administer to The Party's beliefs but never voiced his opinions. To satisfy the requirements, he would join with reservations.

And there was, of course, the concern of stationing a novice agent in a foreign country for his first official job. Nevertheless, after he joined the Nazi Party, it appeared he could qualify for such an assignment based on his records.

The one observation that impressed Heckler the most about Lötz was his knowledge of the English language and the lay of the American landscape. Another good quality was his physical appearance; he could easily fit into American society as one of their own. While Lötz had a good selection of business contacts, it was doubtful their use would fit into his operation. He would have to recruit disgruntled and potentially disloyal Americans from within the states.

At the end of the meeting, which lasted most of the day, Heckler told Lötz he would reply within two weeks. He gave no indication, one way, or the other, as to his thoughts on the matter. Fritz and Otto then motored to a fine restaurant where they imbibed on French wine and feasted on German cuisine. They decided to stay the night and leave the following morning. In Otto's opinion, he felt Fritz performed well in speaking his mind and conveying his thoughts. He had a good feeling his newfound buddy was soon destined for operational status in the United States.

Word finally arrived that Lötz was accepted to become a foreign operator with the Ausland SD and would be classified as an "A-man—trusted." He was to return to Berlin and enroll in a lengthy training session learning the tricks of the trade. It was determined that, when he got to the East Coast of the United States, he was to establish a residence, with his wife, in an apartment located conveniently within the area of the Chesapeake Bay as this was a region where the SD wanted a spy. It had been earlier established, in other types of communiqué, that Hampton Roads was an important naval harbor. If war broke out, there would be a hubbub of activity in this area.

For Lötz's cover, his company, with the urging of the SD, would set him up in business and provide the cameras and photographic equipment necessary for a retail store. This was prearranged by the SD without his knowledge. When he suitably arrived and established his residence, he was to arrange to rent a small retail space in a privately owned building to sell these photographic wares as a ruse to conceal his real intentions.

Not only was Lötz fluent in English, though with an accent, he was also fluent in Dutch because a substantial amount of his customers were in the Netherlands and Belgium. And for his final disguise, he was assigned a new persona as an entrepreneurial Dutchman and given the name Arnold von Stapele. A new passport, and all other relevant papers, would be issued prior to his departure. His wife's persona would be known as Aleta. She was not considered an actual operative but merely to help establish the ruse and provide support for her husband.

For his link back to Europe, Lötz's main contact would be in Berlin with a secondary contact in Amsterdam. He would be able to communicate to these associates by overseas telephone and speak in coded language lest the line be tapped. If the lines to Europe were severed, his third contact was stationed in England. It was believed that, with these three contacts so spread out, he should be able to connect with one. If by chance these resources failed, he was to reach Josef Klein, an operative with the Frederick Duquesne underground network in New York, and communicate from there back to Germany.

Josef Klein was a photographer and a lithographer who had built a short wave radio for communication to Germany. With his background in photography, it was not likely to raise a question if they met. But Lötz was told to use this means only as a last resort and only in an emergency.

By August 1939, Fritz and Traudl were prepared for their voyage. They packed their clothes and several cherished items and withdrew all their personal savings in the amount of 35,910RM and soon thereafter converted it to British pounds equaling £7,182. Lötz's company had prepacked numerous large containers of wares that would travel with them.

For the trip to America, the SD made arrangements for them to travel on the small French ocean liner *Winnepeg*. It was an old ship built in 1918 and originally named *Jacques Cartier*. It was scheduled to arrive in New York on Friday the first day of September. From there, they were to purchase a car and travel to Virginia and the Chesapeake Bay. The SD had given them £60,000, to be converted to American dollars when they arrived, so they could purchase necessary items, locate to a modest apartment, and rent space in a building for his new

175

business. The rest of the money was to build a small network of infiltrators in and around the harbors of Hampton Roads. But his first concern was establishing themselves in the community keeping a low and modest profile. He had to be careful in how he spent the money.

The timing of their arrival in America was unexpectedly good as far as their situation was concerned. After arriving in New York, they read the following day in the newspapers and heard radio broadcast reports that Germany had invaded Poland; and two days later Great Britain, France, and Canada declared war on Germany; the Second World War had started. For the moment, they were out of harms way; nonetheless, Fritz Lötz, now known as Arnold von Stapele, had a job to perform and needed to focus on that. He had to prove his worth.

By the end of September, they found a nice small two-bedroom apartment in the town of Norfolk on the south side of the James River, which flowed into the very southern end of the Chesapeake Bay. The river actually formed a harbor and this was known as Hampton Roads. Fritz had previously researched the entire area finding this section to be conducive in starting their operation. He also discovered Norfolk was where the United States Navy had a large flotilla of warships. The Norfolk Naval Station was one of the oldest of the American Navy.

By the end of December, Fritz found a small building where he could set up shop to sell his wares. Traudl would assist him in the store. He didn't need to spend much money as the space he rented had previously sold jewelry and much of the specialized displays he needed were already in place. He planned to keep the little shop modest.

During the last three months of 1939, a great deal had happened in Europe: In early October, Hitler offered peace to the Allies and they refused; in early November, Hitler escaped an assassin's bomb at the Bürgerbräu Keller in Munich after giving a vociferous speech on British perfidy; and in late November, Russia attacked Finland and was expelled from the League of Nations.

And in the following six months of 1940, it was going to get worse for the other European nations: In January 1940, Britain began rationing; in February, Jews were being deported from Germany; in March, Finland made peace with Russia becoming an Ally, and a German submarine infiltrated Scapa Flow sinking Britain's famous Revenge-class battleship, the 620-foot *HMS Royal Oak* (08); in April, the Nazis invaded Denmark and Norway; in May, Belgium, Luxembourg, and the Netherlands, including Holland, all capitulated; and in June, France was invaded and occupied. The world was now truly at war; but where were the Americans?

During these past six months, Fritz set about observing the Hampton Roads harbors and all its activities. At first he took his best camera and his beautiful wife out and about the area photographing her with the Chesapeake Bay and its naval infested harbors as her backdrop. This, at first, seemed a good ploy without raising questions, but he knew this tactic could not last forever.

During this ploy, Fritz and Traudl met many of its citizens who were friendly and talkative, but they met nobody of interest. He needed a closer view to the workers in and around the docks. Even though he had yet to find a worthy prospect, he had gathered a significant amount of intelligence to send back to Germany.

There was an organization within United States that was made up of ethnic Germans who were marked by a pro-Nazi stance. It was called the German American Bund and was headed by Fritz Kuhn. They disseminated their propaganda, relating to their anti-Semitic and anti-Communistic views, through published magazines and glossy brochures. They even organized demonstrations demanding the United States remain neutral in the European conflict. Because of their radical and unpopular stance, they found themselves continually at odds with the general population.

This organization was not particularly appealing to Lötz, but he thought there might be a chance to recruit somebody for his network. When a rally was announced in New York City, he decided to look and see for himself what this organization was really all about. As his disguise, he took one of his cameras and carefully paraded about as a newspaper photographer. By doing so, he was able to close-in on the action and talk to its members.

After a tiresome day at the rally photographing and talking to its members, Lötz realized this radical group was far too left for his wants and needs; he really saw no fit for any of its members within his organization. What he desired were low-profiled individuals with quiet socialist beliefs. Surely in the landscape of America there was someone to fit his criteria. But where, he didn't know.

* * * * * * * *

During the 1930s, the United States passed a series of neutrality laws with the aim of keeping themselves from war. Such legislation prohibited the trading or loaning to belligerent countries. But with the outbreak of war in 1939, Congress enacted a new law requiring belligerent nations, including Great Britain and France, to purchase arms only on a cash-and-carry basis. It was appearing that, no matter how hard the United States was trying to stay out of war, all indications were they were heading straight for it.

By the summer of 1940, Britain began purchasing American made arms to replenish their losses when their British Expeditionary Force retreated to the shores at Dunkirk, France in late May and early June. Fortunately, a large fighting force of men escaped. But their armor was destroyed and their military might was weakened.

By the first of July 1940, German U-boats began operating in the North Atlantic routes sinking American and Canadian freighters going to England to resupply their needs. This information caught Fritz's eye, and he began paying closer attention to the actions in all the harbors. It was now becoming critical and he needed to find some help. Germany's conquest for world domination was developing sooner than he had expected. Even though he had made several attempts at recruitment, all had failed for one reason or another. At the time he hadn't felt pressured—now he was.

* * * * * * * *

One pretty Sunday morning in August 1940, and purely on a whim, Fritz and Traudl decided on a picnic to clear their cluttered minds. Through a friendly neighborly chat, they heard of a beautiful section of North Carolina beach where the sand was as pure as freshly fallen snow. To them, this was the place to go. With a basket full of goodies, and two bottles of wine, they headed to the reaches of the Outer Banks.

Once crossing the Wright Memorial Bridge over the Currituck Sound, they continued south along the narrow coastal road. The scenery was dazzling and it never seemed to end; a beautiful blend of pearly white sand melding into the deep malachite green colored sea so effervescent against a light powdery-blue sun-swept sky. It was a dream for any artiste. However, the view dissolved the further south they drove; they happened upon a smattering array of cottages, stores, and long ocean piers. Nevertheless, it was still the scène à faire.

But what they didn't see were any strands of trees. With a sizzling hot sun on a pleasant summer day, a picnic in the open without any shade would not be a pleasurable affair. But what they did see, to the west and across the Roanoke Sound, was a large green island with plenty of trees. They continued driving south until finding a passage to the island—Roanoke Island.

Following the road from across the bridge, they turned north at a junction and headed into Manteo. While slowly passing through the downtown waterfront area, they happened upon a constable. It was Deputy Sheriff R.W. Scoggins on his Sunday morning foot patrol. They explained their wish to quietly picnic and were seeking a place with trees. After a brief and friendly chat, R.W. directed them to the north end of the island where there could find all the grass and foliage they desired. The deputy wished them well, and they drove off.

It was indeed a lovely place just as the constable had described. They found a grassy open spot near a shallow sandy shore overlooking the tranquil Roanoke Sound where the view was the essence of heaven. Here they unfolded their blanket beneath a shady grove of trees and opened a bottle of wine. It was a wonderful place to relax and unwind the muddled mind.

After refreshing their thoughts and enjoying the beauty, they packed their basket and headed for home. After wending their way through town and back to the barrier islands, and driving north up the coastal road, by happenstance they noticed a very large grassy knoll topped with a very large stone monument. The structure gave the appearance of a large art deco vertical wing preparing for flight. How they missed it going south was in itself a downright mystery. But for whatever the reason, they noticed it now.

With time on their hands and curiosity on their minds, they turned left off Highway 12 onto Colington Road and drove the one-half mile to the structure's entrance and then to a small sandy parking lot located on the east-side base of the mound. They left the car and puffed their way the ninety-feet to the top of the dune. It seemed so unusual to have such a massive stone structure in an area so desolate of people.

Upon reaching the top, and realizing the triangular edifice was considerable larger than it appeared from below, Fritz was astounded to discover that this was the birthplace of aviation and the monument was a memorial to the brothers Wilbur and Orville Wright who were the first ever to take mechanical flight. This was in fact the exact location in which their feat occurred just thirty-seven years before— the year he was born in 1903. He quickly realized this structural icon was not only a monument to a nation—but a monument to the world.

After slowly walking around its base mesmerized by its mass, an older gentleman suddenly appeared from behind the south side of the monument. He briefly startled the couple. He had been inside the structure making a minor repair and quietly exited one of the large heavy double metal doors to the rear.

Introducing himself as Alfred Winters, the monument's caretaker, he casually chatted with the couple explaining the various details of the structure. He then cordially invited them inside for a personal guided tour to the top. He thought they might enjoy the view from the top.

And that they did and were amazed at how far they could see. But Alfred chuckled explaining they could see no further than eighteen miles out to sea. Because of the curvature of the earth and their height above sea level from the observation deck where they were standing, approximately one hundred and fifty-eight feet at eyelevel, that was the distance to the horizon. Nevertheless, the view was exquisite. They could even spot, with a little neck bending, their picnic area six miles away across the Roanoke Sound to the west.

After slowly descending the monument via its narrow metal spiral staircase and narrow concrete and granite steps, they went to the outside on the patio area and sat atop the small wall that acted as benches that were part of the tower's star base. They continued talking.

Fritz, introduce himself as Arnold von Stapele and explained that he and his wife, Aleta, were from Holland now living in Norfolk where they had opened a small retail shop selling cameras and equipment. With the Nazis currently occupying the Netherlands, they feared they would never see their homeland again.

After ten minutes talking about the Nazi regime, Alfred explained his views on National Socialism. He then went into a monologic diatribe that he was a retired political science professor from one of the larger state universities. Because of his adverse political viewpoints in promoting the totalitarian beliefs of the National Socialist German Workers Party (the Nazi Party), the university felt his views created entirely too much controversy and suggested he retire before being fired. He reluctantly did so with considerable regret. However, he still believed that one day the United States' capitalistic government would eventually implode and become a socialistic state.

It was only by happenstance that a former student, who was also the previous caretaker of the monument, helped him secure this job. As the caretaker, Alfred was responsible for keeping the rotating beacon light lit and the double metal doors locked. If the power went out, it was his responsibility to engage the gasoline-powered generator located in the small bunker-like granite building at the base of the steep south side slope of the mound. While sitting atop the wall, Alfred pointed towards the building that could easily be seen from where they were sitting.

It was an interesting turn of events. Even though Fritz had joined the Nazi Party only to secure his job, he thought he may have found an individual who might fit the bill for working in his network. But how he was going to use him was another matter. They continued talking with a very hot afternoon sun bearing down upon them.

To get away from the heat, Alfred casually suggested they continue talking at his cottage, which he pointed to on Colington Road only three hundred and seventy-five yards behind the monument, where they could sit inside his screened in porch and drink iced tea. Beginning to feel comfortable around Alfred, the couple accepted his offer and spent the rest of the afternoon enjoying each others company.

Over the next several months, Fritz and Traudl visited with Alfred as often as they could to squabble over politics and quibble about the war. And for a change of pace, they talked about angling as Alfred had learned to surf fish. He also learned to prepare and cook his catches and on many occasions he would light up his fire pit and cook his morning catch-of-the-day. Fritz always brought at least two bottles of wine.

* * * * * * * *

One day in early April 1941 the following year, Fritz received a disconcerting message from the Ausland SD acknowledging they wanted him to start sabotaging the heavily ladened military freighters inside the harbors before they could set sail to England. It was an order well beyond his means; he became quite nervous. While the German U-boats in the North Atlantic were already destroying and disrupting the freighters, far too many were still getting through. As England was beginning to run out of money, the United States, the month before, passed the Lend-Lease Act allowing more matériel to be shipped to the island. Something had to be done to slow this down.

In June, there was a major news story that rocked the nation. Thirty-three members of the Frederick Duquesne German spy ring, secretly operating in New York, were arrested when a swarm of FBI agents pounced on their organization. It was reported that William Sebold, a German acting as a counterspy, was directly responsible for their arrest. While Fritz had no direct dealings with anyone from this organization, he had introduced himself to Josef Klein. Fortunately, Lötz gave no significant information that could possibly connect him to the ring. Though, for safekeeping, he stayed low and kept out of sight. After a fretful two weeks, he realized he had escaped implications. But during this time, he developed an idea to sink the freighters.

Instead of sabotaging the freighters at port, why not let them leave the safety of the harbors where they could be exposed to German torpedoes at the mouth of the bay. If Fritz could find a way to identify the targeted ships in port and relay that information to an already awaiting submarine, then the possibility of that freighter being sunk would be that much more enhanced.

Because of his inexperience with explosive and trying to build a local network of traitors willing to perform such tasks inside a well-protected area with the chances of capture accelerated, that idea did not come to fruition. It was better to plant individuals clandestinely inside the shipping operation as opposed to exposing someone on the outside operations. The idea seemed plausible. But how could he get the signal to the U-boat without detection? Radio transmissions from the shore to the U-boat surly would be monitored causing warships to hide in waiting within the kill zone.

After contemplating the idea for several days, Fritz came up with a communication idea that might just work. But first he had to return to the Outer Banks and see Alfred Winters.

The following Sunday, Fritz visited alone with Alfred at his cottage. By now Fritz knew the penchant of Alfred's political philosophies and believed he might be willing to help. Getting straight to the point, Fritz revealed his true disposition, but not his true

181

identity, as a foreign espionage agent working for the Ausland SD stationed in Germany. His plan was to build a small network of agents to work for the Fatherland with the sole purpose of disrupting American shipping departing the Chesapeake Bay. It was imperative to forestall the supplies going to England.

Fritz outlined his plan explaining he wanted to use the beacon light atop the Wright Brothers Monument to send specially coded signals to an awaiting submarine positioned off the coast. Those signals would broadcast specific information as to which ships needed destroyed. Alfred would be responsible for allowing access to the monument in the wee hours of the morning. As further details developed, more responsibility would be doled to Alfred.

Fritz's part was to devise the codes and a flapper device, along the lines of an Aldis lamp, so it could easily fit over one of the three-sided Fresnel lens. This would allow a Morse code type signal to be sent. The codes, of course, would have to be developed, studied, and learned. But with his training in codes and his expertise with cameras and how they worked, he felt confident he could adequately design a mechanism that could send the signals.

Alfred mulled the matter in little time and readily accepted the challenge. To symbolize the release of his pent-up state of mind, he brought from the kitchen an unopened bottle of wine that Fritz had brought a month before. For now, Alfred had the opportunity to exact his revenge and prove his political theories.

While drinking their wine, Fritz questioned Alfred if he knew of anyone willing to help with his plan. He related that some former students, who had developed similar ideas to his, might show an interest but had since moved away; he felt it unwise to contact them. But he felt there was someone on the island who might be right for a job if the money was good. He considered her as an uncompromising self-serving individual who lacked emotion and had no allegiance. Her name was Jenny Smith—the Postmistress of Dare County.

The following week, Fritz contacted the Ausland SD that he had started working on a complex plan to disrupt the American shipping. The SD believed his scheme was doable. They would contact Admiral Dönitz to make arrangements for a special submarine mission. The codes needed routing as soon as possible so the SD could train an agent, to be positioned on the submarine, to receive and decode the signals.

By mid-August 1941, the flapper device was finished. Fritz had taken his detailed drawings to a small metal workshop where his design was carefully crafted. It was so meticulously devised that it could easily be taken apart and stored inside a businessman's briefcase. Fritz, again disguised as a photographer, told the employee, who was manufacturing the device, that he had specially designed this piece of equipment to control the lighting inside his studio. The employee was none the wiser as to what he was really making.

Through his earlier training in Berlin at the SD Headquarters, Lötz methodically developed the special codes. He took them to Alfred and to Jenny; who subsequently had agreed to join the network for a healthy sum of money. Alfred would be responsible for coding the manifest for transfer and Jenny would be responsible for its conveyance.

Earlier Jenny had provided the name of a lady, Joy Lund, who was working in the main shipping office in Norfolk that was responsible for the manifest of outgoing ships. With knowledge and accuracy, she could properly identify and pinpoint the specialty cargo. Her boyfriend, Dale Conner, who worked on the docks loading the ships, would deliver the manifest to the Outer Banks contact, Hank Larson—the intercity mail carrier to Manteo. The Hampton Roads network had mostly been established.

The only remaining chore left to do was transferring the codes to Germany. Because of their complexity, it was impractical to relay them by telephone or wireless; so he contacted his Ausland SD agent in Germany saying he was sending them to his contact in England. The codes would be packaged in a specially prepared non-descript envelop. He wanted his agent aware it was on its way.

* * * * * * * *

As all types of ships were still being torpedoed in the vast North Atlantic, there was concern the communiqué might not make it to England. Nevertheless, that was the chance that had to be taken. If within two weeks it had not arrived, Lötz was to send another package. There simply was no other way.

Even though Germany didn't declare war on the United States until 11 December 1941, an undeclared war between the two countries was already in the making. Not only were U-boats targeting belligerent nations but also American merchant ships and destroyers. On 21 May 1941, the U-69, commanded by Kapitänleutnant Jost Metzler, torpedoed the freighter *Robin Moor* off the African coast after ordering its crew and passengers away from the ship. This was the first American freighter sunk prior to the United States entry into war. It wasn't the last.

The following month, President Roosevelt froze Axis funds in the United States and ordered German consulates closed and their diplomats expelled. On that same day, the U-203, commanded by Korvettenkapitän Rolf Mützelburg, stalked the 573-foot World War I New York-class battleship *USS Texas* (BB-35) south of Iceland. It was unable to sink her.

On August 18, the U-38, under Kapitänleutnant Heinrich Schuch, sent two torpedoes into the unarmed and unescorted Iceland-bound U.S.–Panamanian freighter *SS Longtaker* sinking her within a minute. Twenty-four of the twenty-seven crewmen drowned.

Early the following month on September 4, the U-652, commanded by Oberleutnant Georg-Werner Fraatz, using his hydrophone sound equipment and not raising the periscope, fired two torpedoes at the 314-foot Wickes-class destroyer *USS Greer* (DD-145) missing with both. The *Greer* in turn began chasing and depth charging her attacker. After three hours, the submarine herself escaped.

Seven days later, and on the same day Roosevelt delivered his "Shoot on Sight Speech," the U-105, under Kapitänleutnant Georg Schewe, sank the U.S.–Panamanian freighter *Montana* carrying lumber from Wilmington, North Carolina to Reykjavík, Iceland killing eighteen of twenty-five crewmen. She was unescorted; that was about to change.

Six days later, and for the very first time, five U.S. Navy destroyers began escorting eastbound convoys all the way to England; it had little effect. On September 20, the U-552, commanded by Korvettenkapitän Erich Topp, sank the cargo ship *Pink Star* going to Liverpool, England killing thirteen of her thirty-five crew. Up until now, all ships sunk had been merchant ships. That changed in the middle of October.

The 348-foot Gleaves-class destroyer *USS Kearney* (DD-432), reinforcing a slow fifty-two ship east bound convoy, was attacked by a Wolfpack. One of three torpedoes from the U-568, commanded by Joachim Preuss, slammed into its hull forward of the boiler room exploding and ripping through the deck. Eleven sailors were killed and were America's first war casualties. Fortunately the ship did not sink and was towed to safety for repairs. But that did not happen to its sister ship.

The 314-foot Clemson-class destroyer *USS Reuben James* (DD-245) on October 23 sailed from Newfoundland with four other destroyers as convoy escorts. On October 31, and nearing the mid-Atlantic, she maneuvered between an ammunition ship and a known U-boat Wolfpack. At 0530 that early morning, Korvettenkapitän Topp and his U-552 sent one torpedo into her port side, forward of the magazine compartment, and ignited her ammunition. The ship instantly exploded splitting her in half with the bow section quickly going to the bottom. When the stern section sank five minutes later, the depth charges, stored inside its hull, exploded killing most of the survivors in the water. With a crew of 144, only forty-four were rescued.

For the next month and up until Germany and Italy declared war on the United States on 11 December 1941, four more tankers and cargo ships were mercilessly sunk. But now that America was in the war, a new plan of attack was on the agenda.

* * * * * * * *

When Admiral Dönitz was approached in late summer by the Ausland SD about stationing a submarine on the East Coast for the sole purpose of receiving specially coded signals and directing it to heavy military cargo, Dönitz was intrigued and receptive to the idea. This he believed could be incorporated into an arrangement he had already devised. His only impasse, in implementing the plan, was to get permission from Hitler and his own commander, Grossadmiral Erich Raeder, to approve the scheme.

A year before, Admiral Dönitz had visualized a bigger and faster flotilla that could transit the Atlantic and position themselves on the Eastern Coast to sink the freighters going to England. Unfortunately, at the time, his idea was rebuked. It was believed that war should remain on the ground and in the air. But with the United States forced into the war, the situation had drastically changed.

With courage and persistence, Dönitz successfully argued his point that his operation, and that of the SD, could be successfully accomplished. Given that most of his current ninety-one submarines were already in use, he found a small group of five long-range Type IX boats that could set sail on Christmas Eve. The SD, requiring more time for preparation for the qualified code reader, asked Dönitz for time. He agreed and the sixth submarine would not sail until the third week in January 1942.

When the U-491 arrived on the American coast and sank her first tanker on Saturday night February 14, they immediately prepared themselves to receive their first coded signal at 0215 the following day. Everything went according to plan and the first heavily laden military freighter, leaving the Chesapeake Bay, was mercilessly sunk.

By April 12, she had spent her last torpedoes. To resupply their food, ammo, and fuel they would relax from the kill zone for one week. Their next scheduled signal was planned for 0215 Monday April 20.

"Jenny, I just got word our U-boat has been reloaded and is now back to full strength. They should be in position within the next two days. I understand from our Norfolk contact a very large shipment is in the works. Are you ready?"

"Well hell Alfred, you know I am. I ain't missed one yet. You bring me the damn paperwork, and I'll be ready. In the meantime, I'm gonna go drink a beer! Want'a join me?"

Chapter 17

On this dull gray overcast Sunday afternoon, the cold green waters of the Atlantic Ocean were wildly swirling with abnormally high breakers uncharacteristically crashing onto the white sandy beaches of the Outer Banks. Somewhere, out-and-about in the vast open sea, many miles east, a vicious storm was a brewing.

But, in the far reaches of a calm and crystal clear blue western sky, the setting sun vigorously threw its vibrant rays beneath the gloomy clouds turning the landscape into a variety of vivid colors aimlessly stretching far and wide. It was this spiritually inspired view that signaled the end to another glorious day.

Heading east across the Wash Baum Bridge towards Bodie Island and the township of Nags Head, R.W. was again mesmerized by the vibrant colors prancing off the windblown whitecaps of the Roanoke Sound. This awe-inspiring picture confirmed his already emotionally charged spirits. For, this afternoon, he was on his way to Claire Belle Charboneau's cottage for dinner and drinks and maybe a peck on the cheek. But, more importantly, and for the very first time, it was a chance to be alone with the enigmatic woman that caused his heart to flutter. But the murky question echoing throughout the back of his mind was entirely not clear. *"What is she thinking?"*

After two months of casual courtship and nary a kiss, Claire, suddenly and unexpectedly, while serving R.W. a late Friday afternoon chicken salad sandwich, invited her friend to dinner. Seemingly bewildered and caught off-guard, and trying his best from slipping off the stool and crashing headlong into the adjacent magazine rack, the deputy heartily accepted the invitation. He promised to bring a bottle of wine. Claire, smiling of joy, was blissfully delighted and was looking forward to regaling her friend.

After the Friday invitation and heading to the office, R.W. was walking on air. In a sense, that was a good. Had he not, he would have stumbled on the same set of courthouse steps he had taken a thousand times. His mind was not focused on work. It was focused on Claire. He pondered long and hard and reminisced.

"Well I be dog. If that just don't beat all! Hell, that's the second time she's asked me out. The first time was to take her to the Casino for the dance. Of course, I was planning on asking her first ... but she beat me to the punch. I guess in a sense, that sort of was a special night. But since then, I've been asking her ... at least to a few movies. Had her over for dinner at Mom and Dad's a few times ... but you know how that goes.

"Been sometime since Emily Mae up and left ... and after that I just really haven't had that much desire to go hunt'en for somebody whether it be temporary or permanent. It all just seems so futile. If'n I do go to rush'en in to something, that can only end up causing a lot of worthless pain ... naw, I don't want'a do that.

"Ol' George now, he said he'd discreetly go with me to Elizabeth City, but I reckon too many soldiers and sailors would've already been that route long before me. Naw, my urges ain't been that strong. Nope.

"But this Claire Belle now ... she is something else! Yes sir, no doubt about it. Now this here is a lady ... and I do mean lady! She's 'bout the sweetest thing I ever met or even laid eyes on ... damn near like a goddess! And that's my problem. Hell, she ain't a goddess. She's human and got human needs ... just like me.

"I tell ya what I'm gonna do. I'm gonna take each moment as it comes. And then the next moment and the moment after that. And when I run out of moments, well ... I'll just start over again with new moments!"

Upon reaching Claire's cottage, R.W. grabbed his bottle and a small bouquet of violets he had slyly picked from his neighbor's flower garden. After closing the door of his car, he looked to the west to savor, one more time, the fading glow of sunlight that had so dramatically painted a portrait of beauty. After further etching the view in his mind, he ambled beneath the cottage, past a shiny new trashcan, and up the steps to her screened front door. Already standing on the deck, and gazing at the choppy seas, Claire welcomed her guest with a warm and open smile.

"Well, hello there R.W.! It's so good to see you again."

"Howdy there Miss Claire! Sure is a pretty sunset today. Ya happen to glance back to the west and see all them purty colors danc'en 'round on those clouds."

"Yes, I did ... just not too long ago. I believe it's one of the prettiest sunsets I've ever seen. We had some pretty ones back in the hills of Virginia, but I believe this one tops all the others I've ever seen."

By now, R.W. had walked up and onto the deck. In his left hand was a brown crumpled sack. In the other, which was hidden behind his back, held the small bouquet of flowers. Claire curiously looked at him.

"And what do you have behind your back? Claire asked quizzically.

Pulling his arm from behind, he presented her with the violets.

"Oh, R.W. ... these are so pretty! Here, let me have them, and I'll put them in a vase of water. My, these are fresh!"

"Yeah, they're pretty fresh!"

"Well, I hope you didn't leave any footprints! May I ask..."

"No! And let's just leave it at that! No harm was done. Besides, I mowed her lawn last week on my day off, and she said I could have some if'n I wanted to purty-up my house. But, I think they'll purty-up your place a whole lot better!"

"Well thank you R.W.! That's very sweet of you. Let's go inside and I'll put 'em in water. What have you got in the other hand? *Please* tell me it came from the store," Claire asked as they walked inside.

"Well, sort of."

"Sort of what?"

"Well, I'll be honest with you Claire Belle. After you invited me for dinner tonight, my head went sideways and I plum-ass forget to get us a bottle of wine. And of course, wouldn't ya know the stores are all closed today and that purty much put a damper on that idea."

"And...?"

"How do you like bourbon?"

"Bourbon?"

"Yeah, bourbon."

"I like it just fine. But how..."

"Back in late February, George and me had a little row with some Georgia crackers that come up this way to go deep-sea fish'en. Only trouble was, the day before they was to go fish'en, they were stand'en out in front of Shanklyn's beer joint drink'en whisky from a bottle out in the open. I gave 'em all the options to stop and go on 'bout their business ... but, they got ugly."

"What did you do R.W.?"

"Well, it wasn't so much as to what I did than what George did."

"Oh Lordy!" Claire said putting her left palm to her mouth.

"When these ol' boys started get'en ugly with me, George quietly got out of the car and walked around to the trunk with his pump shotgun. After he got their attention just by stand'en there, he cocked that sucker one good time and lowered it straight at 'em ... and, well, nature just sort'a took over and those good ol' boys all-sudden like got real nice and decided to hand me over all their whisky. When they did that, I told 'em to get on back to Georgia and not come back."

"But, what if George went to shoot'en?"

"Aw ... George wasn't gonna do any shoot'en. Just wanted to scare 'em a bit and I believe he was successful when he cocked that sucker. It sure made a racket. But had he pulled the trigger, nothing much was gonna happen no how."

"And how's that?"

"George later told me he forgot to put shells in the gun. But them crackers didn't know it was empty. Come to think of it, at the time, neither did I! Anyhow, I told 'em to go on and get the hell out'a here and never come back. I just let 'em go. In the meantime, I stuffed the liquor in the trunk and plum forgot about it till this afternoon ... been there all this time. So, in the meantime, that's *sort of* how I come upon our drinks tonight. Now that I'm think'en 'bout it ... wouldn't mind having a little shooter right now myself. Can I fix you one?"

"Sure, why not!"

Claire opened up a metal kitchen cabinet door over the counter and retrieved two glasses. R.W. in turn opened up the little freezer door inside the small refrigerator and pulled out a tiny tray of ice and then fixed each of them a drink. The late afternoon sunset was just finishing its romantic act, and the couple adjourned to the deck to watch the finale. It was, to say the least, a most fascinating climax to a gloomy day.

After a short while of general conversation about the weather, the local happenings around the Banks, and a short discussion on the merchant shipping still being sunk by the German U-boats, R.W. fixed them each another round of drinks. Claire then brought up the subject of dinner.

"How do you like your steaks cooked R.W.?"

"Oh! We're having steaks?"

"Yes. I picked them up yesterday. They're rib-eyes. I hope you like that cut of beef."

"Claire, I like *any* cut of beef cooked anyway it can be cooked. But how in the hell did you get rib-eyes? I thought steaks were hard to come by these days."

"Oh, that's my secret and let's just leave it at that. Now, would you like for me to roll 'em in flower and cook 'em in the frying pan with lard, cook 'em in the frying pain without the flower and lard, or cook 'em straight-up over a fire pit? Your choice!"

"My word! Well, if I had my 'drethers,' I believe I'd choose the fire pit."

"Good choice. I was hoping you'd say that. I've already dug a little pit near that small dune over there and filled it with wood and a few pieces of coal to help it stay hot."

"When did you do all this?" R.W. asked wide-eyed.

"R.W., stop being so dad-blame nosy! I did it this afternoon. I really wanted mine cooked over the pit so I was hoping you'd choose that option. You can help me light the fire. It's a bit windy and I'll need some help."

"Oh, we'll get it started! I promise you that."

"Well, I tell you what. Let's have another cocktail and enjoy this twilight and then I'll go in and put the baking potatoes in the oven while you go light the fire. It'll take about forty minutes for the 'taters to get done ... so the timing seems about right. Sound good to you?"

"Yeah, that sounds good to me. Here, let me go get us that cocktail now."

R.W. went to the kitchen and fixed another drink. He noticed Claire Belle was getting a little tipsy so he cut back on the liquor and added a touch more water. He himself was feeling fuzzy headed but felt well within his faculties. He wasn't interested in going over the limit. But he knew that after they had something to eat, they'd both settle closer to earth. Though, for the moment, they both were enjoying themselves quite well.

By around seven-thirty, they finished their cocktails. Claire went to the kitchen and prepared the stove for the baked potatoes, and R.W. went to the pit to start the fire. The wind calmed some but was still whipping the sea oats sprouting from the dunes. He did have trouble getting the fire started; but once he got it lit, the wind fanned it to perfection. He stood there and watched the flames.

About five minutes later, Claire walked from the cottage with two more drinks and a lightweight blanket stuffed under her right arm. R.W. noticed her as she was coming down the steps barefooted, and he quickly traipsed through the soft sand to help by taking the drinks from her hands.

"I thought it'd be fun to sit by the fire and watch it. I remember doing this as a little girl and thoroughly enjoying it. Besides, we gots some time whilst 'dem 'taters is a cook'en!" Claire said seemingly a little tipsier than before.

"Claire ... you okay?

"O' ... I'm okay there R.W., just hav'en a little fun with you. Here, let's get this blanket spread out so's I can sit down 'for I fall down!"

R.W. handed the drinks back to Claire, took the blanket, and then let the wind blow it open as he laid it on the sand. He took the drinks back from Claire. She promptly sat down with a thud causing her to roll off to the side. She let out a little girlie giggle, straightened herself up, and then sat ladylike on the blanket. R.W. sat down handing Claire her drink.

"Oh, R.W., don't think ill of me for get'en tipsy."

"No ma'am, I don't think ill of you a'tall! We've shared some good laughs and had some good times."

191

"Do you like me R.W.?" Claire said cutting to the chase. R.W. was gobsmacked.

"Mercy me Claire Belle! You sho' as hell caught me off guard with that one!"

"I know I did ... but you don't have to answer that."

"Well, I..."

"R.W. ... you are without a doubt the most kindest, most sweetest, most good-hearted man I have ever met in all my dear born days. I *really* wished I had met you twelve years ago and all my problems would have never happened."

"Well, I..."

"Where *were* you in my life?"

"Well, I..."

"You don't have to answer that! I know where you were. You were trapped in my dreams with no where to go. Oh how I wish I could have found a way to release you! Did you know that you've always been in my dreams?"

"Well, I...

"But now I have released you from my dreams and I'm so glad! I am so glad you have finally been released because now you are going to save me from misery. You know that don't you?"

"Well I ... I am?"

"Yes, you are! You are going to save me from my despairs."

At that moment, Claire nestled her glass into the sand. She took R.W.'s glass and nestled it within the sand next to hers. Then she bent over from her sitting position, looked him squarely in the eyes, cocked her head, and kissed him smartly on the lips. His hat fell off.

While being kissed, R.W. reflected on his earlier thoughts and how he was going to take each moment as it came. In his way of thinking, there was to be a small building of moments. But the one thing he hadn't counted on was the biggest moment coming first.

He took his right arm and gently hugged her in a lost, but not forgotten, romantic embrace. They flattened out on the blanket; their bodies tightly woven as one. The fire's embers were glowing red-hot. After a few moments of petting and kissing, Claire whispered to R.W.

"Let's go inside. I'm ready!"

"You want'a go in *now*! Well, I reckon them 'taters are 'bout ready, and I'll have them steaks cooked in a jiffy!"

"No you dummy. Me! I'm ready! The heck with them steaks and 'taters. We'll cook 'em later. We need to go in now. You hear me!"

"Oh ... oh, I see what you mean!"

As they walked to cottage and in through the kitchen, R.W. remarked, "While we're in here, let's take them 'taters out of the oven. I don't want'a overcook 'em."

"Oh R.W.! You are so funny! Come on you lug. After you've had the main course, I'll give you some freshly homemade peach cobbler for dessert!"

"Will that be 'a la mode,' Madame?" R.W. humorously said remembering the first time he had ever heard that expression.

"Honey, you can have it any way you want!"

"Well, I reckon a little ice cream would liven things up a bit."

"I knew you'd see it that way!"

"You want me to go back and get the blanket?"

"Naw. Leave it."

* * * * * * * *

It was after one o'clock in the morning, Monday, April 20. Jenny Smith was in her little house waiting for Hank Larson to return from Elizabeth City. Tonight they had another important signal that needed to be sent. The U-491, having completed their side mission of replenishment, was ready. Hank Larson was not. He was late.

"Hank, where in the hell have you been? You're late again. You knew what time you were supposed to be here."

"Ah hell, Jenny ... stop razing me! I was drinking beer with Dale Conner. We got to talking about the cargo that's gonna go 'kabloowee' tonight."

"You idiot! Do you not know how dangerous that is? You shouldn't be seen with him. What the hell were you thinking?"

"Well, I'm gonna tell you what in the *hell* I'm thinking! I'm thinking I'm get'en the short end of the stick around here when it comes to a paycheck. I'm get'en screwed!"

"Now Hank, we've already talked about that. It's all in accordance with each person's importance to the job. You're position just ain't high enough on the totem pole to warrant any more."

"Hell, Conner's get'en twice what I'm get'en and half the time I got'a go up to Hampton Roads to get the packet. Shit, that sumbitch is supposed to be bringing it down to me in Elizabeth City! Hell, that don't seem fair!"

"Now Hank, I don't set the scale and I don't set the rules. The 'Boss Man' does that."

"Yeah, on your recommendations I'm sure!"

"I've had nothing to do with that!"

"Yeah, I bet you didn't!"

"Do you not remember me tell'en ya awhile back 'bout hold'en up your end of the stick and if'n you don't, how you gonna end up float'en in the Albemarle?"

"Yeah, hell I remember."

"Well, you better stop complaining and keep that in mind. You hear me?"

"I hear ya ... I hear ya."

"Did you get the gasoline like I asked you?"

"Yeah, yeah ... three jugs. Just like you *ordered*. It's in the car. What the hell we gonna do with it anyways?"

"After we send the signal, we're gonna have a weenie roast."

"You're kidd'en me! Where?"

"Hank you idiot! I told you last week. That cottage down below the monument where the beacon signal shines. Right now the folks haven't moved in for the summer, and I want'a get rid of it before they arrive. If'n they arrive before we torch it, it's gonna make the job harder, and I ain't in the mood to be torching nobody."

"You bitch! How can you sit there and say that when every time you send a damn signal, at least a hundred men go up in flames scream'en and holler'en when their ship get's blown up? You make no sense!"

"Ah hell Hank, you don't understand."

"I understand perfectly. I'm just a measly ol' idiot, I don't make enough money, and the worst of it, I got *some* sense of compassion. Yeah you're right, I don't understand."

"Hank, Look. I know you're upset. Let's have a beer and calm down. You want'a beer sugar?"

"Well, I reckon so. No since going to *earn a paycheck* when ya all pissed off. Yeah, sure, let's drink a beer. Do we have time?" Hank asked sarcastically.

"Yeah, we got a little more time. Here, come sit next to me. Let me rub your shoulders and take the tension out," Jenny said patting her hand on the couch next to her. She continued.

"You got us squared away for a room up in Elizabeth City tonight?"

"Yeah, I told my roommate to sleep somewhere else tonight. We're staying in my apartment."

"When that cottage goes up in flames, we don't need to be seen around here at that hour. That's why we need to stay up there tonight. You know, when that cottage goes up, people'll start com'en out along with the police and fire department. They might see us if'n we go back to Manteo so we need to be far away in another direction. If'n somebody does happen to see us, they'll wonder why we're out so late and our asses will probably be grassed. So after we torch it, we got'a move quickly back across Currituck Sound and get on up to your apartment. You got that?"

"Yeah, yeah. You've already told me. I got it. Hell, I ain't that stupid."

* * * * * * * *

"R.W., what time is it?" Claire said barely awake.

194

"It's time for me to get on home. It's best I not stay all night. It's not good to get the neighbors a talk'en," R.W. said sitting in the edge of the bed putting on his socks.

"Well, if I'm not mistaken, I think they probably already know by now, you little animal you!"

"Now Claire, cut that mess out!"

"You ready for some dessert?"

"I think as it is I've already had three help'ens with the 'a la mode'." But, if'n you don't mind, I'll probably be com'en back over later this afternoon and work on that steak and baked 'tater."

"Oh honey, I forgot. We never did get around to dinner, did we? I'm sorry! You want me to fix you something to eat right quick. I've got some ham salad in the fridge."

"Naw, that's okay. It's 'bout two thirty-five. Time for me to be get'en on back home. Time I get there it'll be 'bout time to be get'en back up anyways. Besides, I'll just head on over to Bessie's and grab some breakfast with the fish'en crowd."

"Well, don't wake up Josh when you go in."

"Aw, the little fellow's sleep'en over at his grandparent's house."

"You sly dog you!"

"Well hell, I didn't know what was gonna happen tonight. I just played it safe."

"Smart think'en. One of these day's you'll be sheriff. You know that don't you?"

"Well, we'll have to see 'bout that. Ya have to be elected for that position."

"You got my vote big guy. Then, I'll see you tomorrow … okay?"

"You got it! I'll see ya tomorrow." R.W. said now fully dressed. He leaned over and kissed Claire on the forehead.

And with that, R.W. quietly slid out the front door and made his way to the car. The wind was still howling but that was almost normal for this time of year. But what wasn't normal, the wind was blowing due east. Then again, there was a storm a brewing far out in the Atlantic. It was questionable if it was to turn west and pummel the islands. Nevertheless, it was refreshing even though it was a bit cool from the early morning darkness.

When R.W. got into his car, he lit a cigarette and pondered. And what he pondered were those moments. It was most invigorating. This for sure, he imagined, was never going to happen. The way his relationship had been going, a little light peck on the cheek would have made for a complete evening. Then of course, a medium-rare steak and baked potato would have made it just that more complete.

Pulling out of the driveway, R.W. casually backed into the coastal highway angling his car to the south. Putting the three-speed Pontiac stick shift in first gear, he lightly let off the clutch letting the car slowly ease forward. After about ten miles per hour, he shifted into second gear and built up his speed to twenty-five miles per hour. While at this speed, he noticed a car coming towards him at a high rate of speed. With his car's engine building, R.W. shifted into third gear where the car loosened up and pulled forward a little faster. Within seconds, the facing headlights shot past him like a bolt of lightening.

"Jesus H Christ ... what in the hell was that! That sonofabitch was cruising! I better turn this boy around and go find out what this feller's up to. Som'en just ain't right for that to be happen'en this early in the morn'en!"

Quickly slowing his car, he turned hard left into a driveway, threw the car in reverse, and looked out the right passenger window as he released the clutch. Before he could fully turn around, he noticed a faint red-orange glow coming from the beach side row of cottages. That didn't look good. He hesitated for just a moment deciding it was best to head for the glow. He angled back around and headed towards its direction.

As he got closer, he realized a beach cottage was aflame and quickly being engulfed. Parking across the street, he quickly got out and frantically looked around to see if anyone might have been in the cottage. At this point, there wasn't much he could do about trying to get inside. He then hurriedly headed back to Claire's cottage to use the telephone to call Roscoe. He pulled into her driveway with sand flying everywhere.

"Claire! Claire! Open the door! Quickly, I need to use the phone!" R.W. said pounding on the six-paneled glass-pane door with his fist.

Claire had not yet fallen back asleep and hurriedly ran to the knocking door with a worried look on her face. She opened it and R.W. flew in with abandon and grabbed the telephone.

"R.W.?" Claire said dressed in a partially closed robe.

"Goddamnit, a cottage is going up in flames down the street! I need to call Roscoe!"

"A what?"

"Molly! Listen, this is an emergency! Get with Elmer and Roscoe *now* and tell 'em to get the fire boys together! We got'a cottage in flames up past Nags Head ... on Highway 12 directly across from the monument. They can't miss it! Tell 'em to hurry and I'll meet 'em there. Got'a go!"

* * * * * * * *

"Hank, do you know who in the hell's car that was?"

"Nope, can't says that I do." Hank was now approaching the turnoff to the Wright Memorial Bridge traveling well above the speed limit.

"Goddamnit, it was R.W.'s car ... it was R.W.! Can you believe that shit?"

"Think he recognized us," Hank said with a slightly worried look on his face.

"I sure as hell hope not. Hey! Slow the car down. He's not chasing us. He must'a turned around and headed back to the burning house. Look, let's be cool about this now and don't act suspicious. If'n we get pulled over now by *anyone*, somebodys gonna put two and two together."

"What the hell was R.W. doing out this way at all hours of the night anyway?" Hank asked slowing the car down.

"Hell, I don't know ... best I can figure, the ol' boy was probably over at Claire Belle's get'en a little nooky and then going home."

"You reckon?" Hank said.

"Well, why else would he be out this far on the Banks at this hour. These guys don't patrol this late ... hell, there's noth'en go'en on out here at this hour."

"Except'en us," Hank said.

"Yeah, well ... I hope like hell he wasn't snooping in that direction. If that's the case, then our little deal's been compromised. I feel sure we've covered all the bases?"

"Maybe it was just a coincidence ... I mean like you said, being at his girlfriend's house get'en a little nooky and all."

"Yeah, that has to be it ... just a coincidence and a little nooky. Yeah, that's it."

Chapter 18

Later that Monday morning and just after sunrise, Roscoe, George, R.W., and the eight volunteer fireman from the Roanoke Island Fire Department were milling about the smoky burned out structure. Nothing was left but smoldering hot ashes and pieces of charred wood that had fallen away from the structure. The only remaining parts of the cottage still standing were a few telephone-sized pilings that supported it off the ground.

But there was good news. Because the wind blowing earlier that morning was oddly coming directly from the east, it fanned the flames towards the coastal road and away from the cottages on either side sparing them from the same fate. Typically, at this time of year, the wind blew from the northeast and the chances were that three other cottages to the south could also have gone up in flames. Just past the third cottage, there were several vacant lots and it was doubtful the flames could have jumped any further than that to reach houses on the other side. While still a tragedy, luck was on their side.

When the fire department arrived thirty-five minutes after Roscoe alerted them, the house had already collapsed to the ground sending not ash and embers high into the sky and blowing towards the Wright Brothers Monument. Fortunately, there were no structures in that area other than Alfred Winters' caretaker cottage behind and below the monolith.

199

Because fire hydrants had never been installed on the islands, water wasn't available to extinguish the fire. To combat fires on the isles, the department used a tanker truck; but, at the time, it was in for repairs and couldn't be used. The only other option was using their old drafting engine to pull water from the Atlantic. Unfortunately, that notion swiftly faded when they remembered they had tried that once before. It mired deeply in the sand taking two days to have it removed. Nobody in the department was ready to suffer that ordeal again and quickly dismissed the idea.

When the firemen received the call, and were on their way over the Wash Baum Bridge, they realistically knew the cottage would be impossible to save at this point and would be a total loss. Their goal now was to keep the fire from spreading to the adjacent cottages. To accomplish that, they would use their shovels, sand, and sweat—lots of sweat.

Aside from Dare County's finest, many of the nearby residents came to the site to watch and ask questions with no real answers: *"We don't know just yet, but we're certainly gonna be look'en into it."* Many of the folks brought water, coffee, toast, and jelly to the fireman who had been so diligently working for the past four and a half hours. Bessie, who had also heard about the fire from her early morning fishing crowd, had one of her cooks bring to the firemen four large platefuls of hot freshly made cathead scratch country ham biscuits and a gallon jug each of freshly brewed coffee and iced tea.

"Roscoe, you do realize of course this fire could've really gotten out'a hand if'n that wind had'a come in from its regular direction, don't you," R.W. enlightened his boss.

"Yeah, no shit. It could've been bad, real bad, no doubt about it. You know, we've been real lucky with fires since the 'Big One' back in September '39. George, you weren't here back then but that one damn near wiped out downtown Manteo. The one in '32 was bad, but that one was worse."

"That bad, huh?"

"Yep, sure as hell was. Ol' R.W. hadn't been with me long. Somehow a fire got started in a gasoline storage warehouse down on the waterfront and it didn't take long before twenty-one stores, fish'en houses, and some fine homes went up in smoke. Hell, even our courthouse caught fire and had to be extinguished three times. That was a mess!"

"Three times, huh?"

"Yep. Post office didn't make it though. Had to build ol' Jenny a new one. She helped design it. This time with brick. Come to think of it, everything that got burnt went back up in brick."

"Speaking of Jenny, there's the ol' 'Mouth of the South' herself. Wonder what the hell she's do'en up and about in these parts of the county this early?" R.W. wondered.

"Well, she's slowing down. Why don't you ask her R.W.," Roscoe said.

Jenny slowed to a stop right in front of R.W. who had walked from the side of the road with his left palm halfway in the air facing her. The bright early morning sun caused her to raise her left hand to shield her eyes from the sun as R.W. walked to her window. The pungent smell of burning wood was heavy in the air.

"Damn, I can't be gone for one night and the whole place goes up in smoke! What in the hell happened, R.W.? Jenny asked.

"Looks like we had us a little fire early this morn'en."

"Well hell, I can see that, but it don't look all that little to me. You got any clues as to what happened just yet?"

"Well, I was hop'en you'd tell me."

"Me?"

"Yeah, you! Hell, you're the one who always seems to know stuff before anybody else does! Think you can put your secret little powers together on this one?" R.W. said sarcastically inching closer to the driver's window to block the sun on Jenny's eyes. He then put both hands over the window-well and bent down to get closer to Jenny's eye level. While doing so, he casually peeked inside. She began fidgeting with a large brown envelope on the passenger seat turning it over covering the address.

"I don't think I can help you on this one. I was up in Elizabeth City last night at Hank's place," Jenny said matter-of-factly.

"Oh?"

"So what! Not doing anything different than you are ol' buddy!" Jenny said defensively.

"Whose car is this? Hanks?"

"Yeah, he picked me up at my place last night. Thought we'd have a change of scenery and go to his place and drink some beer. I was all out. He'll pick it up later this morning when he brings the mail down. He'll have somebody with 'em so's he can take it back. Why the third degree R.W.?"

"Ah Jenny! You remember who owns this cottage?"

"Right off the top of my head, I think it's Tommy Matthews from Nash County, but I'm not all that sure. I can call ya later and let you know after I open up. How soon you need to know?"

"Well, sometime today. I'll need to be call'en 'em and let'en 'em know what happened. But I don't know when I'll be back in the office. I'll just stop by your place later when I'm back over that way ... maybe in a little while."

"Anything else R.W.? I got'a be going," Jenny said slightly agitated.

"Naw, I'll be talk'en to you later."

Jenny then drove off and R.W. walked back over to Roscoe and George. He had something on his mind but didn't allow for the others to know just yet. He was going to bide his time.

"She have anything interesting to say?" asked George.

"Not much. Said she was up in Elizabeth City last night with her boyfriend Hank. Though, she did get a little tetchy with me on the subject ... thought I was giv'en her the third degree."

"Were you?" asked Roscoe.

"Naw, not really ... but maybe I was a little. Sometimes that little bitch gets under my skin something fierce. She did say she'd get me the name of the owner of the cottage so we can give 'em call. I believe this is gonna be one phone call that'll light up their day," R.W. figuratively said speaking with a light laugh.

About this time, Elmer Duval, the Dare County Fire Chief, walked over to Roscoe with a cup of coffee and one of Bessie's country ham biscuits. The embers were still too hot to poke around to see what started the fire.

"Well, that's okay Elmer. But we really need to keep a few of the boys around to make sure it doesn't flair back up. How 'bouts I meet you back over here later this afternoon. Maybe by then it'll be cool enough for you and me to get our paws dirty look'en 'round for some clues."

"Yeah Roscoe, that sounds purty good to me. I'll keep a coupl'a boys here till then. They can give us a hand too. You get one of Bessie's biscuits?"

"Yep, I sho' did."

After the fire chief walked back to the ruins, Roscoe point-blank asked both R.W. and George if they thought this was an arson fire. George didn't speculate. R.W. did.

"Roscoe, yeah. To me it reeks of arson. So much was happening help'en put out the fire and all, I didn't really have a chance to tell ya, but now I do."

"Go ahead, I'm listening."

"I was head'en south down the road here 'bout quarter to three this morn'en when a car came fly'en by me ... and I mean he was pick'en 'em up and lay'en down. As I was turning around to give chase, I noticed a faint orange glow over top the roofs of the cottages. I debated whether or not to chase the car or head for the glow. Well, as you know, I headed for the glow and here we are. There is no doubt in my mind that, whoever was in that car last night was the culprit who set this puppy on fire. There is no doubt in my mind!"

"Interesting. With info like that, I believe you're probably right. Could you tell what kind'a car it was?" Roscoe asked.

"Roscoe, it went by me so damn fast ... I just couldn't tell. But it definitely was a car. But by the time I had mine half way turned around, it was gone like the wind. You know damn good and well it had to have left the islands over the Wright Bridge. God knows where it went from there."

"Well, where did it pass you?"

"About a half mile north of here. After driv'en back down here to see what was go'en on and realizing we had a fire, I rushed back to Claire Belle's house to call you Roscoe."

"*Back* to Claire Belle's house?"

"Aw shit Roscoe, don't be going there. Hell, you want me to draw ya a picture?"

Roscoe slightly grinned looking over at George who was shrugging his shoulders and slightly shaking his head with a light smile. He took a sip of coffee and a bite of his ham biscuit and looked off into space.

"Well that car is something to go on. How we're gonna find it's another. I reckon we'll just have to keep our eyes and ears peeled for some kind of lead."

"Roscoe, when those ashes stop smoldering and we can get in there and start poking around, I feel sure we'll find something. Look, George and me'll come back this afternoon. You just stay put in the office. We'll take care of it. In the meantime, I'd like to run to the house and shower up a bit and maybe take a short nap. I'll be back in before noon."

"Yeah sure, R.W. That'll be fine. On the way, why don't you take George here back to the office and drop him off there. I'll stick around here for awhile and poke around what I can poke around for ... see'en if I can found something that might help us out."

"You ready to go George?"

"Ready as ever. Let's go."

On the way back over to Manteo, George quizzed R.W. about his get together with Miss Claire Belle in a humorous sort of way. Being they were close friends, R.W. was receptive and cut a few jokes himself on a crazy evening. He did mention that if Miss Bessie hadn't sent over those ham biscuits, he probably was going to faint. He was starved. George laughed. But then R.W. changed the subject revolving around the fire and his chat with Jenny. She's always had a funny way about her, but this morning she acted differently and R.W. couldn't quite put his finger on it. He asked George to do something for him.

"I told Jenny I was gonna stop by the post office and get the name of the folks who own that cottage. While I'm in there keep'en her occupied, I want you to sneak around back to where she parked Hank's car and sniff on the inside. Don't ask me why or what you're trying to sniff for, just do it. I'll catch up with you later this afternoon when we go back over to the ruins. You can tell me then."

"I hear what you're saying. But why don't you let me off on the corner and I'll walk from there. She might notice me getting out of the car in front of the office. You just take off from there and I'll walk back to the courthouse."

"Yeah well, that's even better."

* * * * * * * *

Settling to the bottom of the continental shelf at daylight in his home quadrant of CA79, Kapitänleutnant Vogel was not pleased with last nights mission to the upper reaches of the Chesapeake Bay. The targets he was given were nowhere to be seen and the area was swarming with patrol craft. What ships that were available were less than 2,000 tons and not worthy of a torpedo.

"Herr Kaleun, I don't understand what could have happened. There was nothing in that area. Do you suppose Herr Krech might have misread the signal?"

"Nein, Herr Staats. I talked with him in the strictest of terms and I am assured he did nothing improper. Yes, the seas were rough but not to the point where he could have misread the signal. I was in the tower also and the signals were clear to me. The problem must have come from the purveyor supplying the signal. Fortunately this was only the first mishap. In two days we will have another signal. Hopefully, any miscues have been solved. Even though we are now fully restocked with food, fuel, and torpedoes, we must be careful and not waste. I fear the Americans are now fully reacting to our presence on the littoral and we must be careful in our attacks when they do come our way."

"Ja Kaleun, I believe you are right. The radio reports from the other boats are now reporting that ships are beginning to travel in pairs with trawlers in close tow, and they are also observing a much larger presence of attack craft and airplanes. I believe our future missions are going to be tougher," said Oberleutnant Staats.

"Ja, ja, I believe you are correct."

Not only were the missions going to be tougher sinking the vital military cargo, they will be doing so with two less crewmembers. When transferring the fourteen G7e torpedoes from the U-1059 torpedo carrier to their boat, one sailor accidently drowned when his foot was caught in a drain hole on the superstructure that released water from the inner hull through to the outer hull. When the U-491 lowered its bow section to float the torpedo into position, the sailor was unable to escape as the bow went under.

Several hours after this mishap, and while it was still very dark in the early morning hours, another crewman was accidentally killed when two floating 3,400 pound torpedoes came into contact with each other crushing his skull. While attempting to save the sailor, the raft holding the torpedo collapsed sending the torpedo to the bottom of the ocean. It did not explode because its arming device had been dismantled for transfer.

With the loss of these two seamen, the U-491 had now lost a total of five crewmen while on their long patrol to the East Coast of the United States. Three were known dead while the fates of the other two were unknown—one was in critical condition from crushing his head into a bulkhead while the other, Jürgen Oehrn, who took him to shore in hopes of obtaining adequate medical help, didn't return. Did he defect, was he killed, or was he captured?

* * * * * * * *

The following morning after the fire, Deputies Dawkins and Beatty were performing their normal patrol duties while Roscoe and R.W. were in the office having a discussion relating to the fire.

"Roscoe, yesterday morning when I was talk'en to Jenny, while she was in Hank's car, I bent over her window and peeked inside. She seemed a bit fidgety ... fiddle fart'en with an envelope beside her. I couldn't tell what it was, but what mostly got my attention was I could smell the hint of gasoline on the inside ... or at least that was my first impression. With the burnt smell from the cottage so strong, I couldn't really tell after the first whiff. But anyway, that's what I thought. Well, later that morning when I took George back over here to the office, I stopped by the post office to get the name of the owner of the cottage. At any rate, while I was keeping Jenny occupied at the front counter, I had George sneak around back to the car and sniff the inside for himself."

"And...?"

"He smelled gasoline too. No doubt about it."

"You suspect Jenny and Hank torched that cottage?"

"Well, other than the smell, we certainly don't have any evidence pointing in that direction, but I do have my suspicions now."

"You and George find anything poking around yesterday?"

"Naw, it was still too hot. We're going back over this afternoon."

"Well R.W., what's her motive for burning the damn place?"

"That's the million dollar question. But, what I do know, in the last month or so, she's been acting different. Hell, I've known that ol' gal for years, her antics and personality, and what I've noticed, she's act'en different ... like she's 'stove-up' 'bout something. I don't know exactly what it is, but I can tell ya she's got something weighing-in heavy on her mind."

"R.W., you been here long enough to know we can't be haul'en her ass in here for something that flimsy."

"Aw hell Roscoe, I know that. I know we need more than supposition. But I think it's a starting point."

"You got an idea then?

205

"Yeah, I do."

For the last two months or so, the officers had suspected that Rose Ellen Harris, the Sheriff's Office secretary, had been feeding Jenny bits and pieces of information on the goings on inside the office. It had just been too coincidental for Jenny to know certain things. That private information had to have been coming from an inside source. Having decided it was time to confront the situation, they decided to turn the tables.

"Sheriff Simmons, I am so *sorry*. I *really* didn't mean to pass on anything important. Jenny has just always been so sweet to me and well, you know, I guess a little girl talk just got out'a hand. But I've already stopped passing anything to her. I sort'a had a feel'en ya'll knew, and I stopped a short while back. But, she keeps asking anyway."

"Rose Ellen, what you did wasn't very good. I ought'a fire ya for it, but ... I know you're remorseful and I believe you."

"So, I'm not fired?"

"No Rose ... no, you're not fired. But, things have recently changed and R.W. and me want you to go back to doing what you were doing with her?"

"*What*? I don't understand?"

"You will. This time we're gonna tell you directly what we want you to tell her."

"But I..."

"Rose, listen. We're not setting you up. We're setting her up. This is serious. Do you understand that?"

"The situation ... no, I really don't. But your voice! *That* I understand perfectly well! This is serious isn't it?"

"Yes Rose, it is."

"Well, I'll do whatever you ask me to do. You just name it."

What the two officers wanted was for Rose Ellen to hint to Jenny that R.W. had smelled gasoline inside Hanks car when she stopped by the fire yesterday returning from Elizabeth City.

"And that's all you want me to say?" Rose Ellen asked.

"That's it. No more, no less. When you go to the post office in the morning to get the mail, strike up a conversation with her about the fire. She'll probably still be ask'en you what we think we know. You pass on that tidbit of information. That's all you need to do. Got it?"

"Yes sir. I got it! This isn't going to get me fired is it, Roscoe?

"No Rose ... no it isn't. Not if you stick to what we're tell'en you to do."

Chapter 19

Four days after the fire, the owner of the cottage, Tommy Matthews, agreed to meet R.W. and the Fire Chief, Elmer Duval, at the burned out site. The meeting was meant to combine their minds and hopefully find a reason as to why this fire happened. Several days ago when Mr. Matthews was contacted by phone, his displeasure of hearing the news was evident by his voiceful tone. He, his wife, and little boy were planning on opening the cottage in a few weeks and using it until the end of summer. While waiting for Mr. Matthews to arrive at the site, Elmer and R.W. were poking through the ruins. The information about the suspect car and the gasoline smell from Hank's car was withheld from Elmer so he could objectively investigate the fire. Just as they were walking back to their cars, Mr. Matthews pulled up, got out, and looked at the ruins.

"Damn, there ain't nothing left, is there?"

"Yeah, it's purty well burnt. Not much left! But we do appreciate you com'en, Mr. Matthews," R.W. said as he and Elmer walked over to shake his hand.

"You fellows got any ideas yet what may have caused this?"

"Not yet Tommy, but we're purty well lean'en towards arson because of the burn pattern we saw while it was in flames. Other than speculation, we don't have any evidence otherwise, but we're still investigating. Hopefully, we'll find something out purty soon."

"Well, my wife Willa Jo is all upset about this ... just heartbroken she is. This area of beach was where I proposed to her back in '34. We always had a notion one day to buy us a place here, and we did a few years back. Oh Lordy mercy. What a damn mess!"

"Mr. Matthews, we need to ask you some questions that might help us out. We don't need to be prying, but we got'a eliminate you as a suspect first," R.W. said.

"Well, I understand that. I'm an Assistant District Attorney you know, and I know the drill. So, to start with, no I didn't torch my own property ... had no reason to. The insurance I had on this place wouldn't cover the cost to rebuild near as to the way it was. But with the war and all going on, I doubt seriously that'll happen any time soon anyway with so much material now being requisitioned. And the money from the insurance won't even payoff the mortgage I have on it. So, what happens after I pay to have the place cleaned up, I end up paying the balance on a lot full of sand with a damn good view. Does that help you out there any fellows?"

"Well, yes sir. Yes it does. We're off to a good start. Now, in your line of work ... you think maybe you made somebody mad enough to take revenge?" R.W. asked.

"I'm just a junior DA and mostly handle petty theft cases, nothing serious yet. I just don't think I've pissed anybody off bad enough to cause this."

"That right?"

"Well, that's what I believe anyway. I'm just not that outlandish in court, and I get along fine with everybody in the office. I've been there going on four years now."

After a little while longer of these types of questions and answers, they walked over to the ruins. Elmer wanted Mr. Matthews to give him a detailed layout of the cottage as well as the cottage's contents. Other than the typical furniture and the usual items used in the kitchen, the place was clean. All clothes, towels, and bed linens were taken back to their home in Nash County when they last left.

"You know, before I closed her down for the winter last fall, I cut the water off, drained the hot water heater, and cut the power at the electrical panel. If it was an electrical fire, it would have had to come from this area where the panel was located," Matthews said pointing to a particular place in the ruins. They all walked over to that location which was charred like everything else around it. It did not appear the fire had started in that location.

After spending about an hour and a half at the site, Mr. Matthews thought he'd drive over to Bessie's Café for a bite of lunch before heading back home. He invited both R.W. and Elmer to join him, but they declined as they had other commitments.

"Fellows, I hope I've been of some help to you and I hope ya'll can get to the bottom of this. I'll be back in touch with you from time to time seeing how things are going. Of course, you can let me know if you find anything of interest I need to know about," Matthews said and continued.

"You know, it's going to be real sad not being able to come back out here and see the ol' place they way she used to be. I remember last fall when we came out on a weekend to close her up for the winter, my seven-year-old son remarked how he was going to miss watching the beacon light. Every night, he'd lie in his bed and watch the light go 'round and 'round till it put him to sleep. He always said it was, 'God's light to safety.' I guess in a sense it was when a pilot has lost his way in the sky, or maybe when somebody is just plain lost."

"Well, there's no doubt ya'll had a great view of that beacon light from here. I never paid much attention to it myself. But, maybe one of these days when the war's over, you can rebuild and your son can go back to the way it used to be. Dreams can last forever and I don't think a little charred wood can destroy that," R.W. said solemnly.

"You're very kind Deputy. I'll stay in touch. By the way, what's on the special at Bessie's today?"

"The Thursday special is ... help me out here Elmer."

"It's fish Mr. Matthews ... probably Alligator River bass."

"Thanks fellows. I'll be talking with you."

After Mr. Matthews left, Elmer and R.W. briefly chatted. R.W. related that when he saw the cottage burning, the thickness of the flames were on the opposite side of the house dismissing the notion it could have been an electrical fire. As they further talked, Elmer was beginning to believe that some sort of an accelerant had to have been used to start the fire. If that was in fact the case, it's doubtful the perpetrators would have taken the container with them; they more than likely would have left it in the house to be destroyed along with everything else. If the evidence was in the pile of rubbish, every piece needed to be scrutinized. For that to happen, they were going to need help. But before splitting up, both agreed to keep quiet on the notion it might have been arson. There was no need for anybody else to know what they were speculating.

Elmer headed back to Manteo and R.W. headed towards the Nags Head Casino. He wanted to see his friend John O'Hearn. As he turned his car around, he glanced up at the monument thinking, *You know that ol' beacon light has been twirling since 1932 and I guess I just seem to have forgotten all about it. I guess I've been around for so long I've just gotten used to it. I guess when some things become old hat, stuff like that can happen. Oh well....*

Inside the Casino, there was a modest crowd. Several patrons were sitting at the snack bar drinking beer, some were shooting pool, and a few were playing pinball with palms lightly tapping the sides of the machine eventually causing the dreaded "Tilt" lamp to flash. Rags, the owner, came from nowhere to greet R.W.

"Well ol' buddy, how ya been do'en these days! Hadn't seen ya awhile. Where ya been hiding out?"

"I reckon I been kind'a busy and just hadn't had much chance to stop by Rags. Been recently work'en on the cottage fire right now trying to figure that mess out."

"Come up with anything yet?"

"Naw, not really. Got with the Elmer just a little while ago. Looks like it might'a been some kind'a electrical problem that caused a spark. That's what we're thinking anyhow. Probably have it wrapped up by first of the week."

"You here to see John?"

"Well, as a matter of fact I am. I want'a see how the ol' boy's doing!"

"Ah, he's doing just great. He's in the back working on a small project for me. I'll go get 'em for you."

"Yeah, that'll be great Rags. I'll just slide on over here to the counter and grab a Coke and a ready-made sandwich."

"Hey, try the ham salad. Claire Belle dropped some by this morning. Sho' is a good sandwich."

"Yeah, so I've heard!" R.W. said with a slight chuckle.

While Rags was getting John, R.W. stood by the counter with his soda and sandwich. A few minutes later John appeared and, as usual, was smiling and glad to see his buddy.

"Hello there Mr. R.W. Good to see you again! Rags said you wanted to see me."

"Sure John. Let's go somewhere and have a seat. My legs are killing me right now! You had something to eat yet?"

"No sir. Not too hungry right now. I'll grab something in a little while. Let's go upstairs and talk. Nobody's up there and it's quieter."

R.W. had something on his mind and sought John's help. With suspicion falling on Jenny for torching the cottage, he wanted, as best he could, to keep an eye on her. He knew it was going to be difficult keeping a tail on her full time, but he at least thought it feasible to keep one on her at her regular hangout—the Casino. John was perfect for the task.

"Yes sir, I can do that. I already know who she is. She comes in quite often with her boyfriend Hank. I think that's his name. Yeah, they drink a lot of beer, and they do argue a lot. Come to think of it, they argue all the time. But lately it seems to have gotten worse."

"How lately?"

"I'd say it started a couple of weeks ago. It got so bad one night, Mr. Hank just got up and left her. She stuck around a while longer. I saw her use the phone. Then a little while later Mr. Winters, you know him, the monument caretaker, he came in for a beer and sat with her. After awhile, they seemed to be fussing a bit themselves but nothing like her and Hank. He must have said something to her because she calmed down fairly quick. After that, everything was okay, and they drank a few more beers and got up and left."

"You reckon they left together?" R.W. asked.

"Yes, I think so. He lightly grabbed her by the upper arm and walked her out. She drank a lot of beer and was probably woozy. You see that around here a lot!"

"Well John, where there's beer, there's gonna be woozy!"

"Yes sir, that's for sure!"

"John, I'm impressed. It looks like you're already keep'en your eyes open and I didn't even know it. What else you been notic'en?"

"Like what? Around here you have to be specific. I notice a lot of things."

"Well, how 'bout Mr. Winters then?"

"Usually comes in about three, maybe four times a week mostly just after five o'clock. Drinks a few beers standing at the counter. Likes to listen to the phonograph of the 'big bands' a lot. He's usually by himself, but every now and then he comes in with a tall nice looking gentleman. They drink some beer, shoot a few games of pool, then they leave."

"This tall feller, does he have slick-back blond hair."

"Yes, he does and he talks with a Dutch accent. But if I bet money, he's really German. I've heard him a few times, but I swear I catch a Low German accent mixed with his Dutch. If he's German, he's disguising it quite well. He does look more Nordic than German and that's what throws me off a little bit."

"Low German accent?"

"Yes. Actually it comes from Northern Germany somewhere between 'Lower Saxony' and 'Schleswig-Holstein'."

"And where is that if I can get my geography lesson for the day?"

"Hamburg. Hamburg Germany. South of Denmark, east of the North Sea, and west of the Baltic Sea. Aside from Berlin, it's probably the second largest city in Germany."

"Well, I guess you would know all that. How do you know the accent?"

"Because I'm from Hamburg. I myself have a similar accent. That's how I picked it up. Dutch is a difficult language to master. But no matter what the language a person speaks, the accent is always going to go along with the language. Just like the Gaelic brogue most everybody speaks around here. It could be spotted a mile away, especially yours R.W.!"

"Ahhh, no kidd'en!"

"Don't lose it R.W. It's beauty to my ears. I just love to hear it!"

"John, you seem to have a hanker'en for what I need. Now if you see something unusual, you let me know as soon as possible. Just call the operator. Her name is Molly Hassell. Just tell her you need to get in touch with me and that it's important. I'll leave word with her. She'll know how to get in touch with me. Now what I'm ask'en you to do is real important so keep this under your hat. Got it?"

"Oh yes sir, I got it!"

"One day next week, I'll come over and pick you up and we'll run over to Bessie's for a big lunch. How's that sound?"

"Sounds like you've got my undivided attention!"

Chapter 20

From the first of April to the middle of May, the inbound U-boat attacks on coastal shipping in the Eastern Sea Frontier were at fever pitch. The United States Navy and the undersized and undermanned Coast Guard were overwhelmed with anxiety—helpless in their cause to stop the madness. During this time, twenty-eight different U-boats had exacted eighty-one kills on various type ships with tankers the number one target. In toll, well over 2,000 merchant sailors and civilian passengers met their fate when well-directed torpedoes sent them to a watery grave; many burning alive when ships exploded; many drifting in rafts never to be seen again.

But the patriotic American public was dumbfounded as to what really was going on. Radio broadcast reports and newspaper accounts did little in accurately defining the sunken or damaged vessels. And to confound matters even worse, Navy Public Affairs circulated misleading reports that those *twenty-eight* submarines had *presumably* been sunk by Navy surface craft and Army B-18 Bolo bombers. While folks in heartland America had no choice but to believe such reports, coastal Americans believed otherwise. During the day, U-boat sightings were as plentiful as ever and every night there were numerous faint glows painting the horizon yellow, red, and orange signaling yet another death had just occurred. When was it ever going to stop?

Working in favor for Germany's assault was the earlier Japanese attack on Pearl Harbor. Many American ships were shattered and destroyed and it was questionable as to what to do with the remaining Atlantic fleet. Many key destroyers were already guarding the hostile North Atlantic while the remainder of the fleet was confined to the safe harbors of the Chesapeake until some rational decision could be made. While that decision was being made vital American and British raw materials were quickly succumbing to the depths of the sea because American intellect failed to recognize one vital piece of data.

In late December 1941, British intelligence forewarned American intelligence that a small fleet of five German U-boats were in fact heading for the northern coast of the United States with an arrival date the middle of January. Unfortunately, the warning went unheeded and *Unternehmen Paukenschlag* was off to a rousing head start by slamming Uncle Sammy to the canvas with a blistering one-two punch. Before staggering to his feet by the end of the month, twelve different U-boats battered to the bottom forty fully loaded freighters and heavily ladened tankers. More than 500 sailors and civilians were killed outright. The sea was aglow in crude.

When Uncle Sam finally came to his senses, he began prioritizing his well-established strengths. Topping his lengthy list was radar, sonar, and high-frequency radio directional-finders more commonly referred to as "Huff-Duff." Aside from the desire to whip the Boche with weapons he already possessed, these new technological marvels were eventually the unraveling of the godforsaken *Unterseebootes*. Given the fact their submarines were far superior in comparison to anything the Americans or British produced, the Germans did not possess these weapons.

While these wonders were being produced, with radar in the final stages of development, Admiral Andrews had been pleading for three whole months—without success—to gain cooperation from the cargo and tanker ship's masters. Ever since the U-boats had arrived, these men, in hardheaded, stubborn, and disrespectful fashion, continually ignored well-thought-out suggestions and oft-proven tactics to safely get them safely to port. Each master, mindful only to himself, had his own set of rules and how he thought he could outfox the wolf. In most cases, bad decisions were made and many a captain succumbed to his own miserable fate.

It wasn't until 11 April 1942, when the brand new one-month-old 8,081-ton fully ladened *Gulfamerica* tanker was torpedoed by the U-123, commanded by Kapitänleutnant Reinhard Hardegen, that all gasoline and oil tankers were ordered into port and held there until a convoy system of sorts could be implemented. But it was this type of fate, one time too many, that finally forced the government's hand. Cargo would no longer travel alone but in the cradle of support.

Admiral Dolly Andrews, in complete support from Admiral Ernest King, now Commander in Chief of Naval Operations (COMINCH), and Admiral Royal Ingersoll, now Commander in Chief of the Atlantic Fleet (CINCLANT), was given full power to integrate and operate a convoy system and deal with the agencies involved. After months of aggravation and preparation, Andrews now could implement a plan he knew would work in saving the ships and fighting the subs.

Andrews knew he didn't have the proper patrol craft for a full-blown convoy system; that is, running the length of the coast. But what he did have was enough power to move ships from port to port in a leapfrog manner. He called this makeshift convoy the "Bucket Brigade." The convoys would travel only during the day. At night, the ships would anchor safely in the harbors. While the ships were out of harms way, the patrol crafts could scour the coast at night. By the first of May, the bait was taken and it soon began to pay. The U-491 was deftly aware of what they were about to face.

* * * * * * * *

Late Monday afternoon on April 13, the 314-foot Navy Wickes-class destroyer USS Roper (DD-147) left the Chesapeake Bay and headed south. Based on sketchy intelligence reports from the Fifth Naval District, a U-boat was spotted working the coast off Nags Head. At 2238, and diligently scouring the area, Lieutenant Commander Hamilton Howe had a solid sonar contact. Without sounding an alert, he dropped one depth charge. Afterwards, and assuring himself everything was in order, he retired to his bunk fully clothed turning over the deck to Ensign Ken Tebo, a well-liked and trusted officer.

Six minutes after midnight, there was another peculiar blip on the ship's radar 2,700 yards off the bow. Sonar revealed a large, solid, chunk of iron. With the commander's consent, Tebo followed the blip soon coming upon a curiously strange wake. Believing it to be that of a submarine, he maneuvered his ship starboard of its wake. Slightly increasing his speed, to only twenty-knots to avoid losing his sonar capability, he noticed a shift in the wake to port and then to starboard. Whatever he was following was taking evasive action.

At 700 yards from the target, a torpedo narrowly grazed the port side of the destroyer. Staying starboard of the wake was a lifesaving move. Going to general quarters, Tebo ordered full speed ahead. At 300 yards, he turned on his twenty-four inch searchlight and aimed it at his target. The illumination revealed a Type VIIB German submarine.

Turning quickly to starboard, and placing themselves inside the turning radius of the destroyer, the U-boat prepared to fight. After completing a 180-degree turn and only 200 yards starboard of the Roper, the Germans manned their guns. With the Roper's beaming

215

light steadily trained on the conning tower of the sub, one three-inch gun, and one fifty-caliber machine gun quickly cut loose killing and scattering the Germans from the deck. Within minutes, the submarine began to sink and sailor after sailor clambered from the conning tower to abandon the boat.

As the *Roper* continued its turn, they prepared a depth charge barrage atop the sub. Many German sailors, now bobbing in the water with yellow life jackets and clamoring at the side of the ship as it passed them by, hopelessly screamed for help. *"Bitte! Bitte! Kamerade, Bitte!"* "Please comrade" was not what the *Roper's* sailors wanted to hear. They had no sympathy for their foe. *"They deserved this misery for all the misery they've caused,"* was the common thought amongst the Americans.

But all the yelling came to a halt. The *Roper* rapidly launched eleven depth charges imploding the submarine and rupturing the organs of the water bound Germans. After the last of the geysers came splashing down, it was deathly quiet. Only the rumble of the engines and the moaning of the guywires were audible. By sunrise, seven airplanes and a blimp were flying overhead. By 0830, the British trawler *HMS Bedfordshire* arrived to help recover the bodies. Of the forty-six U-boat crewmembers, only twenty-nine were eventually recovered. The U-boat's commander, Oberleutnant Eberhard Greger, was not one of them.

Later that morning, identification papers found floating on the surface acknowledged the submarine as the U-85. After the bodies were recovered, they were then transferred to Norfolk where, later that night, they were given a military funeral at the National Cemetery in Hampton, Virginia. Following the service, three volleys were fired, taps were played, and the graves were filled with dirt. [To this day, the German sailors are still buried in that cemetery in numbered plots and a memorial service has been held every April 14 since. *Ed.*]

Twenty-five days later on Saturday May 9, the 165-foot United States Coast Guard Cutter *Icarus* (WPC-110), the sister ship to the USCGC *Dione*, was en route from New York to Key West to act as an escort for the southern end of the Bucket Brigade for ships heading north. When twenty miles south of the Cape Lookout cusp at 1615, soundman William Rabich picked up in his earphones what he thought was a submarine noise one hundred yards away. Before calling general quarters, Executive Officer Lieutenant Ed Howard, who had the bridge, alerted fifty-two year old captain Lieutenant Maurice Jester.

By 1630, Jester had still not come to the bridge. By now the sound had faded and was placed 2,000 yards away. But several other sonarmen were in agreement with Rabich that the *Icarus* had picked up the propellers of a submarine, and it was maneuvering into a position of attack.

Just as Seaman Santiago Quinoñes, head sonarman, was calling the bridge verifying what they knew, a huge explosion 200 yards off the port quarter heaved the ship. At this moment, Captain Jester entered the bridge and immediately ordered his ship towards the large swirl of the explosion. It was believed that either the torpedo detonated early or it stuck in a rising shallow shoal of the seabed. Either way, the sea was the color of burnt sienna and dirty white foam.

When Kapitänleutnant Hellmut Rathke of the U-352, a Type VIIC boat, peered into his periscope, he was expecting to see a burning freighter. What he saw was a boiling dark reddish-brown sea of foam and a fast, armed, gray naval cutter bearing down his throat. Lowering the scope, he ordered the boat to dive and hide in the swirl of dirty sea. Unfortunately for him, the depth at that point was only twenty fathoms deep—shallow for submarine.

Seconds after the explosion, the *Icarus* was en route to the stained rusty foam and ready to attack. One hundred and eighty yards from the mud, the sonarman lost the contact. Jester then estimated the distance to where he thought the submarine might be hiding and unleashed five depth charges in a diamond pattern set for a depth of one hundred feet. Inside the U-boat, the underwater explosion shattered the glass of the gauges in the control room and thrust the Executive Officer, Leutnant Josef Ernst, headfirst into a control panel knocking him to the deck instantly killing him with a broken neck. The main lights flickered off leaving only the dimly lit glow of the emergency lamps; the electric motors were dislodged from their mounts. Any thoughts of escaping were now diminished. Rathke's only hope for survival was rolling over and playing dead.

But unbeknownst to Kapitänleutnant Rathke, because his instruments had been demolished, his boat was slowly on the rise. The depth charges, dislodging the heavy 88-millimter cannon from the foredeck and blowing away a good portion of the heavy metal surrounding the tower, had compromised her buoyancy. On the sonar scope, the *Icarus* noticed the boat's slow movement and prepared for another attack.

Captain Jester then unleashed three depth charges in a "V" pattern killing the boat's leading engineering officer (*Leitender Ingenieur*) Heinz Teetz and causing the U-352 to heel to port with a ruptured ballast tank; air wildly gushed to the surface in boiling like fashion. Seeing the bubbles, Jester dropped one last charge over the fizz forcing Rathke to blow his remaining tanks and surface. He had no choice if he wanted to survive.

While turning about, and from 1,000 yards away, the crew if the *Icarus* saw the ill-fated U-352 surface from the bow and resettle back down with the stern section beginning to sink leaving eight feet of bow exposed. The cutter opened up with her three-inch guns and fifty-caliber machine guns raking the deck and hitting the first few men jumping into the sea. During the horrific shelling, the crew continued abandoning through the hatch fearfully diving into the water. As the boat began to plummet, eleven live crewmen never made it through the hatch succumbing within the hull. Rathke was the last man out before his boat sank. While the crew was swimming away from the sub, *Icarus* gunmen continued pelting the bow of the boat giving the predilection they were shooting at the crew. That may have been true; but the firing quickly stopped when cooler heads prevailed. No one in the water was hit. The time was 1717. The day was warm and overcast.

With thirty-three survivors floating in the sea, the *Icarus* turned around and very slowly began to leave. Rathke, believing the Americans had left them to drown, encouraged his men to stay together and help support the wounded. In reality, Lieutenant Jester was beginning a series of frustrating radio calls inquiring about the rescuing of their fallen foe. Because no regulations or precedents had ever been set for retrieving enemy prisoners, Jester was at odds with what to do.

Norfolk station made no effort in responding to his request. The response to the matter from the Charleston station said they had "no message" meaning they had "no comment." The final call, to the commandant of the Sixth Naval District, finally answered at 1749 ordering him to bring the survivors to Charleston. Upon receiving the message, Jester immediately turned his ship around and rescued the waterlogged Germans. Unfortunately, Gerd Reussel, a sailor who had his left leg blown off at the hip while escaping the boat, died four hours later while on board the *Icarus*. He was later buried in the National Cemetery in Beaufort, South Carolina. The final survival toll now stood at thirty-two men.

There was one interesting fact about the U-352. In a total of three short patrols and seventy-six days at sea since her commissioning on 7 June 1941, and with only seven days on the Eastern Sea Frontier arriving off the coast of New Jersey on May 2, the boat sank nary a single ship—not to say it didn't try as witnessed by the Swedish crew of the freighter *Freden*.

On the night of May 5, Kapitänleutnant Rathke, 300 miles off Cape Hatteras, fired four torpedoes, over the course of one and a half hours, at the hapless non-zigzagging Swedish freighter. Two torpedoes passed in front of the bow while two other torpedoes went completely under the ship.

The captain of the *Freden*, fearing the so-called inept U-boat commander was sooner or later going to sink his ship, turned his stern towards the paths of the forthcoming torpedoes narrowing the submarine's target to give him extra time to abandoning ship. Rathke, on the other hand, not pleased with his actions, felt the freighter was running away, and decided not to chase. Not thinking clearly, he left the scene looking for another target neglecting to consider using his powerful 88-millimeter cannon on his foredeck to blow holes into her hull.

The following morning at sunrise, the *Freden's* crew, drifting in their lifeboats, was overwhelmed to see that their freighter was drifting beside them. Feeling confident the danger had passed, they reboarded the ship and continued onward towards New York unscathed and incredibly lucky.

* * * * * * * *

To say that twenty-eight submarines had presumably been sunk was, at best, spirited propaganda. The Navy was presumptuous in releasing those reports probably in hopes of boosting the American morale. Nevertheless, since the first day of March, the fact remained that only four U-boats had actually been sunk killing a total 156 German sailors—a paltry figure compared to what they and their comrade brethren had caused.

Two boats, the U-656 and the U-503, were sunk by American aircraft off the Canadian Coast of Newfoundland. This was not considered part of the Eastern Sea Frontier. But the other two boats, the U-85 and the U-352, were actually the first two submarines sunk in American jurisdiction—certainly a far cry from the *twenty-eight* boats the Navy had *presumably* claimed. Nonetheless, it wouldn't be the last. By the first day of August, basically before it was over on the Eastern Sea Frontier, five more U-boats would never again see the shores of Germany.

From the middle of May to the middle of August, thirty new and different U-boats would sink a total of fifty-six more merchant ships bringing the grand total since the middle of January and the beginning of *Unternehmen Paukenschlag* to two hundred and sixty-four merchant ships sunk by one hundred separate U-boats. But what these figures don't represent is the devastation inflicted by the U-491 from information sent via the "Beacon on Kill Devil Hill."

Kapitänleutnant Hans Vogel had been off the North Carolina Coast since February 15 and he, along with his fellow submariners, had caused tremendous amounts of damage to the Americans and British by sinking heavily laden secret military cargo destined for the British Isles. Having been freshly reloaded and fully restocked, Vogel was now as ready as ever to continue his rampage against the Americans. Except for one badly timed miscommunication, or so he thought, on a large military target, and a few faulty G7e electric torpedoes from the replenishment boat that failed to explode, everything was status quo ante and running smoothly. While this crew had been at sea longer than any other crew in the U-boat fleet, they were in remarkably good spirits. And to keep those spirits high, Vogel, now affectionately known as the "Old Man" and uttered only behind his back, began allowing American swing music to be piped in over the loudspeakers throughout the boat from the radio station WBT in Charlotte, North Carolina. Now with fresh food, clean sheets, and plenty of rolls of toilet paper received from the U-459 *Milchkuh*, the big band music was an added bonus and just the ticket to keep the morale of the crew reposed.

* * * * * * * *

Admiral Andrew's convoy system was not foolproof. Many ships, approaching the East Coast of the United States from all over the world, refused to join up with a convoy preferring to travel alone. It was these maverick ships the Nazi seawolves continually preyed upon and sunk. But, by the end of May, when the system finally caught the fancy of all inbound skippers, nary a ship was sunk while rounding the dreaded Diamond Shoals—the Eastern Sea Frontier's main killing field.

Because the convoys were now a threat to the submarines, Admiral Dönitz ordered his fleet of wolves further south to the Florida Coast, the Caribbean, the Gulf of Mexico, and to the mouth of the Mississippi River. But, a few submarines were ordered to continually roam the Eastern Seaboard in an effort to keep the Coast Guard patrol spread thin. In making the Americans believe the Germans still had a formable presence, the Americans were forced to remain on station along the Atlantic coast. Dönitz did not want his adversaries to believe his fleet had moved south. Though, one specific submarine was still ordered to stay on station and continue his deadly mission: the U-491. As far as Admiral Andrews and Lieutenant Fleming were concerned, that boat had done its deed and retreated back to France. The American command had no reason to believe it was still floating around.

On Tuesday, May 12, Admiral Andrews, with hands clasped behind his back, was pacing the fourteenth floor of 90 Church Street gazing at the large one-story map in front of him. The chart depicted the whole Eastern Sea Frontier with the Caribbean Sea extended below plotted on the floor. He was contemplating the next move Herr Dönitz, his Nazi counterpart in arms, was feasibly going to make.

Lieutenant Fleming, on the other hand, was pacing his office floor contemplating what he was going to do for lunch. He picked up the telephone.

"Molly ... this is Lieutenant Fleming at the Coast Guard Station. I need to get in touch with Deputy Scoggins. Know where he is this morning?"

"Yes sir. I think he's still at the courthouse. Let me try him there first."

"Okay." A few seconds passed and R.W. came on the line.

"Mark! How's it going? What's on your mind?"

"Hell R.W., where ya been lately? You don't seem to come by and see me anymore!"

"Well, lately I've been right busy Mark. Been work'en on a few cases, but things have slowed down a bit. Been scratch'en my head the last few days try'en to figure it all out. What'cha ya got on your mind?"

"Bessie's! What's the special today?"

"Well let's see ... today is Tuesday ... let me think."

"You mean to tell me ya got'a think what the specials are? I thought you knew those puppies by heart."

"Mark, I ain't been eat'en over there as much lately. Been tak'en my lunches over at the pharmacy."

"What'cha been eat'en over there... aspirins and diuretics?

"Well, it's not that bad. Why don't I meet you over there 'bout one o'clock? My little cook friend's got a dynamite chicken salad sandwich with hot 'tater salad on the side that'll knock ya out!"

"Yeah well, sounds okay I guess. But ya don't know what the special's over at Bessie's huh?"

"No Mark, can't say that I remember. Just come on over to Ned's, all right?"

"Okay ... Okay. See ya 'bout then. No fried chicken huh?"

"That's Wednesday's special!"

"You dog you!"

Lieutenant Fleming didn't have anything important he wanted to impart other than to see him and find out what's been happening on the civilian frontier. His beachfront protection was status quo with nothing unusual to report other than some jetsam that had floated to shore from the blown up cargo carriers running the coast. So far no bodies had been recovered.

R.W. didn't have much to report either. His investigation into the cottage fire had come to a screeching halt except for finding one small clue. After filtering through every piece of debris on the site, the investigators discovered two one-gallon glass bottlenecks in the ruins. Being what they were, it was out of place based on the information from what Tommy Matthews, the cottage owner, had said. The bottlenecks were suspected of being the remnants of some kind of gallon jug that held an accelerant which probably started the fire. For the moment, the office had a suspect but no hard evidence or motive pointing to her or her boyfriend. It had become frustrating. Around one o'clock, Mark pulled in front of the pharmacy.

"Say R.W., who's the cute 'chicky' behind the counter?"

"Ah, she's the cook ... the one who makes the sandwiches."

"She's a looker, that's for sure! Now I see why ya come here more often."

"I reckon."

Claire Belle saw R.W. had a friend for lunch. Seeing the young officer in his khaki uniform walking alongside her beau, she suspected he was the commander of the Coast Guard Station based on the numerous conversations she's had with R.W. After they took a seat at one of the little round tables, she walked over with a pad and pencil to take their orders. R.W. played coy. Mark spoke first.

"Well there sweet thing! What'cha got hot today other than you?"

Claire just laughed mentioning that most folks got the chicken salad sandwich with the hot potato salad. He ordered that along with a glass of sweet iced-tea and a wedge of apple pie for dessert. She turned towards R.W. and spoke.

"Well how about it, you ol' animal you!" R.W. played along for fun. He wanted to see the expression on Mark's face.

"How 'bout some of that raw meat we had for dinner last night. Sho' was good, wasn't it babe!"

"I'll say it was!" Claire Belle said with a slight grin.

"But, on the other hand, I think I'll just have an egg salad sandwich and a Coke. No, make that two sandwiches."

"You got it sugar. You coming over this evening?"

"Sure thing ... 'bout the usual time?"

"Sounds great! See you then."

At that moment, Lieutenant Fleming felt smaller than a flea on the tail end of a barking coon dog. He was totally embarrassed and heartily apologized to his friend. R.W laughed lightly punching Mark on his upper arm. When Claire brought their orders, Fleming meekly apologized asking her to change his order to crow. She giggled and later brought him an extra helping of potato salad.

She sat down at the table and talked for a few minutes flashing her wonderful smile. Mark just melted. He knew he had been had. After a few more minutes of laughter, Claire went back to the counter, and Mark and R.W. carried on conversations on various subjects. Then Mark rehashed the story about the two fishermen who came into contact awhile back with the German U-boat. They both chuckled imagining Mr. Webber's head in the toilet bowl.

"Yeah, that was about as funny as it gets. You reckon those two ol' coots ever told their wives?" R.W. said laughing.

"I think they kept purty quiet. I don't believe their wives would've believed that fish tale no how. You reckon?" Fleming said also laughing.

"If'n it was me, I believe I would've kept it quiet. Why bring up something ya can't prove," said R.W.

"Well, I imagine when his wife went to wash'en his clothes, I reckon she probably figured he'd been rolling around in some 'hog essence' or something. She definitely would've smelled them clothes."

"Yeah, he was right potent smell'en ... that's for sure!"

"But you know R.W., I keep going back to where he mentioned about them Germans asking him about the monument. Something seemed a bit odd about that. You think?'

"Yeah, it did seem strange. Why would the Krauts ask something like that?"

"I don't know. It's certainly something to ponder," Fleming said.

"I wonder why they would've wanted to know 'bout that. Is the monument that popular worldwide?" R.W. asked.

"Damned if I know. I wouldn't think so. Although, it is the birthplace of aviation. Maybe it is that popular," Fleming said hazarding a guess.

"Yeah, but those guys were seaman. Why would that interest them?"

"Hell, I don't know. Oh, R.W., by the way! You hear about that U-boat sinking this past Saturday?'

"No, I haven't."

"Yeah, the U-352. Sunk by one of our Coast Guard cutters ... the *Icarus*. Even brought in some prisoners of war! Got 'em down in Charleston. About thirty-two of 'em."

"No kidd'en! How many subs sunk now ... 'bout thirty or so?"

"Don't believe that crap the Navy's put'en out! That's pure-tee-bullshit! I know for a fact that ain't true."

"Well, how many then?"

"Four!"

"You're jok'en me! Just four?"

"Yeah, only four. Two back in March off the Canadian Coast, one back in April off Nags Head no less, and the one this past Saturday south of Cape Lookout. One, two, three, and four! No more. That's it buddy."

"Well, I'll be damned. I had a feel'en those figures from the Navy weren't quite right when they came out. Still see'en too many ships go down though."

"That's right buddy. There's still a whole damn fleet of them sons-of-bitches out there killing our seaman and sinking their ships. Seems like a whole new wave of 'em moved in."

"Is it get'en worse or better out there, Mark?

"Actually, I think it's getting better. You been notic'en more planes in the sky now haven't ya?"

"Yeah, come to think of it, I have."

"Well, not only we got'a better presence with those ancient B-18 Bolo Bombers and those float'en PBY's, we even got a presence of civilian planes from the Civilian Air Patrol ... called CAP."

"What can they do? They're not loaded with ammo or bombs are they?"

"Naw, nothing like that. Just a radio. Hell, just being in the air spooks them subs. They can't tell whether or not they're civilian or

223

military. When they see a plane, any plane, they head for the bottom like a rock."

"Now that you mention it, I have seen a little more activity on that airstrip by the monument."

"R.W., if'n you didn't know it, that beacon atop the monument is an airplane beacon. It's not a lighthouse for ships. You knew that though, didn't ya?"

"Well, sort'a. I just never paid that much attention to it one way or the other. It's just become old hat to me. I know it's there, but that's about it. Went to the top of it back in '33 ... hadn't been back up there sense."

"You know they've ordered all lighthouse lights shut down, haven't you?"

"When did that come about?"

"First of May. We've already shut down Currituck, Bodie, Hatteras, and Ocracoke. The Wright Memorial, we've got no jurisdiction over that. Word should've already reached the caretaker. I think with that particular beacon, he need only black out enough just so you can't see it from the east and up and down the coast. Coming from the west, you should still be able to see it. But coming from the east, it should be dark."

"No, I didn't know that. I'll get with the caretaker and make sure he complies. Yeah, I'll get with him today as a matter of fact and see what's going on. Come to think about it, I saw it flashing last night com'en back from Miss Claire Belle's cottage."

"Yeah, you do that. It needs to get blacked out."

Just after overhearing this piece of conversation, Claire Belle brought over a wedge of apple pie for each of them.

"Hey, you got ice cream on yours!" Fleming said.

"Yeah. Kind of a standard order with me. It's called 'a la mode'."

"'A la' what?"

"Aw shut up and eat."

After they finished their meal, Fleming went back to the Coast Guard Station and R.W. walked back to the courthouse. He met up with Roscoe in his office. George was patrolling the Outer Banks in R.W.'s car. Sam was on foot around town.

"Well, how was lunch with the Lieutenant?"

"Ah, we laughed a bit. Not much going on out his way. He did tell me 'bout a U-boat the Coast Guard sunk this past Saturday that had survivors. They took 'em to Charleston for interrogation. I'd like to be a fly on that wall!"

"No kidd'en! A sub, huh? It wasn't the U-491 was it?"

"Nope, the 'U-three-fifty-something.' That's 'bout all I know. He also told me all the lighthouses have been ordered shut down except the Wright tower. You know anything 'bout that Roscoe."

"Haven't heard a word on that one."

"Fleming said word should have already reached Alfred through the Quartermaster Department. Only the east portion needs to be blacked out. Everything took effect the first day of May. You want me to take care of that for you Roscoe?"

"Yeah, sure. You take care of it. If it needs blacked out, by god we need to get it blacked out!"

"Yeah well, I'll get with Alfred this afternoon. Did Rose Ellen pass on to Jenny that last piece of scuttlebutt about the glass bottlenecks we found in the fire ruins?" R.W. asked Roscoe.

"Yep. She passed it on this morning at the post office. Said she didn't react too much about it which in itself was a bit unusual."

"Yeah, you're right. That is unusual. I've noticed since Rose passed on that first tidbit of info about the gasoline smell in Hank's car, she's been a lot quieter than usual. Even seems she and Hank are seeing less and less of each other."

"That what John been tell'en ya?" asked Roscoe.

"Yeah. Says she usually goes to the Casino by herself. Drinks a few beers, shoots some pinball. Leaves 'bout nine, maybe nine-thirty. Probably goes home but not too sure 'bout that. Sometimes Alfred sits with her for a beer or two."

"Well, there's no doubt something's going on with her. If she's guilty, sooner or later she'll slip up somewhere. Hopefully we're there to catch the slip."

"Yeah, I hope you're right."

Just about that time, George walked in from patrolling and turned the car keys over to R.W. so he could go find Alfred Winters and get him to take care of blacking out the beacon. First he would go to his cottage. He could call first but this type of information was best served in person.

\

Chapter 21

By sunset R.W. had traveled all around the Outer Banks looking for Alfred Winters without success. He decided it was time to head for his parents house for a bite of supper and to pick up Josh. It had been a long and frustrating afternoon, but he knew sooner or later he'd find him. After dinner and just before heading back to his house, R.W. received a phone call from his young friend John at the Casino. Alfred had just walked in along with Jenny and the tall blond Dutchman. They ordered a round of beer and were sitting at a small table at the end of the snack bar.

R.W. told John he was coming over and to just sit tight and try to keep an eye on them without arousing suspicion. R.W. thought it might be sometime before he returned and thought it best for Josh to spend the night with his grandparents. In the meantime, the three bar patrons began talking keeping their conversation just loud enough to hear over the music and the crowd of about fifty people who where bowling and shooting pool.

"We might have a problem," Alfred said to the other two after taking a swig of beer.

"And what kind of problem might that be my friend," spoke Fritz Lötz, the German infiltrator and head of their small Nazi organization. Even though Jenny and Alfred knew he was German, they only knew him as Arnold von Stapele and playing the roll of a Dutchman. They knew very little else.

"About a week or so ago, I got word from the Quartermaster Department, who is in charge of the monument, telling me I've got to blackout the beacon light dome so it doesn't shine east and up and down the coast. Being an airplane beacon, I have to keep the backside towards the west lit and still rotating."

"You knew this last week? Why didn't you say something? Surely the local authorities know something about this ruling," Arnold said in an agitated state.

"Yes, yes ... I know. I should have said something sooner. But you both know since the first of May, we've had three signals to deliver and I thought it best we get those signals off. At the time I felt things were moving fast, and I didn't think there was enough time to do something that quick. But now I know I can't hold off much longer without somebody in authority noticing. I think it's best I get that section blacked out tomorrow. That's why I called you together tonight."

"Alfred, you've subjected our organization to serious risk! If the authorities get wise to your mistake, they may look into the matter," Arnold said firmly.

"Yes, I know. But the message came through the mail service. I can always claim I didn't receive the notification in time. I don't think it was that big a deal. I still thought it was best to get those signals off without going to so much trouble!"

"Yes, that's true. But somehow we could have worked around that to get them off. What is your plan to block off that section of beam?"

"Well, I don't particularly want to paint the glass. I want to make it so that we can remove the coverage quickly and return it back to dark. Right now, I think I can probably use some dark blankets over the glass and hang it on the dome frame ... the same kind of thick blankets we're currently using to block off the beams from the other two lights. That seems to work fine. This way it can be quickly removed and replaced. That's the only idea I can think of so far."

"Yes, that might work. Jenny, do you have any thoughts on the matter since you're the one performing the signal?"

"Well, I reckon it'll work okay. It's already tight as hell up there anyway so it's gonna take some extra time. Anyway you look at it, the beam of light's gonna be shinning through that section when, in fact, no light should be shining at all. Somebody who's paying attention, and knows the new ruling, might just notice. There's really know other way we can get around that."

"What about getting a third person to take care of the dome blanket?" Arnold asked.

"Hell Arnold, you've been up there. You know how damn tight it already is in that dome. A third person could get in there but I think it could cause problems when I send the signal. If I accidently get bumped working the leaver, the signal becomes worthless ... kaput! One wasted mission and one pissed off Kapitänleutnant."

"Yes, you do have a point. I see what you mean," Arnold said.

"What about a window blind system ... you know, like in a house?" Jenny suggested.

"Interesting idea," Alfred said.

"Yes, maybe that might work best. But with a 1,000-watt light bulb, I think the light will still permeate through the blinds. Still, I think it's something we need to consider," Arnold stated.

228

"In the meantime, let's hang the blankets and we'll put some more thought into the blind system. Based on what Joy has told me, it looks like we won't have another target for about four days. She tells me the ships are now beginning to work in a convoy system and that in itself is beginning to cause problems for our U-boat commander. I think he already should have noticed the ships as they move up and down the coast. The scuttlebutt is they've stopped moving at night. I'll see if I can get more information on that."

"Who's ready for another beer?" Alfred asked.

Just as he got up to get the beers, R.W. walked into the foyer outside the door of the main room. There he met Rags and began a short conversation. As Alfred was at the bar getting the beer, R.W. looked through the door and spotted him. By the time he could excuse himself from Rags, Alfred had already walked back to the table with three beers. He had a gut feeling R.W. was going to walk over to the table. He forewarned the other two so they might be ready to receive him. After everybody took a swig of their beer, Alfred's premonition came true. R.W. walked to the table. Alfred spoke first.

"Good evening there Deputy. How are you this evening? Out on patrol tonight?"

"Yeah, I sure am. Just can't seem to get it all done during the day. Jenny, how are you this evening?"

"I'm doing fine R.W." Jenny replied in a friendly tone. R.W. noticed she was a bit more upbeat than usual. It was probably the beer. Then he looked over at Arnold and stuck out his arm for a friendly handshake. He introduced himself.

"Howdy there ... Deputy Sheriff Scoggins." Arnold reciprocated by standing and shaking hands with R.W.

"Yes, Deputy. How are you? I'm Arnold ... Arnold von Stapele."

"I haven't had the pleasure although I've seen you around a few times. You and your lovely wife find a cozy spot for that picnic awhile back, I gather?" Arnold looked dumbfounded.

"Why yes, yes we did. We had a splendid picnic overlooking the sound area. It was a most beautiful day as I recall. Thank you for pointing us in that direction!"

"A Sunday it was. Yeah, I thought ya might find it pleasant up that way. Look, take your seat. I don't mean to bother ya'll, but I do need to have a private word here with Mr. Winters if'n you don't mind."

"Sure Deputy, what's on your mind?" Alfred said standing up in front of R.W.

"Why don't we just step out to the front here, and I'll be done with ya in a jiffy."

While Alfred and R.W. walked to the foyer and out of earshot of anybody standing nearby, Arnold and Jenny had a conversation themselves.

"You have any idea what that's all about?" Arnold asked.

"Best I can figure it's what Alfred has just mentioned about the beacon light. I reckon them *authorities* have already caught wind it should've been blacked out ... and it ain't. R.W.'s probably *reminding* Alfred to get it blacked out. I'm sure we'll find out in a minute or so when he returns."

"Yes, probably so. Your Deputy seems rather sharp. I find it interesting how good a memory he has. It was last summer when my wife and I came over this way to have that picnic. I remember talking with one of your officials, but I don't remember him."

"So, you're married huh?"

"Yes. Her name is Aleta."

"Well, I hate to hear that. I was hop'en one day to get in your britches."

"I don't think so my dear. I don't screw-around with the hired help. You do understand me?"

"Yeah, I hear ya. But you're missing out on some good stuff!"

"And your Hank. How is he these days?"

"Aw, he's all right. A little moody he is, but he's doing okay."

"He's not happy with his pay, I hear."

"He runs his mouth sometimes when he ought'a be keep'en it shut. I've got'en him squared away though. I keep 'em happy, if ya know what I mean!"

"Yes, so I hear. But he doesn't seem happy now?"

"Like I said ... he's moody. He'll keep his mouth shut."

"The cottage fire. I hear rumblings the officials think it was arson."

"Well, what the hell do you think? Of course it was. We had already talked about torching the place ya know. You agreed if I recall ... right!"

"Yes, that is true. But you weren't supposed to make it look like arson."

"Well, I guess it didn't work out that way. We used three gallons of gasoline. Lit up the mattresses first ... spread the rest on the walls and floor. We needed to light 'er up fast and get the hell out'a there. If'n we'd let it smolder, somebody might have seen it and put it out. That was our thinking anyway."

"Anybody see you leave the scene?"

"No ... nobody! We got away clear and clean and went to E City. *Nobody* saw us!"

"But the newspapers are insinuating otherwise?"

"The Sheriff's Department don't have shit, I tell ya! The place was burnt to a golden crisp. Hell, nothing was left. Nothing I tell ya!"

"Okay ... okay, I believe you. Calm down. If they don't have anything, then they don't have anything. I am sure the officials are playing games. But the fact is you and Hank did do it, so stay low. How well do you know this Deputy Scoggins character anyway?"

"Aw, we go back a long way. We tolerate each other, but that's about it. And no, R.W. ain't stupid. Sometimes he looks and acts stupid, but he ain't stupid. He knows what in the hell he's doing."

"Those kind of officials are dangerous. We must start being more careful."

About that time, Alfred came back to the table. He seemed normal.

"Is it what I think it was?" Jenny asked.

"Yep, it was. He found out about the blackout from the Coast Guard. I told him I'd take care of it first thing in the morning. So, tomorrow it looks like it's going to get blacked out!"

"What did you tell him?" Arnold asked.

"Just what I said I would ... that I received nothing in the mail. He was none the wiser and seemed to have accepted that as the truth."

"And that's all there was to it, yes?"

"Arnold, that was all there was to it. This place isn't like Germany or Eastern Europe. As long as I get it blacked out, everything's going to be okay."

* * * * * * * *

Two days later on Thursday, Hank showed up at his usual time at the main post office in Manteo with the regular morning mail. Jenny grabbed the sack and slung it to the large table in the backroom and started sorting the letters and packages.

"I hear tell Alfred's got'a blackout part of the dome window? How's he gonna do it?" Hank said.

"Well, at first he was gonna use a blanket but then decided it might be best to paint the section with black paint. He didn't paint a two-foot diameter section in the due east direction. He just covered that section with a thick piece of dark cloth hanging it from two screws he put into the dome frame with a hook just over it. So, when we're ready, all we got'a do is lift that piece of cloth from the bottom and hang it on the hook. When we're finished, we just pull it off the hook and let it fall back into place. It looks like it'll work just fine. He showed it to me last night. I don't think it'll take anymore time than what we're already doing."

"Am I supposed to hook and unhook it?"

"Naw, I can do it. You know how damn tight it is up there. You'll be crawling all over me. I can do it ok."

"When are we on again?"

"From what I hear, in a couple of days. Seems most shipments these days are going out after sunrise. I don't think they're gonna be anymore night shipments going out."

231

"How's that?"

"Convoys are get'en started. Patrol craft go along the outside of the freighters trying to protect 'em from the subs."

"How's our guy gonna handle that."

"Damned if I know. But from what I hear, he's a purty crafty commander. He'll probably handle it okay.

"You com'en over tonight?" Jenny asked.

"Naw, I won't be com'en over tonight. I'm gonna meet Dale up in his neck of the woods tonight. Says he's got a new bar he wants to go to."

"Well, don't get your ass drunk and run off the road. You run into some of the ditches up that way, the snakes'll eat you alive! You know that don't ya?"

"Yeah, yeah, I hear ya. I'll be all right. Look, I need to get on the road. I got some more deliveries to make. I'll see ya in the morning, okay?'

"Yeah, you take it easy ... okay, sugar britches!" Jenny said as she pecked him on the cheek.

* * * * * * * *

Early that same morning at the courthouse inside the sheriff's office, Roscoe, George and R.W. were going over busy paperwork and discussing various items about police work and the happenings around town. Then the topic turned towards the war and rationing.

"Well, looks like the Office of Price Administration (OPA) finally put the hammer down. We got our gas stickers in the mail today," Roscoe said.

"Where do we stand with that one?" R.W. asked.

"We got the 'C' sticker. We can get just the amount of gas we need to do the job we need to do which is a bit better than the 'A' and 'B' stickers."

"How much gas can those stickers get, Roscoe," George asked.

"Well, the way I read it, the 'A' sticker is for the general public and they can only get three to four gallons per week and the cars can't be used for pleasure driving. That's gonna hurt a lot of our cottage owners so it's a safe bet we won't be see'en a lot of 'em out here this year."

"Yeah, I reckon you're right there, Roscoe. What 'bout those 'B' stickers?"

"That's for the folks working for the war effort ... you know, industrial and defense plant workers and such. I reckon it'll take care of some of them guys working in that small shipyard over in Wanchese."

"What else has been rationed so far?" asked Rose Ellen who was listening in.

"Well, aside from freezing prices on everything, tires and rubber, stoves, typewriters, here's the biggy ... sugar!"

"Oh shit, not sugar! What about coffee? I hope coffee's not on the list!" Rose Ellen said with her eyes wide open.

"No Rose ... coffee's not on the list yet. But I can assure you it's probably com'en," Roscoe said with a slight chuckle. In all the years Rose Ellen has worked for him, that was the first time he has ever heard her say a nasty word. Even George and R.W. had a bit of a smile on their faces. [Coffee wasn't rationed until November 1943. *Ed.*]

"Well, that's it so far. R.W., you reckon Alfred's covered up that dome window for the beacon light?" asked Roscoe.

"He probably has. He assured me he was gonna do it. Maybe George and me ought'a go over there and double-check with him and make sure he did it. George! You been to the top of the monument yet?"

"No, can't say that I have. But it looks like I'm about ready to! You know R.W., I'm just a little afraid of heights ... you know that don't you?"

"Aw shit, George. You be walk'en those twelve-inch 'I' beams in New York City thirty floors up. I believe you like ya got a hole in your head. Come on you big lug, let's go!"

After their little meeting, Rose Ellen went to the post office, Roscoe fixed his fourth cup of coffee, with sugar, and R.W. and George jumped in the old faded green Pontiac and headed over to Alfred's cottage. R.W was hoping he'd be there because he wasn't much in the mood to go looking for him again. It was still fairly early in the morning, and he had a feeling he was probably there. When they pulled in front of his cottage, his car was there. They went to the back door screened-in area and knocked.

"Morn'en Alfred," R.W. said in a friendly way.

"Well, good morning fellows! What be it that brings both of Dare County's finest to see me this morning?"

"Just came by to check to see if'n ya got that dome section atop the monument covered up."

"Yes sir ... did it yesterday just like I said I would."

"Well, I guess that's all well and good. You mind if'n we might go take a look-see ourselves"?

"What, you guys don't trust me?"

"Oh, no sir. Nothing like that! No sir, we trust ya. It's just that we'd like to actually to see it and verify it's been tak'en care of ... you know, so I can tell Roscoe we've actually seen it. You know, from way down here, it's kind'a hard to tell. As a matter of fact, you can't see it. You don't mind do you?"

"Well, I see your point. Let me get out of my slippers and put on some shoes, and I'll be right with you."

"Sure thing. Take your time."

A few minutes later, Alfred came out into the screened-in porch with the key to the double metal doors. He knew what they were going to see and his mind was clicking as fast as his heartbeat.

"You fellows want to walk up the back way or walk over to the side to where it's not so steep?"

"I reckon we'll take the long route where it ain't so steep."

"Good, I'm glad you suggested that route. I'm too old to be climbing up the back way even if it is a bit shorter. But this way is still a little steep too. When was the last time you were up there?" Alfred asked R.W.

"Well, George here ain't never been up there ... the last time I ventured up this way was somewhere 'round '33 or so. Don't have too much memory of it though."

"It's not changed much. We did put a fresh coat of paint on the metal stairwell a few years back ... changed the light bulb a few times ... worked on the rotating motor once or twice when it stopped. Beyond that, it's about the same."

The monument was directly behind Alfred's cottage about three hundred and ninety yards. Because the way the sand dune had formed eons ago, the backside was very step and quite cumbersome to climb. Walking around to the side of the mound to the east, the incline wasn't as severe and definitely an easier walk. Once around to the side, they were able to easier walk on the concrete path to the top of the monument platform. Once to the top of the mound, the view was magnificent. The mound was, after all, ninety-feet tall.

The monument was built on a platform that consisted of a circle sixty-four-feet in diameter with five star-points projecting twenty-five-feet from the circumference pointing towards the north, west, southwest, southeast, and east. The base exterior is defined by sections of fabricated granite blocks that extend five-feet to ten-feet above the grade.

The base of the monument is triangular and centered on a platform that is forty-three-feet long on the east and west sides and thirty-six-feet long on the south side where the double metal doors are located to enter the structure. At the north end, it is six-feet wide at the base with the word "Genius" carved into the granite about five-feet up from the base.

The monument is tapered at the top and is a total of sixty-one-feet tall to base of the stainless steel and glass dome where the beacon light rotates. At the fifth level, the topmost section where people can enter the observation platform, it is only fifty-three-feet from the base of the structure. On the east and west sides, where it has been tapered, it is twelve-feet wide. On the south side, it is eight-feet wide and encompasses mostly the five-foot diameter light dome. On the north side, there is the observation platform measuring a paltry three-foot on the sides and two-feet at the small double door entrance comfortably allowing just three people to observe the countryside sand dunes and ocean. It was here that Jenny and Hank would relax with a cigarette before and after sending the signal to the submarine.

"Wait till you guys get to the top and look out over the area from the observation deck! It's even a grander view. From the fifth level, where the observation deck is, you're a total of one hundred and fifty-eight feet from your eyelevel to sea level. It's about the highest point all around for miles and miles."

After walking around the base of the structure and looking to the top with their heads bent backwards, Alfred opened the right double door through the serrated brass door handle. He walked in first groping for the light switch. Once he had the lights turned on, the foyer was aglow. Alfred then unlocked the metal bar-door on the right granite staircase, and they began walking to the top with Alfred leading the way. When they reached the first landing, George let out a light grunt.

"Think your knee can handle it to the top George?" R.W. asked his buddy.

"I'll give it a try. I think once I get to the top, coming down might be a bit easier. I think I can make it though."

Pass the third landing they came upon the narrow spiral staircase leading to the top. The rails were easy to grasp making the climb much easier. In the meantime, Alfred had already skedaddled to the fifth level and opened up the two small twelve-inch-wide metal doors leading to the observation deck. The inside was a trifle warm and he wanted to get the cool Atlantic Ocean breeze swirling to the inside. It was a welcomed relief to George as he worked his way to the top of the tower.

"No doubt 'bout it Alfred, it's a great view from up here. Think you can make it there big George?"

"Yeah, I'm right behind you. Be there in a second. Boy, that cool breeze sure feels good!"

Because it was so tight at the top in the dome area, George went directly from the steps to the observation deck, hunching over to get through the five-foot nine-inch tall doors, so Alfred could show R.W. the painted section on the dome glass. The dark cloth was obvious to R.W. hanging from the screws attached to the dome.

"What's with the cloth there, Alfred?"

"Well, there was a small section I didn't paint just in case there was some odd reason we had to let the light through. What reason that would be I don't rightly know just yet. But as you can see, if I did have to let some light out, I'd have a whole lot of paint scraping to do off that glass in an awkward position. So, I left a small section and just covered it up with that thick piece of dark cloth to keep the light from shinning through. I checked it last night and no light is shining through."

"Well, I reckon that might be thrifty idea, but I can't imagine what reason there'd be for allowing light through when everything is supposed to be blacked out. But maybe it's a good idea. It would save ya a little extra work if'n ya did have to briefly open 'er back up. At least ya got that heavy cloth over it. Seems to be attached well ... don't look like it'll blow off or anything. At least ya got it painted so ya can't see it from up or down the coast. I reckon that's good."

"Yeah, that's what the letter said."

"Oh, so you got the letter huh?"

At that moment Alfred realized what he had just said. He quickly reacted.

"Uh ... yeah, it came yesterday. Must have gotten lost in the mail and then found. But, yes ... it came yesterday. Said, 'Block off the light so it couldn't be seen up and down the coast but could be seen from 180 degrees from the west side.' Yep, that's what it said."

"Well, no doubt you have complied. At least those damn U-boats can't see it anymore. Maybe it'll save a few lives ... you never know."

"Nope, you never know."

"George, you got enough fresh air yet? You ready to slide back down those steps?"

"Yeah, slide's a good word. Let's go."

* * * * * * * *

Friday, the following morning, it was bright and cool. There were some townsfolk out and about going in and out of local stores. Claire Belle had arrived early at the pharmacy to help Ned sort through a delivery of new stock that had arrived the previous day. Roscoe was buttoned up in the office handling paperwork over his fifth cup of coffee, George was patrolling the Wanchese boating area, Sam was patrolling the downtown waterfront area, and R.W. went to the Coast Guard Station to get new information from Mark about the Eastern Sea Frontier. Jenny, in the meantime, was at work in the post office waiting for Hank to show up with the regular morning delivery. He was running late.

About ten-thirty, his truck pulled to the rear of the building. Jenny was inside cleaning up and had the door to her back when it opened. She didn't look up when she spoke.

"Damn it Hank, you're late. Where the hell ... hey, you're not Hank! Where the hell is Hank? And you're late yourself!"

"I know, I know. But there's a reason. The supervisor had to pull me away from the line to get this mail to you. It's been crazy as hell this morning!"

"Well then, what's so damn crazy about it other than you're late. I got'a mess a work to do! Well, don't just stand there with your dick in your ear ... speak up!"

236

"Jenny ... Hank's dead!"

"He's WHAT!"

"He's dead, Jenny. Hank *is* dead!"

"Oh no! ... What happened? He get drunk and run into a ditch?"

"It might'a been a bless'en if'n he had."

"What'a you mean?"

"The police found him inside his car outside of E City early this morning."

"And...?"

"And he was in the trunk ... and the car was engulfed in flames. It was totally gutted."

"My poor Hank! Dead! Ah shit! I knew that son-of-a-bitch run his mouth too much."

"What was that Jenny?"

"Aw, never mind."

Chapter 22

As typical as it was on the Outer Banks at this time of year, a rainsquall came through the area just before dawn soaking the area with an inch of rain. By sunrise, the clouds had dissipated with the sky becoming unusually clear. Because the rain had packed the sandy road heading south to the Coast Guard Station from Whalebone Junction, R.W. felt he could safely get there without having to reduce the air pressure in his tires to the usual eighteen pounds for traction keeping the big four-door Pontiac from miring in the sand. That was one less headache he had to deal with today.

When he pulled in front of the station, Lieutenant Mark Fleming was on the front porch of the Coast Guard Station administration office smoking a cigarette and talking with Chief Bleu.

"Glad you could make it down this morning R.W. Let's go on over to the mess tent and grab us a cup of joe. We'll just talk there."

"Wouldn't happen to have any leftover eggs and dried toast would ya, Mark?"

"Well, I reckon I could get our stewburner to cook ya up a few. Didn't make it to Bessie's this morn'en, huh?"

"Naw. I took the notion to stay in the bed an extra hour this morning. Hell, this past Wednesday, George and me walked up top of the monument to check it out and to make sure ol' Alfred Winters, the caretaker, complied with the blacking-out order. On the way down, I slipped on one of those damn tiny metal steps and jammed my back. It's been sore as a sumbitch ever since."

"Well, I do sort'a notic'en ya walk'en around like ya got on wooden underwear. I'll get ol' 'Doc Fingers' here to take a look at ya.

With all the work 'round here, we get'a lot of sore backs he revitalizes with a little tweaking."

"Yeah, that might be a good idea. Ol' Doc Wheless in town just gave me some pills and said to stay off my feet awhile. Hell, I can't do that!"

"I know what ya mean. Come on, let's walk on over ... or should I say hobble!"

After walking inside the mess tent, Mark had his mess cook rustle up a plate of fresh eggs and toast for R.W. The day before the station had received a case of raspberry jam for the toast. While R.W.'s breakfast was being prepared, they sat at a clean table each with a cup of coffee. Mark enlightened the deputy with some fresh news.

"R.W., looks like our 'ol' pal,' the U-491, is still around."

"How's that? I thought you folks said he was long gone by now."

"Well, we thought so too. But I believe our Kapitänleutnant Vogel screwed up. Late last week a military cargo freighter outside the Chesapeake went up in smoke, presumably by 'our friend.' Fortunately, the freighter didn't blow up completely and there were quite a few survivors. Where the torpedo entered the hull and exploded, some men were killed outright but many guys were able to get away in lifeboats."

"Well, that's good news to hear for a change."

"The sub surfaced near the wrecked ship and asked some of the sailors what the name of the ship was and what it was carrying. Seeing how those Germans were manning the guns, our guys were a bit skittish in not tell'en 'em the truth."

"Well, I reckon that makes sense. But I haven't heard tell the Germans doing that before ... asking for the name of the ship and all."

"Yeah well, we have. A lot of these U-boat captains do this and sometimes actually give the survivors some rum and cigarettes and steer 'em in the right direction to get home."

"But Mark, how'd you know it was Vogel?"

"After the sailors passed on their ship's name and cargo, one of our boys hollered back wanting to know, 'Who is the son-of-a-bitch that just sank our ship'."

"You're kidd'en! Boy, that was ballsy."

"Yeah, weren't it though? Anyway, the captain laughed aloud and hollered back in broken English, 'This is Kapitänleutnant Hans Vogel of the U-491. Tell your President Roosevelt he can kiss my ass anytime because I am going to personally sink every military freighter you send out and there is nothing you can do to stop me. Heil Hitler'!"

"Mark, I believe we've heard that before!"

"Well, that's how we know it's him. And it's puzzling to figure out how 'our guy' has lasted this long in one spot. He seems to have an unlimited supply of firepower and food. We knew for a fact when these subs run out of ammo and torpedoes, they hightail it back home.

A lot of 'em reload and then come back. But that takes time ... at least fifty days for a turn-around. From our last contact with Vogel and now the one last week, he ain't had the time to return to France and come back so quick. We think Vogel must be going out to a supply ship somewhere in the Atlantic."

"How do you know that?"

"Well, the Brits have been furnishing our headquarters with all the communication between the U-boats and their command headquarters in France. Then, by the first of February, it all came to a screeching halt. Nada ... nothing! Everything's been shut down. They must'a changed their codes or something 'cause the Brits can't read 'em anymore. But before the signals got shut down, we knew different subs were coming and going ... and there was a message about a supply ship. But just after that, the signals went dead and we don't know any more than that."

"Mark, that's interesting. But what's that got to do with me?"

"Admiral Andrews' staff of thinkers believes there's a leak somewhere feeding this vital information regarding these military freighters to some sub out there in the Atlantic. The theory right now is that it's the U-491 and, as you know, he's damn near impossible to catch. So, they're going through the entire inside organization from top to bottom trying to find some sort of link. But they're still befuddled as to how in the hell the information is getting to the sub. They're beginning to believe there has to be a small organization that has infiltrated into the system."

"And with all the tech-wonders you boys got, ya'll can't figure it out?"

"We've got this marvel from Signal Intelligence called 'Huff-Duff.' It's a high-frequency radio-directional-finder gizmo that can triangulate a signal and give us the general direction from where the radio frequency is being transmitted from."

"Well, ya lost me after triangulate, but go ahead." R.W. said, swabbing the last bit of eggs on his plate with a piece of toast.

"The only signal we can pick up and triangulate is coming from the Diamond Shoals area. Time we get out there, whatever it is, is gone. But the puzzling part is there's no signal that can be detected coming from the shore. So whoever is sending the signals to Vogel, it ain't coming from a radio signal on our shores. Somebody has got to be taken him the info from a local boat."

"Any chance the sub is sending a man in by raft to pick up the info?"

"Well, we thought that. We know we're spread thin, but I don't think so. I mean there's no way that German sailor could come ashore in the exact same spot every time. Sooner or later one of my men would catch 'em."

"You think maybe one of your men might be involved?"

241

"I doubt it. We rotate our guys around so that they don't patrol the same are twice. This makes it so they become familiar with the whole section of island and not just one particular stretch of beach. I mean if'n it was one of our guys, the sub would never know where he's gonna be. You know, we're spread out over forty miles. By water, that's a lot of distance."

"Yeah, I see your point."

"What about some fish'en boat? I assume you got a man or two stationed around Wanchese don't you?"

"Absolutely ... and there is nothing coming or going we don't have our eyes on or know about. We got them guys covered like flies hovering dead dog meat."

"Mark, I still haven't heard ya tell me what this has got to do with me!"

"Well, with this new information to go along with the previous information from our little German friend John, about him knowing for sure the sub receives some kind of signal from somewhere along the coast, command thinks those signals are getting to the sub from somewhere south of the Oregon Inlet to Cape Hatteras, and I got'a pull some of my men from up your way and put 'em further down south. Headquarters ain't gonna send me any more men, and I got'a make due with what I got. I even called my sister, but she can't help me. Hell, I got a boatload of shrimp and a small warehouse of Jim Beam bourbon to trade for some help and I can't get any takers. Can you believe that?"

"That is hard to believe. But I know you had some men about as far north as Nags Head. How many you gonna be pull'en?"

"All the way down to 'bout five miles south of Whalebone Junction. About twenty-five men. R.W., you're gonna be exposed up there without any help from my guys. I'm sorry as hell 'bout that but there ain't a damn thing I can do about it."

"Mark, I know you're doing your best. We'll just have to deal with it and pull up the slack. Fortunately, and I do mean fortunately, we ain't had no trouble there. Now you know if'n we do get into a mess, we're in deep shit don't you?"

"I know that. But Intelligence has to go with their best hunch, and they think this is it. R.W., I wish there was something else I can do for ya."

"Well Mark, yes there is. Seeing how we're all gonna need to be healthy, you can take me to see ol' 'Doc Fingers' and see'en if'n he can straighten me up!"

"Yeah, let's go ahead and do that."

"Now what's he gonna do to my back?"

"He's gonna *adjust* your back. He's gonna move some bones around and put your spine back into alignment."

"How's he gonna do that? Put me on some kind'a medieval rack and make me a foot taller!"

"Naw, nothing like that. Actually, he puts you on a table on your side and spreads your arms and legs every which way so they look like noodles on a spaghetti plate. Then somehow he torsions your body with his arms and hands and you'll hear your back 'snap, crackle, pop' and after that you'll be as good as new."

"Gee, that don't sound like a whole lot'a fun. How you know all this?"

"Because he's done it to me and it's a miracle I tell ya ... it's a damn miracle!"

* * * * * * * *

Later on that morning, Alfred Winters went to the post office to see Jenny. Nobody else was in the office when he went inside. Jenny was somber. He had a feeling Hank had been killed. But his main reason for the visit was he wanted to let her know that she needed to come by his house later that evening. Arnold was coming down from Norfolk and they were to have a meeting concerning Hank's replacement.

"Jenny...?"

"Alfred."

"I'm sorry about Hank. I had nothing to do with that."

"Hell, I know that Alfred. Hank brought this shit on himself. I told the idiot to keep his mouth shut. But no, he wouldn't listen to me! He had to keep on run'en it. I thought I had 'em calmed down, but I guess I didn't. I bet that Dale Conner had something to do with get'en 'em all riled up again when they sat around drink'en beer. I believe that's what done it."

"Well, I wouldn't know about that. I really don't know what was going on other than I do know that Arnold wasn't pleased with his attitude, and he was afraid he might compromise the operation."

"Then you knew enough!" Jenny said with a tear in her eye.

"Maybe I did then. But then again, you know, you and I have had some lengthy conversations over Hank. You told me you had him straightened out."

"Well, I thought I had him straightened out. That's why I think ol' Dale had something to do with firing his ass back up. That's what I believe anyways."

"Look, Arnold's coming over to the house tonight. He's got some information on how things are going to be run from now on. I think because of Hank's death, things are going to change and we had better listen."

"Alfred, do you have any clue who might'a killed 'em?"

"Jenny. No I don't. I really don't know who could've done it because I don't know how deep this organization really is. But what I do know, Arnold is nobody's fool and he is somebody to reckon with. We, ourselves, better be careful or we'll end up like Hank."

"Yeah, I reckon you're right. We got'a be careful. You know Alfred, I been think'en. I'm beginning to believe we might'a screwed up when we signed on to do this mess. Do you actually realize what we've got'en ourselves into?"

"Jenny, I hear what you're saying. But we've already talked about that and have even already tried to do something about it. We're stuck unless we carry through with our plan. There's only one way we can get out of this mess now and still stay alive."

"That's for fuck'en sure!"

"Look, you be over to my house about eight o'clock. Arnold said he'd be there about eight-thirty. I'll go to the store and have you some beer on ice when you get there."

"Thanks Alfred, I'll see ya 'bout then."

"Jenny, keep a cool head tonight. This is serious business," Alfred said clasping her hands within his. He then winked and walked out the door.

* * * * * * * *

Much later that afternoon, R.W. was finishing up his rounds on the islands and was idly talking to a few of the local residents. Before finishing up with one neighbor, he noticed a regular summer couple he knew arriving from Greenville, North Carolina to open up their cottage. After finishing his conversation, he walked over to greet them.

He was a doctor at the local hospital in Greenville and used his "C" gas-rationing sticker to get him to the coast. He had been on duty for twenty-one straight days and told the administrator of the hospital he had to take some time off to refresh himself. The physician was frazzled and confided to his wife he was thinking about leaving the hospital for private practice to lessen the amount of work hours he had to perform. The leave to his beach cottage was just the ticket to give him the time to contemplate that decision. R.W. stopped by to chat while he unpacked the car.

"Dr. Culp, good to see ya again."

"R.W., how long's it been?"

"I reckon since last summer. How's the wife?"

"Ah, she's doing fine ... inside right now making the beds and fixing me a drink, I hope! I hear tell you folks out here have had some activity lately?"

"Yeah, those damn U-boats just ain't giv'en up. Probably during your stay, you'll no doubt see the horizon light up signaling another ship just got blown up."

"So I've been hearing. But I understand the Navy's been sinking those subs right and left."

"Well I hate to tell ya, it ain't nothing like what you been hearing. If you've heard that twenty-eight have been sunk, well ... that just ain't so."

"No! Really?"

"That's right ... had a meeting with the Coast Guard commander this morn'en and he told me that so far only four have hit bottom."

"Really!"

"Yep, that's what he said ... just four."

"Well, I'll be. Ain't that something! What about that burnt cottage we saw coming in? Germans didn't have anything to do with that did they?"

"I don't think so. We're not entirely sure what happened there ... still investigating that but we think it might'a been an electrical problem."

"Whose cottage?"

"Tommy Matthews from Nash County."

"Damn, I hate to hear that. We used to get together some with him and his wife, Willa Jo, and cook out. Nice fellow. I assume he knows about it."

"Oh yes sir, he does. He's just heartbroken about it ... came down a few weeks ago to see it. We talked a right good while. He's help'en us out the best he can but there's just nothing to go on right now. I reckon with war break'en out and all, I doubt he'll be rebuilding anytime soon I'm afraid."

Yeah, that's a shame. I'll have to give him a call. Say R.W., I notice you're walking a touch funny. How's you're back?"

"Actually, it's a lot better. Slipped a few days ago com'en down the monument steps and threw it out'a whack. Had ol' 'Doc Fingers' down at the Coast Guard Station 'readjust' it this morn'en. It's a whole lot better now than what it was, I tell ya that!"

"That ol' Doc Price you talking about?"

"Yep, it sure is. You know 'em?"

"Yeah, sure do. We were classmates at Duke University. Damn fine doctor."

"No kidd'en!'

"I didn't know he was doing chiropractics now."

"I reckon. All I know is he torqued me up on that table and I can walk straight-up now. It feels a whole lot better."

"Yeah, that's an interesting science. Not many medical doctors believe in all that bone crack'en 'voodoo.' Actually, I do. If you can keep a patient off pills, it's that much better. Those pain pills can hook you."

"Ol' Doc Wheless said the same thing. Said vodka works purty good too to ease the pain, but ya end up 'snockered' half the time. I'm not ready for that."

"Yeah, vodka's not a good idea. You keep seeing Dr. Price. He's a good man and a good doctor. He'll get you straightened out okay, no pun intended. You might have to see him a few more times, but that's okay too. Sometimes it takes more than one visit."

"Well, thanks for the advice," R.W. said turning towards his Pontiac.

"What's the Friday supper special at Bessie's tonight? I don't think the missiz's is gonna be cooking," Dr. Culp asked to R.W. as he was walking to his car

"Well Doc, it's usually the pork ribs. But I'm not entirely sure. I think she's changed up her menu a bit because of the war ... so I really don't know. Actually, I'm going over there myself in a little while. I promised a friend I'd take 'em. Maybe I'll see ya."

"Yeah, okay. Thanks for stopping by."

* * * * * * * *

Last week R.W. had promised to take John to Bessie's for lunch. But because he had been so busy with the fire investigation and other police duties, he was unable to do that; though, he did make arrangements for a supper this evening. After talking with Dr. Culp, he drove over to the Casino to pick up John. Because it was Friday, Rags was expecting a large crowd tonight and it was best for John not to be gone too late. When R.W. pulled in front of the Casino, John was already waiting in the foyer and met his car in the parking lot. As was usual for John, he was in a chipper mood. He always made R.W. feel good.

"How's it going there John? You ready for a big meal tonight?"

"Yes sir, Mr. R.W., I sure am! But I better not eat too much. We have a big crowd coming in later and I got a feeling it's going to be a long night. If I eat too much I get sleepy, and I don't think that would be too good for tonight."

"Well, I understand that. Ol' Bessie's food can put ya right to sleep if'n you're not careful. I think I'll cut back a bit myself. But I'm gonna save a little room for some of that sweet 'tater pie though."

"Oh yes sir! You have to save room for that. It sure is good!"

Upon arriving at Bessie's, R.W. noticed the usual Friday evening crowd was much smaller than normal. No telling what it was but R.W. figured it was because Bessie might have changed the special. But Bessie told R.W. that the Friday special was still the same as it always had been; though, today, she had an unusually big lunch crowd and

246

they devoured all the pork ribs. So, she came up with country ham, hominy grits, and green beans. Nevertheless, it was as delicious as ever. After finishing their meal, it was time for dessert.

"You ready for some of that sweet 'tater pie now, John?" R.W. asked.

"Yes sir, I believe I left just enough room for a small wedge."

While they were eating their dessert and having general conversation, John arbitrarily brought up an observation that caught R.W.'s attention.

"Say, I bet that view from the top of the monument is quite dramatic. Maybe one day I'll have a chance to get up there myself. While I'm there, I might take a look at the rotating beacon mechanism and see how it works. Sometimes it seems to run amiss."

"How's that, John?"

"Well, some nights when I lay in bed, I notice the flashes seem to run out of sequence ... but not for long. Maybe about a minute or so."

"Is that right?"

"Yes sir. When I can't sleep, I sometimes mentally count the time between flashes. It normally rotates so that each flash is just over three seconds till the next flash. Most of the times, it's right on the money. But every now and then, it gets out of sequence."

"How bad out of sequence?"

"Oh, not much. Sometimes it's two seconds, sometimes it's four seconds or longer. Though, after about a minute or so, it gets right back to normal. But one night the light beamed for well over ten seconds. I just figured the rotating mechanism somehow got hung up or something, but it always gets back to the normal sequence. Maybe the guy taking care of it doesn't know there might be a problem. It is late when it occurs."

"About what time?"

"Well, when it does occur, which is not every night, it's usually after two o'clock ... I think around two-fifteen or so. But like I said, it's not every night. Actually, it's quite sporadic."

"When was the last time you noticed it out of sequence?"

"Well, I can't say for sure. It's such a mundane thing. I really don't pay all that much attention to the days it occurs. I mean, the only time I really think about it is when I see it. When you brought it up tonight about going to the top of the monument, it refreshed my mind. But now that I think about it, there were three times last week it occurred, but I don't remember what days."

"Well, that's certainly interesting."

"You want me to say something to Mr. Winters? I understand he's the caretaker."

"No John. No, I'll take care of it. But do this for me. Don't mention this to anybody else, and when you do see it running 'catawampused,' I want you to let me know immediately by phone even if it is after two o'clock in the morning."

"'Catawampused?' That what you said Mr. R.W?"

"Well, you know what I mean ... out of sequence."

"Mr. R.W., I don't think I'm ever going to learn all your Southern American colloquiums! Mr. Rags is full of them, and he confuses me to death."

"John, you're doing just fine. Don't even try to learn 'em 'cause it'll just drive ya crazy! But you listen ... you keep me informed immediately when you see that light out of sequence. Ya got that!"

"Oh yes sir ... yes sir I do. Is this important?"

"John, I'm just not too sure right now. But you keep this quiet, okay?"

* * * * * * * *

Later that evening after R.W. dropped John off at the Casino, he decided to head back to the sheriff's office to talk with Roscoe and George about John's revelation on the beacon light. It all seemed unusual and, for the time being, he really couldn't make heads or tails out of the information other than it was something that needed attention.

At dusk, Jenny went to Alfred's cottage a little earlier than the specified eight o'clock to talk with him and wait for Arnold. Just like Alfred had promised, he had a large cooler of beer iced down. When Jenny showed up, Alfred was already drinking one.

"Jenny, yes ... come right on in."

"Eve'ning Alfred."

"You ready for a cool one I imagine."

"Yeah, sure. I could use one ... or two ... a dozen! Sure not gonna be the same now with Hank gone. I'm gonna miss that SOB."

"Jenny, I am so sorry."

"Yeah, I know you are Alfred. You know I loved 'em didn't ya?"

"Yes, yes I did. Ya'll had a funny way about it with each other, but yeah ... I could tell you loved him, and I knew he loved you too. It's really all so tragic, but you know that already. He seemed like a good ol' boy with a good heart."

"I should've never got'en him tied up in this mess. All he was supposed to do was bring me the package with the regular mail and then I was to pass it off to you. At that point, he was none the wiser to what the hell was going on. If'n I had left it at that, probably none of this crap would've happened. I should've never got'en him up there in that tower to help me. I should've figured another way 'round working the other two beacon lights myself in a different manner. Was I stupid or what!"

"Jenny, you didn't know. You can't blame yourself. He knew better ... hell you even told him yourself."

"Yeah, I know. But Hank was one brick shy of a full load and I knew that. I knew that all along and should've handled it differently. I was hop'en by giv'en him more responsibility it might make him concentrate more. I just screwed up. I should've known better and I knew it! I should've never put him in that position. His mind just seemed to work different than ours."

"You really think so, Jenny?"

"What'a you mean, Alfred?"

"I think you know what I mean. Hank wasn't stupid. He certainly didn't play his cards right about the money, that's for sure. But he realized long before us that we all screwed up by turning traitor. I think when you put the fear of God in him that one night, and how he could never go back to the way it was, I think deep down he knew his days were numbered. You just scared the shit out'a the ol' boy."

"You think so?"

"Based on what you told me, yeah, I do. You know Jenny, I was doing this dastardly deed for revenge, and you were doing it for the money. Hell, ol' Hank didn't have a reason. He was just like a lost puppy dog following along. At some point, he just didn't know what else to do except asking for more money and trying to feel more important. I just think it was his way of saying he wanted more recognition. Unfortunately, Arnold didn't see it that way."

"Well, I never thought of it like that."

"You know Jenny, Hank is really the one who put the fear of God back in us ... remember? He's the one who really got us to thinking of just what in the hell we were doing ... and deep down we listened to him. You know that because of what we did. We talked about it back then and agreed. Why it's taken us another month to get where we are is beyond me, But, I'm see'en much clearer now."

"So, what'a you want'a do now?"

"I think we should just go ahead and implement our plan now to the fullest. We've already sent one bogus signal. Hell, let's go ahead and do 'em all that way and bug out'a here as soon as we can and leave Arnold holding the bag."

"You think so, huh?" Jenny said taking a large swig of beer from her bottle.

"I don't see that we really have any other choice. Arnold's turned into a littler Hitler now and, sooner rather than later, somebody's gonna get wise to our little scheme, and we'll end up in front of a firing squad. If our plan works, we can escape Arnold, he'll be implicated, and we'll be long gone ... and alive," Alfred said reaching into the cooler for another beer for himself and Jenny.

"But to get ourselves organized and bide a little more time, I think we ought'a send at least one more good signal. That way, things'll look on the up-and-up and Arnold won't know any different for right now. I think we need to be careful on how we plan our escape and the little extra time wouldn't hurt," Jenny said working the plan in her mind.

"Yes, I think that might be a good idea. Let's plan on that then," Alfred said taking a sip from his beer.

"Well, you know Alfred ... we *did* talk about this for a right good while. Maybe the time has come."

"I think so, Jenny. Look, Arnold's got a bigger stake in this than we do even though we're in it up to our eyeballs, but we can get out of this with our lives. All we got'a do is kiss his little ass for a little while longer, and we're home free."

"I guess you're right, but I ain't all that excited 'bout kiss'en that heinie's butt for anything. I know he killed Hank."

"Jenny, you're probably right. But when he get's here, keep a cool head! The last damn thing we want'a do is let him know *we're* disgruntled or we'll end up like Hank."

"Well, what'a ya know. The sumbitch just pulled up. He's got somebody with him. Probably the guy who's gonna replace Hank."

Jenny was right. Arnold just pulled in and got out of the car with Dale Conner in tow. Just that alone immediately told them who was going to replace Hank. They came into the cottage. There was an air of tenseness. Alfred offered them each a beer while they spent a few minutes of idle chin-wagging before Arnold got right to the point.

"Unless you don't know who this is, it's Dale Conner. Jenny, he's going to replace Hank in helping you with the beacon lights. Also, from now on, he's going to bring the package from Norfolk directly here, to your house Alfred, on the same night the signal is to go out. In turn, you will contact Jenny and proceed from there."

"Can we not get the package a bit sooner, Arnold? It takes a little time to prepare this thing you know," Jenny piped in with concern in her voice.

"You will have to make do with the new procedure. There is no other choice! It's an order!"

"When do you expect another signal?" Alfred asked as pleasantly as he could.

"Dale tells me that Joy is currently processing a ship movement manifest as we speak and one should be ready for tomorrow night. So plan on Sunday morning at the usual time."

"I thought Dale worked on the docks?" Jenny said.

"He no longer works there. He will now be working directly under me. He will be the one that will be contacting you from time-to-time and giving you instructions. It is doubtful I will be coming here any more. Are there any more questions? Jenny, do you have something to say?"

"Well Arnold, I was going to ask you one but after seeing your singed eyebrows, I believe you've just answered my question!"

"Come Dale, we shall go now. I have said all that needs to be said. Now, if you will excuse us...."

Before leaving, Dale snidely walked over to the cooler of beer and grabbed five bottles to take with him. He said nothing as the screen door closed behind him. Jenny took one large gulp from her bottle and looked out at the car as it was turning around.

"I had a feeling it was that blond haired heinie son-of-a-bitch who 'fried' my Hank. Alfred, get me another beer and let's sit down and do some cogatat'en on this!"

Chapter 23

When R.W. returned to the courthouse after seven o'clock from his dinner date with John, Roscoe was the only one in the office. With Roscoe's permission, George had taken a job that night working at the Casino to help Rags, the owner, keep the antics of the servicemen in check. It was rare for Roscoe to be in the office on a Friday night. He heard R.W. walk into the office and sit down at his desk and look over his mail and paperwork. Roscoe hollered through his open door.

"Is that you, R.W.?"

"Yeah, it's me Roscoe. What you doing here tonight?"

"Aw, thought I'd give George a chance to pick up some extra bucks over at the Casino tonight. Besides, he could use the dough and it seemed like a good idea. Things been purty quiet around here today and, when he's over there, it usually stays just that more so. Besides, my wife has her garden club over to the house for dinner, and I wasn't much in the mood to be 'round them cackling hens if'n ya know what I mean."

"Yeah, I know what you mean 'bout them cackling hens!"

"Come on into the office R.W. Let's have us a little shooter!"

"Well, I don't mind if'n I do ... been kind of a long day. Say, where did ya get this liquor? Looks kind'a familiar."

"Well hell it ought'a! It came from the trunk of your car."

"Aw shit Roscoe. I forgot all 'bout that except'en the time when I got a bottle out for Miss Claire Belle and me when I had dinner with her awhile back. Hell, it's been in there since

February when George and me run them Georgia crackers out'a town."

"I know that but don't worry about it. I had George bring it on into the courthouse the other day when he had your car. I asked him to run me an errand, and I had a mess of stuff to put in the trunk. Sam had my car that day. Ain't no big deal."

"Ya got some ice?"

"Yeah, Ned gave me a bucket full before he closed up awhile ago. It's over there on the table by the filing cabinet near the door. Here, put some ice in my glass too. So, what's been happening down at the Coast Guard Station? Anything interesting?"

"Yeah, well ... there's been some activity. Lieutenant Fleming's pull'en a good portion of his men off our section of beach from just south of Nags Head to just above the Oregon Inlet and mov'en 'em further on south down towards Cape Hatteras. Their Intelligence somehow believes information is get'en to our U-boat friend from the shoreline down that way."

"Who? The U-491? Hell I thought that sumbitch was back in Germany."

"Well ... so did everybody else. It appears he never left."

"What the hell's keep'en 'em alive? Bessie's country ham biscuits and corn dodgers!"

"Yeah, that's it Roscoe. Bessie's the link! But naw, Fleming hear tells they've been get'en resupplied from a boat somewhere out in the Atlantic. Don't know anymore than that. Anyway, what Coast Guard support we had out that way is now gone. Mov'en 'em on out tomorrow."

"Well, we're gonna be neeked as a jay bird with them gone. I guess he knows that."

"Oh yes sir, he knows."

"Not much we can do 'bout it anyway though. Anything else? Roscoe asked.

"Mark also told me that all those U-boat's the Navy's supposedly sank is pure bullshit."

"Well, I never believed those numbers anyway. He give you a figure how many?"

"Yeah ... four, just four been sunk."

"I thought maybe there'd be a few more, but I reckon that's probably about right."

"Yeah, kind'a shocked me a little too. Maybe things'll turn around soon."

"Maybe. Say R.W., I notice you're walking a little straighter. You run into some voodoo magic today?"

"Yeah, the doc down at the Coast Guard Station. Aside from being a medical doctor, he also does something called chiropractics."

"I heard 'bout them guys. Somehow they take their hands and adjust the bones. Looks like he helped you out!"

"Yep, sho' did. I feel fine. But he did say I might have to come back down for a few more adjustments. Didn't hurt at all what he did. Heard my back go 'snack, crackle, pop' and the pain was gone ... just like that!"

"No kidd'en!"

"Yeah, just like that."

"Well I'll be dog. Just like that, huh."

"Anything happen 'round here today Roscoe?"

"Naw, real quiet. How was your supper with our little buddy John? He do'en okay?"

"Aw, he's doing fine. Really likes his job and work'en with Rags. He did pass on something of interest though."

"And what would that be?"

"He's been noticing for quite awhile now that the beacon light sometimes gets off sequence."

"How's that?"

"Well, he said it normally takes just a smidgen over three seconds between flashes but sometimes it's less and sometime more ... sometimes as much as four seconds."

"What does he do ... count the time with a second hand on a watch in the dark?"

"Naw, you know like we did as kids ... one-Mississippi, two-Mississippi, three-Mississippi, and so on and on."

"Yeah, I remember that! Not quite like a second hand but it'll do in a pinch. I reckon if'n you do it enough it's fairly accurate."

"Well, that's how he was do'en it."

"You know, we better get Alfred to fix that."

"Roscoe, I'd hold off on that right now."

"Why's that?"

"John says that when it does occur, it's usually at the same time every night, or I should say every morning ... around two-fifteen," R.W. said.

"Well, I'd figure if the rotating mechanism was screwed up, it'd probably happen more often and not at the same time. Is that what you were thinking?" Roscoe suggested.

"Exactly. But what's odd about it, it's not every night and it's always around two-fifteen. He did say last week it acted up three times. He doesn't remember what days. But they were all at the same time when it screwed up."

"How does he know this?"

"John's rent'en a room from Wally Palmer over there off Kitty Hawk Bay and, from his bedroom window, he's got a perfect view of the beacon. He says when he gets in late from work and can't sleep, he lies there and counts the seconds between flashes to put himself to sleep. I reckon it's like count'en sheep, but he's using light flashes."

"And we're just now hear'en 'bout this?"

"Roscoe, it is kind of a mundane thing, and he just never thinks about it till he sees it. He only mentioned it to me tonight because I happen to bring up that I went to the top of the monument earlier in the week. That just happened to refresh his mind."

"Well, I reckon you're right. But it's Alfred's job to keep that sumbitch work'en right. You think he knows about it?" Roscoe asked.

"It's hard to say if he does or not ... but he *should* know about it. Like you say, it is his job to know regardless of what time of night it is."

"Well, what'a you think'en then?"

"I asked John to keep an eye on it for me and to let me know the second he sees it's out of whack. I told 'em to call me no matter what time it is. First, let's see if'n it's still happening and also verify the time. If that is in fact the case, there's got to be something going on we need to find out about."

"You reckon we ought'a station somebody there?"

"Well, not just yet. Let's see what happens first. Then we'll go from there. Besides, if we do station somebody there, you'll have a sleepy deputy or two the following day?"

"Yeah, you got that right. You think John's tell'en us the truth?"

"Roscoe, I see no reason for the boy to lie. Hell, he brought it up to me. What's he got to gain from it?"

"Well, I guess you're right. Let's wait and see. If'n this light thing's been happening all along, it'll probably go on a happening again," Roscoe said.

"Right now, I think that's the smart thing to do."

"Hey, let's have another shooter and play a few hands of gin rummy to pass the time."

"Yeah, that sounds good. How much you owe me now Roscoe."

"Aw shut up and get the cards!"

* * * * * * *

Early the following Saturday morning, R.W. stopped over at George's place to pick him up. They had earlier made arrangements to go to Bessie's for breakfast. R.W.'s back was feeling much better. George, on the hand, was now limping.

"Well, good morning there George! What you limping about?"

"Aw, threw my damn back out last night!"

"How's that?"

"One of the Guardsman from Coastie Station had a few beers too many and started getting boisterous. I went over to calm him his butt down, and he took a swing at me."

"Well, that wasn't too smart!"

"Time I got his arm behind his back and subdued him, he jerked and that's when I felt a twinge in my back."

"Well, I know just the ticket to get that puppy fixed."

"You do?"

"Yep, ol' 'Doc Fingers' over at the Coast Guard Station. I was down that way yesterday and Mark had 'em work on my back. I'm almost as good as new."

"'Doc Fingers' huh?"

"Actually it's Dr. Price. Good man. I'll take ya over there later today and have 'em crunch you up. He's got magic fingers he does."

"Well, if you say so."

While at breakfast, R.W. enlightened George on the recent news from yesterday. Based on what R.W. imparted, George also felt something was up. When they got back to the courthouse, Roscoe had more interesting news. When they walked in, Roscoe called them into his office.

"You boys have a good breakfast this morning?"

257

"As usual. You know ya just can't eat one cathead scratch country ham biscuit. It takes 'bout three before ya have to stop. What's up Roscoe," R.W. asked

"Got a call this morning from Sheriff Wiggins over in Currituck County saying they found a burned out car Thursday night with a body in it. It looks as though the fellow was murdered."

"Murdered? How could they tell?" George asked.

"Well, he was found inside the trunk. The lid was closed."

"Sounds like that purty well defines murder to me," R.W. piped in.

"Anybody we should know," asked George.

"It was Hank Larson ... Jenny's boyfriend."

"Holy smoly!" R.W. said with a startled look on his face.

"Yep, I think now things are start'en to get complicated with her, and him, being a suspect in that cottage fire," Roscoe said.

"You reckon she knows about it, Roscoe?" R.W. asked.

"My guess is she does. But why don't you boys go and find out. Even though today is Saturday, she might be at the post office this morning doing some work. I think she comes in sometimes."

"Yeah well, we'll start there first and go from there."

"Say George, I see ya walk'en like R.W. did the other day!"

"Yeah. Casino wound! R.W. tells me he's got a fix though."

The post office was the first place George and R.W. looked and she wasn't there. Another employee, who was inside, said he had no idea where she was. He did mention that he had talked with her earlier that morning and said she would be back in on Monday. Other than that, there was no other information. The employee, when asked, had not known of Hank's death and was unsure if Jenny knew. He was shocked to hear it.

From the post office, the two deputies drove to her house and Jenney's car was gone. Both officers looked around the perimeter and noticed nothing unusual other than her yard was beginning to look ratty from lack of care. From here they scoured the rest of Roanoke Island without success. They then decided to roam the barrier islands. While they were there, R.W. took George to the Coast Guard Station to get Dr. Price to have his back worked on. By lunchtime, George was walking upright with very little pain. For the next few hours, they continued covering the island with no success. By mid-afternoon, they were back to the courthouse reporting to Roscoe.

258

The rest of the afternoon was quiet and by seven o'clock R.W. was at Claire Belle's house to pick her up for an evening at the Casino to drink a few beers and maybe roll a few games of duckpins. There was no band tonight.

As a rule, R.W. rarely talked to Claire about the happenings in law enforcement or any of the cases he was working on. But tonight he brought up the discovery of Hank's body in the trunk of his car.

"Oh R.W., that's awful! Have you had a chance to see or talk to Jenny?"

"No, not really. George and me hunted 'round all day for her. We couldn't find hide-nor-hair of her chinny-chin-chin anywhere on the island. You got any ideas?"

"Wouldn't you imagine maybe she went up to Elizabeth City to see his parents? I mean, she and Hank were going together you know."

"Well, yeah ... we didn't think 'bout that. Maybe that's where she went."

"Sure it is. She'll probably be back in to work on Monday."

"Yeah, I reckon you're right. I wonder how she found out about Hank though?"

"Maybe somebody with the postal system told her. I mean, if Hank didn't come in to work on Friday, somebody had to bring in the mail and maybe that person told Jenny."

"Well, that makes sense too. Have you talked to Jenny lately?"

"Me? No. I haven't seen her since the first part of the week. Why?"

"Oh, no reason. I just know you talk to her some ... that's all."

"Well, yeah ... I talk to her some, just like other folks do. She's a little crusty at times but, you know, I think she has a good heart. Sometimes when we shoot pinball, she can be right friendly."

"You see her down here sometimes do ya?"

"Yeah, I told you that a long time ago. Right after I moved in she got friendly and invited me to come over here and drink some beer with her so we could get to know each other a little better. I don't do it very often, but every now and then I do. Sometimes she get's a little depressed and calls me and we meet here. Somehow I have a way of cheering her up."

"Claire Belle ... that is, for sure, a fact. You could cheer up a swet'en man set'en in the 'lectrical chair just before the warden flipped the switch."

"Well that's a little extreme, but thank you R.W.! I appreciate that. Now let's bowl another game. How much is it you owe me now?"

About ten-thirty R.W.'s back was beginning to flinch and asked Claire if they could call it a night. He needed to head back to Wanchese and pick up Josh at his parent's house. He also had to get up early because he had the Sunday morning watch at the office.

When they pulled into her driveway, Claire invited him in for coffee and maybe a back rub to help ease the pain. R.W. was quite tempted but begged off knowing he might not end up leaving until much later that night. Claire was understanding of his pain and didn't pursue the matter. R.W. did promise he would come back over Sunday afternoon and visit. She suggested he bring Josh along and he could play in the surf. The water temperature was beginning to warm up.

After crossing over the Wash Baum Bridge, R.W. decided to stop by the courthouse first and see how George was doing. His back was feeling much better. He reported the area was very quiet and there had been no calls. R.W. then proceeded to his parent's house to pick up Josh and head for home. Josh himself was very tired and fell asleep in R.W.'s car even before they reached their house only a few blocks away. R.W. carefully picked him up and carried the little fellow straight to his bed. His grandparents had already dressed Josh in his pajamas. With that chore done, R.W. undressed and fell asleep on his bed within seconds of his head hitting the pillow. With what seemed like minutes, his telephone rang. Molly the operator was on the other end.

"Deputy Scoggins?"

"Yes."

"This is Molly. You have a call from a John O'Hearn. I know it's late, would you like to speak with him?"

"Yes Molly, I'll take it."

"Sir, go ahead. He'll speak with you now."

"John?"

"Mr. R.W., I am sorry to call you so late, but you said it was all right to call you no matter what time."

"Yes John, I did. Are you call'en about the beacon light?"

260

"Yes sir, I am. It happened again just a few minutes ago and this time the sequence was terribly off!"

"Have you noticed anything else?"

"No sir. But just like I said, after about one minute the sequence went back to normal."

"John, you did just fine. Now go on back to bed and don't worry 'bout anything. Okay? And don't mention this to anyone."

"Okay, Mr. R.W. I will."

As tired as R.W. was he could not go back to sleep. His mind began twirling like a windblown whirligig. While there was nothing he could really do at the moment, he called the courthouse to see if George was still there. He was.

"George!"

"R.W.? Is there a problem?"

"When you leaving?"

"Actually in just a few minutes."

"Look, how 'bout stopping by my house before you head home. I just got a call from our little friend, John. He noticed the beacon sequence amiss again at exactly the same time. We need to talk. I think we got us a problem."

"Sure thing. I'll be over there in about fifteen minutes. You want me to call Roscoe?"

"Naw, not yet. We'll get up with him tomorrow morn'en. I think we need to start work'en on a plan."

"You need me to bring anything?"

"Yeah, bring over one of those liquor jugs we got from them Georgia crackers."

"Okay, see you in a few minutes."

Chapter 24

By three o'clock the following Wednesday morning May 20, George and R.W. packed up from their early morning surveillance of the monument and headed back to the courthouse. This was their third straight night of observation duty with nary a bit of activity. There was no telling how much longer they were going to have to continue their watchful eye. It was beginning to become frustrating; not to mention very tiring. It made the daylight working hours just that much more exhaustive.

"Hell George, let's just go on home and grab some shuteye. We don't need to go back to the office, you think?"

"I think that's a good idea. I don't see any reason we need to. I'm beginning to wear out myself. Yeah, just drop me off at the house. Why don't you pick me back up say about eight o'clock and we'll go grab some breakfast over at Bessie's."

"Well, that sounds like a plan."

After breakfast later that morning, the two deputies went to the courthouse and met with Roscoe reporting that it had been another uneventful night. They all agreed to continue their surveillance until something broke. Roscoe was feeling a bit antsy about getting in on the action, or lack of action, and told George he would replace him for that night's work. George thought it was a nice gesture but said he'd continue for the next couple of nights. He suggested if Roscoe wanted to take over Saturday night that would be fine with him. He wanted to work the Casino and, trying to work those two jobs in the same night, it would be a stretch on him physically. Roscoe agreed.

Around three o'clock that afternoon, Jenny received a phone call from Alfred Winters. Dale Conner had just delivered a packet to his house.

"Jenny?"

"Yeah Alfred. What's up?"

"We just got a new package a little while ago. You want to come by the house after work and we'll go over it."

"Yeah, sure. You got any beer?"

"I got a few left from the other night. That Conner feller took most of 'em."

"Well, I'll stop by the Midget Market and pick some up for you when I come over.'

"Aw Jenny, that's not necessary. I'll run out and get some for you. It'll save you some time. We got some stuff here to talk over."

"Yeah, I know. I'll see ya then. Thanks for calling."

* * * * * * * *

About the time Jenny had received the phone call from Alfred, R.W. had the notion to head over to the pharmacy to see Claire Belle and grab a late afternoon lunch.

"Well, hello there R.W."

"Claire, how are you this afternoon?"

"I feel a whole lot better than you look! You look like something the cat drug in! What have you been up to?" she said with a perplexed look on her face.

"Aw, I can't talk 'bout it. George and me been work'en late on something and I haven't got caught up on my sleep."

"Well, it looks like it. You're a damn sight for sore eyes if I've ever seen. You know that! You ready for something to eat?"

"Don't mind if'n I do. What'cha got today?"

"How about a couple of ham salad sandwiches and a bowl of fruit?"

"Yeah, that sounds purty good. Ya got any pie for dessert?"

"Made up a couple of egg custards this morning. Still got some left."

"Yeah, that'll be good too. So, what've you been up to the last couple of days?"

"Aw, not much. About the same as the day before and the day before that. I did see Jenny. She went to Hank's funeral in Elizabeth City last Wednesday you know."

"No, I didn't know that. So, how she do'en?" R.W. asked.

"She seems to be doing well. For some reason she seems a little more at peace with herself and a whole lot more friendlier."

"Oh yeah?"

"Well, it's just that woman's intuition thing. You men would never understand."

"I reckon not. But what's different with her. I saw her Monday, and she seemed the same to me."

"Oh, I don't know. She just seems a lot calmer and not so jittery like she had been. She actually seems to be smiling a genuine smile now and not that same ol' shit eat'en grin she had all the time. I guess that sort of stuff is what I meant."

"She misses Hank doesn't she?"

"Oh, she does at that! I think she's realizing now just how precious life really is and how quickly it can go. I certainly haven't known her as long as you have, but she has changed within the short time I've known her."

"Well, I have giv'en her lots of shit through the years, but she's brought a lot of it on herself, you know," R.W. said.

"I can imagine. She can be crusty. But you give her a chance when you next see her. She is still in mourning."

"Well, that would be the proper thing to do I reckon."

"Sure it would! It doesn't take that much effort to be nice."

"Yeah, you're right. I'll work on it," he said studying over a plate of sandwiches Claire just put in front of him.

"Good, now eat your sandwiches."

"Okay ... okay. Say you got any chicken salad sandwiches left?"

"I've got enough left to make a few. You want that on top of these?"

"Naw, fix me up two to go. Me and George'll eat 'em later tonight. We get kind'a hungry where we are."

"You can't tell me what you're doing?"

"I better not. It's police work and you know I don't really talk 'bout that stuff."

"Yeah, I know. But whatever you're doing ... you *be* careful now. You hear me!"

"I hear ya ... I hear ya."

"By the way. I enjoyed last Sunday. That was a lot of fun. It was good to get to know Josh better. You've done a real nice job in raising that boy."

"Yeah, he's a good kid. Thanks!"

* * * * * * * *

Later that afternoon, Jenny showed up at Alfred's house about six-thirty. Alfred had, as promised, purchased more beer. He knew Jenny liked the suds. Though, what amazed him the most was how well she maintained her weight with the amount she drank. She was still as trim as ever with a hard body to match.

"Thanks for getting the beer, Alfred. I sure could use a cool one."

"Tough day today, Jenny?"

"Aw, no tougher than any other day. Though, for some reason now, since Hank's death, the days do seem to fly by a whole lot quicker."

"Again, Jenny, I am so sorry."

"Aw Alfred. He's probably in a better place. I just wish he could've got'en there on his own without any help. He didn't deserve what he got. But, one of these days ... one of these days, I'm gonna pay that heinie back ... just you wait and see!"

"Yeah, his due is coming. Hell, I'm about get'en to the point I don't even like being around him anymore. And that Dale Conner fellow is a real pain in the ass," Alfred replied taking a swig of beer.

"What the hell does Arnold see in that son-of-a-bitch? He's tak'en to him like a green fly on a dog turd."

"Damned if I know. When he came by the house here awhile ago to drop of the codes, we got into a bit of an argument ourselves."

Jenny's curiosity was piqued.

"Over what?"

"Well, he's not coming tonight to help you. He said as much crap as you gave him on that last signal this past Sunday morning, from now on you'll have to handle it all by your lonesome."

"Hell, Alfred. When that son-of-a-bitch was up there with me, he just royally screwed up. He didn't know his ass from a hole in the ground. He didn't even come close to working those

266

blankets right. He had those lights flash'en so far off sequence, it had to have stood out like a sore thumb. His help was worthless. I'd just as soon he didn't help. If'n I didn't know better, somebody may have noticed *that* screw-up. Even if those other two beacons stay dark for the whole minute, that'll be much better than what the hell he did. I wonder what ol' Arnold would've thought about that?"

"Jenny, I wish I could help you, but you know that's not safe."

"I know ... I know. We've talked about that more times than I can count. But we need to have you down here, away from the danger, so to speak. You'll be able to escape if need be."

"I don't know what good it'll do. All I got is this thirty-eight caliber hand pistol ... and you, what'a you got?"

"Same damn thing you got! Shit, time we fire off a coupl'a rounds, we'll be full of lead before hit'en the ground."

"Well, I sure hope we never have to fire 'em."

"Yeah, me too."

"Look, let's go over these signals Dale brought down and make some adjustments."

"Yeah, let's look 'em over. I wanted to talk to you first so we agree to the set up. We don't want that sub to miss tonight, do we?" Jenny said sarcastically.

"No, that we don't ... *do* we? We want that Nazi SOB to be right ...on ... target!" Alfred replied with a smiling smirk.

"Say, Jenny, why don't you just stay here with me this evening until you got'a go up the hill later tonight. No sense you going all the way back over to Manteo and then come back. I got a coupl'a fresh flounder I caught this morning. Let me put 'em in the frying pan with some butter, and we'll have us a nice supper. I'll make some coleslaw and we'll have some corn on the cob, too. I bet you hadn't eaten too well lately."

"Yeah, you're right. I hadn't eaten too good. Mostly junk and beer. Sure Alfred, that'd be nice. Is there anything I can do to help you?"

"Naw, you just sit tight. I got everything covered. You're doing fine just by being here. I'll take care of everything. You just sip awhile and I'll do all the cook'en. Look, why don't we go ahead and look at those special codes I made up, all right?" Alfred said from the kitchen.

"Yeah well... let's do it later. What's the rush?"

"Yeah, what's the rush! Say, why don't you turn on the phonograph, and we'll listen to some big-band music."

"Okay, what'a ya want'a hear?"

"How about some Glenn Miller. I got an album over there in the box from 'The Chesterfield Shows 1939 to 1940.' I want'a hear 'The Woodpecker Song'."

"You got it!" Jenny said picking the album out of the box.

* * * * * * * *

At exactly twelve-fifteen Thursday morning, R.W. picked George up at his house for their twenty-five minute trek over to the Wright Brothers Monument to start their surveillance. The plan was the same. They would park their car near the airstrip to the west side of the mound behind a small grove of pine trees and brush. From there, to the monument, it was three hundred and fifty yards and ninety-feet up a mostly thirty-eight degree incline from that side of the mound.

Once they left the grove of trees, they would be exposed in the open on the mound because, other than a few spindly bushes, there was nothing else to really hide behind. Fortunately, the mound was irregular towards the south side and it was possible to get within a hundred and fifty feet from the base of the monument by nestling down in some potholes formed by erosion. From that position, they had a very good view of the double metal doors, Alfred's cottage, and a probable path someone would take to get to the monument. As long as the deputies stayed close to the ground, it was doubtful they could be seen. But tonight there was one glitch working against them: the moon was waxing and it was almost a half-full. There was enough moonlight reflecting off the surrounding sand that could cause a problem. But if they stayed still, it wouldn't present a problem. By ten minutes after one o'clock, they were hunkered down in position.

"You think we ought'a split-up tonight, R.W.?"

"I don't think so. We've got a good position here and it's a great view of the door so we definitely can see somebody com'en and go'en. Besides, we really don't have any way to communicate if we're separated."

"Yeah, I guess you're right. You did bring you're gun didn't you?"

"Yep. All the crap you gave me the other night for not bringing it, I didn't want'a go through that again," R.W. chuckled.

"Now R.W., you know it's the smart thing to do, don't you?"

"I know, I know. Yeah, I got it and it's loaded. Your shotgun loaded ain't it?"

"Fully and with a few extra shells in my pocket. Ought'a get somebody if need be."

Just then George saw a flash of light come from inside Alfred's cottage.

"You see that?"

"What? Where?"

"Alfred's cottage. I saw a light come on and then go off."

"Hell, he's probably go'en to the bathroom to take a leak. It's about two-o'clock."

George's eyes were focused on the house. He corrected the time.

"Not really. It's one-forty-five."

"Oh, well I don't have my watch on."

"Well, if Alfred's gonna take a leak, he's gonna do it in the field right behind his house. He's walking outside."

"How in the hell can you see that good?"

"I'm Indian!"

"Yeah, well ... what's he do'en now?"

"R.W. was frustrated his eyes couldn't keep up with George's.

"I don't know but he ain't stopping to take a leak. He's walking over towards that little building that houses the generator."

"What, he's gonna piss in the generator room! He ain't got indoor plumbing!"

"Hell R.W., I don't know. Can't you see him?"

"Not very well. All I see is a fuzzy figure. I can't tell who it is or what he's do'en."

"Well, I really can't either. But if it's Alfred, he ain't walking like Alfred. Whoever it is just went inside the building."

"Not Alfred, huh? I wonder who in the hell it is then?"

"Whoever it is, he's coming out now. Looks like he's got something under his arms and carrying a small suitcase."

"Where's he going from there?" R.W. asked finally realizing his eyes weren't focusing very well.

"Best I can tell he's walking straight up the steep slope from behind the generator room. I can't see him now. He'll probably be to the top in a minute or so ... purty steep climb ... it's gonna take some strength get'en up that baby! You did bring the key with you didn't you?"

"Yeah, I got it right here in my pocket. I'm glad Roscoe found it. We might need it."

Years back when the monument was built, the Quartermaster Department had several keys made to unlock the large metal doors. They specifically gave one to the Dare County Sheriff's Department in case there ever was an emergency. Through the years, Roscoe had it stashed in his top desk drawer. He never had cause to use it and it was only by happenstance he remembered where it was amongst all the junk that had accumulated in that drawer.

After two minutes, the figure crested the top of the mound and was walking towards the brick-covered star base the monument rested upon.

"R.W.! You ain't going to believe this!"

"What?"

"It's Jenny!" George said in disbelief.

"Oh shit! You *are* kidd'en me aren't you! *Please* tell me you're kidd'en me."

"I wish I was but I'm not! It's Jenny all right. You can't miss that body!"

"Holy cow! What next?" R.W. said slowly shaking his head.

"I think you're thinking the same thing I'm thinking?" George said.

"I think so. This is where those damn signals are com'en from going to that U-boat. How could we have missed it? Hell, the clues were there all along and we just blew it. Damn! How could we have been so stupid?"

R.W. was now focused on the same thing George was seeing.

"Because it was so damn obvious, that's why! We, like everybody else, kept thinking it had to have been coming from somewhere else. Even the Coast Guard thought so. Hell, that sumbitch has been right here in our own backyard all the time. Now we know why Alfred left that unpainted section on the glass dome. He sweet talked us and it flew right over our heads."

"Damn! How could we have been so *stupid*?" R.W. said again.

"We were played, R.W., that's why. Hell, if it hadn't been for John...."

"Shhhh. Be quiet, she might hear us," R.W. said in a hushed tone.

Moments after Jenny disappeared inside the monument, she turned around, closed, the door, and locked it. Immediately George and R.W. released from their crouched position in the sand dune depression and scurried to the short set of steps leading to the star base and then to the steps leading to the patio area fronting the metal doors. After quickly looking the area over, they rushed to the metal doors. R.W. put his ear up against the doors in hopes of hearing something. He could hear nothing.

"What time is it now?"

"It's exactly two o'clock," George replied, checking his wristwatch against the faint glow of the moon.

"If the signal is regular at two-fifteen, we got fifteen minutes. Let's wait and give her a few minutes to get to the top and set up. Then I'll go on in and sneak up there as best I can. I got'a see how she's do'en this thing. I think that's important."

"What you want me to do?" George asked.

"I don't know what's gonna happen up there. She may be armed and blow my ass away right after she sees me ... hell who knows. But if'n there is gunfire, ain't but one of us com'en back down. If'n it ain't me, you'll know what to do ... you understand that don't you?"

"Yeah, I got it."

Five minutes later, R.W. inserted the key into the door lock. He knew it would work because they had tried it Monday night on their first night of surveillance. The lock easily opened with the door just barely scrapping the concrete as it opened inward. It was doubtful Jenny could have heard it if she was already at the top.

"Don't close this sucker," R.W. said turning to enter the dark room.

Once entering the foyer, R.W. found it pitch dark except for a very faint pale blue moon glow around the edges of the door. Because it was so dark, he flickered his flashlight on and off to give him his bearings to the steps leading him to the next landing. He favored the entrance to the right where Jenny had already unlocked the bar-door.

Here R.W. cautiously climbed to the first landing where a single set of steps in the middle of the structure angled him to the level over the foyer's roof. At this point, there was total darkness. His memory told him to work his way to the left where another set of single steep concrete steps would take him to the third landing. He tightly grabbed the brass rail with his right hand. The risers were taller than normal and it was possible to easily stumble. He had to be careful with each step.

As R.W. reached the third level, he could hear the hum of the beacon's rotating motor cut off. From this level, the steep and very tight winding metal spiral staircase began its ascent to the top. He thought he heard Jenny let out a few cuss words but wasn't quite sure. But what he was sure of, it was very dark and very quiet. His every breath was deeper and faster; his hard-thumping heart began pounding through his ears. He concentrated on his breathing. The climb was breathtaking even in a slow manner. He gritted his teeth as he took his first step on the metal steps afraid his leather-soled shoes might make a sound. They did but not to the point of alarm. He grasped the railing pulling himself upward to help soften the noise from his shoes. It worked. He made it to the fourth level without being detected; he paused. From there, he knew it was just one more rotation of steps to the top.

From this landing, R.W. could hear a flapping noise of sorts echoing throughout the interior. He could only surmise the signal was being sent.

"Damn, it must be two-fifteen. It's taken me longer to get up here than I expected," R.W. thought to himself as he paused. He debated whether or not to rush to the top and stop the signal from being sent. He also knew he might catch an unwanted bullet, so he quickly dismissed the idea. He decided to continue sneaking upwards.

As he continued his climb to the fifth and topmost level, he heard the flapping noise stop. Putting two-and-two together, he surmised it took only one minute to send the signal.

"Maybe I should have made a bigger effort to stop it. It probably would have saved lives. But after tonight, they'll be no more signals regardless," R.W. thought trying to make himself feel better.

Just after the signal stopped, R.W. took another step. It loudly crunched. Jenny had scattered peanuts on the step to warn her that somebody unannounced was climbing the staircase. He froze in his tracks. Jenny hollered from the dome.

"Who's down there? Is that you Alfred? Whoever it is, don't you dare come any further unless you want your head blown off!"

R.W. had no choice in the matter. He had to speak.

"Jenny! Jenny! Hold your fire. It's Deputy Scoggins. Don't shoot."

"R.W.? *Goddamnit,* it *would* have to be you!"

"Jenny, George is at the bottom. He has his shotgun. If you shoot me, you'll never make it out alive. Let me come up. We'll talk."

"It's a little late to be talk'en now, R.W.," Jenny said very perplexed.

"I'm com'en up Jenny. Hold your fire."

R.W. could hear scrambling inside the dome. Jenny opened the observation deck doors and moved to the outside. Before doing so, she removed the blanket that was covering the two other beacon lights. The flapper mechanism was still attached to the eastward bound light. She did lower the heavy piece of cloth covering the hole in the painted dome glass. It was now very bright with a fixed beam of light shining just over the observation deck.

"You can come up now R.W. I still have my gun pointed at you though. Don't you do anything stupid or I'll shoot ya!"

At this point, R.W. moved to the top of the stairs which led directly to the outside platform. He was just inside the doors at the top of the staircase. From there, he could see Jenny standing on top of observation deck's thick wall. To his right, he could see the beacon light and the flapper device attached to the housing. He looked back over at Jenny. His gun was holstered. He raised his arms to just above waist level.

"So, this is how it's done ... huh?"

"R.W., *why* did it have to be you?"

"Who else were you expecting?"

"Anybody but you. How in the *hell* did you find out. I thought we were careful! Who ratted on us?"

"Actually nobody. A nosey neighbor reported last week he saw the sequence of flashes out'a whack."

"Well, I knew sooner or later somebody would probably notice that. I have to admit ... that was a flaw we never got quite right. But the last signal *was* the worst. My helper didn't know his ass from a hole in the ground. Who was the nosey neighbor?"

"You really don't need to know. You didn't know him anyway."

"Bullshit! I know everybody on this island. Tell me, who the hell was it?"

"Actually a German."

"A German on this island! Bull, there's no German's on this island."

"Well, actually there is. He may have even served you beer over at the Casino."

"I don't know who you're talk'en about! Rag's has a bunch of people work'en for him. Who was it?"

"John."

"Yeah ... yeah, I remember him. Good kid. But how ... aw what difference does it make. Shit ... don't even tell me!"

"You remember the injured German sailor the Coasties found on the beach awhile back?"

"Yeah."

"The guy who brought him ashore decided to defect. I later found him and got him a job at Rag's place."

"Boy, he must've sweet talked your purty little ass!" Jenny said shaking her head.

"Well, I reckon he did some. He came from the U-491. Is that who ya'll been sending the signal too."

"Yeah, it was. How did you know that?"

"Well, let's just say once in a blue moon, the seas release their secrets. The Coast Guard knew about him too. As a matter of fact, Naval Intelligence had it figured the signal was com'en south of here ... down 'round Cape Hatteras."

"Well, I'll be! At least that part of the scheme worked out well. It was a diversionary tactic to throw the heat away from here. I didn't have anything to do with that though. All I was supposed to do was send the signal ... nothing else."

"What about Alfred. He's tied in too, isn't he? We saw you com'en from his house."

"Ol' Alfred. He's a good man. Yeah, well ... he gave us access to the monument here. He was also responsible for taking the coded signal we received from Norfolk and translating it into a language I could use to send it through this beam of light ... kind'a like a Morse code. It's worked well. Even tonight's signal went rather well."

"You know your little plot here has really hurt America and Britain in their plight against Germany, not to mention the scores of helpless people you've already killed."

"Well, R.W., you can take this for what it's worth! But the signal I just sent ain't gonna kill a soul," Jenny said as she pulled out a cigarette from her pant's pocket. She offered one to R.W. He took it and lit up with her. She was still standing precariously close to the outer edge of the wall. From there it was fifty-seven feet to the brick granite base.

"How's that?"

"Alfred and me decided we didn't want any more to do with these Nazis and figured we were gonna do something about it. We took it upon ourselves to rearrange the codes and send a bogus signal. It took some time, but we finally got it. That's partly the reason I stayed over at Alfred's this evening. We sent a fake signal about two weeks ago to test it out. It worked, but we didn't find out about it until recently. After we found out it worked, we organized our own little escape plan."

"And tonight's signal was...?"

"This was to be the first in a series of bogus signals. We sent the sub to some part of the Atlantic where we knew there'd be no ships. If he finds one, it'd have to be some rogue bastard not traveling in a convoy."

"Well how's that going to bring down the organization? I don't understand?"

"We felt if we could start sending fake signals to the sub, and he was exerting a lot of wasted energy going out to never, never land so to speak, we figured sooner or later the powers in Germany might start putting pressure on our contact up there in Norfolk. Then we figured they might do something to get rid of him."

"But wouldn't your man go to ya'll first?"

"Yeah, we had that figured that. Our plan was to wait until the last possible minute and then just up and disappear. We had it all worked out. Hank and me were going to Florida. I don't know where Alfred was going. He hadn't made up his mind yet."

"Who killed Hank?" R.W. asked.

"Aw, it was that heinie boss son-of-a-bitch of ours. Hank got antsy about some things and started running his mouth. The heinie thought he was going to compromise the organization and he up and killed him."

"You know that for sure?"

275

"Well, the son-of-a-bitch had singed eyebrows when I saw him later! So yeah, I think so but he never admitted to it. Sure pissed me off!"

"That heinie boss of yours. He that the tall blond feller I've seen 'round here?"

"Yeah, that's him."

"Where's he now?"

"As much as I want'a give 'em up. I'm not. Alfred and me still have a plan in place and we still need him. You'll see. You'll catch on. And when you catch that creepy son-of-a-bitch with the goods, I hope you plug his ass!"

"What about the cottage fire? You do that?"

"Yeah, me and Hank did that. That was the only cottage in the line of sight of our beacon signal where we felt somebody might notice the signal going out. Hell, we spent more time worrying about that beam than the ones that nailed us! You tell Mr. Matthews I'm sorry for what I done."

"Well if ya'll were get'en out of the organization, why burn it?"

"Damn R.W., don't you see? We had to! For our plan to work we still needed to send the signals, and we didn't want it compromised. We had no choice."

"You know we suspected you and Hank don't you."

"Yeah, that was purty stupid of Hank to put those jugs of gasoline inside the car. I told 'em not to do that, but he did it anyway. Then when I came home the following morning from E City and you stuck your head in the car window, I saw your nose sniffing like a thirsty bloodhound. I was stupid too. I never should've stopped to talk to ya'll ... should've just waved and moved on." Jenny continued.

"You had Rose Ellen pass on those tidbits about the gasoline smell and the glass bottlenecks didn't ya?"

"Yeah, I did," R.W. admitted.

"What the hell were you expect'en after that?"

"Oh, I don't know. Just wanted you to know we suspected you. We had no evidence or motive ... just supposition."

"Well, it did get me a little nervous, but we knew you didn't have anything on us."

"Let me ask you, Jenny. If'n ya'll were want'en to get out of the organization, why in the hell didn't you just go to the authorities like us, or even the FBI and report it? I'm sure you'd get some leniency."

"Now, R.W., I want you to listen very closely to this. We wanted out of the organization *and* be free. If we went to the authorities, how long you think it would've been before they put us in front of a firing squad? Twenty-four hours? Shit, I made a bad decision get'en involved with those damn Germans, I admit. But I'm not totally stupid. No matter how you look at it, we were tied in very deep with those bastards and we wouldn't have had a snowball's chance in hell of escaping with our lives."

"I see your point. But with what all you've told me, I still think they'd listen and be fair with you. Jenny, ya got'a give it a chance."

"With this war going on! I doubt it. Look, I made my own bed, now I got'a go sleep in it. Let's just let that sleep'en dog lie, okay."

"Jenny! Listen to me ... Jenny! Why don't you come down from that wall? You're mak'en me a bit nervous stand'en there!" R.W. said as he inched closer with his left hand reaching out towards her.

"I don't think so R.W. You just step back now, ya hear. Don't come any closer. This gun's loaded I tell ya!"

"Jenny, you're not gonna shoot me. Now come down, please?"

"Naw, I reckon not. Hell, Clare Belle would have a shit-kick'en fit if'n I did. She loves your ass, but I reckon you already know that don't ya?"

"Yeah, I believe she does. She's a sweet lady."

"I know she's a sweet lady. Got a good heart. I wish I'd met her a whole lot sooner than I did. Woman's got a good head on her shoulders and a smile to kill for. You take good care of her. She's gonna need it!"

R.W. noticed Jenny inching closer to the outer edge of the wall.

"Jenny, don't do it! Jenny, we can talk this out!"

"R.W., we done talk'en. You'll soon figure out the rest of our plan. You get with Alfred. But you get that heinie SOB for me! You hear!"

"Jenny ... NO!

At that moment, Jenny put the gun to the base of her neck just below her jaw and gracefully leaned backwards over thin air. As her feet left the backside edge of the wall, she pulled the trigger plunging a thirty-eight caliber slug squarely through her brain. She was dead before hitting the outcrop granite monument's base two and a half seconds later. R.W. quickly crawled to the top of the thick wall and glanced down. He could barely make out the crumpled figure sprawled out below on the small white granite bricks. There was no chance for survival.

George had just walked to the east side of the monument and was looking upwards when he heard the gunshot. Within seconds he saw a body hit thirty feet from him with a slapping thud and bounce into a contorted position. Her gun bounded over the shallow star base wall onto the grass. He could tell it was Jenny and not R.W. Not knowing exactly what had happened, he immediately ran to the south side facade and quickly entered the door. He took his flashlight and shined it up the stairwell. The light could transmit no further than ten feet because of the curved staircase. He hollered loudly.

"R.W.! HEY R.W.! YOU OK BUDDY?"

There was a moment of silence because R.W. had just crawled down from the top of the wall after looking at Jenny. He entered the dome and heard George.

"GEORGE! YEAH, I'M FINE. I'M ON MY WAY DOWN. JENNY"S DEAD!

A few minutes later R.W. appeared at the foot of the steps in the foyer. They both had their flashlights burning. George grabbed R.W. by the arm and helped him outside to the patio area. His back was flinching badly. They sat on one of the small granite portions of the supporting wall to the monument's star base just below the patio.

"I heard the gunshot. Did you have to shoot Jenny?"

"No George ... no I didn't. When I got to the top, I frightened her a bit and she moved from the dome to the top of the wall of the observation deck with her gun on me. It purty much looked as though she had no intention of com'en back down here alive. After we talked awhile, she looked me straight in the eye with a subtle smile, put the gun under her jaw, leaned backwards over the edge of the wall, and pulled the trigger just as her feet left the granite. Is that what you saw?" R.W. asked his friend and partner.

"Not in that much detail, no. I heard the gunshot and saw her fall. For a moment there, I thought she may have shot you and then jumped."

"She did have the gun pointed at me as we talked just so we'd have some distance. But no, I don't think she had any intentions of shooting me. She and Alfred had some sort of plan to retaliate against the Germans and they were in the process of implementing it. By us discovering her, it was thrown out'a whack. But in a round about way, I think she wants us to get with Alfred and finish it off. So now we got'a go down and talk to Alfred and see what he can tell us. He's tied in with those Germans as deep as she was."

"So this really is where the signal was taking place, huh?"

"Yep. The whole shit'en caboodle is there at the top. We'll need to go back up and get that mess and look it over. But I'm gonna leave it just the way it is till Roscoe gets here so's he can see it."

"What about Jenny's body?"

"I'll call Roscoe and get him to get the meat wagon over here. We got'a keep this quiet 'cause it's still hot as a firecracker right now. Till we get it all figured out, we got'a handle this with kid gloves."

"Yeah, I believe so," George said, shaking his head in agreement.

"Well, let's go on down and wake ol' Alfred's ass up unless he hasn't already committed suicide. I'm sure he knows something's amiss now that Jenny hasn't returned and the beacon light ain't twirling."

"How's your back buddy?"

"Sore as hell ... but I'll make it okay."

Chapter 25

After George and R.W. walked over and looked at Jenny's body at the base of the monument, they trekked on down the steep south slope of the mound and walked across the open field towards Alfred's cottage. The door to his porch was partially opened. As quietly as they could, they walked in and over to the main door of the house which was also partially opened. They could see the living room portion dimly lit from a lamp inside an adjacent bedroom. They tapped on the door.

"Alfred! This is Deputies Scoggins and Dawkins. Are you in there?"

There was no answer. They tapped the door again. Still nothing. They opened the door fully. R.W. walked in first with his gun drawn. George was two steps behind with his shotgun lowered to waist level. After entering the room, they noticed Alfred sitting in a leather-covered armchair in the far corner of the room with a beer in his right hand. He stared straight ahead; he softly spoke.

"Is Jenny dead? I heard a gunshot."

"Yes Alfred, she's dead!" R.W. answered back.

"Did you kill her?"

"No Alfred. No, I didn't kill her. She killed herself by fall'en backwards off the observation deck wall and shoot'en herself just before falling."

"I had a feeling she would kill herself before being taken into custody."

"Well, she did. Alfred, we need to use your phone. Where is it?" R.W. asked in a straightforward demeanor.

"It's in the kitchen."

"George, keep an eye on Alfred. I'll give Roscoe a call."

R.W. walked into the kitchen and turned on the overhead light. It was bright and he momentarily had to adjust his eyes from the darkness of the night and the living room. He picked up the telephone. It took a moment before Molly the operator answered her line.

"Molly, this is Deputy Scoggins. Will you ring Roscoe's house for me?"

"Yes, just a moment." It took a few moments before Roscoe finally answered.

"R.W.?"

"Roscoe ... you need to get over here to Alfred's house on Colington Road. It's real important. I'll discuss it with you when you get here. Also, call the hospital and have them bring over the ambulance."

"What happened R.W.?"

"I'll discuss it with you when you get here. Tell the ambulance driver not to make any unnecessary noise. Just tell 'em to drive normal and don't do anything irrational. Have him come to Alfred's cottage too."

"You can't tell me what's going on?"

"Roscoe, not over the phone. But things have got'en complicated. George is okay so don't worry 'bout him. Ya'll just keep it quiet when you come over. We don't need to be wak'en everybody an' his aunt and uncle. You understand?"

"Yeah. As a matter of fact, I'll personally go over to the hospital myself and have them follow me. We'll be there as soon as we can."

"Good. We'll be wait'en."

After hanging up the phone, R.W. grabbed a glass from the metal cupboard over the counter, turned on the sink faucet, and filled it with cold water. He finished it in three big gulps and filled it again drinking it a bit slower this time. He walked back into the living room and sat down on the couch. He told George where the glasses were if he wanted a drink of water.

"Alfred, I'm sorry about Jenny. I truly am. I tried keep'en her from jumping but it looked as though she had already had her mind set to do it anyway."

"Well, we have gotten ourselves in purty deep as it is and the only real escape *is* death. We had talked about that before but never really believed it would come to that."

"Before she died, she mentioned to me that you and she were plotting your vengeance against the Germans. What's that all about?"

"She told you that, huh?"

"Yeah … yeah, she did.

"We wanted to destroy the organization from within. We were heading in that direction until you came along."

"What's this about bogus signals?"

"What'd she tell you?"

"That ya'll were sending fake signals to the U-boat directing him away from their targets."

"Yes, that's correct. We were sending him away from the known target we were supposed to be sending him to. We figured sooner or later somebody in Germany would get wise and might end up putting pressure on our German contact."

"But ya'll had an escape plan?"

"Yes. We knew the German would come after us first after he got wise that the U-boat kept missing his specified targets. But by then, we were planning to be long gone, and he'd be left holding the bag, so to speak. I don't know what's going to happen now. I suppose when he finds out his little Nazi organization has been compromised, I'm sure he'll up and disappear like a fart in a breeze. When that happens, we won't be able to carry through with our own little plot."

"What if the heinie doesn't find out?"

"How's that?"

"I mean, what if we plan it so the heinie doesn't know his operation has been compromised?"

"Are you saying you're willing to help finish out our plot?"

"Yeah, well, I reckon that's possible. I mean no sense let'en that sumbitch up and fade away. We might as well try to capture him and bring down the organization too. If'n we can stop some ships and sailors from going to the bottom in the mean while … well, that's just an added bonus."

"Well yes, that could work. Arnold did train a backup in case something happened to Jenny so the operation wouldn't come to a complete stop."

"Arnold's the heinie?"

"Yeah, you briefly met him that night at the Casino when you came to see me about blacking out the dome. Remember?"

"I remember. Met him and his wife 'bout a year ago too. They were looking for a picnic area over on Roanoke Island."

"That's him. He's a hell of a lot more ruthless than he looks."

"Jenny's backup. You met him?"

"No, I haven't and have no clue as to who he is. But in as much as trying to do something about that submarine, we have no control over him other than the signal's we send. I guess once he realizes there's not going to be any more signals, I suppose he'll do whatever else them other subs are doing ... you know, start taking potshots at whatever they find floating around out there."

"Yeah, I see what you mean. But maybe we can at least get Arnold and whoever else we can. You have any idea how many others there are?"

"I really don't know how many there are in total. Of course, there was Jenny and Hank and myself responsible for this end of the operation. There has to be some more people spread out within the Hampton Roads area responsible for gathering the information for the high-grade shipments that were the targets. I know that Arnold and his wife, Aleta, have an apartment somewhere in Norfolk, but I don't know where 'bout's it is. All I have is a phone number. And what Aleta does for the organization, I don't know. She used to come down with Arnold quite a bit but stopped coming awhile back. I haven't seen her in months and Arnold makes no mention of her anymore."

"Don't know, huh?"

"Not really. She must be tied in somehow up in Norfolk, but that's a guess. I still believe she's around, though."

"How did the operation work?"

"Someone from Norfolk would hand Hank the signal packet and he would relay it to Jenny through his regular morning mail deliveries. I would then pick it up at the post office and code the information so that Jenny could send it using that flapper device. I guess you saw that up there?"

"Yeah, I did. It's still up there just the way Jenny left it. Can you think of anybody else tied in to the organization?"

"Well, now that Hank's gone, Arnold did recruit this fellow named Dale Conner from somewhere within the organization to take over Hank's position. Arnold changed the format a little and the packet was then supposed to come directly to me. He decided to cut down the time I had to decipher the packet. I became hard pressed to get it organized in time for Jenny. Though, tonight was only the second time he brought it to me and, actually, it made no difference anyway because we had already designed a bogus signal to send. But, if I'm not mistaken, I *think* Dale's girlfriend's name is Joy Lund who is one of the persons responsible for gathering the shipping manifest from up in Norfolk."

"You haven't met her?"

"Nope. Have no clue what she looks like. Haven't even spoken with her on the phone."

"Jenny said she sent a bogus signal tonight?"

"She was supposed to. Did she get it off before you got to her?"

"Yeah, she got it off."

"Well, that's good. You know this Conner fellow was also supposed to help her tonight in the dome, but she got all pissed off at him the last time he helped because he screwed up so badly. He told me this afternoon, when he dropped off the packet for tonight's signal, to tell her he wasn't coming to help her anymore. If'n he had'a come tonight, you probably could've have nailed his butt too."

"And you don't have *any* idea who Jenny's replacement is?"

"Nope. And probably won't unless you come up with some kind of plan to keep Arnold from finding out about what's happened tonight."

"Yeah, well I'll be studying on that before daylight. I'm sure we can figure something out. I'll get with Roscoe on that.

"What made ya'll turn traitorous?"

"My political beliefs and the way the Nazis were running Germany. At first I thought Hitler was good for the Fatherland. I soon realized he hoodwinked his own people, and I fell out of favor with what I used to believe. By then, I was already hooked in here.

"Now Jenny ... I recruited her because she was self-centered with no loyalty and she liked money. But she got to thinking real hard after awhile and realized she had made a mistake. We both soon figured that our only redemption was to destroy the organization from within and then disappear with our lives and try to live happily thereafter somewhere else. That seemed to be our only hope for escape. We just saw no other way out ... and there was *no way* to go to the authorities least we be put in front of a firing squad. Like I said, we were in the midst of our plan until you happened by."

"What about Hank?"

"Poor guy. He loved Jenny so much he'd go to hell and back for her. But he was nothing but a puppy dog following her along and get'en into mess he had no clue about. At first, he didn't know what he was doing and then caught on. That was his undoing. He should've never gotten involved. But he did and, in his own little way, he showed us the light. He's the one who really got us to think'en about getting out of this mess in the first place. Unfortunately, he's dead now."

"Well, I hate to hear all that but maybe you can find a way to redeem yourself. I doubt seriously it'll keep you out'a prison or maybe even from a firing squad, but at least you're see'en the light. There is something to be said for that in the eyes of the beholder.

"Does that monument have a water spigot?"

"Why?"

"There's a lot of blood there that needs cleaning up. I think you should do that before people start going up there tomorrow. It won't be good for them to see it, and it'll cut down on trying to make false explanations."

"Yes, I suppose that would be a good idea. But no, there's no spigot up there."

"Well, after the ambulance picks up Jenny, you can haul a coupl'a buckets of water up there and clean it up. Take a brush and some soap with you.

"Do you have any weapons here in the house?"

"Uh ... no, no I don't."

"Where are your car keys?"

"On the table there beside you. R.W., I'm not going to run. It wouldn't do any good and if you want me to help get Arnold, I will."

"Well, I just want'a keep an honest man honest if'n you don't mind. As far as help'en to catch Arnold, I'll let you know about that."

About three-forty that morning, Roscoe, and the ambulance with a driver and two medics, quietly pulled in front of Alfred's cottage. R.W. went outside to meet with them and briefly talk with Roscoe. He returned to the cottage and told George to stay with Alfred while he rode with Roscoe up the slope of the mound with the ambulance following behind. While the large sand dune was fairly steep, it was possible to safely get vehicles to the top by traversing the northwest quadrant at an angle. When they arrived at the top, it was not possible to pull the cars onto the star shaped foundation, but they could pull up next to it. Upon parking and getting out, they stepped atop the three-foot star foundation wall and walked over to Jenny's body. Everybody had their flashlights turned on. What they saw was gruesome.

"Damn R.W., you said it was bloody! I reckon a fall like that would cause a mess."

"Yeah, she died hard. The bullet didn't help matters."

"Sheriff, you want us to get pictures first?" asked one of the medics.

"Yeah, I reckon so. I hate to do it fellers, but I think it's necessary."

After taking ten photos of the body from different angles, as well as the six-foot outcrop of the base where her head hit before crashing onto the granite brick just under the carved word "Genius," the medics went about their grisly chore of removing Jenny to a stretcher and carrying her to the rear of the ambulance. Roscoe talked to the men.

"Fellers, I want all the three of you to keep this quiet. We're investigating a serious matter here and it's *imperative* this doesn't leak out. If'n by chance it does, I'm holding ya'll directly responsible and I promise you I'll throw your butts in the jailhouse for compromising this investigation. When I get back into town, I'll talk to the coroner. But in the meantime, ya'll tell 'em he needs to be quiet about this. Is that understood?"

"Yes sir, no problem. We'll keep it quiet. We'll just keep her on ice till we hear back from you," one of the medics assured.

"Fellers, I appreciate that. As I said, this is real important. Its nature is very serious!"

The two officers stood on the slope by the wall and watched the ambulance pull away and disappear to the south side of the mound towards Colington Road. Afterwards, Roscoe wanted to climb to the

286

top of the monument and see the mechanics in how the signal operated. Before stepping back onto the base, Roscoe's flashlight accidently picked up Jenny's gun lying ten feet in front of him. R.W. walked over to pick it up. It had blood on the barrel.

"That the weapon Jenny used on herself?" Roscoe asked already knowing the answer.

"Yeah, I believe so. Took a purty good bounce to get all the way out here."

After climbing back over the small wall to the base and before going inside the monument, R.W. took Roscoe to the south side slope and pointed to where he and George hid and watched Jenny approach the monument. Their view was ideal for observing. From here, they walked to the patio and the double metal doors and went inside.

While in the foyer, R.W. found the light switches that lit up the entire interior making it easier to move up the steps. The last time Roscoe had been to the top was in 1935 when he took a small group of Boy Scouts from the piedmont area of the State that were visiting.

Before reaching the top, R.W showed Roscoe where Jenny had sprinkled peanuts on the steps to alert her that someone was approaching. From this position R.W. could barely see Jenny by the flapper device. When reaching the top of the staircase, R.W. moved to the observation deck allowing Roscoe the full view of the beacon light. He noticed the dark piece of fabric hanging over the unpainted section of dome. Ironically, she lowered it over the hole before moving to the observation deck when R.W. approached.

"So this is it, huh?" Roscoe said with his eyes glancing all around the dome focusing in on the flapper device.

"Yep, this is where it all happened ... right under our damn noses."

"Well R.W., let's not beat ourselves up too badly over this. Sounds like the organization was well oiled and everything else just slipped by us. But, as you know, every well-oiled machine sooner or later gets a little grit in the bearings. Sounds like our little buddy John just happened to be that piece grit."

"Yeah, kind'a funny a German who defected unknowingly unraveling a treacherous plot designed by his own people. I wonder what Der Führer would have to say 'bout that?"

"Probably wouldn't be too pleased! John deserves a medal, you know. But I'll be honest with you R.W., I had my doubts about him back then ... but your hard-headedness and intuitiveness about him paid off. I tip my hat to ya. Nonetheless, I still think we got lucky.

"You know, you could've put a lot of people's lives at stake as well as some careers not to mention jail time if'n this thing hadn't worked out the way it did. Hell, Lieutenant Fleming was hotter than a pair of bride's britches that you talked him into going along with you. You know he called me on the phone the following Monday after ya'll had lunch over at Bessie's. He was about ready to renege on the deal and haul John's ass in!"

"What stopped him?"

"Me! I told 'em I believed in ya and told 'em to lighten up ... that I knew you had a good handle on the situation and you weren't going to let it get out of hand ... that I'd known you way too long not to put my trust and respect in ya!"

"You said that?"

"Yeah, I sho' did. And from here on out I ain't gonna be blowing any more smoke up your skirt. So get a grip! Now what's this crazy ass idea of a plan you told me about driv'en up here about trying to corral the rest of this here German operation? And can we do it without bringing in the goddamn FBI?"

"Well hold on just a minute and let's first take this flapper device down and get the lights back to twirling so's we don't attract any more attention. I'll discuss it with you when we get back down to Alfred's cottage. I want him to come back up here and clean Jenny's blood, and time's a run'en out. After we discuss the plan, we'll go back over it with Alfred and work out the details. I think it'll work Roscoe ... I *really* think it will."

"You think Alfred'll go along?"

"Yeah, he'll go along. I know he'll go along."

* * * * * * * *

The biggest news story in Friday morning's local paper was the death of Jenny Smith, the Dare County Post Mistress, from the result of a car accident late Wednesday night on Highway 158 on a desolate section of road near Harbinger about four miles north of Point Harbor. Her car had veered off the road and crashed into a drainage ditch where she was thrown through the windshield. She was dead at the scene.

In the courthouse that same morning, George and R.W. were in Roscoe's office drinking coffee and reading the article. Rose Ellen was at her desk typing away totally unaware of the real cause of Jenny's death. Roscoe got up from his chair behind his desk, walked over, and casually closed his door.

"Good article there Roscoe. You handled that quite well," R.W. said.

"Yeah, writing is not a profession I care to get involved in, but it'll suffice for what we're doing. Is everything ready?"

"So far everything seems to be on go. Alfred called Arnold yesterday morn'en about ten-thirty and told him about Jenny's 'accident.' He had a lot of questions about her death, but Alfred did a good job tell'en him just what we wanted him to say. I'm sure if Arnold happens to see today's paper, he'll take it as fact," R.W. said.

"You think Arnold's none the wiser to what's going on?" Roscoe asked.

"I think so. I was there when Alfred called and he sounded convincing to me."

"Do we know if Arnold has already called Alfred back yet?" Roscoe asked.

"Nope, not yet. Alfred has instructions to call here just soon after he gets the call. But so far nothing. He told Alfred on the phone yesterday he was gonna have to get up with the new signal guy. He said he was planning on bring'en him down here when they got a new ship to sink. Though for the moment, we just don't know when that's gonna be."

"Well, I reckon it's just a wait'en game now boys. Sam still over guard'en Alfred," Roscoe asked.

"Yeah, he's still there. You want me to go relieve him?" George said.

"Naw, let's wait till lunch and then you can go over. I need to get you boys back out on the street and do some patrolling. Why don't ya'll get on out there and check back in to the office every thirty minutes or so. We can't do anything till we hear back from Alfred. Anything else there fellers?"

"I can't think of anything," George said.

"Me either. We'll be check'en back in," R.W. said yawning putting his hand to his mouth.

Much of the day passed with very little happening. At lunchtime, George went over and relieved Sam at the cottage bringing them both a sandwich and a Coke from the Midget Market. After Sam ate his sandwich, he drove Jenny's car back to the courthouse parking it behind the building out of sight of prying eyes. As a safety precaution, he removed the license plate.

During the day, R.W. was antsy and decided to patrol on foot around the downtown waterfront market areas to help stay awake. He stopped into many of the businesses and chatted with the owners and customers and catching up on the local gossip. He received many questions about Jenny's accident making him uncomfortable when he responded. About four o'clock that afternoon, he decided to walk back to the courthouse and see if he could grab a quick nap on a sofa in the backroom of their office section. He had been up for almost sixty-four straight hours and was wearing thin in his disposition. Maybe Roscoe would let him run back to the house and take a quick shower and a shave.

"Anything yet Roscoe?"

"Nary a whimper ol' buddy."

"Mind if'n I grab a quick nap on the sofa in the backroom?" R.W. asked.

"Hell, why don't ya just run on back over to your house and take a cold shower and a nap there. I'll call ya if'n I hear something."

"How's ol' George hold'en up?" R.W. asked with droopy eyes. Roscoe laughed.

"I called over there a little while ago and asked Alfred if I could speak to George. He said the ol' boy was sound asleep on his sofa. 'Did I want'a wake 'em?' Can you believe that?"

"Well, me and him have purty much worked the same hours, so I reckon he's 'bout as wore out as me," R.W. said.

"Yeah, that's what I thought. So I told the ol' buzzard not to wake 'em. I mean if Alfred was gonna escape, I reckon he'd already done so by now?"

"Probably. But I think ol' Alfred's seen the light and wants to get to the end of this mess about as bad as we do. He ain't gonna run. Hell he ain't got nowhere to run to. You know what I mean?"

"Well if he did, he wouldn't get too far. Look, go home and get your ass cleaned up and I'll see ya back over here 'bout six-thirty."

Just as R.W. was heading to the courthouse front doors, Roscoe picked up his ringing phone. R.W. stopped in his tracks and looked back over his shoulder into his office. He could see the phone to Roscoe's right ear and his left arm motioning for him to come back.

"That the phone call?"

"Yep, it sho' was."

"And?"

"Arnold's coming over to his house at nine-o'clock tonight and he's bringing the new person who'll be sending the signal. There's a good chance he'll be bringing Dale Conner. If that's the case, we can get all three of 'em. Of course, we've already got Alfred."

"Almost a home run. The only one's left will be the folks in Norfolk. But at least from this end, there won't be any more signals going out and the Coast Guard ought'a be ready to pounce on that damn sub if'n everything goes according to plan. Fleming ever calm down after you went over there to talk to him and give him the information we put together?"

"You know R.W., he really didn't act too badly. Then again he might not've wanted to show his ass in front of me like he does in front of you. I know you and him have an ongoing friendship and that's understandable how he jumps around and raves at you. I know he respects ya. But you know with me, it's different. I mean, I have the star on my chest and he damn well knows it ... and he also knows I ain't screwing around."

"Well, that's one reason I asked you to go instead of me. I know he always gets a little sideways about John and I could see him jumping all around with that again."

"Actually I brought that up. I told him if it wasn't *for* John and his observations, this whole thing could've gone on for god knows how much longer. I told him that we've got everything in place for a sting operation and we can probably knock this thing out in one big swoop."

"He ask many questions about it?"

"Sho' as hell did! I told 'em to stay the hell off my section of the beach and that he needs to take care of his section of the Atlantic. I said that goddamn submarine is in the ocean and if everything goes right, he can chalk-up one dead Nazi submarine for his Coastie Station. Except'en for the date, I gave him the coordinates of where and what time the sub'll be there and told 'em not to screw it up. I told 'em we'll take care of our business ... for him to take care of his business!"

"What'd he say to all that?" R.W. asked.

"Not a damn word! He knew I was right! Now if'n that submarine don't show up like we said it was ... well, I'll have to eat crow. But I don't think I'm gonna have to do that. As a matter of fact, I need to call him right now and tell 'em we're on for tonight so's he can get his people in position. I'm glad we had a better notice than what I was expect'en. I'll also call George and tell him we'll be over to his way 'bout seven o'clock. You go on back over to your house and take care of business there and be back over here at six-thirty. We got a little time before we need to get over there. I got a feel'en it's gonna be another long night."

"Yeah, I believe so. I'll see ya then."

"Oh ... and R.W. Tonight I want you and George to wear your badges. This is an official operation. Also, make sure your gun's loaded and take some extra bullets. You hear me?"

"Yes sir. George has already got'en on me 'bout my gun. It's loaded now."

"Good! Now get out'a here!"

* * * * * * * *

At seven o'clock, Sheriff Simmons and Deputy Scoggins pulled in front Alfred's cottage and met George as he came out of the house. Alfred was inside taking a nap on his bed. Roscoe motioned with his arms for everyone to go inside so they could go over the plans one more time. After this, they would all move into their positions.

"George, you get a good snooze this afternoon?" Roscoe asked in a jovial way.

"Sorry about that Roscoe. I was sitting on the couch talking to Alfred and the next thing you know I got level with the cushions. I won't let it happen again. It was as though my body just gave out."

"Don't worry 'bout it George. I think we all did the same thing earlier today ourselves. But we're ready now, aren't we?"

"Yes sir. Yes, we are," George and R.W. said in unison.

"Good. Let's go over the plan one more time. Now, at eight o'clock, I'll move my car back down to the end of Colington Road here and park under the second cottage south of the intersection with the Highway 12 so's I'll have a good view of Arnold's car when it pulls onto Colington. You guys are going to take the other car and move it back around the mound towards the airstrip and park in the same position you did the other night. Is that right?"

"Yeah. From there we'll move to the same position we had before on the mound. Sunset tonight is at eight-o-nine so we should be okay while we're getting into position. I've noticed some clouds moving in from the southwest which should help us out."

"Okay then, when I see Arnold's car pull onto Colington, I'll wait about five minutes for him to drive the sixth-tenths down here to Alfred's place. I'll then move my car down to that shrubby area short of the entrance to the monument and park it there. I'll work my way the remainder three hundred and fifty yards to the cottage by foot and get behind one of the cars in the driveway or in front of the house depending on where they park."

"After we see Arnold's car come down the road and park, George and me'll work our way down the mound and over to the porch side of the cottage and split up. George'll go to the west side and I'll go to the east side. Roscoe, you should see me at this point."

"What's next?" Roscoe asked.

"From here, Roscoe, we sort of play it by ear. We'll listen in through the windows and get a feel as to what's going on. When I think the time's right, I'll burst in through the porch door with my gun drawn and get everybody on the floor as quickly as possible. At that point, George'll follow me in with his shotgun. Roscoe, you're the backup guy. If somebody happens to not get on the floor and flies out that front door, you'll have to take care of it. Are you ready for that Roscoe?"

"Got the same Remington shotgun George has and it's loaded for bear! Ain't nobody get'en by me."

"What about the walkie-talkies that Fleming gave you while you were down there Roscoe?" R.W. inquired.

"Yeah, they're in the trunk, charged and ready to go. I'll get 'em when we go back out. When we get into position, we'll do a radio check."

"Good. Well, that's purty much about it fellers. Any questions?" R.W. asked.

"And the beacon signal's a done deal, right?" George asked.

"That's a done deal George. It doesn't need to be sent tonight. All we really need to do is open up that cloth fabric and shine the beacon light through the hole in the dome to give the preponderance that a signal is ready to be sent. Hopefully, while the sub is concentrating on receiving it, their attention will be diverted and should give the Coast

Guard the edge they need in catching 'em off guard and, with any luck, blow his ass out'a the water. As long as Fleming has taken care of his business, that submarine ought'a be history at o-two-fifteen!" Roscoe said.

"With the coordinates we gave him, 36° 1' north, 75° 25' west, this puts the submarine due east in shallow water ... about twelve fathoms deep twelve miles out from what Fleming told Roscoe. If the submarine happens to dive before our Coast Guard guys can move in, he'll never make it to deep water in time. The depth charges in that shallow of water ought'a get him. Maybe if we're lucky, we might see or hear some activity out there," R.W. added.

"You want'a add anything Roscoe?" R.W. said.

"Yeah, just to say that me and the coroner had a long chat this afternoon and he's on call. Something tells me these boys ain't gonna go peaceful like."

"That's something we need to be concerned about. It's gonna be dark and we need to be watching out for each other and who we're shoot'en at. No sense blast'en each other," R.W. said with trepidation.

"Yeah well, we're just gonna have to be careful there. Everybody knows where they're supposed to be. There shouldn't be any problems," George also added.

"Anything else?" Roscoe asked.

"Yeah, we need to wake up Alfred. He's out like a light!" said George.

"Well, let's wake his ass up! He's the main attraction tonight."

* * * * * * * *

By nine o'clock, everybody had been in position for an hour and were anxiously awaiting for Arnold's car to show up. There was an air of anxiety surrounding the officers hoping the operation would go off without a hitch. If there was one thing working in their favor, high puffy white clouds had moved in across the sky dissipating the faint glow of the moon from the west.

"Well, they ought'a be get'en here any minute now. I understand those Germans are punctual when it comes to time. Did you raise all the windows in the house George?"

"All except one on the east side of the house towards the road. It was stuck purty good and I couldn't get it to budge. But all the others are opened so we should be able to hear what they're saying."

"Damn, I hate this wait'en game. It's working on my nerves."

"You'll be all right R.W. Once we start working our way down that hill, it'll go away."

"Yeah, I reckon so. Look, I've been thinking after looking over the area from up here. Why don't we both move together to the west side of the house. The east side is a little more exposed than I thought.

They might see me if'n I try to get over there. I'll have to go by the back porch and there's really nothing back there I can hide behind. I should've paid more attention to that."

"I see what you mean. Yeah okay, let's move together. There is a window on the west side that has a good view into the living room. We should be okay there."

"Well, let me notify Roscoe we've made an adjustment. Hand me the walkie-talkie."

George reached behind him and handed it to R.W.

"RS, RS ... this is RW ... come in, over."

"This is RS, over."

"We've made a slight adjustment in plans to cover the house. I'm mov'en with GD to the west side of the house, over."

"Copy that. Is there a problem? Over."

"We've decided it's a safer move. You won't see me on the east side, over."

"Copy that. Sounds like a good move, over."

"Any activity your way? Over."

"Negative, over."

"Keep us in touch. RW out."

"We'll do. RS out."

Fifteen minutes had passed and it was still very quiet. George looked through his binoculars and could see that Alfred had gone out the back porch door towards the open field to smoke a cigarette. Apparently he was getting antsy too. Just as he had finished his cigarette, a crackle came in over the walkie-talkie."

"RW, RW ... this is RS ... come in, over!"

"This is RW, over."

"Two cars pulling onto Colington. I repeat two cars, over."

"Copy that. Do you recognize our target car as one of them? Over."

"Affirmative. It's the lead car. Do not ... I repeat, do not recognize the following car, over."

"Copy that, over."

"This is it boys. Let's do it! RS out."

"RW out!"

Forty-five seconds later, George and R.W. observed the two cars approach Alfred's cottage from the east. From their height on the mound, they could barely see over the cottage. They noticed the cars park on the street but could not see how many individuals exited the cars.

They waited thirty seconds before moving off the mound. Once they reached the base of the dune, they still had a two hundred and ninety yard jaunt to their position by the house. It took them about four minutes to get there carefully crouching along the way. Once there, they nestled up to the outside wall near the open window

George had earlier mentioned. R.W. ducked and cautiously moved to the opposite side of the window. They could hear loud voices coming from within but could not see anyone other than Alfred. Alfred subtly looked in their direction and raised his eyelids and eyebrows.

George stayed in his position but R.W. moved to another side window to see if he could get a better view inside to the living room. By moving, he could not see Alfred but he could see Arnold, and he could tell the German spy was very unhappy. At that moment, a figure moved into R.W.'s view and he could not believe whom he saw. It was Claire Belle Charboneau. R.W. immediately went back to the window where George was standing. He whispered lightly but firmly to him.

"Jesus H Christ, George! You ain't gonna believe this!"

"What!"

"That third person. It's Claire Belle!"

"Oh shit! You're kidding!"

"No! What the hell's go'en on here?"

"I don't know ... let's listen. Ain't nobody real happy in there right now."

Claire Belle Charboneau was in fact part of this German Nazi organization that was sinking American and Allied shipping. Unfortunately, she had been coerced into her position in a highly unusual way over which she had absolutely no control. After listening to Arnold speak, she began screaming at the German.

"Arnold, I've told you before and I'm telling you again. I am *not* going to betray my country. Even though you have a hold over my head, I am NOT going to do it. Do you understand me?"

"But Miss Charboneau, if you don't ... you know your daughter's life will be in jeopardy. You do understand that don't you?"

"Yes ... I truly believe you heartless bastards would kill an innocent child. But as young as she is, I think she understands the word *loyalty* and would gladly *die* for her country knowing what you wanted me to do!"

"Those are just words that have no meaning. You Americans are too foolish to understand loyalty. All you people care about is good wine, soft beds and good sex! You don't know the first thing about suffering and will do anything and everything in your power to keep that from happening. You are so weak it is pathetic."

"Arnold, I think you underestimate the overall American spirit. Some traitorous Americans would sell their souls to the devil for a few bucks ... but not me nor millions of others!" Claire Belle shot back.

"But you are wrong Miss Charboneau! You have already accepted our offer, and you have already accepted our gifts. Do you not remember?"

"Ha! So you think. Here, take your goddamned money and put it where the sun don't shine, you slime ball!" Claire reached into her purse and threw a wad of dollars into his face scattering it all over the floor in front of him. She continued.

"I only agreed with you to buy more time to save my daughter. I've despised you from the moment I met you, you son-of-a-bitch! At the time, you forced my hand and had a tortuous grip on me, I had no choice then but to agree. But now I do have a choice!"

Arnold's face grew grim.

"But you still have no choice in the matter now my dear. If you continue to refuse, I will kill you and have your daughter slaughtered in a most unpleasant way. You have no idea what our Gestapo is capable of ... or me for that matter. So you see my dear, I still have you under my spell."

"Again you have misjudged me. My other choice *is* death, and I will gladly accept that rather than satisfy you and your scurrilous cause!"

"Those are only spineless words words, my dear. You have no courage. When the time comes, you will change your mind. Pain has a way of changing one's needs. You will not sacrifice your daughter because of your simplistic silliness and you know that."

"Bullshit!"

R.W was totally shocked at what he was hearing but was relishing the dressing down she was giving the German spy. He had never seen Claire in such a stupefied state and was taken aback at what he was seeing and hearing. For the moment, he didn't know what to think, but he knew he had to do something quick before the situation got out of hand.

While this exchange was transpiring between Claire Belle and Arnold, George and R.W. quickly readjusted their plan so as not to get Claire Belle injured. Instead of R.W. bursting into the room in combat fashion, he decided to enter the porch door slowly and then into the main door to the living room with his gun aimed directly at Arnold. At that point, R.W. would move away from the door and direct Claire Belle from the cottage. When she was safely outside, George would enter the same door as the one R.W. had entered and holler for Roscoe to come in through the front door.

Arnold continued taunting Claire.

"My dear lady, you are getting rather emotional. Perhaps you should calm down and follow our instructions. We have a large target tonight and you must follow our instructions. Now, wouldn't you like to be part of our Führer's triumph? I think once you get used to killing, you will like it. Isn't that right Dale?"

"Yeah, the more the merrier," Dale grunted.

"Dale, you shithead! This son-of-a-bitch has hoodwinked you too. I feel so sorry for you."

"You see my lady...." Arnold stopped in mid-sentence and looked towards the porch door. He knew somebody was out there.

"What was that? Dale, there is someone on the porch! You ... on the porch ... show yourself now or I will shoot the lady. Schnell, schnell!"

At that instant, Arnold grabbed Claire by the arm and pulled her towards him putting his Walther PPK to her right temple. Dale pulled out his thirty-two caliber pistol and pointed it at the door to the porch.

"Show yourself or I will kill the lady. Come out now I say!" Arnold said.

R.W. had no choice. He gradually stepped from outside the left doorframe to the opening of the door and walked a few steps inside the room with his arms partially raised. His gun was loosely held in his right hand.

"Well Miss Charboneau, if it isn't your cowboy beau! My, my ... isn't this convenient! Here to save your damsel in distress are you sheriff? Now, slowly drop your weapon to the floor."

"R.W.?" Claire said bewilderedly.

"Yeah well, what can I say there Arnold. Ya got the drop on me," R.W. said in a John Wayne like manner.

"Well, I say it looks as though you've been a rather busy boy lately. Shall I think otherwise?"

"No. I think you're right on the money there honcho. It's all over for ya."

"Maybe for you and the lady."

"No, Arnold. I think for you and the rest of the boys here."

"I doubt that seriously ol' friend. You see, we're the ones with the guns."

"Well, you do have a point there. But you don't think for one minute I'm gonna let you boys just walk out'a here, do ya?"

"Of course you are! Because now you are a bargaining chip. Whoever you have out there with you will see to that. You people have no gumption whatsoever. Dale, pick up the cowboy's weapon."

As Dale moved from the front of the room to the rear and was just bending over to pick up R.W.'s gun, Alfred Winters, thinking quickly, grabbed Claire by her left arm and pulled her from Arnold's grasp towards him. The motion startled Arnold whereby he momentarily took his eyes off R.W. The deputy took advantage of the surprise and swiftly punched Dale in the jaw sending him sprawling into a wall by a bedroom door. During the commotion, Arnold torqued back around towards the deputy and aimlessly fired a shot at him as he bent down to pick up his gun a few feet in front of him. The bullet struck him in the left side of his chest throwing him hard to the floor by the door entrance to the porch. Alfred quickly pulled Claire to the floor by the sofa and shielded her body with his.

Just as R.W. fell by the doorway slamming his head hard against the porch doorjamb, George burst into the room stepping over R.W.'s body and pumping two twelve-gauge blasts directly at Arnold striking him in his upper chest and neck. The gun's powerful velocity sent the spy crashing backwards into the front door with his arms wildly flapping above his head. He was cold dead before cascading onto the floor at the foot of the front door.

As George was unloading on Arnold, Dale quickly regrouped and disappeared through a nearby open bedroom window landing on hard-packed sand. Swiftly getting to his feet, he frantically scrambled towards his car. Roscoe, with his shotgun aimed directly towards him from behind Arnold's car, ordered him to halt. Dale turned and rapidly fired three rounds into the sheriff's direction blowing out a passenger window on Arnold's car.

Roscoe quickly ducked behind the car. Seconds after he fired, Roscoe cautiously rose to his feet and unleashed two powerful shotgun slugs sending Dale crumbling into the sand. The resounding echo of the powerful twelve-gauge in the still of the night air was awesome and deafening.

While seriously wounded, Dale faintly rolled to his right and barely able to fire two more shots in Roscoe's direction. By then, Roscoe had moved from behind Arnold's car to the front of Dale's car. Despite not having any gun fighting experience, Roscoe pumped two more rounds into his hapless body completely removing his face from his jaw to his forehead. The dyeing man's left leg, bent at the knee, jerked flat at the moment of death. Vapor from his open body wounds wafted through the air like breath on a cold winter morning.

Roscoe agilely moved to Dale's body lightly prodding it with his left foot ensuring all life was spent. He then ran to the front door of the cottage muscling aside Arnold's dead body frantically entering the room to see the fate of his deputies. He instantly noticed Claire Belle, George, and Alfred hovering over R.W.'s body on the far side of the room trying to stop the bleeding from a terrible wound to the chest. He was barely alive.

Chapter 26

On this bright and sunny Saturday morning May 30, Decoration Day, Deputy Sheriff R.W. Scoggins was, for the first time in a week, comfortably propped up in his bed since being admitted to the hospital with a bullet wound to his chest, a half-cracked open skull, a broken left ankle, a fracture to the fifth metacarpal bone in his right hand, and tender lower back. Aside from feeling terribly sore from his toenails to the follicles in his hair, he was surprisingly in good spirits and feeling downright chipper.

Sitting by his side, and holding his left hand, was Claire Belle Charboneau. She had vigilantly been staying by his bedside soothing his tired and weary soul. Also in the room were his fellow officers Roscoe Simmons and George Washington Dawkins. Standing beside the officers was Bodie Island Coast Guard Station commander Lieutenant Mark Fleming. They were spread out at the foot of the bed grinning and cutting up bringing a welcomed smile to their friend's face. They were ever so glad to see their close comrade-in-arms pull through surgery and learn he would be fine and healthy after a lengthy recovery.

"What you bums grinning about?" R.W. asked with a beam.

"Buddy, you gave us quite a scare! We were worried about you," Roscoe replied.

"So I hear. Mind tell'en me how I got here?"

"You don't remember?" George asked.

"Not too much. The last I remember was that tall, blond haired Nazi point'en his gun at me. By see'en all these cards, letters, and flowers spread out all around here, I reckon he pulled the trigger. How long have I been here?"

"One week, darling. One *very* long week!" Claire Belle said looking into his eyes.

"That long?" R.W. said smiling back tightly gripping her hand. He then cut his head back towards the foot of the bed and his friends.

"So, Arnold's bullet caused all this, huh?"

"Well, R.W., you were knocking purty hard at the Pearly Gates. If we hadn't got'en ya here when we did, you'd be walk'en through 'em right now. Miss Claire Belle here never left your side and kept shut'en them gates every time they stated to open. Her willpower gave you the strength to stay alive. You're a lucky man," Roscoe said with wet eyes.

"Ah Roscoe, don't be get'en mushy on me now."

"Actually R.W., if Roscoe hadn't told us to wear our badges, chances were you wouldn't be here right now," George chimed in. "The bullet ricocheted off your badge entering just to the outside of your heart and, as the doctor told us, missed it by one centimeter. It still did quite a bit of damage but had you not been wearing it, well...."

"What's a centimeter?" R.W. asked not having a clue as to how small that was.

"It's about the width of your pinky fingernail," Claire Belle, the former math teacher said, holding up the backside of her hand so that R.W. could see her pinky fingernail.

"Boy, I guess that was purty close. Roscoe, you done real good there buddy. Thanks!"

"Yeah, I've got the badge at the office. You'll see it when you come back."

"You know I will Roscoe. It might be awhile, but I'll be back!" R.W. said assuring him. "Now, will somebody please tell me what happened? I'm still in a fog here."

"Okay, well uh ... a few moments after Arnold told you to drop your gun, Alfred pulled Claire Belle away from Arnold distracting him. Just as he did, you slugged Dale Conner up against the wall," Roscoe continued.

"Would that be the reason for this broken right hand?"

"Yep, that would be the reason," George said.

"Then what happened?" R.W. asked.

"As you were reaching down for your gun after whacking Conner, Arnold fired at you hitting you in the chest, and then you crashed hard to the floor," Roscoe continued.

"Is that to be the reason for this little head wound?"

"Yep, you fell hard up against the doorjamb to the porch," George added.

"Well, I'm afraid to ask, but what happened next?"

"George burst into the room and planted two quick shotgun blasts into Arnold's chest," Roscoe said.

"You don't suppose George stepped on my ankle do ya?"

"Sorry about that R.W. I didn't mean to. I tried to miss you, honest. Arnold was just about to fire again, and I had to nail him before he was able to get off another round. I talked to the doc about your ankle, and he said it wasn't too bad broke."

"Well George, I reckon if you sacrificed my ankle to save lives, I guess I'm okay with that," R.W. said slightly moving his left leg. He continued.

"So, Arnold's dead huh? What about that Conner feller?"

"After you went down and George crashed into the room, Conner got up and hightailed it through a bedroom window," Roscoe continued.

"He didn't get away did he?"

"Well he tried, but Roscoe was where he was supposed to be. He hollered for the ol' boy to halt but answered Roscoe back with three quick rounds," George continued.

"You duck Roscoe?"

"Yep, but he missed me purty good though. When I popped back up, I pumped 'em twice ... once in the legs and once in the hip. He went down hard, but he rolled back over and was able to fire twice more at me. Just after that, I pumped two more into him and ... well, that did 'em in."

"Got 'em good did ya?"

"Well, maybe a little too good. We'll talk 'bout that later."

"How 'bout ol' Alfred? You say he pulled Miss Claire Belle away from Arnold?"

"Yes he did ... probably saved my life too R.W. Once he got me to the floor, he shielded his body to protect me against any stray bullets. Once he had me on the floor, I really didn't see anything after that. The whole shoot'en caboodle was over in less than a minute, but it seemed like hours," Claire said.

"He in jail now Roscoe?"

"No ... no he's not. After the shoot'en was over with, he got some towels, bandages, and some sulfur and helped with your wound and made you comfortable till the ambulance got there. When they did, they immediately took you on to the hospital here and came back later for the other two. When the medics finally arrived again to get Arnold out of the house, and pick up what was left of Conner, he cleaned up a bit, excused himself to the bedroom, and put a bullet in his head. He must've had a gun hidden in there somewhere. Then, when that happened, we had to call the ambulance back again to get him! It was a purty crazy night, no doubt 'bout it."

"Damn! And I asked 'em if he had any weapons in the house and, of course, he said no. Hell, I should've looked," R.W. said feeling slightly remorseful.

"Now R.W., don't be beat'en yourself up over that. If he was gonna kill himself, one way or the other he was gonna do it regardless," Roscoe said.

"Yeah well, I reckon you're right. I sure do hate to hear that though. But I guess he finally found his peace. Better his bullet by his own hand than one standing in front of a firing squad. That's probably what he was think'en," R.W. reckoned and then continued.

"Mark! Just don't stand there. Tell me, did you guys get that sub?"

The Coast Guard officer swelled up with pride and began telling his story.

"Lock, stock, and barrel there good buddy! Got a present here for ya too." Mark reached into a crumpled brown paper sack and pulled out a white-peaked black-billed cap trimmed in gold braid on the brim that was worn only by German U-boat captains.

"Well, I'll be! Don't look like the ol' boy'll be mak'en any trips to Washington to have Roosevelt kiss his ass, huh there Mark?"

"Naw, I don't think so. Vogel's there in the depths with ol' Neptune himself. Let's see if he tries to get the 'God of the Sea' to try and kiss his little ass!"

"Hell, I think it'll be the other way around! Where did you get this ... I mean I know where you got it, but how did you get it?"

"Well I want you to know we found that sub just about where ya'll said it'd be. We had two Coast Guard Cutters and two PC [Patrol Coastal] sub-chasers on his four corners. At exactly o-two-fifteen, we sent three Bolo Bombers screaming in from the north, south, and east. The first two dropped their charges but missed. The third dropped his charges and a yellow dye marker. He missed with his charges too but the dye markers did a good job for the PC's to locate the spot where he submerged. Of course the phosphorescence from her submerging helped a lot too.

"After she plunked down below the surface, we poured on the charges where those markers were and thirty minutes later large surges of fizz and oil came bubbling to the surface along with a lot of debris. They circled the area again and again dropping more depth charges but not much surfaced after that. She was only in about eighty-feet of water so the resounding effects of the charges from the seafloor really put the hammer to her.

"Two ships hung around 'til daylight. Then they put in a coupl'a whalers to pick up the debris and see if'n they could find anything to signify it as our sub. Yep, they found quite a bit of debris and there was no doubt it was our U-491! That's where they found the hat. The captain of one of the PC's got ahold of it and thought it was best to pass it on down the line to the person who gave him the coordinates. And, well ... that'd be you ol' buddy! That's how I got it."

"Any bodies float up?"

"Nope. They're all entombed on their killing machine. Damned if'n I know how this hat floated up though."

"What about that preliminary signal? Ya'll get that off okay?"

302

"Yeah. Claire and George went up there with the flapper device and Claire sent the prep signal that Jenny taught her. But that was it."

"Claire Belle did?"

"Yep, she sho' as hell did!" Roscoe said.

"Claire Belle?"

"She's kind of a secret local hero right now R.W." George said with a wink.

"Claire Belle! Well shit ... now I'm stupefied. What am I missing here?"

"I guess you don't remember, huh?" George spoke again.

"I guess I don't. But I reckon you'll fill me in."

"When you and me got beside the cottage after coming down the mound, we discovered Claire Belle was being forced to be part of the Nazi plot. But after listening to her rant with Arnold, we knew otherwise and adjusted our plan about get'en her safely to the outside. Then Arnold heard you on the porch trying to sneak in and that's when he pulled his gun on you. We just told you that part."

"Well, things *are* still a bit fuzzy...."

"Let me finish George," Claire Belle interrupted.

"R.W. It's a very long story, but I'll give you the jest of it. You see, I was coerced into joining the Nazi organization because the Gestapo in France was holding my daughter hostage."

"*Your* daughter?"

"Now be quiet and listen! I'll get to that in a minute. While I was in Hillsville, Virginia several years ago, I got tired of teaching school and decided to move to Norfolk for a change of scenery. I ended up getting a job there working in an office for a company that built ships. While I was there, I became good friends with a lady named Joy Lund."

"Now that name rings a bell," R.W. said with wide eyes.

"Well, what I didn't know was that she had just gotten tied in with Arnold's organization. One day at lunch, and in casual conversation, she asked me if I was interested in making more money. She told me, without going into much detail, that Arnold's organization was looking for a person to back up someone's position if that person became incapacitated. I showed a little interest. I really didn't jump at the bit."

"But where does your daughter fit in to all this?"

"Just about now. Before I left Hillsville, my former father-in-law suggested that Charlene...."

"*Your* daughter?"

"Yes ... go to school in France. You see, we discovered at an early age she was a gifted artist and my father-in-law wanted to cultivate that talent. So, he was willing to pay for her schooling by sending her to a well-known art academy in Paris. As I had earlier told you, he's from France and very wealthy. He thought that would be the best place for her to learn under the masters. I thought it was a great

303

opportunity. She did too but wasn't too thrilled about leaving her friends. But, she thought it over and decided it would be a great adventure. So, we made the plans."

"How long ago was this?' R.W. asked.

"She entered the academy in France in the spring of 1938. She was fourteen at the time. Anyway, she loved it and wrote beautiful letters home telling us how much she enjoyed it. Then when war broke out in the fall of 1939, we decided to bring her home but everybody at the time felt it would be over with fairly quick so we held off. But before we knew it, Germany moved on France in late spring of 1940, and she got stuck there and we couldn't get her out."

"So I assume Joy knew all this?" R.W. asked.

"Yes, she did and told Arnold. In the meantime, he had the SD get with the Gestapo to keep an eye on her. This information was told to me to pressure me into getting involved ... and if I didn't go along, they would kill her. I had no choice, so I went along just to bide my time. That's how I ended up here on the Outer Banks and working with Jenny."

"She trained ya, huh?"

"Yes. I went through the motions with her, but I never had any intentions of ever sending a signal ... but yes, she taught me. At first we didn't get along too well, but after awhile we started hitting it off purty well and were actually becoming close friends. Within the last month or so, she came to realize she had made a big mistake and wanted to get out of the organization but was in too deep. When Hank was killed, that was purty much the last straw. She then told me that she and Alfred had devised a plan to bring down the organization and safely get out of town. When the time came to disappear, she was going to notify me so I could escape at the same time and not be caught. As you can see, that didn't quite work out."

"So I see. You were gonna leave, huh?" R.W. anxiously said.

"Yep, I sure was ... but I wasn't going too far away from you, and I certainly would've gotten back in touch with you as soon as possible."

"What about your cottage?"

"Arnold gave me the cash for that and some other things. The car was mine all along, but I never used any of his money. Everything I spent was my own money. I put his money away. Last week when he picked me up at my place to go over to Alfred's to send the signal, I brought the money along to throw back in his face."

"I think I remember that. What happened to it then?"

"Well, when Roscoe called the FBI..."

"Now wait a minute! Roscoe called the FBI! You're jok'en me! Roscoe...!"

"Yeah R.W., I broke down and called Agents Jones and Johnson the following day. I realized it was the only way to get the rest of the operation. We had no way to tackle that problem in Norfolk. They immediately came down here and we told 'em what all we had, what'd been going on, and what we'd done ... filled 'em in on everything and even gave 'em the flapper device and the codes we found in Alfred's cottage. But we didn't tell 'em everything."

"How's that?"

"We didn't tell 'em 'bout Claire Belle's involvement! The money she got from Arnold, the same money she threw back at him, we put it in Alfred's sock drawer for the FBI to find. Seeing how he was already involved up to his eyelids, it seemed like the logical thing to do," Roscoe said with a smile and glint in his eye.

"Now Roscoe ... you know if'n you had turned her in, we'd *never* be able to replace those chicken and ham salad sandwiches we enjoyed so much!" R.W. said laughing then grimacing from the pain of the exertion.

"Yeah well, that was in the back of my mind!" Roscoe said with a grin.

"I thought it would be! Any luck on them agents catching anybody up in Norfolk?"

"They closed in on Joy Lund, but she, too, committed suicide before they nabbed her. In as much as Arnold's wife was concerned, she up and disappeared. Based on the phone number Alfred provided, the agents ascended on the apartment. Unfortunately, it looked as though it had just recently been vacated. So right now, we don't know where she is," Roscoe said.

"Well, I guess there is one more thing I'm curious about. What about our little buddy John. Did he escape the scrutiny?"

The room got real quiet with the three men all looking back and forth at each other, and in Claire's direction, not knowing what to say or who was going to speak. Then Lieutenant Fleming spoke up.

"Uh, well ... ah ... R.W., things with him got a little more complicated than we expected. The FBI had no choice but to haul him in. We tried our best but..."

"Bullshit! You turned him in? How could ya'll do that! Hell, he's the one who gave us the clue to solve this damn thing in the first place. How *could* ya'll?"

"Well ... we didn't have much choice."

"Sure you did. Hell, you saved Claire Belle!"

"Yeah, but that was different."

"How in the *hell* was that different?"

"Well, first off she's already an American citizen, and she can't be naturalized."

"What the hell are you saying?"

"Uh Roscoe ... you want'a help me out here?"

"What Mark is trying to say is that John wants to become an American citizen. Under his circumstances, and with the war and all, it would've been next to impossible for that to happen. We told 'em all

305

about John and embellished what all he did to help uncover the beacon. So, we asked the FBI to intervene and help him out and … well, with a little arm twist'en, they agreed."

"Say what?" R.W. said incredulously.

"The FBI is gonna help John cut corners with the authorities to have him become a naturalized American citizen of the United States. When he becomes one, he's gonna join the United States Navy and go to work in their Intelligence Department. Being a German, and of course thinking like one, the Navy believes he can provide some excellent resources in helping sink the subs. After that, who knows? War with Germany looks like it's gonna be around awhile, and I think he's gonna be busy," Roscoe said with a smile.

"Are you guys pulling my chain right now?"

"No R.W., they're not. Before John left with the FBI, he gave me this note to give to you," Claire Belle said with a small lump in her throat handing him the envelope.

"I'll read it shortly," R.W. quietly said tucking it under the sheets.

"He thinks the world of you R.W." Claire said.

"Hear, hear!" said his friends.

At that moment, the door to the room opened. A nurse entered to change the dressing on R.W.'s surgical wounds and thought it was best for everybody to leave. The nurse motioned to Claire Belle that she could stay. But before they left, the boys passed on some comical talk wishing R.W. well and they would return later to see him.

* * * * * * * *

After the nurse changed R.W.'s dressing, checked his temperature, and puffed-up his pillows, she left the room. Claire went to a table by the wall, poured herself and R.W. a glass of ice water, and returned to her chair.

"You wouldn't happen to have a shot of bourbon in that pocketbook of yours would you? I sure could use a belt right now!"

"I bet you could with what all you've been through! When you get well enough, you can come sit with me on my deck and we'll have one whilst we look out over the ocean. You remember that wonderful evening?"

"It's etched in my memory. How shall I ever forget it?"

"Do you remember that same night while we were on the blanket with the fire-pit burning and how I told you that one day you were going to save me from my despair?"

"Yeah vaguely, but at the time I didn't know what you meant."

"You understand it now don't you?"

"I do now. Funny how things seem to work out though. But your daughter … have you heard from her?"

"Not directly, no. But this week I received information through one of my father-in law's relatives that she had escaped the Gestapo surveillance and had moved somewhere into Southern France. But we don't know where she is."

"So ... you ready to go look for her?"

"R.W., I've already made the arrangements. My father-in-law has agreed to finance our little operation and Lieutenant Fleming is going to make arrangements for us, through some of his Coastie buddies, to get us on a convoy leaving Halifax, Nova Scotia to Liverpool, England. After that, well ... we're going to be on our own in getting into France. But, as soon as you're fit and well enough, our 'tickets' are ready."

There was a moment of silence with each passionately looking at the other. R.W. could not restrain himself and leaned over to her as close as he could. He spilled his ice water on the bed.

"Will you marry me Miss Claire Belle?"

"Well now there, Mr. Scoggins ... I *reckon* I just might!"

* * * * * * *

The End

Printed in the United States
154328LV00004B/6/P

9 780977 911950